SALES MANAGEMENT

The Wiley Marketing Series

WILLIAM LAZER, Advisory Editor *Michigan State University*

Sales Management

George D. Downing

Professor of Marketing

Arizona State University

John Wiley & Sons, Inc. *New York · London · Sydney · Toronto*

Library of Congress Catalog Card Number: 69-13678
SBN 471 22030 2
Printed in the United States of America

To Jean

Preface

In the exciting, changing world of business, the nature of sales management is changing. As business firms adopt the "marketing concept" and become systems adjusting strategically to changing market environments, the selling operation becomes increasingly crucial to the firm's success.

This book is based on the premise that the success of the selling operation—which determines the success of the firm—depends significantly on the effectiveness of its management. The role of the sales manager, both at headquarters and in the field, is more important than ever before. Moreover, *it is changing, becoming different*. The focus no longer is on "things to do"—setting quotas, recruiting and training salesmen, analyzing number of calls per customer—even though these are important technical skills, which must be capably performed.

Instead, the role of the sales manager *as a manager* is becoming increasingly important, and this function is the main thrust of this book. The book develops a *managerial and strategic* framework for thinking about the sales manager's job. It proposes that as a manager of people, money, and things, he must think and behave as a manager within the sales sphere.

Therefore, the book is organized around managerial and strategic concepts, rather than technical skills. It consists of four parts.

Part I presents the contemporary view of the firm as a "marketing system" and discusses its impact on the management of the selling operation.

Part II develops one major thrust of the book—the *managerial and strategic* framework—using managerial concepts translated into the sales idiom.

Part III discusses three administrative techniques, which actually deserve separate treatment. The discussion is broad, however, rather than encyclopedic, in order to keep the managerial frame of reference.

Part IV focuses on the second major topic of the book—the *management of people*. A far cry from the orthodox view of management as "supervision," it deals with the strategic influence of others' behavior. It draws basic concepts from behavioral science to gain insights into how the other person perceives, thinks, and responds. It proposes ways to translate these concepts into meaningful strategies for effective leadership by the sales manager.

The book does not try to cover everything in the world about sales management. Procedure, policies, practices, and problems; objectives, organization, and operational processes; style and ideology; markets, customers, channels, and competitors—all these vary greatly from industry to industry and from firm to firm. What is important for an electronic component manufacturer may be unimportant for a linen supply business. The book does try, however, to develop a set of pervasive, relatively universal sales management concepts, into which different "contents" can be put and which can be applied in different situations. It is therefore a managerial "framework for thinking" book.

Many people have provided inputs to my thinking about this book. I am particularly grateful to three. First, my friend and colleague Professor W. J. E. Crissy has been an unceasing source of provocative and creative new ideas about professional selling and sales management, ideas that have considerably influenced my thinking. Second, I am much indebted to Professor William Lazer who strongly encouraged me to write this book. Finally, I owe much to Professor Robert M. Olsen of the University of Kansas who reviewed the original manuscript, and contributed many significant ideas for improvement.

Tempe, Arizona   George D. Downing
September, 1968

Contents

SALES MANAGEMENT

The Marketing Concept and the Selling Effort

The selling operation of the business firm does not exist in isolation. It is no longer—as it once was—a rather autonomous, tail-end function of some productive operation. It is an integral and important element of a *system of business action.*

The contemporary, provocative view of *the firm as a marketing system* is having great impact on the firm's selling operation and on its management. The chapters of Part I develop the view of the selling operation working as a vital subsystem within the greater, market-oriented total system of the firm.

Chapter 1 sets the stage, viewing the firm as a marketing system. Chapter 2 expands this view, detaching the interacting elements of the process of marketing and introducing the selling operation. Chapter 3 focuses on the selling operation itself, establishes its relationships to the systems of the firm and of the marketplaces, and in so doing emphasizes its critical and growing significance to the success of the market-oriented firm. Chapter 4 then turns to the managing of the selling operation, developing a "model" of the sales manager's job in this contemporary systems concept. Thus Chapter 4 sets the stage and provides a framework for the rest of the book, proposing that a new managerial and strategic view must be taken of the job of the sales manager.

I

The Firm
as a Marketing System

Selling is playing an increasingly important role in the business firm in today's highly competitive and complex world. The effectiveness of the selling effort—and of its management—is becoming more and more significant to the achievement of the firm's objectives.

The whole nature of the selling operation is undergoing a subtle but sweeping change. As the managements of firms increasingly embrace the "marketing concept," the role of selling—and its management—is changing. Within this concept, the knowledge or prediction of customers' real or potential needs and problems becomes both the *starting point* and the *target* for all the activities of the firm. As the entire firm adopts this market-oriented philosophy, the very nature of the selling operation changes with respect both to the market and to the firm itself.

The nature of management of the selling effort—that is, the job of the sales manager itself—is changing. The effective sales manager of today must perceive, think, and act differently from his predecessors. He no longer operates an element of the firm that is relatively independent. Far beyond this, he now manages a *system* that is an integral element or subsystem within the greater marketing system of the firm.

This new systems concept, now becoming widely used in understanding and managing a firm's behavior, is a main thrust of this book. Here a simple definition of a system can be given. A system is an organism, or an entity, consisting of a number of separate, semiautonomous, interacting parts—with established relationships between the parts and with a control mechanism that exerts forces to maintain these relationships, should they become upset. Hence the firm can be viewed as a formally organized, goal-seeking system, consisting of a number of separate, but interacting "subsystems" (production, finance, sales, etc.) . Furthermore, the firm is an "open" system. That is, forces outside the system can penetrate it. When this happens, the subsystem that is penetrated responds, but as it does so, its response "trickles" over to other subsystems, requiring them to flex somehow.

Within the systems concept, the sales manager is responsible for much more than "running the sales force." He still must, of course, learn and utilize the "tools of the trade"—such technical skills as forecasting, recruiting, training, and setting quotas. But now he occupies a position of vital importance as a key link in the loop of customers to firm to customers. He coordinates selling activities with the total marketing effort of the firm. He keeps constant surveillance over the forces in the marketplaces and feeds this market information into the firm, so that the firm's marketing system may adjust to it—either to exploit opportunities or to defend itself. Within the profit and sales revenue objectives of the firm, he creates and implements innovative strategies. He continuously observes, assesses, and predicts the activities of competition and develops batteries of counterstrategies. Pervasive to all this is his role as a motivator and leader of people.

Paradoxically, to say that the effective sales manager manages a subsystem within a greater system does not mean that the value of his role has decreased; rather, it has sharply increased. To say that the sales operation is part of a team and must coordinate with it does not imply that it has become somehow subservient; rather, its efficiency, productivity, and strategic creativity have become more essential than ever to the firm's success. All this does mean, however, that the effective sales manager must be systems-conscious and have insight into the analysis, management, and coordination of systems and their strategic behavior.

THE MARKETING CONCEPT

An understanding of the rationale behind the "marketing concept" and the marketing system within which the selling operation exists is vital to the effectiveness of modern sales management. Despite the popularity and growing use of the term "marketing" as more and more firms embrace its basic philosophy, some haziness exists with regard to what it really is and what its meaning is to sales management.

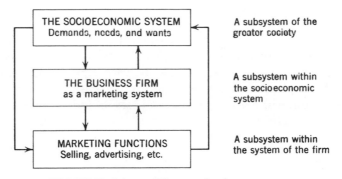

FIGURE 1-1   The marketing system.

What is Marketing?

No simple, concise definition of marketing can be put forth. Certainly, it is something more than just selling, or the soliciting of customers for the purpose of getting orders. Elements other than sales are involved— advertising, sales promotion, physical distribution, and packaging, to name a few. Thus marketing has been more broadly defined as all those services necessary to move goods from production to consumption.[1]

Yet this definition, even though it implicitly includes manufacturers', wholesalers', dealers', and even customers' activities, is not sufficient. Marketing is something more than this; it is a complex of three major elements:

1. The socioeconomic system
2. The business firm as a marketing system
3. Marketing functions

Each of these is an aspect or element of marketing, subject to marketing theory and study. All three represent in broad-brush terms the total of what "marketing" is. Note that they are arranged in a descending or "macro-micro" scale. That is, they are interrelated and interactive systems and subsystems (Figure 1-1).

The real key to this broader concept of marketing is that the firm is viewed as a marketing system. Of course, the firm itself has many subsystems—a financial system, a technological system, a social system, a marketing-function system. But this view holds—and this is the heart of the "marketing concept"—that *the entire firm as an entity is a marketing system*. To understand this more fully, consider first the firm's objectives.

[1] *Marketing Definitions: A Glossary of Marketing Terms,* developed by the Committee on Definitions, The American Marketing Association, 1960, p. 15.

Objectives of the Business Firm

The executive managements of essentially all firms have objectives for the firm to attain. These objectives may be very explicit and definitive or they may be implicit and tacit. Although firms will have differing mixes of objectives and will place differing emphases on individual ones, typical objectives may include:

Profitability
Volume
Market share
Growth and expansion
Corporate image

Profitability. Profit is universally regarded by business executives as the primary objective of a business. Nevertheless, it is a rather illusive and loosely defined objective, subject to widely differing criteria. How the firm's executive management sets profit objectives is an essential input into the sales manager's calculus. Does the firm seek to maximize profit (which it rarely does) or to optimize profit? What are the criteria for measurement: net to sales, net to investment, or both? Is profit determination broken down to individual product lines? To organizational groupings? What is the balance sought between short-range and long-range profit? Obviously, the mix of these profit elements will vary materially from industry to industry. For example, because of the nature of their business—their markets and their technologies—General Motors, General Mills, Swift and Company, and J. C. Penney may have very different profit criteria. The criteria will often vary from firm to firm within an industry. For example, the differing views in the past of profit criteria of Sears, Roebuck and Company and Montgomery Ward helped to lead to quite different market strategies. A thorough understanding of how the firm sets its profit objectives is a necessary ingredient in the sales manager's own goal-setting, planning, decision-making, and controlling processes, which are discussed in later chapters.

Sales revenue. Many firms vigorously seek increased sales revenue—volume of orders, or volume of units demanded—as a prime objective. As will be discussed in Chapter 6, this quest for sales revenue becomes a prime input into the objective-setting and strategy-creating aspects of the sales operation. Furthermore, as will be proposed later (when we discuss break-even analysis; see Figure 3-4), in today's highly competitive and increasingly technological business world the sales revenue objective is assuming increasingly important proportion in the objective mix of the firm. And, as we shall see, this is putting great pressure on sales management.

Market share. Market share is the percentage that a firm receives of the total available business in the markets for its own products and for similar products of its competitors. Many marketing and sales executives feel that it is the most meaningful of all objectives, other than perhaps profit itself. This is particularly true for those products or services for which market demand is not increasing or is not sensitive to efforts to increase it. Getting increased sales volume (given no price changes) with stable demand can be done only by increasing market share, at rivals' expense. Certainly, it is often one of the most significant objectives for the selling operation. Proper focus on market share avoids some possible traps. For example, the management of a firm may happily observe increasing sales volume. Yet it is completely possible, and often happens, that demand in the markets is increasing at a greater rate. Competitors are gaining position and reaping greater harvests—hence this firm's reactive strategies in the marketplaces are inadequate. Definitive market share objectives help to keep the blinders off marketing and sales management eyes. To be sure, quantification of market share is more difficult in some industries than in others. Sometimes it can be calculated quite closely (e.g., in the automobile industry, in the primary metals industries, or in industries most of whose firms participate in a trade association that legally assembles and disseminates such data). At other times it may have to be estimated. In any case, market share is a basic objective for the whole firm as a marketing system—and it becomes a highly important input to sales management's objective framework and strategy. Chapters 6 and 7 will show how a "hierarchy of objectives" such as market share culminates in the planning of strategies and tactics by the individual salesman for individual customers. The important point here is that the efficacy of objective setting and planning at the customer level is diminished if the market share objective is not clearly defined at the firm's top management levels. Furthermore—though admittedly this has more import for marketing management than for sales management—decisions on market share objectives have great interacting impact on decisions for other areas: pricing policy, promotional strategy, market selection, and so on.

Growth and expansion. Firms seek to grow and expand in order to become more firmly entrenched in selected markets, to increase volume, to increase market share, and to increase profit. Yet for a number of reasons (see the discussion of break-even analysis, p. 38) the vigorous seeking for growth in many firms becomes almost a fetish. Many an executive has exhorted his management, "We've got to grow. We can't stand still: You either go ahead, or slide back." This has defensive overtones, which will be discussed later, but such rationale does exist as a driving force in many managements. Growth is sought in many ways: sheer physical growth in volume and output; geographical growth in expanded plant, spatially; market growth in entry and penetration of new markets (market diversification) ; product growth in the increasing array of products and services offered. The growth objective is a dynamic one to which sales management must keep tuned, for it impinges a strong force on the plans and actions of the selling operation.

Other objectives. Somewhat less quantifiable and to some extent less forceful in shaping the firm's strategies are a variety of other "contributing" objectives—new product lines, a good "image" of the firm among its publics, healthful employee relations, and so forth.

The importance to the firm's management of all these objectives can not be overstressed. They are the starting point in the firm's planning and actions, and the bases by which the firm's organizational components set their goals (see the discussion of hierarchy of objectives in Chapter 6) . In some mix of emphasis, they set the stage, so to speak, for everything that sales management does. They create a guiding framework for the planned behavior of the selling operation.

Yet the most important objective, exerting the most power over the actions of management is one that was not included in our listing; it is *survival of the firm*—to stay in business, to remain alive, to maintain continuity. In many firms survival, as a primary objective, may be considered only tacitly, inferentially, or semiconsciously. Yet it is there, at work. Often, however, it is openly expressed and specifically designated as a primary objective.[2] Furthermore, it is proposed here that in the increasingly competitive world, with its mushrooming technology, sheer survival is becoming more and more potent as a driving force behind firms' behaviors.

Some firms that are in apparently healthy condition today will not survive. It is fairly safe to predict that some major, nationally known companies, with stock on the "Big Board" in New York, may not be around twenty years from now. They will be gone—out of business, dismantled, or their assets gobbled up by other firms. Some firms will flourish; some will wane and die.

Lest this seem overdramatic, let us consider a few actual cases and some possibilities for the future. For example, whatever happened to Packard?

2 At one time, R. J. Cordiner, then President of the General Electric Company, said at a meeting of company management: "General Electric must innovate and grow if it wants to survive. If it doesn't it could die." It is hard to visualize the great General Electric Company dying, but it could!

The Packard Motor Company was one of the great industrial firms of a generation ago, producing a prestige product of high quality. But this great company made mistakes, hence failed to survive as an entity.

What would have happened to the railroads if the United States Government had not helped to keep them alive? [3] They probably would not have survived, because most railroad executives made the mistake of thinking that they were in the business of running railroads. Actually, they are in the business of marketing transportation services—and this simple turn of mind may spell the difference between successful survival or failure of a firm as it exists among the changing forces of its competitive world.

Similarly, the advent of television nearly torpedoed the movie industry, because the movie executives made a mistake. They thought they were in the business of making movies, but, again, they were not. They are in the business of marketing recreation or entertainment—and they recognized this business rationale barely in time.

Firms may wane and die not only because their managements are unable to perceive them as marketing systems. They may experience difficulty in surviving because of failure to adjust to changing conditions in their external environments. This is particularly true for the technological environments. For example, it is difficult to imagine Standard Oil waning and dying—but it could happen if such a company regarded its business only as that of oil production and refining. After all, the fuel cell has been invented, has winged around in space in the Gemini missions, and, for that matter, is powering golf carts around the fairways. Some believe that it is only a matter of time until the gasoline engine will be an obsolete power source for the automobile. How will Standard Oil adjust to the changing technology, if it is to survive? Certainly it must adjust somehow—and here we are at the heart of the dynamics of marketing and the concept of the firm as a marketing system. To survive, the system which is the business firm must do much more than decide on a product or service to produce and market. It must constantly adapt and adjust to changes in its external environment—and all this has great meaning to the management of its selling operation.

Note, too, that the achievement of essentially all these objectives—certainly the prime ones of profit, volume, market share, and sheer survival—*significantly hinges on actions that take place in the marketplaces, as customers make purchase decisions.* Here is the payoff. This is the point at which every activity of the firm must be aimed. Again, this has

[3] Here and in the next several paragraphs, we are following Theodore Levitt, "Marketing Myopia," *Harvard Business Review,* July–August 1960.

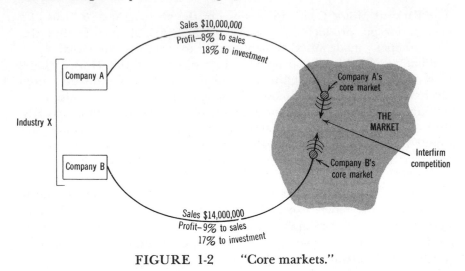

FIGURE 1-2   "Core markets."

great meaning to the management of the selling operation. And again this leads to the view of the firm as a marketing system.

THE "CORE MARKET" CONCEPT

To crystallize the key thought that success and the very life of the firm depend on its market actions, consider a simplified account of what really happens [4] (Figure 1-2). A company, which we shall call Company A, produces and sells some line of products (or services). Over time, customers have regarded these products as capable of satisfying needs and as fairly priced. They have come to consider the firm a good one with which to do business and one that provides adequate service. As a result, Company A has penetrated the market and won for itself a following of loyal customers. It has acquired a chunk of the market. This is its "core" market, consisting of those loyal customers who keep doing business with it. If Company A were Ford Motor Company, these would be the Ford owners who, when purchasing a new automobile, simply buy another Ford. If Company A were Florsheim Shoe, these would be the customers who, when purchasing new shoes, look for the Florsheim sign. If it were

[4] For the "core market" concept that follows I am indebted to Donald A. Taylor of Michigan State University. It is probably a bit oversimplified, but, judging from observations over many years in sales management in a large industrial corporation, I think it is a real "fact of life."

Maxwell House Division of General Foods, these would be the house-wives who, when in the supermarket, do not check prices, but simply find the familiar red-and-blue can and pop it into the basket. Every firm has its core market, its piece of the market (at least for some given period of time). Furthermore, for many firms the core market may provide an adequate and even substantial volume of business, enabling the firm to achieve its profit and volume. For example, as shown in Figure 1-2, Company A is enjoying a volume of $10 million in annual sales, with attractive profit returns. Its chief executive could understandably be quite satisfied with the state of affairs: the firm has loyal customers, it has a profitable flow of business, it is meeting the payroll, it has healthful relations with employees, its stock options look good, and so on. All is well. It would be a most human response to "let things be." Why rock the boat and upset everyone? [5]

But something disturbs this *status quo*. For one thing, Company A has competitors. It will normally have many, but Figure 1-2 shows only one—Company B—for the sake of simplicity. Company B produces and sells a line of products which, in the eyes of customers, are substitutable for those of Company A. If A is Ford, B is the Chevrolet Division of General Motors; if A is Florsheim, B is French, Schriner, and Urner; and so on. And over time B, too, has offered good, fairly priced products and good service. It, too, has won a core market, a set of loyal customers who continue to do business with it. It, too, might find its core market generating a satisfactory volume of business at satisfactory profit.

Of course, there are customers on the fringes of or outside the core markets. These are customers who divide their business and for various reasons patronize one firm at one time and another firm at another time. Certainly, firms hope to embrace such customers into the core. But it could well be that the core market itself represents an adequate share of the market for the firm to exist in relative comfort.

Thus a "don't rock the boat" condition could exist even in a competitive situation. What happens to upset this *status quo*? What triggers the fierce competitive activity that we observe in today's markets? Many things do, of course, but to simplify a bit in order to develop a competitive framework of thinking, let us imagine that the executive of Company A is meditating about his business. He thinks: "Everything looks fine down at the office. . . . Sales are good; we've gained a couple of notches on profit, and the plant is busy. We've got good loyal customers. No problem there . . . or is there? What would happen if we lost some of

---

[5] Admittedly, in some firms in some industries, some executives may reason and act in this manner. But it is my earnest opinion that they have blinders on, and are in potential trouble.

our market chunk, if sales dropped for some reason to nine million? We can't let that happen!" He begins making notes for the special management staff meeting. At that meeting he is likely to say something to the effect that "Gentlemen, we've got to grow. We can't stand still. We've got to expand. I want each of you to go back to your respective departments and come up with ideas on how we can increase our volume."

Of course, this little drama has a defensive note. Certainly the *status quo* can be upset and severe competitive activity generated for positive reasons. For example, the management of one firm may see opportunities in the market that can be exploited. However, it is my belief—and this is a debatable point—that much of the driving, aggressive market behaviors of firms is really quite defensive in basic purpose.

Whatever the generating force, the kind of thinking just described is the wellspring of innovation and of the creation of aggressive competitive strategy for the purpose of pushing out the market beachheads and enlarging the core. From this sort of rationale come technological innovation,[6] manufacturing-process innovation, organizational innovation, and marketing innovation. From it come new strategies, new plans of action by the firm, all culminating in new market actions. Again we see the firm as a marketing system, with all elements of the firm responding to the need for actions in the marketplaces.

Meanwhile, the executives of Company B may independently pass through the same thought process. Alternatively, they may perceive Company A's changing behavior in the markets. Or, they may merely begin to suspect that Company A is maneuvering strategically to enlarge its market share. All this is threat, and Company B embarks on its own programs to innovate, sometimes imitatively and sometimes creatively, in order to solidify its market position and to protect and enlarge its core.

This is interfirm, intraindustry competition. Often (perhaps even usually) it is less focused on price than on nonprice strategic programs of market action. Such vigorous competitive strategy and counterstrategy are quite easy to see (and very interesting to follow) in many consumer product industries. Observe, for example, the strategic reactions and interplay between such companies and products as Ford's Mustang and Chevrolet's Camaro, Coca Cola and Pepsi Cola, Hertz and Avis, Gillette and Schick, NBC, and CBS. These forces are just as potent, if less easy for the casual observer to note, as those in the industrial marketing sphere—

---

6 To be sure, much technological innovation evolves from its own impetus rather than from market-derived forces. Yet it can be argued that it flourishes significantly because of favorable marketing environment and because of the drive by firms to enhance their market position.

du Pont versus Monsanto, General Electric versus Westinghouse, or Alcoa versus Reynolds. Here again, the competitive strategic flexing that firms must devise to survive and meet objectives places great import on the effectiveness of the selling operation and its management—more, probably, than ever before.

Other Market Forces

Direct interfirm competition is not the only force to which the firm must adjust. Many other forces are at play and are in flux in the firm's market environments. The firm must detect these uncontrollable environmental forces and strategically adapt to them either defensively (to protect itself against inroads in its core market) or aggressively (to take advantage of new market opportunities) . These forces, shown in Figure 1-3, are touched on only briefly here.

The tremendous impact of *social change* on firm's marketing futures is becoming well recognized by many marketers. Certainly the society of tomorrow, with its changing standards, morals, and expectations, will have changing demands. Styles and patterns of living will change, and so will wants. Furthermore, the changing demands and expectations will echo back through the consumer markets to the industrial markets.

Akin to and mixed with social change is *economic change*. Real incomes will increase, working time will contract, and "leisure" time will expand.

Almost beyond comprehension is the force of new *technology,* which is growing exponentially. The firm must be prepared to be technologically innovated out of its marketplaces. Hence it constantly must be preparing

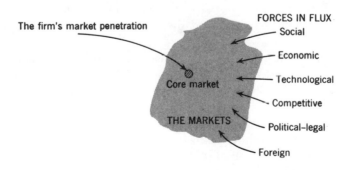

FIGURE 1-3   Forces in flux in the marketplaces.

itself to enter new markets or to adapt its products to changing demands. It must also constantly scan new technology that may seem quite foreign to its own marketing system, so as to adopt and adapt it to advantage before its competition does. Consider Teflon, for example.

Competitive forces are also mushrooming—that is, competition other than direct interfirm, interproduct competition. In our vibrant economy and technology and with the resulting massive array of goods and services available to the society, competition for the customer's disposable dollars is rife. For example, a vacation trip to Hawaii competes with a home air-conditioning system. Hence one might say that United Airlines is increasingly in competition with Carrier Corporation, and the marketing systems of both must be tuned to this fact. This is also true in the industrial markets. An industrial customer does not have unlimited funds and must allocate his resources. For example, his consideration of a new computer may create competition for a new boring mill. Hence IBM really is in competition with Cincinnati Milling, and somehow the marketing system of each must be aware of this.

Political-legal changes directly affect the firm's marketplaces and actions. The role of government is a very real force. Beyond the direct impact of government on the firm's behavior, governmental social, fiscal, monetary, and military programs have tremendous force on markets. New firms and even new industries will unquestionably spring into being as an indirect result of governmental actions. Existing firms and industries must keep tuned to such actions and be prepared to flex with them.

The forces of *foreign trade* pose many problems, both positive and negative, to domestic firms. Certainly, the economic relationships within the world are not going to stay as they are. Many firms may gain considerably, from a market standpoint; many may suffer if this input to their marketing systems is not properly treated. Consider, for example, how Honda and Yamaha have affected the marketing system that is Harley-Davidson.

Thus the firm must do more than create strategic programs of market actions to hold its position or gain position vis-à-vis its direct competitors. It must continuously observe and forecast changes in many other forces in its markets, which are in constant flux. It must strategically adjust to such changes. This places a particularly important demand on the selling operation. The effective sales manager must develop an analytical framework of thinking about all this, because in many cases it may be the selling operation that first becomes aware of environmental changes. The selling operation may be the primary input of such dynamic information to the firm.

Interindustry Competition

Another great force impinges on the firm—that of interindustry competition (Figure 1-4). Consider again Company A and Company B, direct competitors in a specific set of markets. This is Industry X in Figure 1-4. Now assume that there is another industry (Industry Y in the Figure), which has two companies, Company R and Company S, that serve a completely different set of markets with completely different products. They, too, experience vigorous interfirm competition, each seeking to enlarge its core market by innovating and by programming strategic market actions. Each detects and adapts to changing forces in its shared market—perhaps the same forces that exist in Industry X's markets, but with differing effects. At some point, the firm-to-firm competitive struggle begins to offer diminishing payoff. There are economic and legal limits to such competition. Hence Company S, still seeking to enlarge its core market, casts its eyes about and looks at Industry X's markets. It observes and analyzes the needs and wants of customers in these markets. It evaluates the products of Company A and Company B, and how effectively these products satisfy customers' present and potential needs and wants. Simplifying somewhat (but not much), Company S might say: "Aha! We can take our products, modify them slightly, and invade Industry X's markets. We can do a better job of satisfying needs and wants than A and B can with their products."

This is interindustry competition. Company A and Company B wake up one day, shocked to find an "invader" in their markets, drawing customers into his core, threatening, perhaps, their very existence. Dramatic examples: the aluminum industry invading the steel industry, the airlines invading the trucking industry, the steel industry invading the glass bottle industry, the paper industry invading the tin can industry, and the chemical industry invading almost everyone's industry. This competitive phenomenon is likely to increase rather than decrease, because of severe competitive pressures and because of expanding technology.

THE FIRM AS A MARKETING SYSTEM

All this brings us back to the concept of the firm as a marketing system. Within itself, the firm has many interacting components, or subsystems. But the firm in total is an organism that exists in and reacts with its external environments. Its very life, let alone its objective achievement,

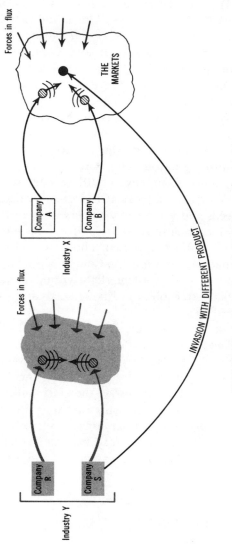

FIGURE 1-4   Interindustry competition.

depends on how it reacts with these environments. These environments are the complex of the firm's marketplaces. As a system—a *marketing system*—the firm strategically reacts and adjusts to the ever-changing forces in these market environments. This concept is not restricted to industrial manufacturing types of firms. It applies to all kinds of firms— wholesale firms, banks, retail stores, service organizations, and others. The next chapter discusses the process by which the firm does this, and the meaning of this process to the management of the selling operation.

QUESTIONS AND PROBLEMS

1. What is the difference between "marketing" and "selling"?
2. What is meant by the expression: "The firm is a marketing system"?
3. Does the fact that "marketing" has become a vital concept and process for the firm not diminish the importance of "selling"?
4. Take a stand on this statement, and defend it: "Marketing makes sense for a manufacturing firm like General Electric or IBM, but not for small nonmanufacturing enterprises like a local retail store, laundry, or a real estate agency."
5. Why is "volume" an important objective for almost all businesses and what meaning does this have for the selling operation of the firm?
6. Select three business firms by name—one that manufactures physical products, one that markets services, and one at the retail level. For each of these firms, show how the "systems concept applies"—that is, how does each appear to adapt to changing external environments and how does each contain internal, interacting "subsystems"?
7. What are the three great external forces that the firm must detect and react against in order to successfully meet its objectives? How do they affect the sales operation of the firm?
8. For each of these three external forces, cite an example now occurring in the business world.

2

The Process of Marketing and the Selling Subsystem

The concept of the entire firm as a marketing system centers on the idea that the system is always capable of adjusting to forces in its environments. This brings us to the "marketing concept" itself. *Marketing is the process by which the firm accomplishes this strategic adjusting.* That is, marketing is the process, ideally, by which the firm accomplishes the following:

1. Detects the needs and wants of selected customers in selected markets.

2. Analyzes all forces in those markets that have the potential to change these needs and wants.

3. Tailors, therefore, an array of products or services to satisfying these needs and wants.

4. Informs and influences customers' perceptions of the firm and its products and their purchase decisions through strategic programs of market action.

5. Keeps surveillance of what happens as a result of this market action, and constantly adjusts the product array and the programs of market action to make them more effective than are those of competing firms.

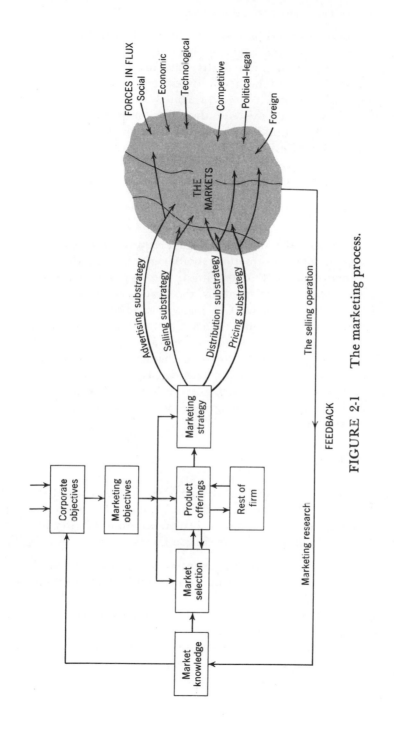

FIGURE 2-1   The marketing process.

The interworkings of this process are shown in Figure 2-1. Understanding of the marketing process and insight into how the selling operation meshes into it are essential for effective sales management.

Analysis of Figure 2-1 begins at its extreme right, with the markets. Again note that the markets are represented by wavy lines, since they are dynamic and not static—they are always in the process of change. Note also the use of the plural word—markets—rather than the singular. For most goods and services the total marketplace is complex enough so that more than one uniquely different market can be identified—an important factor in marketing and selling strategy, as will be seen later.

FEEDBACK MECHANISMS

As in any system, the marketing system requires *feedback mechanisms,* which transmit vital information about variables and their changes in the firm's environments. This key link in the loop of customers to firm to customers is at times activated by the marketing function of market research. But in the judgment of many marketing executives, it is the selling operation that provides the continuous flow of vital market intelligence. This is discussed in somewhat more detail in Chapter 12, but it must be stressed here that feedback mechanisms for market intelligence must not be allowed to evolve haphazardly. It is a subprocess assigned to the selling operation that must be carefully created, with specific objectives, plans for accomplishment, and systematized techniques.

MARKET KNOWLEDGE

Knowledge of many aspects of the markets is the base input to the firm, as seen in Figure 2-1 and as discussed in Chapter 1. Although the kinds of market intelligence required vary considerably from industry to industry, some of the types of questions needing answers are the following:

1. Who are the customers and potential customers in the market? How can we describe them along various dimensions? What are their relevant characteristics?

2. What are their needs and wants in the general areas of customer behavior that we might be able to serve? Are these needs and wants relatively stable or relatively capable of change? How are they changing or how might they change?

3. How are these needs and wants now being satisfied? Can they be better satisfied?

4. What relevant external forces of change are at work—social, economic, technological, political, and so on—that might change the answers above?

5. Are there regional variations in the answers to these questions?

6. How do customers or potential customers perceive us as a firm, and our products and services?

7. Who are our direct competitors in these markets? For each, what is his product offering? What are his apparent strategies? What is his capability for change in strategy? How has he reacted in the past to competitive pressures? How might he react in the future?

8. What kinds of indirect competition are there or might there be in the future?

Because of the great diversity of markets and industries, this description of kinds of market intelligence needed is necessarily overgeneralized, but it may serve as a framework of thinking for the sales manager as he considers and analyzes this important element of the selling operation's task.

MARKET SELECTION

The next logical step in the marketing process is *market selection*—an analysis and decision process that has great meaning to and input into the firm's strategies. To get at it, however, a basic underlying idea must be developed, the simple philosophy of which pervades the entire marketing and selling effort of the firm. Its sense will also pervade this book.

Consider the question, *What is a product?* Now, a product can be described in many ways. It is a physical thing with physical characteristics. One can put calipers on it, measure it, weigh it. One can feel it and sometimes taste it or smell it.

A product can also be described as something salable. It is a unit of the physical output of the firm, which is the revenue generator for the firm. It is the culmination of the firm's productive effort.

But a product is much more than this. What the product is physically, is actually beside the point. To understand what it really is, one must forget its physical aspects and consider its *function in use*. Put another way, a product is nothing more or less than the utility it provides in use. That is, a product is something that satisfies a need, or fills a want,[1] or solves a problem.

---

[1] Here the word "need" is used in the sense of a *psychological motive*—for example, the need for "prestige." The word "want" is used as an *object* that will satisfy a need—for example, "I want a Cadillac because I have a need for prestige."

But in whose eyes? *In the eyes of the user.* This dynamic view of a product as a need satisfier or a problem solver focuses on the *customer's perception* of what the product will do for him. We can look at it this way. A customer has needs, wants, and problems. In this moment of time, he perceives a product—the physical entity. But in his mind, he projects himself out into the future and visualizes himself *using* the product, thus focusing on *what the product will do for him.* If he perceives that it will satisfy his needs better than they can otherwise be satisfied, he may decide to buy. If he does not perceive the *use* of the product in this positive way, he will likely decide not to buy.

For example, when you buy an automobile, what do you buy? The physical product is very obvious—3000 pounds of iron, steel, copper, glass, nylon, and the like. But is this what you visualize when you trade your $3000 for it? No, what you really buy (and what shapes your decision) is transportation, or recreation, or mobility, or status, or some mix of these things.

Thus in a very real sense the success of any business firm depends entirely on decisions that customers make about the firm's products or services. And, in turn, these customer decisions depend on how the customer perceives his future use of the product with regard to its ability to satisfy his needs, wants, and problems. Following the concept of the firm as a marketing system, this reasoning would seem to dictate that the firm, therefore, must present product offerings so that each of its many, many customers also so perceives these products.

However, this poses a serious dilemma. A market is made up of many individual customers, each one of whom is completely unique. Each has his own set or his own mix of needs; each has his own way of perceiving how these needs can be best satisfied; each has his own view of problems that lie athwart the path to his goals. If the firm literally followed the marketing concept and attempted to create a "custom" package of product offering tailored to each individual customer, it would find itself in extreme difficulty.

For example, suppose that Maytag, a large manufacturer of home laundry equipment, attempted to satisfy each housewife's wants in just one of its products—the automatic washer. From millions of housewives would come a huge number of different combinations of product wants. Some would want top loading, some side loading with right-opening door, some with left-opening door; some would want tumbler action, some agitator; some would want bleach dispenser, some not; some would want a water temperature range, some would not—and so on, in almost countless combinations. It simply would not be economically feasible for Maytag to produce enough models of the product to satisfy every unique customer's unique need set.

This is as true in industrial marketing as in consumer goods. For example, The American Blower Company serves many kinds of industrial customers, each with its own unique processes and its own specific operating problems, in such widely different industries as iron foundries, automotive plants, coal mines, office buildings, and lumber mills. Obviously, it would be impractical for American Blower to design, produce, and market a specific model of blower to match each individual customer's operating requirements.[2]

Does this dilemma mean that the customer-need orientation of the "marketing concept" is fine in theory but useless in practice? Not at all. The total market may be classified into groups or categories of customers, each group distinctively different from others, but the individual customers within each group having *relatively similar* needs or problems. This classifying can be done along many dimensions. For example, in the consumer goods markets it may be based on such factors as age, income, education, or occupation. In the industrial goods markets it is often based on customers' industries. That is, a computer manufacturer may classify or segment his markets into banks, oil refineries, steel mills, and so on. Certainly, individual banks within the banking customer-segment vary in their operating needs, hence in computer application. But they are *relatively* alike, and marketing programs can be tailored to *banks* as one customer grouping.

This classifying of customers into uniquely different categories, within each of which is relative communality of interests, needs, and problems, is *market segmentation*. It is an extremely important element of the firm's strategic planning, and it has special import for the sales manager's planning effort, as is discussed in Chapter 7. There we shall see that the sales manager may even have his own subcategories within the firm's major market segments—an influencing input into selling strategy.

Given the description and segmenting of customers into categories or market segments, the firm now makes its *market selection*. That is, the firm decides which of the market segments it elects to serve. In most cases a firm simply cannot fling itself across all possible markets and attempt to serve all customers in all markets. Most firms select certain markets and zero in on them. For example, in the men's clothing industry, Hart, Schaeffner, and Marx has elected certain market segments (and is in competition with Society Brand, Eagle, GGG, etc.), whereas Robert Hall has elected to aim at different market segments and essentially does not compete with Hart, Schaeffner, and Marx (but competes vigorously with

[2] To be sure, in a few cases firms do design and manufacture a "custom-made" product to an individual customer's specifications. For example, each large turbine generator produced by General Electric and Westinghouse is custom-designed for an individual electric utility.

such firms as Bond). One can examine any industry—publishing, radio broadcasting, automotive, electrical appliance, machine tool, and so on—and find that individual firms within each industry have made market selections.

The subprocess of market selection must be a rational and analytical one, because it greatly affects the firm's product and marketing strategies. A number of factors influence it:

1. *Corporate objectives.* What the firm wants to be, now and in the future, has a direct bearing on the markets that it may want to enter and serve.

2. *Skills and resources available to the firm.* A toy radio manufacturer may want to enter the computer market, but does not possess the necessary "know-how."

3. *Competition.* Market segments presently being very well served by firms that are in vigorous competition may not be likely candidates for selection.

4. *Long-range potential.* In most cases, firms seek to select market segments that will continue to contain customers with ongoing needs for the firm's products—even though the firm may have to adjust these products from time to time.[3]

5. *Tastes.* The managements of some firms may simply make selection of markets based on their personal tastes. Even here, of course, the foregoing steps should have been considered.

This entire market selection process is a vital one, to which, ideally, sales management should contribute, but on which, in any case, sales management bases much of its planning and operations. Furthermore, it is not a process that can be done only once. Markets are in flux. Firms must be constantly alert to the potentials of new markets as the world changes about them. This should never be too far below the surface in the effective sales manager's mind as he constantly analyzes and evaluates his markets.

PRODUCT OFFERINGS

Given the specific, definitive markets the firm chooses to serve, the *product offerings* are created to match the specific needs and problems in

---

[3] Of course, a firm may occasionally deliberately leap into a short-term market. Example: the large but very short-lived market for hula hoops.

those markets.[4] For example, if Hart, Schaeffner, and Marx elects to serve a men's clothing market identified as composed of men in the "upper-middle" social class and the higher-income "executive" category, the styling, materials, workmanship, and so forth, of their suits will be determined accordingly. The matching of products (or need satisfiers) to the needs of selected markets is, within the sense of the "marketing concept," the input to the productive components of the firm. Note in Figure 2-1 the input from "product offerings" to engineering and manufacturing. Note also that the arrows go two ways; technological development by research and engineering may often be the first stimulus for new products. Even in this case, however, the proposed new product ideally should be plugged into the "marketing process" to be certain that it matches present or feasibly potential needs in rationally selected markets.

MARKETING STRATEGY

At this point, broad marketwide and firmwide marketing strategies are developed. As a first step, specific marketing objectives are determined, consistent with and directly contributing to the firm's total business objective. Furthermore, marketing objectives must always be compatible, and at times coordinated, with the objectives of other components of the firm (i.e., production, finance, etc.). Given the objective, alternative broad strategies (or plans of action) are created. Selection of specific strategies is based on expected payoff, cost, feasibility, timing, and alternative anticipated competitive counteractions. Rational and analytical processes and techniques have been devised for this highly important step, but they are beyond the intended scope of this book.[5]

THE "SUBSTRATEGIES"

Spinning off from the broad marketing strategy, and necessarily evolving as a part of the marketing strategy itself, are the "substrategies" for

[4] This assumes that the needs are in existence and that customers are aware of them. Sometimes, of course, this is not the case, and the firm's strategies must create rather than influence demand. This is particularly true of product developments arising from new technology. Example: color television. However, this in no way changes the rationale or the mechanisms of this "marketing process." It simply puts in two-way arrows between "rest of firm," "product offerings," and "market selection" in Figure 2-1.

[5] For an example of one excellent analytical technique for market planning, see W. J. E. Crissy and R. Kaplan, "Matrix Models for Marketing Planning," *Business Topics*, Michigan State University, East Lansing, Mich., Summer 1963, pp. 48–66.

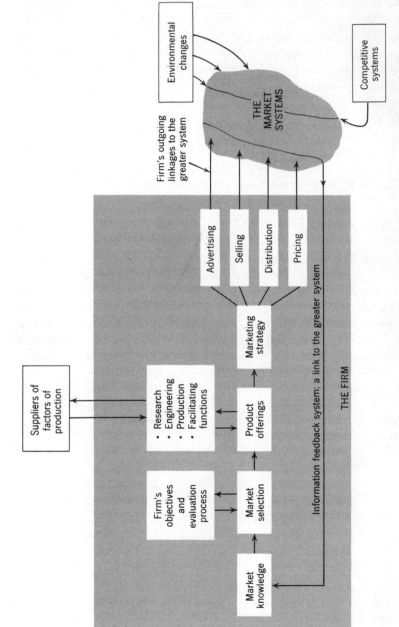

FIGURE 2-2   The firm as a marketing system.

advertising, selling, channels of distribution, and pricing. This is not an exclusive list; some firms, by the nature of their markets or products, may include other substrategies, such as packaging.

Note in Figure 2-1 that each of the substrategies is tailored uniquely to the differing market segments. Note also the highly significant integration and coordination of the substrategies. Later in this book (Chapters 7 and 8) the process of developing selling strategy is discussed in detail; it must be stressed here, however, that the selling effort is a key system *within a system* which is constantly maneuvering strategically. It is essential that the modern sales manager have this framework of thinking.

FEEDBACK, AGAIN

Marketing strategy generates market actions by the firm, resulting in customer decisions and behavior. It would be naïve to believe that such customer behavior will always gain the firm's objectives. Inevitably, changes and adjustments must be made. Equally important are competitors' reactions, to which the firm's strategy and actions must flex and counter. Hence the loop is again closed—with feedback of market knowledge continuing to flow back into the firm.

These are the great dynamics of marketing, the strategic process by which the firm develops and adjusts its behaviors in the marketplaces. The very anatomy of the firm itself may perhaps be more meaningfully portrayed in this way than by the orthodox organizational chart. By merely adapting the marketing process (Figure 2-1) slightly, one can envision the entire firm as a *system* existing in changing environments (Figure 2-2). Again, this is the great framework within which the selling operation plays such a vital role. It is a dynamic "way of life" in the competitive world of today's markets. It sets the stage for *everything the sales manager must think about and do.*

Chapter 3 will lift out selling from this dynamic framework and expand it, to examine its own system workings and its significant relationship to the system of the firm and to the systems of the marketplaces.

QUESTIONS AND PROBLEMS

1. The text proposes that it is essential for the effective sales manager to understand the "marketing process" and how the selling operation meshes into it. Why? Why can he not simply manage the sales force and do the best job possible without such understanding?

2. A highly successful sales manager recently remarked: "An outstanding sales force should be almost as much concerned about its ability to provide inputs as it is about its ability to provide outputs." What do you think he meant by this?
3. Should not the flow of market knowledge back into the firm be the responsibility of market research people, and not the sales personnel, who should be busy calling on customers?
4. Should the sales manager have anything to do with "market selection" or should these strategic decisions be left to marketing management?
5. Select a manufacturing firm. Show how this firm apparently utilizes the "marketing process" model presented in this chapter.
6. Select a firm operating only at the retail level and show how it apparently utilizes the "marketing process" model.

3

The Significance to the Firm of the Selling Effort

Selling is a vital process in our society. Its importance can be viewed from two sides—from the perspective of buyers in the market and from the perspective of the business firm itself. Before examining the significance of selling to the firm itself, and the significance of its effective management, it is revealing to look briefly at the buyer side of the process.[1]

The selling process has economic and social value to the society. As suggested by Harry R. Tosdal,[2] the ultimate objective of all selling is social gain—the raising of standards of living and the raising of goals toward which people strive. Selling influences and powers increases in aggregate demand, making possible higher production, in turn creating more wealth and more income, which in turn stimulates demand. Furthermore, selling provides invaluable help to buyers in identifying

[1] This book focuses on the management of the firm's selling operation, hence is quite frankly taking the firm's perspective, looking out into its markets.
[2] Harry R. Tosdal, *Selling in Our Economy*, Richard D. Irwin, 1957, pp. 79–90, as cited in T. W. Meloan and J. M. Rathmell, eds., *Selling: Its Broader Dimensions*, Macmillan, 1960, pp. 12–20.

wants and problems, in gaining information about alternative solutions, and in evaluating the alternatives. Finally, selling provides a key service to the society by communicating back into business firms the needs (real and potential), attitudes, and means of buyers—so that adapted, tailored goods and services will be forthcoming.

SIGNIFICANCE OF SELLING TO THE FIRM

The *primary* obligation of the business firm to the society is to be a productive, efficient economic unit. To continue to fulfill its social and economic function, the firm must be productive and profitable on a continuing basis; it must survive. Its profit, put simply, is the excess of revenue over cost. The revenue element of this equation is the target for the selling operation—the generation of an adequate volume of sales at a profitable price. Of course, this has always been true. Production itself has never created demand. Even in firms whose management is inwardly oriented, it is the selling operation that influences demand facing the firm and creates the revenue for the firm.[3] But now, with the growing acceptance by firms of the marketing concept, new dimensions have been added to the selling operation.

Within the framework of thinking of the firm as a marketing system, the firm's selling operation has become more important than ever before. The firm's very success depends more significantly on its effectiveness. This does not necessarily mean that selling is the most important activity of the firm. And the often quoted statement that "Nothing ever happens until a sale is made"[4] is fallacious as well as naïve. The selling operation is a subsystem that is interrelated with and reacts to many other subsystems in the greater system of the firm. *But it is the one subsystem*

[3] It may be argued that an innovative product itself may influence demand and thus create revenue. But this is the old "build a better mousetrap" adage, which has been rather well debunked. To be sure, if the firm eliminated or minimized selling effort, some revenue would flow in. But it would be naïve to believe that it would be profitably adequate. In any case, firms do not minimize selling effort but, rather, optimize it. The argument can be posed that in some consumer nondurable industries, the advertising function is the primary demand-influencing and revenue-securing effort. This is valid; in some industries (e.g., cigarette, soap) advertising *expenditures* exceed selling expenditures. But these represent a small percentage of GNP and even here the selling operation is a vital one—to get stocks ordered by wholesalers and retailers, to get effort by wholesalers, promotions by retailers, and so on, all in the face of vigorous rivalry from competitors.

[4] Rather obviously, before a sale is made, the customer wants must be detected, production facilities organized, a product or service created, and an offering made to the market. In fact, the entire system has responded before a sale is made.

that extends beyond the firm into its market environments and personally interacts with customers. The selling operation may be viewed as the one subsystem of the firm that links the system that is the firm with the greater system of the markets.[5]

In this sense, the selling operation is at the very heart of the "marketing concept." Whatever innovations, strategies, and programs of action are created by the firm, the payoff comes at that magic moment when some salesman from the firm sits face-to-face with a customer, influencing that customer's decisions.[6] The more the firm flexes its strategies and marketing programs, the more true this becomes. Here the selling effort is playing its classic role—translating the product offerings of the firm to customers in the markets. This is the classic role of contacting customers, applying the firm's products or services to their needs, wants, and problems, developing and securing orders and sales revenue, and doing all this so that customers will deal with the firm repetitively.

But of at least equal importance in the modern systems concept is the key role that sales plays in *translating customers' real and potential attitudes and activities back into the firm.* Furthermore, though economists, marketing staff, and even management may forecast future changes in many external variables, only the selling operation is intimately keyed into the *actions of the moment* in the markets. Only the sales operation is intimately and directly tuned to the behaviors of competitors (given the fact of no collusion). This aspect of market intelligence—rivals' strategy and tactics—is one of the most important but least adequately managed marketing activities in most firms today. The selling operation is the key link in the customer-firm-customer loop.

As shown in Figure 3-1, the selling operation not only communicatively *links* the firm with the markets, but also provides the medium for *translating the meanings of each to the other.* Translating here is meant quite literally—the transfer from one language to another, and in both directions. This does not take anything away from the normally expressed

---

[5] It may be argued that market research and public relations function similarly. Yet the selling operations' linkages with the market system are pervasive, intimate, personal, and truly *interactive*. Other functions of the firm also have links with the external environment (e.g., the finance function has links with the financial community). But here we are considering the vital links with *market* environments in which exist *customers* who determine the firm's revenue, hence profit, hence survival.

[6] To be sure, in some consumer goods industries the *mix* of advertising and selling efforts weighs heavily toward advertising. Even here, salesmen of the manufacturing firm perform vital activities with wholesalers and sometimes with dealers, getting their orders, providing an array of services, training their salesmen, analyzing their markets, and so on. They implement the firm's strategies in the wholesaler-dealer marketplaces. See Chapter 7 for a more detailed discussion of this.

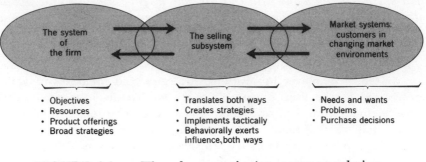

- Objectives
- Resources
- Product offerings
- Broad strategies

- Translates both ways
- Creates strategies
- Implements tactically
- Behaviorally exerts
  influence,both ways

- Needs and wants
- Problems
- Purchase decisions

FIGURE 3-1   The sales operation's two-way translating.

prime *function* of selling [7]—to contact and influence customers so as to produce volume, or a flow of orders into the productive elements of the firm. But in the dynamic markets of today, *sales management* must encompass this greater rationale of the selling operation as a linking and translating system:

1. Translating market intelligence into "the firm's language," thus providing inputs into the firm, so that the firm may (if necessary) strategically adapt.

2. Translating the firm's offerings and strategies into the language of the market systems, so that they may adapt such offerings to their advantage.

The *function* of selling then becomes one of implementing the firm's strategies in the marketplace, strategically and tactically.

This systems concept of selling is relatively new. In the 1920's and 1930's, most manufacturing firms were production-oriented.[8] This orientation stemmed quite naturally from the revolutions in manufacturing processes during that generation. They sufficed for the period. In those times the firm looked somewhat as shown, very schematically, in Figure 3-2.

[7] This is from the firm's viewpoint. Selling fulfills an important function from *buyers'* standpoints, too, in providing a flow of up-to-date information on how to satisfy changing wants and to solve problems. This is well recognized in industrial selling. It is equally needed at the consumer level for many consumer products, but is often poorly accomplished.

[8] Similarly, most service-producing firms were internally oriented or self-oriented, rather than market- or customer-oriented. Examples: banks, railroads, many kinds of wholesalers. Like manufacturers, they focus on *means* (products) rather than *ends* (customer needs and satisfactions). This is the converse of the "marketing concept."

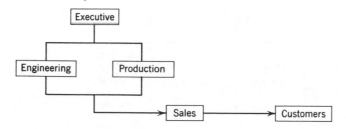

FIGURE 3-2   Rationale of production-oriented firm.

Oversimplifying somewhat, the executive of the production-oriented firm met with engineering management and production management, who then together made the large strategic decisions for the firm. They decided what to produce, how to produce it, how many to produce, what production rates to use, what models, what price levels, what packaging, and so on. They then turned to the sales department and said, "Okay, you sell 'em." And sales departments by and large did a very good job, accepting as their primary (and usually their only) mission that of getting orders and "moving the goods." [9]

Not so today. In today's almost volatile competitive markets, *marketing* becomes the starting point as well as the output end in the spectrum of the activities of the firm, and additionally loops these two "ends" together through the dynamics of the marketplaces. To fit the reasoning discussed in Chapters 1 and 2, the diagram of Figure 3-2 must be changed as shown in Figure 3-3.

Although in Figure 3-2 the sales department *looks* rather independent (and may have been) and in Figure 3-3 marketing seems to be in ascendancy, it must be reiterated and stressed that the place of the selling operation in this rationale is infinitely more significant to the firm. Note again that it is the selling operation that closes the loop—which interprets the firm to the markets by way of its strategies and tactical influence and which translates back into the firm's system the dynamics of the markets. Clearly, the management of this vital element of two systems has increasingly heavy demands placed on its performance.

[9] Unfortunately, there are some industries, both manufacturing and service, and an uncomfortable number of companies in many industries, whose managements and sales departments still operate like this in actual practice. They are likely to have trouble in the future.

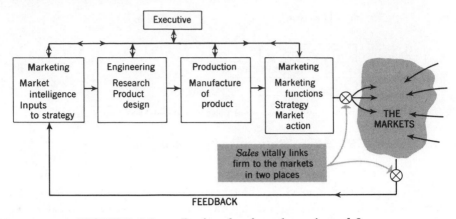

FIGURE 3-3 Rationale of market-oriented firm.

SELLING BECOMING MORE COMPLEX

Although the selling operation and its management are significant to the firm's overall success, selling itself is becoming more complex.[10] This has compounded the drive by many firms for greater and greater competence in selling and in sales management. The reasons for this are not difficult to understand when contemporary marketing and selling are examined in the framework of thinking discussed in Chapters 1 and 2.

Competition

Thinking back to the "core market" concept, and simply observing what goes on in the marketplaces, makes it clear that the vigor and drive of competitors increase the complexity and difficulty of selling. In most industries, competitors are "tough" these days.

For one thing, their executive managements more and more exhort their function managements: "Let's get going! Let's innovate. Let's create new strategies. Let's get a bigger chunk of that market, or we could be in trouble." *It would be naïve to believe that competitors' managements are not or might not be following this natural rationale.* By and large, competitors' strategies are becoming more responsive, more effective, and more difficult to counter.

10 In many selling and sales management seminars conducted by me, the question, "Is selling becoming more difficult?" always receives a resounding "Yes" answer from the professional sales and management participants. The following paragraphs are condensed paraphrases of reasons given by these professional people.

There are also *more direct competitors* in many industries. Because of socioeconomic growth, markets have enlarged, attracting entry. The great technological growth also attracts and permits entry, as the growing complexity of products and product systems encourages more and more specialization. Classic examples are the electronics industry and the space industry, in which hundreds of small firms have entered with unique specialized skills, centering on a very small segment of the industry. Many of these small firms grow and expand, sending competitive tentacles into new markets.

Competitors Are Becoming More Competent. Managements know that to stay alive, performance of all elements of their firms must become constantly more effective. The severe and sometimes almost vicious competition for competent professional people is illustrative. This drive for increasing competence is observable not only in large firms; witness the growing activity of many trade associations in providing highly professional educational programs for personnel of their relatively small member firms. The professional salesmen of today and his district sales manager would be naïve to believe that the personal and professional quality of their rival counterparts is not improving. And this certainly tends to make the selling and sales management job more difficult.

Indirect Competition

Customers of all kinds—consumer, industrial, commercial, and governmental—are spending more money. Personal spending and private and government investment are increasing. Yet the array of goods and services available to satisfy wants and to apply to problems has more than kept pace. Buyers of all kinds, therefore, must allocate their resources. Very few individual consumers and very few business firms can buy anything they decide without an effect on other purchase decisions. Hence, to an increasing degree, "indirect" competition (a second car versus a new electric kitchen, an automatic typewriter versus new dictating equipment, a new power plant versus a renovated power distribution network) is making selling more difficult.[11]

Product Technology

Products, product lines, and product systems have become increasingly complex, because of new technology available to the firm and the stra-

[11] This can be an insidious kind of competition, difficult to detect and to analyze. For this reason, and because a framework of thinking about it is rarely developed, it is often shrugged off or simply not even thought of.

tegic maneuvering of the firm in seeking to enlarge its market core. This may take the shape of an expanded product line, more complex and complicated products, widely diverse products, systems of products, or combinations of these. The increasing complexity may be in the design and application of the product itself, in the processes of its manufacture, in its packaging, in its new distribution requirements, in its servicing, or in combinations of these factors.[12] All this, too, tends to make selling more difficult.

Changes in Customers Themselves

Revolutionary changes have occurred also on the customer side. Consider industrial and commercial customers. Most firms find that a high proportion of their business comes from a relatively small percentage of their customers—those customers who place relatively large orders. But over time these customers grow. Being business firms, they too seek to expand their market positions. As they grow, their organizations grow. As this happens, decision making tends to be delegated to a greater degree. With decision making about purchases being pushed to lower levels in customer organizations, the many new decision makers who operate "under risk" tend to be very careful and highly rational in their decisions. With such delegation, new accountabilities and new policy guidelines evolve. All this poses problems for selling.

Customer Technology

Also operating within the rationale of the marketing concept, the industrial or commercial customer must continually adopt and adapt new technology, altering or adjusting operating processes in all elements of his system. Thus, to the firm selling to him, operating problems and product applications are under continual change and grow in complexity. This may not be a "problem" in the strictest sense to the salesman and his sales management.[13] It may, in fact, be an opportunity that the salesman can exploit (see Chapter 6). But it does place on the salesman demands for new abilities. It does make his job more complex, albeit

[12] These facts are obvious for technologically oriented firms such as Monsanto Chemical or Caterpillar Tractor. But it is equally true for firms with "simpler" products. Consider how these facts apply to a sales representative for a large food wholesaler, whose customers are large supermarkets. Technology in the processing, packaging, transporting, storage, and display of foods is as glamorous and complex as in the "technological industries."

[13] Except, of course, to the salesman whose firm's products have been made obsolete by changes in the customer's technology.

more important. Expanding technology has created changes in attitudes and market behavior of individual consumers as well. Individual consumers are becoming increasingly sophisticated.

Purchasing

The purchasing function has changed greatly in the past twenty years. A new breed of professional purchasing managers has evolved. The day of the old-time, rough and gruff, "wheel-and-deal" purchasing agent is essentially gone. In his place is a highly trained, often technically educated, extremely competent professional, who thinks and behaves as a manager, within a system. The authority to make more and more important decisions is being delegated to the modern professional purchasing agent and his competent organizational group of buyers. Again, this may open great opportunities for many salesmen. But it has changed the nature of the selling job and has made it more complex and exacting.

THE PRESSURE FOR VOLUME

Other forces within the firm itself exert great pressures on the selling operation, particularly *the quest for greater volume*. In most industries, executive managements face serious problems in improving and often even in maintaining the desired levels of profit for their firms. Consider the profit equation:

$$\text{profit} = \text{revenue} - \text{cost}$$

To increase profit, either revenue must be increased or cost decreased, or both. But most industries are in a "price-cost squeeze," in which price levels are drifting downward (at least relatively) and costs keep inching upward. Examining the revenue equation,

$$\text{revenue} = \text{price} \times \text{quantity}$$

we see that revenue can be increased if price is increased or if quantity is increased.[14] But increasing prices is an extremely difficult thing to do in the highly competitive markets and with government watching over

14 Under certain conditions, if prices for a product are *decreased* by firms in an industry, revenue will *increase*. If the industry is operating in the elastic portion of its demand curve, the relative increase in quantity demanded will more than offset a relative decrease in price, and revenue will increase. See any basic economics text on price theory.

managements' shoulders. Hence part of the drive for profit centers on increasing quantity, or volume, and this is the function of the selling operation.

Another part of the drive for profit focuses on reducing costs. Again, this is difficult to do in most industries, particularly because of increasing costs of manpower.[15] But even the drive for reducing costs reflects an additional drive for added volume and, in turn, exerts great pressure on sales management. To see the dynamics underlying this, consider the concept of *break-even analysis*. Figure 3-4 is an extremely oversimplified depiction of break-even analysis. Though the real cost curves are not straight lines, and though the shifts in costs made in the diagram are exaggerated for clarity, the rationale behind this analysis is valid and highly important for sales management to understand.

In the diagram, dollars of revenue and of cost are plotted on the vertical axis, and units or quantity of output are plotted on the horizontal axis. All units produced are assumed to be sold. Selling price per unit is assumed to be unchanging.[16] The "revenue line" starts at the origin (no units produced and sold; no revenue) and rises upward to the right (the more units sold, the greater the revenue).

Somewhat oversimplifying, costs are considered to be of two kinds—fixed costs and variable costs. The *fixed costs* are those incurred by the firm that remain constant regardless of output (the so-called overhead costs, such as mortgage payments, insurance, capital amortization, and depreciation). Because they are constant, they are represented in the diagram by the horizontal line *FC*. *Variable costs* are those incurred directly for the manufacture of the product. Again oversimplifying somewhat, they represent the cost of material and labor going into each unit of product. Hence the more units produced, the greater the variable cost. The variable-cost line (not shown on the diagram) therefore begins at the origin (no units produced, no direct labor and material cost) and runs upward to the right. Since we are interested in *total costs,* the variable costs must be added to fixed costs. This is done geometrically in the diagram by drawing the variable-cost line not from the origin, but from the point where the fixed-cost line *(FC)* intersects the vertical axis, at *A*. The resulting line *TC* represents the total costs at all levels of output.

Obviously, for the firm to make a profit, revenue must exceed total costs. But since even at zero output (hence zero revenue) there are some costs *(FC)*, revenue does not exceed total cost until some level of output

[15] We could say simply "cost of labor," except that here we mean the increasing cost of all kinds of personnel.

[16] If price were increased, the revenue line would swing counterclockwise; if price were decreased, it would swing clockwise.

is reached, where revenue just equals total costs. This is the "break-even point," the level of revenue and output where the firm makes no profit and sustains no loss. This is represented in the diagram by point C, where the revenue line and the total-cost line intersect. Here a sales revenue of R_{BE} and a corresponding production level of Q_{BE} must be achieved for the firm to just break even. At sales volumes below this point, the firm incurs loss (costs are higher than revenue); at sales volumes above it, the firm makes a profit (costs are lower than revenue). Note that as volumes more and more exceed the break-even point the gap between TC and the revenue line becomes greater and greater—that is, more and more profit is achieved. This creates drive for added volume, but it is only one of the factors involved. Other more subtle factors result in even greater drive for increased volume.

Consider, for example, a firm that is operating above the break-even point. If volume can be increased, the gap between revenue and TC becomes larger. Assuming that demand for the product remains the same, to get a larger volume in the existing market, the firm must gain on its competition and increase its *share of the market*. This brings the drive for increased market share that most selling operations experience. And this will be attempted, by way of strategic programs. But it is difficult; competition is likely to be behaving similarly. Another way, therefore, to increase profit (even at the same volume of output) is to enlarge the gap between revenue and TC by rotating one or both of the lines. Given the same costs, if the revenue line can be rotated upward, greater profit will result at all levels of output.[17] However, this means that prices must be raised, and although firms and industries do attempt this, sometimes successfully, it is often very difficult to do.[18]

Still another way to increase the profit is to rotate TC downward, by reducing costs—and great efforts are exerted in this direction by most firms. But here is a dilemma, and its solution has great impact on the selling operation. Fixed costs are very difficult to reduce—they just "sort of stay with you." Turning to variable costs, then, presents a likely opportunity. But here a major element of cost is direct labor, and labor rates keep inching upward. One way to reduce variable costs is to reduce the *amount* of direct labor going into the product. Basically (and again oversimplifying a bit) this means increased use of "laborsaving" processes and the greater use of automated or semiautomated equipment.[19]

[17] Refer to footnote 14 with regard to price elasticity of demand and its effect on revenue.

[18] Recall the difficulties encountered by the steel industry during the Kennedy Administration.

[19] This may not mean that workers are dismissed. It may mean that new capital equipment can increase the volume of output with the same work force—hence reducing direct labor cost per unit of output.

This is the underlying force behind the modernization of plant. Many problems exist here for the executive. Technology is expanding so rapidly that the new plant of today may be "obsolete" tomorrow. This does not mean that the "obsolete" plant is not productive or efficient. It merely means that suddenly new technology and new kinds of plant equipment are available which if adopted *can reduce variable costs*. But in order to use them, the firm must make additional capital investments, and *fixed costs increase*. Here the dilemma intensifies. If the firm does invest in new plant (even though the "old" may be still quite "new" and very functional), it will have to increase its volume for the investment to pay off (as will be explained below). Can the firm do it? Can the sales operation produce added volume? On the other hand, if the firm does not invest in the new plant, a competitor might. And if he does, the competitor might so improve his cost and profit situation that he *could* manipulate his price tactics in the market to gain market share, at this firm's expense. Or his tactics might force the firm to meet his lower prices, hence suffer reduced profit (revenue line swings down toward TC).

As a result of this sort of calculus the *general statement can be made* that many firms today are compelled for competitive as well as cost and profit reasons to continually expand and modernize their plant. But what happens as fixed costs go up because of more frequent investment in continually more sophisticated and expensive plant equipment? The increase in fixed costs is shown in Figure 3-4 by line FC', intersecting the vertical axis at B.[20] Because with the new equipment, variable costs are decreased, the new total-cost line (TC') is drawn at a lower slope than formerly.[21] But note that because of the higher fixed costs, TC' intersects the revenue line farther to the right, at D—that is, the break-even point is now higher. In other words, it now requires more volume to just break even than formerly—a revenue of R'_{BE} and a quantity produced of Q'_{BE}. This is an added pressure on the selling operation.

There are other pressures. Note the obvious fact that with TC' swung down from TC, the gap (or profit) between revenue and TC' is now greater—if the firm can get up the volumes to the point where this occurs. Hence a great drive for volume. But there is a less obvious fact that is often overlooked. Actually, the new break-even point (D) is not the most significant point. Certainly, volume must be held above this

---

20 The increase shown here is exaggerated in order to show clearly what happens to the break-even point.

21 The executive would never rationally incur the higher fixed costs in the first place, unless he was sure that variable costs, *hence total costs,* would be lower at some volumes. For this not to be true would mean lower profit at all volumes, which he would not permit. That is, he would not commit to the new investment.

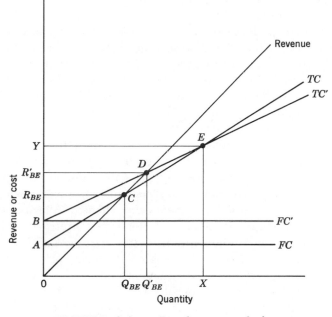

FIGURE 3-4   Break-even analysis.

point. The really critical point is at *E*, the point at which the new total-cost line (*TC'*) intersects the former total-cost line (*TC*). Examination of the diagram will show that at all volumes of sales above the former breakeven point but below that at *E* (sales of *Y* and production of *X*), the former total costs are *lower* than the new total costs. That is, *TC'* is at all points *above* *TC*. It would be foolhardy to install the new capital equipment, unless the firm can be quite sure of achieving volumes not merely above the new, higher break-even point, but *above point E*. Furthermore, it is completely possible that point *E* might be *significantly* higher than new break-even. For example, a plant that is computerized and automated may have to run at significantly higher volume to be more profitable than the former plant. This very clearly places *great emphasis on the volume objective* in many firms today. And with technology expanding, the emphasis appears to be increasing.

These phenomena are not restricted to technologically oriented manufacturing firms. They are operant in all kinds of firms. American Airlines, with increasing investment not only in aircraft but in sophisticated ground facilities, must feel the quest for added volume. A modern retail enterprise (such as Sears Roebuck, Marshall Field, Macy's, or A & P), with its modern "plant" of escalators, complex display facilities, air conditioning, computerized billing service, and automated ordering systems, certainly must experience the drive for added volume because of these phenomena. So do banks, magazine publishers, clothing manufacturers, and wholesaling firms. There seems to be an almost universal and increasing drive for volume, which in turn puts the spotlight on the selling operation and its management. Never has this element of the firm's system been so vitally important and so significant to the firm's success.

The effective sales manager must view these phenomena from two slants. For one thing, of course—and this is the more important slant—he must understand these dynamics within his firm, so that he can more adequately guide the performance of his selling operation. Insight into these dynamics may help him to understand (and even predict) some apparently unconnected side effects on other elements affecting his operations (hence affecting the efficacy of the firm's strategies and market activities). For example, though it may appear to be unrelated to plant modernization and the cost problems of the firm, pricing policy and action may change, requiring sales management to flex and adjust strategies. As a simple illustration consider the following example, based on fact. A large electrical apparatus manufacturer produced and marketed (among other products) a line of distribution transformers. This firm was considered (and considered itself to be) the "price leader" in this market. Its pricing policy was quite rigid; that is, it held to its published prices and, despite occasional price cuts by some competitors, held its prices quite firmly. Efforts by the selling operation to increase market share were (in the eyes of sales management) somewhat hampered by this policy.[22] The manufacturing plant was an old one, having been in existence for over fifty years, but it had been renovated and modernized. Yet the multistoried plant did not lend itself to complete "modernization." Then this firm, a leader in automation of plant, designed and erected a new, completely modern distribution transformer plant in another geographical location, which had a considerably higher productive capacity than the old plant. Shortly after the new plant, with its computerized ordering systems and similar features, came "on line," the pressure on the selling operation to increase sales volume stepped up considerably. Following this, pricing policy began to change. On this product line, the firm became quite competitive in its pricing. It can be hypothesized quite safely that the quest for profit, for market power, and for protection and

---

[22] This is not to say that such a policy was "wrong," under the market conditions of the time. See Chapter 10 for an analysis of situations of this kind.

enlargement of its core market led this firm to modernize plant and reduce variable costs—but with the concomitant great drive for added volume. Furthermore, it *can be hypothesized* that this quest, while it occurs, not only exerts pressure for more volume, but also *tends* to lower price levels.[23] The executive can look to the right of the break-even diagram and see the proportionately large added increment of profit as volume goes up—and he might perhaps "bend" the revenue line down somewhat to reach higher volumes, by selective price decreases.

The possibility of these things occurring might be predicted by the sales manager, and certainly better understood, by his understanding of the dynamics discussed in this as well as the first two chapters.

Such understanding will also increase the ability of the sales manager to predict competitors' behaviors. As individual firms, competitors, too, are enmeshed in the same dynamics. Thinking in the analytical framework presented in this chapter may enable the sales manager to predict in advance how a competitor's selling strategies (including pricing strategies) might flex, hence enable him to be better prepared with counterstrategies. Let a competitor modernize plant,[24] and it is a safe bet that quite soon it will be reflected in a change in behavior in his field sales operation, as his sales management comes under the pressure for more volume.

How to cope with this? The answer is the gist of this book. The sales manager, as the manager of a system within systems, must so think and behave that the strategies and actions of groups and persons in his component result in achievement of the agreed upon objectives of the selling operation. The first three chapters of this book have presented the dynamic background needed for such thinking and behavior, as well as a framework within which such thinking and behavior must develop. Given this framework, the next chapter zeroes in on the analysis of the job itself of the sales manager, the elements of which form the structure of the remainder of the book.

QUESTIONS AND PROBLEMS

1. Comment on the following statement: "Twenty-five years ago, most manufacturing firms had a technical function, a production func-

---

[23] In my opinion, the "low" price levels existing in some industries are going to remain that way, and executive and sales managements must adjust their thinking to it. Strategies must be devised to increase the *quantity* factor in the revenue equation.

[24] This could be an increased investment in warehouses, service facilities, and the like, as well as in manufacturing plant.

tion, and a sales function. The sales manager was on a par with the technical manager and the production manager. Now with 'marketing' in the picture, he is down the line. His job level is organizationally below that of the production manager. Obviously, his job is not considered as important as it was."

2. Comment on the statement: "The success of the firm depends entirely on the successful sale of its products. Therefore, the job of the sales manager is more important than any other in the firm—except perhaps that of the president."

3. If you were a district sales manager, how would you describe your responsibility for "two-way linking"? What elements would you "translate" in each direction?

4. The statement was made that "Selling is becoming more complex— more difficult." Yet, in many firms, the selling job has been split into specialized parts. For example, an office equipment manufacturer may have some salesmen selling only desk-top machines, while others sell computers (product specialization). Or a large food wholesaler may have some salesmen selling only to large retail food chains, while others sell to restaurants (customer specialization). Or customers may "specialize," so that some of their personnel are concerned with some kinds of products, while others are concerned with different products. Should this not make selling simpler and easier? Why?

5. You are a regional sales manager for a firm producing air-conditioning equipment. At a national sales meeting, the marketing vice-president announces that the directors and executives of the firm have decided to launch a vast plant expansion program, to take advantage of the growing demand for air conditioning. The program will include modernization and some automation in present plant and construction of several large new plants. What is the meaning of this to you as a regional sales manager? What can you predict about the requirements that your headquarters will begin putting on you in the near future? Show schematically what happens in the firm's cost structure to cause such changing requirements for your selling organization.

6. You are a regional sales manager for a firm competing with the air-conditioning manufacturer. You read in the *Wall Street Journal* of their expansion plans. Explain in detail what your reasoning about this might be and why—with respect to your own job.

4

The Nature of the Sales Manager's Job

The management of the firm's selling effort assumes critical importance, because the firm's success depends more and more on the effectiveness of this effort. This chapter examines analytically the important role of the sales manager, and the resulting "model" of the sales manager's job can serve as a framework for the remainder of the book.

What is the basic nature of the sales manager's job? What are its essential elements, those common to all sales management jobs? Here the idea of the "job description" gives little help. Job descriptions spell out the very specific duties, authorities, accountabilities, and relationships of specific jobs. They necessarily vary widely from firm to firm. For example, job descriptions will be very different for the sales manager of a chemical company, a linen supply company, a food wholesaling company, or an airline. Furthermore, the job descriptions for different sales management levels within a given company will vary greatly. For example, consider the very different specific duties, authorities, accountabilities, and relationships for a national sales manager, a regional sales manager, and a district sales manager.

But in all these diverse *jobs,* some common, pervasive elements can be identified. These basic elements provide a conceptual underpinning, a *framework of thinking* about the sales manager's job. It is this managerially oriented rather than task-oriented framework on which this chapter focuses.[1]

However, to put this framework of thinking about sales management in the proper perspective, consider first the role of the selling operation itself, within the concept of the firm as a marketing system. Or, just what is it that the sales manager manages?

THE MISSIONS OF THE SELLING OPERATION

The selling operation is a subsystem of marketing. It is an entity that possesses resources—people, money, and things. These resources may be great in large business firms that have far-flung selling organizations, such as du Pont or Metropolitan Life Insurance Company. Or they may be relatively small, as in a local dairy or a screw-machine shop. The management of these resources must always aim at the achievement of the missions given to the selling subsystem.

Every facet of the selling operation's missions or *goals* becomes, in a sense, a base point in the sales manager's job. These goals can be viewed from three different standpoints: [2] the market's, the firm's, and that of the systems-link. Obviously, for some selling operations, certain goals or combinations of goals will be more heavily stressed than others. Furthermore, it is conceivable that some selling operations may have a goal not appearing in this analysis. Or some may legitimately disregard some of those included. This analysis is meant to serve as a framework for thinking.

BROAD GOALS FOR THE SELLING OPERATION

The Market Standpoint

1. To help determine what market segments should be selected and cultivated. Although "market selection" is primarily a responsibility of

[1] It can be argued that the "model" in this chapter is not operational, or quantifiable. This is true. It is also true that job descriptions can be made operational and quantifiable. But job descriptions are designed for unique, specific jobs and provide missions and duties. Here we are concerned with the rationale underlying job descriptions. The job description gives little help with the questions: What is the nature of sales management? What are the elements of the sales manager's job? About what must he think and be knowledgeable? In what realms must he become proficient? To answer these questions, we need a general, conceptual framework of thinking.

[2] Here we are picking up the thread from the preceding chapter and moving more specifically into the goals of the selling operation, from the firm's point of view.

marketing management, the selling operation in intimate contact with market forces must have a finger in this pie.

2. To help select customers within these chosen segments. Again, customer selection may depend on factors outside the scope of sales, particularly the selection of *general types* of customers. But selection of *specific* customers is usually best accomplished by the selling operation (see Chapter 7).

3. To convert marketing objectives into specific sales objectives, which are to be achieved within the selected market spheres. This is discussed in some detail in Chapter 6.

4. To create strategies or plans of action, market by market and customer by customer, for achieving these objectives. This is one of the most vital goals and activities of any selling operation; it is discussed in detail in Chapters 7 and 8.

5. To translate the firm's product offerings and policies into the language of the marketplaces.

6. To develop and maintain contact of predetermined degree of intimacy with customers. The rationale and a method for the "predetermined degree" is presented in Chapter 7.

7. To implement tactically the strategies and translations—so as to influence customers to perceive the firm's product offerings as advantageous need satisfiers or problem solvers.

8. To so behave in the marketplaces as to influence customers to perceive the firm as a good one with which to do business.

9. To create these strategies and to exhibit tactical behaviors in such a way that long-range as well as short-range objectives will be achieved.

10. To influence and direct the planning, action, and achievement of intermediaries who are outside the firm, but in the channels of distribution between the firm and the customers who use its products (see Chapter 10).

11. To represent the firm in the public at large—thus to enhance the firm's image.

The Firm's Standpoint

1. To achieve and maintain a flow of orders such that marketing objectives of sales volume and market share are realized. This, of course, is keyed to the production and profit goals of the firm. Note, however, that this is a primary *sales* goal and probably is the one most often present in the consciousness of sales managers.[3]

[3] This entire part argues, however, that it is the complex of *all these goals* of the selling operation that sets the "job" of the sales manager. It does not detract from the primacy of the sales volume goal to say that the sales manager would be

2. To develop and sustain a predetermined balanced effort and achievement between the firm's various product lines. The necessary knowledge for allocating effort between product lines depends on the profit mix, which may vary from time to time. It usually must be provided to the selling operation by marketing management by way of the control systems of the firm. This is an important input into sales-strategy-creating process and even into such processes as compensation and ongoing training. It should be emphasized, however, that allocation of selling effort among the firm's product lines must not be left to the whim or the taste of sales personnel, but must be rationally and objectively determined.

3. To contribute to profit by achieving sales objectives at optimum expense.[4]

4. To coordinate its objectives, plans, and actions with other elements of marketing (advertising, marketing research, product planning, etc.) and with other elements in the firm (credit, product research and design, inventory control, etc.) .

The Systems-Link Standpoint

1. To maintain a constant (planned and formal) surveillance of all market forces. The purpose is twofold:

(*a*) to flush out potential or actual obstacles to goal achievement, so that plans and actions may be accordingly adjusted, and (*b*) to detect new market opportunities to pursue, so that plans and actions may be created.

2. To feed back into the firm's systems vital information on all market forces in flux—those forces that affect or potentially affect customers' attitudes and behaviors. This must be a way of life, as well as a formal objective and a set of methods for accomplishment.

3. To feed back into the firm's systems its continuing observation, analysis, and, when possible, prediction of competitive behaviors of all kinds.

These three sets of objectives—those oriented toward the marketplace, those oriented toward the firm itself, and those aimed to tie the systems of

operating with blinders on if he did not think of the interrelationship of all these goals.

4 This book takes the stance that the selling operation usually is not to be charged with *profit accountability* per se. That is, the sales operation cannot be established as a profit-and-loss operation, hence with specific, *quantifiable profit objectives*. Of course, in some rare cases this might be done. A "sales division" could "buy" products from the parent company and operate as a profit-autonomous component. Or it could be argued that some entire firms are selling operations (wholesalers, manufacturers agents, etc.) . In these cases, one need only add specific profit objectives to this list.

the firm to the system of the marketplaces—become the real target and *raison d'être* of the sales manager's job. He manages a system composed of people, things, and money in such a way that these objectives are achieved by the performance of the system itself.

THE JOB OF THE SALES MANAGER

Taking these objectives, then, as the job to be performed by the selling operation, and within the systems rationale previously discussed, the anatomy of the job of managing this operation can be examined analytically (Figure 4-1). Again, it is necessary to generalize, since the nature of the

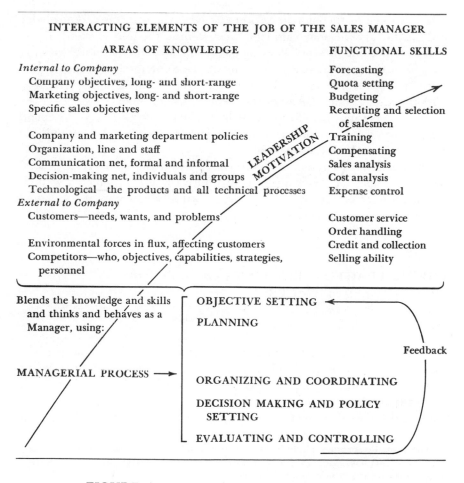

FIGURE 4-1   The job of the sales manager.

selling operation itself may vary widely from firm to firm or between different types of businesses. Again, the model is meant to serve as a framework for thinking, which can be adjusted to fit specific selling operations and, with its overriding rationale holding, whatever specific sales management job is plugged into it.

Note in Figure 4-1 that the job of the sales manager may be broken down analytically into four major categories, all interrelated, interdependent, and interacting:

1. Areas of knowledge
2. Functional skills
3. The managerial process
4. Leadership and motivation

Whereas some of the *content within the elements* of areas of knowledge and functional skills may vary from firm to firm, the four elements themselves are present in every sales management job. Furthermore, viewing the job of the sales manager in terms of these interacting elements provides an overall *managerial orientation* rather than a descriptive or a work-functional one. Because the modern sales manager manages a system and because his effectiveness in achieving objectives will depend more on managerial abilities than on technical or functional skills, a managerial orientation is essential.

The remaining chapters of this book focus on the managerial process element of sales management and introduce the other elements vis-à-vis this managerial orientation.[5] The "broad-brush" discussion of the model and its elements in this chapter is meant to serve only as an overview.

THE INTERACTING ELEMENTS OF THE JOB
OF THE SALES MANAGER

Areas of Knowledge

A logical starting point in analyzing the job of the sales manager is the knowledge that he must develop in a number of aspects. Here is meant simply the intelligent grasp of facts that he must have. This knowledge is not really teachable from books or learnable by deduction. Such intelligence and knowledge must come from experience. These are things that

---

[5] The orthodox manner of studying or training for sales management centers on learning functional skills. In this book these skills will be materially subjugated to the management and motivational elements.

the sales manager learns over time from his company, from his associates, and from the world itself.

However, this does not mean that this important element of the sales manager's job need be or should be left to chance. To analyze within an analysis, so to speak, this element of knowledge can be broken down into subcategories, thus providing a "framework" that the sales manager (or potential sales manager) can use to develop himself rationally and logically.

Many areas of knowledge need to be developed. One broad area divides into a wide array of knowledge that must be obtained about situations and things internal to the firm and a similar wide array of knowledge about situations and things external to the firm. Neither is more important than the other. The sales manager always stands with one foot in the market and one in the firm itself.

The areas of knowledge internal to the firm vary greatly from firm to firm. The listing in Figure 4-1 is therefore only symbolic of what the sales manager must know and must continually keep verifying, amplifying, and amending. *He must have such knowledge to understand how the subsystem he manages fits into the greater system of the firm and how it interacts with the other interdependent subsystems of the firm.*

The areas of knowledge *external to the firm* that must be developed are probably more common to all sales management jobs. Certainly, the competent sales manager must, through market analysis, thoroughly know all relevant aspects of customer attitude and behavior, how they are changing over time, and how they potentially might change. This is a big order; there is no simple procedure for obtaining this knowledge. Chapter 12 discusses certain aspects of market and sales analysis that enable the sales manager to keep plugging market intelligence into this "pigeonhole" of customer knowledge. The purpose here is to stress this important subelement.

Another vital category of knowledge of situations and things external to the firm is *knowledge of competition.* Again, this cannot be developed in a hit-or-miss way. A very systematic logic must be devised to assure the sales manager that information of all kinds about competitors is being fed into this important "pigeonhole." Chapter 8 and particularly Chapter 16 discuss in depth this exceedingly important subelement of the sales manager's job.

Functional Skills

The sales manager's job has a number of unique technical requirements that are not found in the jobs of managing other organizational components. They might be called the "tools of the trade," and to the extent necessary in his peculiar firm, the sales manager must develop ability in these skills. This may not mean he has to *do* each of these jobs; in firms of any size he may well delegate many of them to others under his direction. But even here he must set objectives for the person to whom he delegates, approve programs, evaluate the performance, and measure the cost. In some cases, particularly in smaller firms, the sales manager may literally perform these functions himself. In either case, he must have technical competence in them.

Figure 4-1 presents a listing of functional skills. It is a partial list. In some cases additional skills may be required (e.g., the sales manager for a firm that is heavily involved in selling to defense agencies of the Federal Government may have to develop skills in contract negotiation, quality control procedures, etc.). Furthermore, this book must be general about these skills, since they may vary vastly from job to job. There is no one simple set of techniques, for example, of setting "quotas." Or, consider how different the "forecasting" skill and techniques are for the sales manager of an aircraft jet-engine manufacturer than for the sales manager of toy model-airplane manufacturer. Therefore, these technical, functional skills will be subsumed under the topic of managerial process.[6]

The Managerial Process

Important as knowledge and functional skills are, the effective sales manager must *think and behave as a manager*. He must blend and utilize knowledge and skills managerially. The *managerial process* provides a meaningful framework of thinking within which to do this.[7] Here the sales manager generates thinking and action in the distinctive subrationales of (1) setting objectives, (2) planning actions or programs to achieve these objectives, (3) organizing resources of men, money, and things to implement the programs, (4) coordinating the plans and programs with those of other organizational components, (5) making the necessary decisions after due search of alternatives, (6) setting policies or guidelines, and (7) evaluating the progress of the implemented programs

6 This does not mean that they are of relatively minor importance. Rather, the competent sales manager must possess ability in them. Because they are discussed in this book in rather general "framework-of-thinking" terms, cross-reference will be made to excellent technical publications that can be studied if more detail is desired.

7 The following elements of the managerial process are sometimes called "principles" of management. This probably goes too far. But certainly a "process" is involved. At this point the student should introduce this thinking into his previous studies of management.

toward the objective. The evaluating step thus becomes *feedback* into the process. It detects whether the programs are on or off target—and if off, how much and in what direction. This input enables *controlling,* an adjustment of plans, sometimes even organizational shifts, and new decisions. It is again the systems concept at work.[8]

The managerial process is one of the two major thrusts of this book, and it serves as the framework for Part II on management of the selling effort. It is a mandatory thinking-way-of-life for the sales manager.

Leadership and Motivation

The other major thrust of the book is the topic of leadership and motivation. Management is "getting things done through others"; hence it involves the influence by the manager of others' thinking and behavior. Whether he is consciously aware of it or not, the sales manager is always influencing behavior of his subordinates, of his associates, of his superiors, of managers of other organizational components, and of customers. He influences them favorably (so that their resulting behavior helps him to reach his goals)—or unfavorably. The importance of understanding the basic valid principles of motivation of individuals and of leadership cannot be overstressed, such understanding being a major element of effective management. These principles are learnable; they are discussed, with the help of simple models and in sales management language, in Part III.

Note that in Figure 4-1, leadership and motivation are symbolically spread through all other elements of the sales manager's job. It is knowledge, it does involve skills, and it must be considered within the managerial process. Hence it is a pervasive element.

Thus Figure 4-1 and the preceding paragraphs present a model, or an analytical picture, of the interacting elements of the job of the sales manager. Each of these elements and its subparts can be pulled out and further analyzed and studied, as is done for most of them in Parts II and III. Each, however, must be regarded as part of a larger whole.

[8] The "steps" in the managerial process are not always discretely performed. That is, the sales manager does not set objectives on Monday, plan on Tuesday, and so on. These steps are often interwoven; planning is required to organize, for example. Yet this is a logical framework of thinking. And certainly in practice these steps are often separately and very formally thought about and developed. Note also that there is no common nomenclature for these steps. Various management books and firms attach different titles on them. For example, in General Electric's famous Management Development Institute, they were known as POIM, for planning, organizing, integrating, and measuring. Some listings include the step of "delegating." In this book we shall subsume it under "organizing."

Furthermore, the job itself of the sales manager must be viewed in the larger context of the job of the selling operation. The selling operation itself must be considered as a system within the larger system of the firm, living in an ever-changing set of external environments. Hence we have again gone around the circle, stressing the key concept that the sales manager manages the system within a greater system.

THE JOB OF THE PROFESSIONAL SALESMAN

"Getting things done through others" requires one more critical bit of insight. To effectively plan, organize, direct, control, lead, and motivate a selling organization composed of people doing things, the sales manager must have a thorough and logical concept of *what it is these people do*. The crux of it all is the salesman. How he performs significantly determines the success of the sales manager's own performance. Hence, to round out the picture of the salesmanager's job, it is necessary to consider also the nature of the job of the individual he is managing—the sales-man.[9] This book will not go into a discussion of the salesman's job itself, other than in the paragraphs that follow. The important point here is that the salesman's function is the culmination of everything the firm has planned and done, and the entire ensuing discussion of sales manage-ment must always have as a tacit background a concept of the sales job. Furthermore, a rational concept of the sales job itself is an essential ingredient of such subprocesses as recruiting and training. It is an input into the managerial process of planning and organizing.

Figure 4-2 presents a model of the job of the professional salesman.[10] Note, first, its similarity in concept to the job of the sales manager. This follows the contemporary view that the effective professional salesman is a managerially oriented person, thinking and behaving managerially. He is, so to speak, the "manager of his territory" and operates, ideally, as the firm's marketing tactician in that territory.

Like the sales manager, he must have a base of knowledge and skills. Note the five circles across the top of Figure 4-2. He must have *knowledge of the market*—of forces and trends having effect on his customers. He must have *knowledge of product*—the technical knowledge of everything

[9] Of course, he also manages people in nonselling jobs. But the personal selling activity is the *raison d'être* of the entire selling operation, and its function must be crystal-clear in his mind.

[10] The term "professional" is used to describe the salesman assigned by his firm to contact customers who are other business firms. The model can be adapted to apply to "retail" salesmen, but it will then be less complex, containing fewer elements.

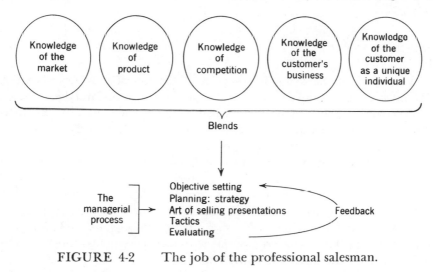

FIGURE 4-2   The job of the professional salesman.

about the product, its application, its servicing, and so on. Included here is knowledge of his firm's policies, facilities, and the like. He must have *knowledge of competition*—everything about competition.[11] He must have *knowledge of the customer's business*—the organizational, technological, financial, and policy facets of the customer's business. He must in fact become an expert in the customer's business and to apply his products to the customer's problems so that the customer will perceive them as needed problem solvers. He must have *knowledge of the customer as a unique individual*—of each person who as a customer directly or indirectly influences decisions about his product, of how that person perceives, thinks, and acts. This is the domain of psychology, to which a major part of Chapter 13 is addressed.

Using this knowledge, the effective salesman then behaves managerially. He *sets objectives*—taking his given quotas or budgets and allocating them by product line and by customer. He creates *plans of action*—strategies, customer by customer, to achieve his objectives. He prepares *selling presentations*—an art of selling, using analytically learnable skills. Then, as he physically visits and faces customers, he engages in *tactics*—the face-to-face interaction and reaction. After this customer interview, he *evaluates*—a check on his planned progress toward his objectives, hence feedback into the managerial process—enabling him to adjust his plans, presentations, and tactics.

[11] This is the important starting point for the vital input to the firm of competitive behavior. Much more about this later, in Chapters 8 and 16.

SUMMARY

This, then, is the dynamic complex of the job of the sales manager. He must have certain technical skills, to some degree, and he must be knowledgeable about many factors inside and outside the firm. Furthermore, he must think and behave as a manager, continuously developing his abilities in the managerial process. He influences the behavior of others, hence he must continuously enhance his insight into leadership and motivation.

Within all this, he must be systems-oriented. He must understand the inner workings of the system he is managing—the selling operation and its component selling jobs. He must understand the interrelation and interaction of his managed system with other systems—those of the market places and those of his own firm.

Small wonder, then, that such a high premium is being placed on the sales management job and such rich rewards are given for its effective performance.

QUESTIONS AND PROBLEMS

1. Since there are many different kinds of firms and many different kinds of sales management jobs, of what sense is it to have a "framework of thinking" about the sales manager's job?
2. Critique the statement: "The job of the sales department is simply *to sell.*"
3. Comment on the following: "The selling operation is a complex organization in many firms. The really key aspect of the sales manager, therefore, is to properly recruit, train, and administer competent people."
4. You are a headquarters sales manager for an electronics manufacturer. What elements of the "job of the sales manager" shown in Figure 4-1 do you think may not apply to you? How would your answer change if you were a sales manager for a toy manufacturer? A radio station?
5. What is meant by the statement: "The sales manager's effectiveness in today's marketing-oriented firms depends more on his *managerial abilities and behavior* than on technical or functional skills"?

The Management of
the Selling Effort

Part I portrayed the milieu in which the selling operation of the firm exists, ranging from broad system concepts to the more specific aspects of the job of the sales manager and of the professional salesman. Part II examines the management of the selling effort itself and analytically discusses the particular elements of this management job.

The discussion here is *managerially and strategically oriented.* Although some attention must be given to certain "technical skills," they are considered as end behaviors or functions that result from managerial processes. Furthermore, because the *practice* of these "technical skills" varies widely from firm to firm and from industry to industry, they are discussed in Part II in broad, simple terms only —and are introduced into the managerial process framework. The structural pattern of this part of the book, therefore, encourages first a framework for thinking about management itself and about strategy. Then, within such a framework, the skills and end behaviors of the sales manager are considered.

Chapter 5 on *sales forecasting* treats the forecasting process as the vital starting point for all planning in all the functions of the firm —production, procurement, finance, and so on. It proposes that although the techniques of forecasting are becoming highly specialized and are usually outside the responsibility of sales management, it behooves sales management to have a knowledge of the process, in a managerial framework.

Chapter 6 on *objective setting* treats the important "target" aspects of objectives as the springboard for planning and action. Beyond this, however, the chapter discusses the more subtle strategic and tactical roles of objectives. Within this framework, the functions of *quota setting* and of *budgeting* are considered.

Chapters 7 and 8 center on the vital managerial processes of *planning*—of creating strategies or programs of action devised to achieve objectives. Given the concept of the firm as a marketing system that is flexing and adjusting to its changing environments, the process of planning strategies is at the very heart of effective sales management. Chapter 7 treats the planning process from a broad managerial viewpoint, at sales management level. Chapter 8 moves to the crucial point of the customer and presents a model for planning selling strategies for each specific customer.

Chapters 9 and 10 deal with the managerial processes of *organizing* and *coordinating*. Broad concepts of organizing as a dynamic process are presented, with a focus on its strategic and tactical elements. Here the deployment of the sales manager's resources is considered as a strategic, not merely a functional, device.

Chapter 11 on *decision making* recognizes that the job of management is "to get things done through others" and that, despite the importance of all elements of the managerial process, programs of action must be implemented. Furthermore, from time to time the actions ensuing from decisions may have to be changed or adjusted, requiring additional decisions. Within the context of the sales manager's job and in his language, Chapter 11 presents some current models of *decision making* and discusses the kindred subjects of *delegating authority* and *setting policy*.

To round out the cycle of the managerial process, Chapter 12 proposes concepts and methods for *evaluating and controlling* the selling effort—providing feedback into the process in order to adjust, if necessary, its interacting elements.

5

The Sales Forecast

One of the most important processes in the management of the business firm is the development of the *sales forecast*—that is, the estimate of the dollar sales of its products which the firm expects to achieve over a specified future period. The sales forecast sets the expected *revenue* of the firm in this future period; hence it is the starting point for all planning in every element of the firm—production, materials procurement, inventory control, personnel, financial, marketing, and others.

The sales forecast is particularly significant to sales management because it defines the primary targets that the selling operation must achieve. Thus it is the generating force behind the managerial processes of objective setting, planning, organizing and coordinating, decision making, evaluating and controlling, which are discussed in turn in the chapters that follow.

Yet, in a way, a discussion of the process of sales forecasting does not rightfully belong in a book on sales management—because under the more or less widely prevalent "marketing concept" the development of the sales forecast is a marketing function and is accomplished organizationally outside the selling operation. However, sales and sales management certainly provide *inputs* of essential market intelligence into the process and are *receivers* of the end result. This in itself necessitates a clear understanding by sales management of the process. Both headquarters and field sales managers need a managerial framework of thinking about specific policies, organizational responsibility, and knowledge of the methods of sales forecasting practiced in their firms.

Sales management must have a clear picture of the sales forecasting process also for a number of other strategic reasons. From the sales forecast come very specific, quantified *sales goals* to be achieved by the selling operation. This not only sets the whole pattern of behavior of the selling operation, but also establishes a potent set of factors in evaluating its performance and productivity. Sales managers may well be individually evaluated against degree of achievement of the sales forecast (as they probably should be). Yet it would be naïve to believe that the sales forecast is always quite accurate or, even if it were, that it will remain accurate throughout the time period involved. It may be advisable, therefore, for sales management to secure some ability or power to negotiate with those managers and/or specialists in marketing who establish the forecast. To do this effectively (or even to earn the opportunity to do it), the sales manager must have more than just an intuitive "feel" about the market variables potentially affecting customers' perceptions and demand for the firm's products. Furthermore, he may seek, in the firm's as well as just his own department's interest, adjustments of the forecast from time to time. Under some conditions, he might even wish to question its validity and to appeal the forecast to higher-level management. For all these reasons he must understand the rationale and method that his firm uniquely uses in its sales forecasting. Hence this chapter views the sales forecast quite broadly, in a managerial framework, and as a significant input into the sales manager's managerial processes.[1]

VARYING CONCEPTS AND METHODS OF SALES FORECASTING

The underlying rationale and methodology for sales forecasting have varied during the past three or four decades from the almost "crystal ball" approach to the use of highly sophisticated mathematical models stemming from computer technology. Even today, one can find examples of use of forecasting concepts and methods from all parts of this spectrum.

In the days of production-oriented executive management (the decade of the 1920's) the sales forecast was really less a forecast than a production and sales budget, which was set up by the executives, often with relatively little regard for factors outside the firm itself. Executive management in a sense decided, perhaps in consultation with production

---

[1] In some cases, the entire sales forecasting process may be assigned to the sales manager. For such a case, this chapter will serve only as a door opener. The suggested readings at the end of the chapter will lead the reader to the more technical methods of forecasting.

management, what would be produced, what quantity, what styles, at what selling prices—and directed the sales department to sell this plant output. In general this worked, largely because demand conditions in the market permitted it, not because it was a really competent management approach.[2] It is rarely feasible in today's world.

Executive Judgment Method

As the complexity of the marketplace increased, the practice of "polling" of executives of the firm was introduced. Even though subjectively, variables beyond just the production objectives are considered in this approach. Managers of different functions, with a diversity of opinion and expertise, contribute to and pass judgment on the estimate for sales for the coming period. Included may be managers of such functions as sales, finance, purchasing, and production. Assuming that these executives have identified within their respective fields the relevant variables affecting sales (both internal and external to the company), this combining and "averaging" of expert judgment can be fairly successful. There is nothing very scientific, rigorous, or objective about this method, however, and it could become a sort of "seat of the pants" technique—hardly good enough in today's vigorously competitive market places.

The Sales Force Composite

Also in the category of "judgment forecasting" is the *sales force composite*. Here the prediction of future sales is built up from estimates by each salesman of the business he expects to secure from his customers. Proponents of the method point to the value of developing the input of direct, firsthand knowledge of salesmen who consult face-to-face with customers. Allegedly, the method thus is based on relatively reliable customer intentions. Opponents of the method point to the many sources of potential error: bias of the individual salesman (who may be overly optimistic, or ultraconservative, or anywhere in between); inability of those individuals contacted in customer companies to accurately predict their own product requirements; technical inability of the salesman to factor into his estimate such variables as changing market structures and competitive forces.

On balance, however, variations of the sales force composite may provide quite reliable sales forecasting, particularly for companies whose markets are well defined and for whom a large share of potential business comes from a relatively small number of customers. Examples: manufac-

2 See Chapter 3, p. 33.

turers of steam boilers, locomotives, or mine-shaft drilling rigs. Or, for another type of firm, an industrial distributor, such as an antifriction bearing distributor selling to the replacement market, may find this method of forecasting fairly successful.

Still another variation of the sales force composite, increasing its validity somewhat, comes from the introduction of executive judgment at each level of its formation. For example, as each district sales manager studies the consolidation of estimates made by each of his salesmen, he "adjusts" the district figures by subjectively considering factors known by him and not by his salesmen. Such factors might include his knowledge of anticipated changes in company policy, of forthcoming promotional programs, or changes of sales manpower, of competitive forces in the district territory, and of individual salesmen's predictive ability. At the next level, as each regional sales manager views the adjusted estimates from each of his district sales managers, he consolidates, but introduces his judgment, thus factoring in his knowledge of variables, both in and out of the company, that he believes apply to his region but have not been considered by the districts. Similarly, at sales headquarters, the manager of sales reviews the estimates from his regional sales managers, and adjusts as he consolidates. At some level—and here we assume that it is the level of marketing management (and marketing staff) "above" sales management—still other adjustments are made in the adjusted sales force composite. These might include adjustments for anticipated changes in pricing or product, for estimates of changing business conditions provided by economists or market researchers, for future marketing strategies of all kinds, and for reallocation of marketing resources.

Buyer Surveys

Buyer surveys involve finding out what customer's intentions are about buying in a future period. This technique is similar to the sales force composite in that the primary input is from the customer.[3] Here, however, the forecast really comes from projecting the expressed intentions of a selected sample. Such information may be secured as primary data—that is, a probability sample survey technique may be used. This method of forecasting is sometimes employed in estimating market potential for a new product in a mass market.[4] Example: a cereal manufac-

[3] Data for the buyer survey, however, must come from the customer, whereas in the sales force composite the salesman may provide inputs of data that he has had to deduce.

[4] Here *market potential* is defined as the total sales for a product that an entire industry will achieve in a given period of time.

turer proposing a new dehydrated product may conduct such a survey. Adequately done, it is a costly and time-consuming method. It may be a valuable investment under some conditions, but is not practical for periodic sales forecasting for all products.

Buyer surveys may, however, be accomplished by utilizing secondary data—that is, data already generated for other purposes. For example, such institutions as the Federal Reserve Board conduct surveys of buying intentions for a variety of consumer durable products, which can be adapted for sales forecastings. Similarly, such agencies as the Security and Exchange Commission and the National Industrial Conference Board survey business executives' intentions to invest in capital plant equipment. The magazine *Sales Management* publishes annually a "Survey of Buying Power," which is widely used in determining market potentials, by territory, for consumer products of all types. By multiplying such territorial potentials by the expected market share, a sales forecast by territory can be derived.[5]

Parenthetically, if the sales forecast is being constructed by an individual or a group outside the selling organization and by methods other than those discussed above, these methods may enable sales management to validate (or reject) the resulting sales targets presented to them.

Projection of Past Sales

Some firms estimate future sales by projecting the data from past sales in a rather simple manner. This is the projection or extrapolation of last year's sales. It assumes that all factors affecting past sales will not change and that sales itself will develop continuously, so that the past may be truly extrapolated.

A variation is "trend analysis," in which it is assumed that the rate of change of the variable will remain constant. On this basis, the past is projected into the future. This is a common practice in many business firms—but, like other methods, it may be inaccurate, particularly when trends change, as they often do!

Still another variation of the projection technique factors into the projection the effect of a number of "conditioning" variables. As put by Maynard and Davis,[6] a forecasting "formula" is developed as follows: future sales = past sales ± changes in business conditions ± changes in

---

[5] Obviously, the human element is again injected: the market share figure must be estimated by the forecaster. He may have it from history, but how does he decide whether it will increase or decrease?

[6] H. H. Maynard and J. H. Davis, *Sales Management,* Ronald Press, New York, 1957, p. 165.

company policies ± changes in competition ± "miscellaneous" changes. The idea here is similar to that in the judgment-adjustments of sales-men's estimates, except that here the forecaster is projecting from past sales rather than from alleged customer intentions.

The several variations of the projection technique are widely used, with varying degrees of accuracy and success. On balance, it can be stated generally that these techniques are somewhat naïve. With the *rates* of change in firms' external environments accelerating, with the complex web of independent and intervening variables becoming more complex, and with the increasing dependence of the firm's strategies on the validity of its forecasts, more sophisticated methods are emerging.

Mathematical and Econometric Models

The development of statistical analysis and of electronic data process-ing has resulted in the application of objective and scientific techniques to forecasting. It is beyond the scope of this book to discuss these models in detail. To reiterate, the process itself is outside the realm of sales management in almost all firms. However, a brief overview may help the sales manager to develop a broad conceptual idea of the process.

Mathematical models: regression analysis. Statistical analysis is becom-ing an important tool in forecasting. A particularly valuable application is known as *regression analysis.* In this technique, a mathematical rela-tionship or equation is developed, defined as a *regression equation.* It describes the relationship that exists when a "dependent" variable varies as one or more "independent" variables change. Thus the demand for room air conditioners may be the dependent variable whose change we want to predict as it varies with such independent variables as mean temperature or income. The independent variables selected all are those that are known to have some controlling relationship with the dependent variable. The selected independent variables may be given different weights, or relative impacts on the dependent variable.

Hence the term "correlation"—or "co-relation." Correlation analysis seeks to quantify the relationship between the dependent variable and the independent variables. If this can be done, a predicted change in any of the independent variables can be plugged into the equation, and the predicted change in the dependent variable can be calculated. Note that this more sophisticated technique *does not eliminate predictions.* It does, however, enable more accurate forecasting by predicting changes in variables *which themselves can be predicted more accurately.*

Forecasting by simulation. For most practical situations, the "regres-sion equation" is a highly complex one, and the subjective weights and probabilities result in very complex *sets* of the equation. Consider this very practical question that a marketing executive might ask: "What will happen to our total sales if we make such and such a change in price in one of our product lines?" Consider for a minute the web of variables that are affected: direct customer reactions, direct competitive retaliations, distributors' and dealers' reactions, other product lines, effect on other elements of the company, changes in probability of governmental intervention, and so on. There is not just one possible reaction in each of these categories; there may be many *alternative* reactions that must be considered. Thus the equation becomes extremely intricate. And it must be solved not just for one price level, but for many. Examples of this kind dramatize the potential use of the computer for complex forecasting. Solution of exceedingly complex mathematical models, the simulation of complex market situations, and the use of econometric models—all are becoming more and more practical in short- and long-range sales forecasting.

THE DYNAMIC ASPECT OF FORECASTING

Whatever the technique used for forecasting and whatever its accuracy, there remains one philosophical or conceptual aspect of forecasting that many firms overlook. In fact, the more sophisticated their techniques, the more possible it might be to overlook this aspect. To understand it, reconsider what forecasting is and what it is meant to be. *Forecasting is predicting the future* with some degree of probability. Furthermore, it is an *estimate* of what will happen in the future. Certainly, in the business world it would be naïve to expect to forecast the future exactly.

A forecast is made at a given moment of time and predicts events in the future or over some time period in the future. But the moment *after* the forecast is made, the future begins to merge into the present. As it continues to do so, the relationships between the many variables may change in ways that would have been impossible to predict. The very fact that the firm creates strategies and actions to achieve the end that is forecast is an input into the market milieu which sets off chains of reaction and counteraction.[7]

[7] For example, assume that Firm A has made its forecast using as one of the independent variables "expected competitive reaction," based on observation of how rivals have behaved in the past. Now the firm embarks on its planned market action. But one major rival, let us assume, has recently committed a large fixed-cost capital expenditure (say, an automated production process). Seriously needing additional volume on its plant (see Chapter 3), the rival may retaliate with counteraction never before exhibited and drastically challenge Firm A's market position. In this case, the previous forecast may become quite worthless. One independent variable has drastically changed.

At the *moment* the forecast is made, it represents the best estimate of the future that the firm can make. And, of course, this best estimate must be the stimulus and the rational base for all the objective setting and the planning for the various components of the firm. *But there is nothing holy about the forecast.* As time progresses, and as the future period being forecast moves toward the present, the forecaster can reestimate with increasing clarity. For example, suppose that in October of a given year a firm estimates sales for each quarter of the next calendar year. The first quarter of the next year is only three months away, and perhaps sales for it can be estimated with a fair degree of accuracy. But the fourth quarter is a year away, and at this distance the estimate is apt to be much more of a "guess," regardless of the technique used.

Philosophically, rather than making a *forecast* (which, so to speak, tends to set some numbers in concrete), perhaps the firm's management should be concerned with *forecasting*—considering it to be a dynamic process that never really stops. The very concept of the "feedback process"—with continuous inputs of market intelligence flowing back into the firm, so that strategies and actions can be adjusted—applies here. Certainly, the astute firm "signals" its production operations when marketing conditions change. Note how quickly automobile manufacturers adjust production if new car inventories become "out of balance." For the same reason, continuing and adjusting forecasting processes should present changing objectives or "a new par for the course" to the selling operation. Of course, the dynamic forecast must be an "evolving" thing, and not flip-flop like a yo-yo. To be sure, the *objectives* developed after the forecasting process must adhere to certain criteria, which are specified in the next chapter. But the firm is in an ever-changing milieu, and in no way must any of its managerial processes forget the elements of time and change.

An example of "dynamic forecasting." [8] In the Apparatus Sales Division of the General Electric Company—the division that markets engineered products and systems of the heavy capital goods type—sales forecasting in the late 1950's had used a sophisticated version of the "sales composite" technique. Forecasts emanated from sales engineers, and culminated in a division-level consolidation. The forecast was made by product line and was broken down by quarter. It was prepared in September, for the four quarters of the ensuing year. Once made, adjusted, and accepted by top management, it became in fact the sales budget.

Difficult problems arose, however, for production planning and marketing planning when significant potential orders (e.g., the electrical apparatus for a power company customer's generating plant, sometimes in millions of dollars) were postponed by the customer to some future

8 Based on my observations and experience in the late 1950's.

date, or when General Electric's estimated probability of securing the order changed considerably because of changing market (and competitive) conditions. Here the primary *raison d'être* of the sales forecast—to make possible effective planning—was endangered.

To alleviate this discrepancy between an "old" forecast and emerging "new" conditions, GE developed what it called a "rolling estimate" instead of a forecast per se. In *each quarter of the year,* a forecast was made for the next six quarters. Thus the forecast for the next quarter out was always a fresh one and had the advantage of increased accuracy, because a closer look was possible. In each quarter, the past quarter was dropped, the next seven quarters reestimated, and a new eighth quarter added in the future. The credence in the next one or two quarters was, therefore, enhanced. That estimate which included the last quarter of one year, four quarters of the following year, and one of the still next year, was used for *budgeting* purposes for the next calendar year. But the dynamic *rolling estimate* kept a continuous freshness in the entire forecasting process, thus significantly assisting all planning functions.

SUMMARY

Forecasting—particularly sales forecasting—is a vital process for the firm, providing the basis for all of the firm's planning and actions. Once an art that was accomplished almost entirely by subjective management judgment, it is slowly emerging into a set of scientifically based methodologies, much as marketing research has done. Like market research, sales forecasting for many firms has become highly specialized and is implemented by technical specialists (often as a part of the market research function).

Even though removed from the technical forecasting process itself, sales management is an essential input into it and is a primary receiver of the results. Furthermore, the results of the forecasting process vitally affects all of the objective setting, planning, organizing, and decision making of sales management. Sales management must have a working knowledge, in the managerial sense, of the particular methods uniquely used by the firm.

SUGGESTED READINGS

Sales Forecasting General

1. Kotler, Philip, *Marketing Management,* Prentice-Hall, Englewood Cliffs, N.J., 1967, pp. 96–123.

2. Zober, M., *Marketing Management,* Wiley, New York, 1964, Chapter 8.

Economic Concepts of Forecasting

1. Dean, J. *Managerial Economics,* Prentice-Hall, Englewood Cliffs, N.J., 1951, Chapter 4.
2. Spencer, M. H., Clark, C. G., and Hoguet, P. W., *Business and Economic Forecasting,* Richard D. Irwin, Homewood, Ill., Chapters 1–4.

Forecasting Techniques

1. Crisp, R. D., *Sales Planning and Control,* McGraw-Hill, New York, 1961.
2. Bass, F. M., et al., *Mathematical Models and Methods in Marketing,* Richard D. Irwin, Homewood, Ill., 1961, pp. 3–34, 461–514.
3. Appelbaum, W., "Methods for Determining Store Trade Areas, Market Penetration, and Potential Sales," *Journal of Marketing Research,* Vol. 3, No. 2 (May 1966), pp. 127–141.
4. Richmond, R. G., *Simulation as an Aid to the Formulation of Pricing Strategy,* unpublished dissertation, Arizona State University, Tempe, Ariz., May 1966.
5. Ferber, R., and Verdoon, P. J., *Research Methods in Business,* Macmillan, New York, 1962.
6. Wolfe, H. D., *Business Forecasting Methods,* Holt, Rinehart and Winston, New York, 1966.

QUESTIONS AND PROBLEMS

1. If the sales forecast is developed by marketing people outside the selling operation itself, why is it important for the sales manager to have a good conceptual knowledge of the process by which it was derived?
2. You are a marketing executive in a major appliance manufacturing firm (refrigerators, home laundry equipment, etc.). State the advantages and the disadvantages of each of the six methods of sales forecasting described in this chapter. Which one would you want to use? Why?
3. Assume that you have selected one of these methods, which seems to best fit your firm. You arrive at a sales forecast for the coming year, which is broken down into quotas to your selling operation's units.

It also is fed to all the productive elements of the firm as a starting point for their planning and operations. What great difficulty still remains? How can you cope with it?

4. What was meant in the chapter by the difference between "making a forecast" and "forecasting"?

5. Consider a manufacturing firm. List as many organizational elements of the firm as you can, on whom the sales forecast has an impact. For each, briefly explain why it does.

6

Setting Sales Objectives

Objectives are the goals or end results that one wants to achieve. They are the starting point for planning programs of action, and they serve as targets against which action is measured.

Objectives are particularly important in a selling operation. Assuming that a firm is rationally seeking profit optimization, it follows that sales volume or revenue to be achieved is a rationally determined, definite objective for the selling operation. Its determination, of course, follows the forecast of market potential and the decision, on the basis of market constraints and opportunities, about the firm's target share of this market.[1]

Sales volume or revenue is not the only objective that is established in this way for the selling operation. Among other objectives, stated in quite definitive terms, may be market share, development of new accounts, and specific sales-expense levels. Still other objectives, less quantifiable, may be perceived by sales management as the targets to be achieved: increased customer goodwill, company and brand image, and feedback of market intelligence. In a sense, all these objectives are a means to the end of "continuing profit," and yet they demand and require the sustaining of specific, rational programs of action.

It is fair to say that this rather simplistic view of objectives as the key determinants of programs of action is debatable. For example, one noted scholar proposes that a set of *constraints* influence the decision maker to

[1] It is also assumed here that these decisions are made by the marketing executive, and not the sales executive—though this need not necessarily be the case.

action, rather than a set of goals. Furthermore, only *certain* constraints motivate him to search for action, hence are "goal-like" in character.[2] It is certainly true that the "discipline of the market"—the actions of customers and rivals—affects objectives and therefore must be inputs into the goal-setting mechanisms of the firm.[3]

Recognizing all this, the thrust of this chapter nonetheless centers on the key importance (if not actual primacy) of objectives as the targets for planned actions by the sales manager. This presumes that predicted market constraints and opportunities will already have been inputs into the goal-setting decisions. It also presumes that changing market constraints and opportunities—which require adjusted market behavior—are a normal strategic and tactical process that can evolve within a given set of goals.[4]

In any case, it can be safely conjectured that at the line-operation level, sales managers do perceive specific objectives that their sales units are expected to achieve and do devise programs of action to achieve them. This is viewing *objectives as targets*.

THE HIERARCHY OF OBJECTIVES

But the "global" objectives that are given to the selling operation (sales volume, market share, etc.) must be allocated to the various sales units in the selling operation's organization structure. This throws a new and different light on objectives—they are something more than simply ends to be met. In the process of allocating the objectives, and subdividing them, a strategic means is developed for influencing the behavior of subordinate sales units.

To understand this, consider an orthodox organization chart for the selling operation of a simple business firm (Figure 6-1).[5] For simplicity, only a few of the elements of the structure are extended vertically. The organization structure shown in the figure evolved over time as a process by which *to get work done*. The breaking down into manageable parts [6]

---

[2] Herbert A. Simon, "On the Concept of Organizational Goals," *Administrative Science Quarterly*, Vol. 9, No. 1 (June 1964) , pp. 2–22.

[3] Even here, the argument is sometimes presented that goals may be an after-the-effect rationalization of decisions made to cope with constraints and opportunities.

[4] This does not mean that sales goals are not sometimes changed. Sometimes they should be. But this does not negate the above stance—that the new goals are new targets, for which new programs must be devised.

[5] A manufacturing company in our example. The same rationale applies to a service company, a wholesaler, or, for that matter, a retailer.

[6] The rationale that lies behind this is discussed in Chapter 9, "Organizing the Selling Effort."

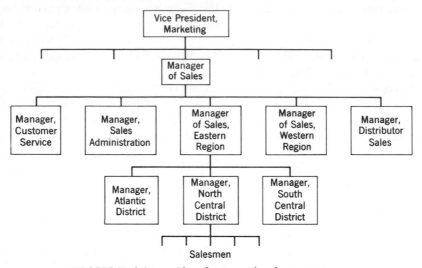

FIGURE 6-1   Simple organization structure.

was done with a work, or task, or *goal orientation*. As an integral part of the organizing process, the executive must consider—and assign—the unique set of missions to be accomplished by the subunits. Why else create an organization structure?

The manager of the subunit receiving these missions perceives them as the *objectives* for his unit. In turn, then, he assigns tasks, or missions, to each of his subordinate units in such a way that if each subordinate unit achieves its tasks, the whole subunit will have achieved its total objectives. Thus, in Figure 6-1, assume that Vice President of Marketing has assigned a specific set of missions to the selling operation. These might include the following, for a given time period:

1. Generate an orders volume of $1,800,000 (usually broken down by product line).
2. Increase market share from 10 to 12 percent.
3. Develop a minimum of 100 profitable new accounts.
4. Improve customer relations.
5. Maintain a sales-expense ratio that does not exceed 8 percent.
6. Develop an ongoing sales training program to improve technical competency and to assure high level of morale.

The sales manager accepts these missions as his objectives. They become "his world," his ends. To achieve these ends, he then *allocates* missions to his subordinate units—to the two sales regions, to Distributor Sales, to Customer Service, to Sales Administration.

Note that the missions assigned to the subordinate units are different from those in the list above. They are "tailored" to the particular expertise, opportunities, and constraints of each unique unit. For example, consider the objective of maintaining a sales-expense ratio that does not exceed 8 percent. If the Western Region, because of peculiar market conditions, is allocated a major share of the "new accounts" objective, a higher ratio than 8 percent may have to be allowed it. Then the Eastern Region must be allowed an appropriately lower ratio. Furthermore, the Sales Administration unit may be assigned specific missions to operate control devices for continually checking the sales-expense ratio performance of the sales region units.

Thus each unit receives its unique set of missions.[7] Now the process repeats itself. The manager of these units accepts these missions as his objectives, his ends. He then considers his own subordinate units and allocates "tailored" missions to them.

In this way, along with the *hierarchy of organization structure,* a *hierarchy of objectives,* subobjectives, sub-subobjectives, and so forth, develops.[8] An important element of the managerial job is an understanding of how a given set of objectives sought by the manager is translated into subobjectives and how these are then retranslated into meaningful sub-subobjectives—with all of them in the entire hierarchy consistent and compatible. Figure 6-2 illustrates such a hierarchy, somewhat simplified, extending down through marketing headquarters to the individual salesman in the field. For clarity, only one branch of the "tree" is shown, no staff organizational units are shown, and a relatively simple marketing organization is assumed.

THE STRATEGIC AND TACTICAL ASPECTS OF OBJECTIVES

Figure 6-2 also leads into another, often unrealized, function of objectives. As we view the hierarchy of objectives, it is easy to see that the

---

[7] The interdependency, compatibility, and possible conflict between these sets of missions requires "coordinating" a managerial process, discussed in Chapter 10.

[8] This discussion views the development of a hierarchy of objectives as rational and deliberate, all the way through the organization structure down to the individual worker. However, the subobjectives may *evolve.* That is, managers "down the line" may not be *given* specific objectives; they may create them themselves. Modern organization theory advances some provocative ideas that question the efficacy of the process discussed. Is it too rigid? Too stultifying? Too "programmed"? This is an area of management that is under close scrutiny by practitioners and scholars alike.

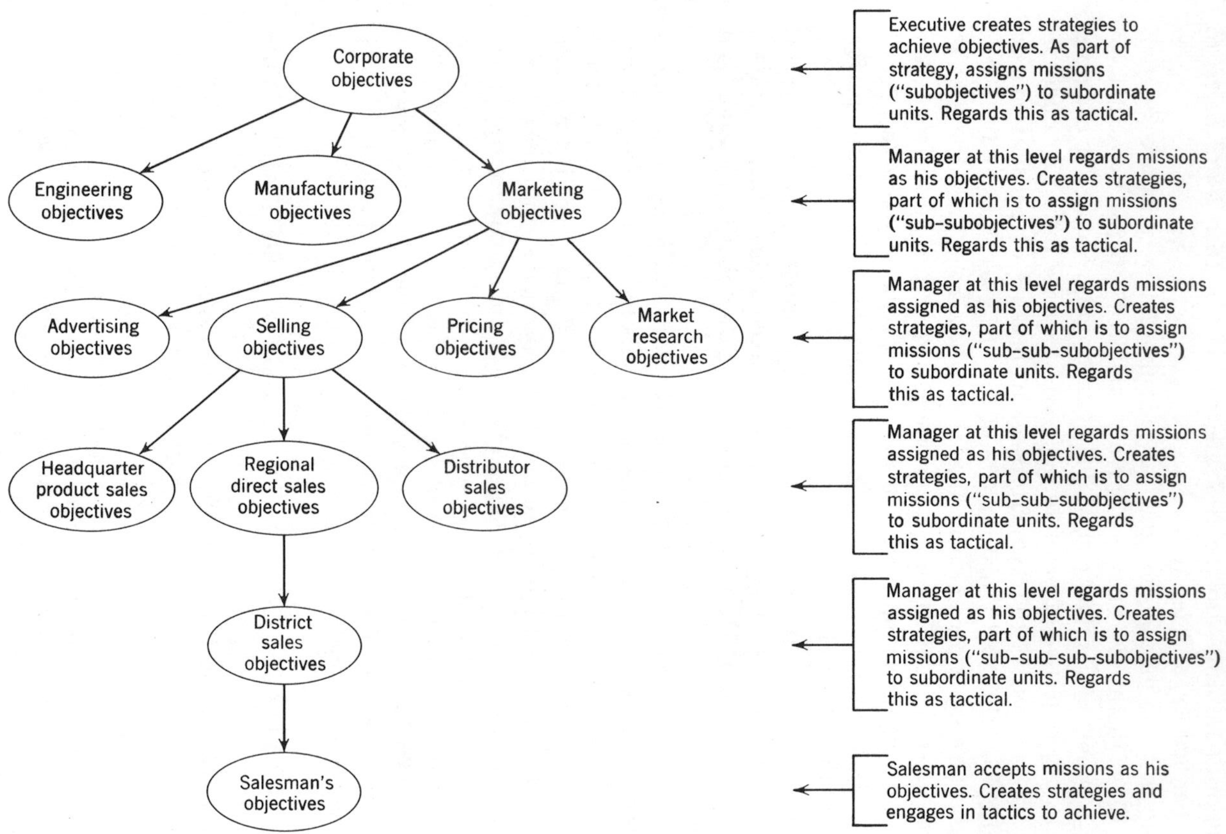
Corporate objectives
Engineering objectives
Manufacturing objectives
Marketing objectives
Advertising objectives
Selling objectives
Pricing objectives
Market research objectives
Headquarter product sales objectives
Regional direct sales objectives
Distributor sales objectives
District sales objectives
Salesman's objectives
Executive creates strategies to achieve objectives. As part of strategy, assigns missions ("subobjectives") to subordinate units. Regards this as tactical.
Manager at this level regards missions as his objectives. Creates strategies, part of which is to assign missions ("sub-subobjectives") to subordinate units. Regards this as tactical.
Manager at this level regards missions assigned as his objectives. Creates strategies, part of which is to assign missions ("sub-sub-subobjectives") to subordinate units. Regards this as tactical.
Manager at this level regards missions assigned as his objectives. Creates strategies, part of which is to assign missions ("sub-sub-subobjectives") to subordinate units. Regards this as tactical.
Manager at this level regards missions assigned as his objectives. Creates strategies, part of which is to assign missions ("sub-sub-sub-subobjectives") to subordinate units. Regards this as tactical.
Salesman accepts missions as his objectives. Creates strategies and engages in tactics to achieve.

FIGURE 6-2 Strategic-tactical sense of the hierarchy of objectives.

The strategic–tactical sequence
of objective–mission changes

1. V.P. Marketing gets new mission from President to increase Marketing's contribution to firm's profit. V.P. Marketing requests Manager of Sales to reallocate effort to increase volume of higher profit lines.

2. Manager of Sales accepts this as new objective. Revises the sales budgets for each region, raising those for the higher profit lines.

3. Accepting this new objective, Regional Sales Manager selectively allocates new budget, considering market and competitive situations in each district.

4. Accepting this new objective, District Sales Manager selectively revises salesman's quotas, considering market potential competitive situations in each territory.

5. Accepting this new quota, the salesman revises his selling strategy and selectively reassings product–line volume goals customer by customer.

```
          Vice President,
            Marketing
               |
               |
            Manager
            of Sales
               |
   +-----------+-----------+
Manager,     Manager,    Manager,
Eastern      Central     Western
Region       Region      Region
   |            |            |
District     District    District
Manager      Manager     Manager
               |
          Salesman
             A
               |
        Customer:
          ABC
        Company
```

FIGURE 6-3   Objective change in a strategic-tactical sense.

perceived meaning of the objectives differs at each level. As already discussed, the manager at each level views the missions (or "subobjectives") given to him as his *primary objectives*. He ideally then creates *strategies* (plans of action) to achieve these objectives, one element of which will be the assigning of missions to subordinate units. He will regard this as a *tactical* device.[9] Thus, along with the hierarchy of organization structure and the hierarchy of objectives, there is a strategic-tactical-strategic-tactical turn.

As a very simple example, consider the Manager of Sales of the company shown in Figure 6-1, one of the several managers who report to the Vice President of Marketing. Figure 6-3 shows a part of the organizational structure. It assumes that a hierarchy of objectives has been previously established. Now assume that the President desires (for some reason) to change the course of the company's direction or to change the company's performance in some way. (Assume that he desires increased profit.)

[9] Here we are using the concept of *strategy* to mean the planning of action and the concept of *tactics* to denote the implementing action itself.

Rather than command specific changes in operations, he may achieve his objective by changing the missions or goals given to his next echelon of management. *He changes their objectives, as perceived by them.* To the President this is a tactical move; to the Vice Presidents it is a change in objective, requiring new plans and programs—or new strategies. In turn, the Vice Presidents respecify, tactically, the missions or goals to be achieved by the next echelon of management, and so on. New strategies and tactical adjustments are generated at every level of the organization structure.

In broad summary—rather than considering objectives as something mechanistic, relatively fixed, and often existing only at high management levels, the Sales Manager must pragmatically view objective setting in *three different conceptual frameworks:*

1. *As targets.* In the orthodox sense, objectives are targets, or goals to be achieved, and as such are guideposts for action.

2. *As a hierarchy.* But the Sales Manager must recognize that beyond his own objectives, the missions that he gives to his subordinate management will be accepted by them as objectives. The subordinate managers in turn will *uniquely* assign missions to their subordinates, and so on. As shown in Figure 6-4, a translating process is involved. It is essential to know how "missions" given to subordinates are perceived by them as objectives and how they are retranslated into other sets of missions for their subordinates.

3. *As a strategic-tactical process.* But the very fact that there is this perception and retranslation of missions to objectives and then to other missions gives the manager a strategic and tactical means of influencing performance. Assuming that some degree of authority for decision making is delegated, it follows that the Sales Manager cannot bypass levels of management and directly influence a change in salesmen's planning and activities. However, he may *tactically* influence them indirectly by changing or adjusting the missions that he gives to his next echelon of subordinate management.[10] Thus it is important for the Sales Manager to develop the ability to change or adjust missions so that the retranslations all the way down the hierarchy are easily and functionally achieved. Ideally, the Sales Manager, after changing or adjusting missions (to better achieve one of his objectives), should be able to predict at any

[10] If adjusting or changing of missions is not recognized as a rational, planned strategic and tactical process, unexpected and sometimes conflicting activities may be generated in lower echelons. It is not uncommon for a Sales Manager to change missions in such ways that the resulting behavior change several levels below may actually be dysfunctional. Changes in missions and objectives should not be made willy-nilly. In this regard, note the criteria for objectives in the following section.

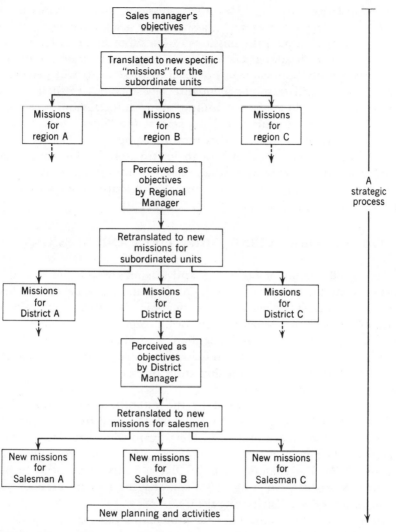

FIGURE 6-4   The translating of new objectives to new missions to new behaviors.

organizational level how his mission change will have filtered down in the perception and retranslating process—and how it therefore will affect behavior and performance of individuals and groups. Note also that if objective and mission changes are employed for tactical purposes (to change performance throughout the hierarchy), care must be taken that the retranslations and new objectives, missions, and behaviors are *compatible at all levels*. For example, assume that a sales manager, to achieve a new objective, adjusts the missions of his subordinate units separately: product sales (a headquarters staff unit), customer service, and the several sales regions. The managers of each of these units will perceive new objectives and will translate them into new missions to their respective components, each in a new way unique to his unit. Obviously, it is important that individual professional workers at the "do-it" end of the hierarchy adjust their activities so that they are compatible. That is, customer service men should not, even though legitimately in their own eyes, do things that are at odds with what salesmen are doing. This, of course, requires *coordinating*, or making sure that activities are coordinated—a managerial process to be discussed in Chapter 10.

CRITERIA FOR SETTING OBJECTIVES AND MISSIONS

The specific kinds of objectives and missions developed by the sales management hierarchy of an individual firm vary widely from firm to firm. Many factors influence the specific objectives themselves—degree of delegation of decision-making authority; organization structure itself; competency, experience, and judgment of individuals; the management style of the firm; nature of products, customers, and competition; and others. Nevertheless, the foregoing three-pronged view of the *process* of objective setting is pervasive.

So also are the *criteria* used in the establishment of objectives or missions—that is, the specific way in which the objectives are framed and presented to the subordinate unit. Here again, the degree to which various criteria are used may vary from firm to firm, and from unit to unit within a firm. For example, a particular objective may need to be less definitively "spelled out" to an IBM sales engineer than to a door-to-door salesman for a book-distributing firm.

Objective-setting criteria fall into four major categories:

1. Operationality
2. Understandability and acceptance
3. Consistency
4. Ranking and balance

Operationality

By this is meant the framing of the objective in measurable, or quantitative, terms. Very generally speaking, the more quantifiable the object-tive, the more meaningful it will be as a target. Quantified objectives either are met "on the nose" or are not—and the amount of deviance is absolutely known by everyone concerned. Obviously, this generates considerable motivation for their achievement.

Quantifying provides another advantage—a base for evaluating performance and a starting point for adjusted behavior. Thus it gives a manager checkpoints, or signals for progress toward goal achievement.

Understandability and Acceptance

Objectives as devices for motivating desired behavior and performance are framed by the sales manager and presented to subordinates. *How they are perceived by subordinates* determines the behavioral responses generated—not how they are perceived by the sales manager. To be optimally effective, the sales manager must carefully frame the assigned objectives so that they are understood and accepted as he intends them to be. This is a simple but critical notion. No "pat" formula exists, but a few broad cautions can be useful:

1. *Definiteness*. Objectives must be clearly spelled out, to eliminate any ambiguity. Particularly for nonquantified objectives (such as "improve customer relations") qualifying and defining statement must be made, so that the subordinate's perception of what is wanted agrees with the sales manager's perception. Furthermore, the objective must be couched in the "language" of the subordinate unit, not that of higher units.

2. *Feasibility*. Normally, effective objectives require some "stretch" to achieve. Ideally they will require better planning, ingenuity, increased productivity. But how much stretch? Obviously, the objective should require reach—but it must be within some reasonable bounds of achievement, or else it will be psychologically rejected.[11]

3. *Acceptability*. This is akin to the feasibility criterion, but adds a different note. An objective may be *feasible* but not acceptable to a subordinate. For example, a district sales manager may receive an objective to operate at a lower sales-expense ratio. This means that he must either increase sales or reduce expenses. If he perceives that he cannot likely increase sales adequately, he must reduce expenses. This, in turn, may require him to sharply curtail salesmen's expenses—possibly even to

[11] A plausible explanation of this psychological reaction may be found in the growing body of knowledge in psychology about "level of aspiration." See D. Krech and R. S. Crutchfield, *Elements of Psychology*, Alfred A. Knopf, New York, 1958, pp. 220–221.

the extreme of eliminating someone from his payroll. He may, therefore, find this objective feasible but not acceptable. This criterion in no way proposes that the higher manager give up the objective. It does propose that he recognize the potential obstacle of unacceptability and thus be able to cope with it—not blindly issue it.

Consistency

Any element of the selling operation, including the salesman himself, usually will have a "mix" or an array of differing objectives. Care must be taken that this set of objectives has *internal consistency*. That is, in establishing the objectives, the sales manager should consider how the possible actions to achieve one objective might influence the ability to achieve all others. If effort to achieve one will endanger the achieving of others, a conflict arises, which should be eliminated *at the level of objective setting,* and not at the tactical level of action. Such possibilities should be considered when the objectives are created.

In addition to being consistent, objectives should ideally be compatible in the complementary sense. That is, effort to achieve one should not only not endanger others, but ideally should enhance the probability of achieving others.

Finally, objectives must be consistent in the sense that they are relatively stable—yet without sacrificing necessary flexibility. This apparently contradictory criterion is important in a *strategic* sense. A sales manager might feel that once objectives are set they should not be tinkered with, because of the possibility of confusing subordinates. Yet there is nothing holy about objectives per se. Why should they not change? Certainly the forces in the external environment are always in the state of change. If objectives do not, within some bounds of reason, flex with them, might not their legitimacy become invalid? When and precisely how objectives are "adjusted" is a matter of managerial judgment and cannot be generalized. Conceptually, however, the process is a valuable strategic device—just as it is in the military.

Ranking and Balance

The devising of the array of objectives itself is not quite enough. Rarely will each objective in the array have exactly the same importance to the sales manager. Also, from time to time, conditions both inside and outside the firm may cause the sales manager to alter his ranking of importance of objectives assigned to subordinate units.

The critical key, of course, is to be sure that salesmen (or managers of subordinate units) rank-order the importance of assigned objectives in the same way as does the assigning sales manager. This must be accomplished by clear communication.

A *temporal balance* must also be determined by the sales manager, and so perceived by subordinate units. The setting of an objective always introduces the element of *time*. An objective is always something to be achieved in the future. This may add complication when a number of diverse objectives are assigned to a sales unit, the achievement of which will occur at different times in the future. Which will receive the greater allocation of effort by the sales unit—the more near-future objective or the farther-out objective? The sales manager must introduce this kind of temporal thinking into his other criteria.

The sales manager must imagine, as he devises objectives, how timing may enhance or threaten their achievement. Two examples follow.

1. In this case, strategy and actions developed to achieve an objective in the near future *enhance* the likelihood of achieving others in the more distant future. Here a conveyor-system manufacturer secures an order today and thereby creates some degree of advantage for the next time the customer purchases a conveyor system—because the customer's operating people have "learned" this system, the maintenance people understand how to service it, the inventory of repair parts can be common, and so on.

2. In this case, strategy and actions developed to achieve an objective in the near future *endanger* the likelihood of achieving others in the more distant future. Here a firm secures an order today from a customer whose policy is to retain several sources of supply. The next order placed in the future may be much more desirable, but the firm's chances of securing it have been decreased.

Proper balance between short-range objectives and long-range objectives varies from firm to firm and from time to time. But it must be considered and communicated to subordinate units.

One last thought about the balance of objectives. Even though the sales manager evolves in his own mind a proper balance between short-range and long-range objectives, a problem may arise in their implementation by the subordinate units. Subordinate managers or individuals are human beings. If they are held accountable for results, if their performance is evaluated, and if this evaluation affects "payoff" to them (economically and psychologically), they will in most cases dedicate themselves to the achievement of short-range objectives *even at the cost* of longer-range objectives. Achievement in the here and now will be paramount.

This focus on the short range will be amplified *if the short-range objectives are quantifiable*. In fact, a general hypothesis can be made that the more highly quantifiable an objective, the more diligently it will be sought. And in sales, it appears that shorter-range objectives are more quantifiable than longer-range. Hence if the sales manager wants emphasis placed on longer-range objectives, he must consider the evaluation that *subordinates* place on shorter-range objectives—and make appropriate adjustments in criteria.

Summary of Criteria

To sum up the real meaning of the criteria for setting objectives, consider again the real meaning and purpose of objective setting as a managerial process. Objectives are conceptually, strategically, and operationally much more than mere mechanistic devices. They are *targets* at which the subordinate group will aim and for which it will plan strategies and implement actions. They result in a whole *hierarchy* of missions and subobjectives interwoven throughout the organization structure. They are, therefore, a *strategic and tactical process* of prime importance to the sales manager. As a managerial process, objective setting must therefore be carefully and thoroughly mapped out—and the criteria listed may be used for some practical "ground rules" in doing this.

OBJECTIVES AT THE SALESMAN LEVEL

The foregoing rationale of the managerial process of objective setting applies to all managerial levels in the organizational hierarchy. A brief mention is advisable, however, of its application at the level of the salesman. As discussed in Chapter 3, the success of the firm's marketing strategies and in a very large sense the success of the firm itself may depend significantly on how effectively the salesman performs during those precious moments when he is face-to-face with a customer. His planning of strategies and his resulting tactics, if effective, must be based on sound objectives. Now, the salesman—just as any other "unit" in the selling organization—will have an array of objectives, stemming from the missions given him by his sales manager and having some ranking in relative importance. Some of these may be in the form of *quotas*, a sales supervisory device so widely debated that it deserves a brief discussion to put it in proper perspective.

Quotas

A quota is simply a goal or an objective stated in numerical terms, assigned to a sales unit (the entire sales department, a sales region, a sales district, or an individual salesman). Here we are assuming that there is a marketing management to whom sales management reports and that the marketing management—not the sales management—has assigned "quotas" of various kinds to the sales management, which in turn has reallocated by breaking the quotas down and assigning shares to subordinate units.[12]

The purpose of quotas is multifold. Quotas are used (1) to set targets, (2) to serve as incentives, (3) as a means of directing and controlling effort, (4) as a basis for compensation, or (5) as a basis for evaluating performance of groups and individuals. They may be established for a number of variables: (1) for sales volume, usually by product line, (2) for sales expense items, and (3) for a host of such quantifiable activities as number of calls made, new accounts opened, servicing calls made, or combinations of all three categories.

The setting of effective specific quotas is not a simple managerial task. A number of techniques can be employed, and the interested reader may pursue these by using the references at the end of this chapter. It must be pointed out here, however, that considerable managerial judgment must be used in this process. The final quota will turn out to be a number, or a set of numbers, and therefore must start from a number. For example, the starting point of a sales volume quota is usually the actual sales observed in the immediate past period. This must be adjusted by a number of factors, most of which are *qualitative rather than quantitative*.[13] Adjustments up or down to past sales must be made for other factors that are *estimated* as affecting future sales—changes in demand, changes in business conditions, changes in marketing and sales policies, changes in territory potential, changes in competitive actions. Furthermore, the specific individual to whom the quota is being assigned may have to be uniquely considered before the final "numbers" are determined. Thus although the quota winds up as a set of "numbers," it is no better a tool for achieving the foregoing purposes than the judgment factors that went into it.

In some businesses, the quota may be a very effective tool as an objective. In others it may not. Furthermore, the sales manager must use caution in placing emphasis on quotas as objectives, if he is also setting other, nonquota objectives that he wants achieved. (Note the foregoing discussion on possible dilemmas caused by a mix of quantified and nonquantified objectives.)

[12] Some sales departments may create their own "quotas." Others may assist higher management in establishing them.
[13] Here we follow generally H. H. Maynard, and J. H. Davis, *Sales Management*, Ronald Press, New York, 1957, pp. 187–188.

SUGGESTED READINGS

The Managerial Process of Objective Setting

1. Newman, W. H., and Sumner, C. E. *The Process of Management,* Prentice-Hall, Englewood Cliffs, N.J., 1961, pp. 373–389.
2. McFarland, D. E., *Management Principles and Practices,* MacMillan, New York, 1958, Chapter 5.
3. Drucker, P. F., *The Practice of Management,* Harper, New York, 1954, Chapters 6 and 7.

Setting Sales Objectives

1. McBurney, W. J., Jr., *Goal Setting and Planning at the District Sales Level,* American Management Association Research Study No. 61, 1963.
2. Jerome, W. T., "Market Knowledge—Source of Objectives," in Britt, S. H. and Boyd, H. W., *Marketing Management and Administrative Action,* McGraw-Hill, New York, 1963, pp. 52–63.

Setting Sales Quotas

1. Brion, J. M., *Corporate Marketing Planning,* Wiley, New York, 1967, pp. 361–362.
2. Risley, G., "A Basic Guide to Setting Quotas," in M. Alexander and E. M. Mazze, *Sales Management: Theory and Practice,* Pitman Publishing Co., New York, 1965, pp. 352–363.

QUESTIONS AND PROBLEMS

1. What is an "objective"?
2. Why is it not satisfactory to tell a district sales manager that his objective is simply to "get all the business he can"?
3. Explain why the objective-setting process has behavioral overtones.
4. What are three different ways in which a sales manager can view the objective-setting process? Why not simply view it as setting "targets for achievement"?
5. A vital process in any firm is the determining of the sales forecast. In Chapter 5, it was proposed that the sales forecast is the starting point

for all planning, and activity in the entire firm. For the selling operation, then, can we say that the sales forecast is synonymous with the selling operation's objectives? Why?

6. Using imagination, devise a list of objectives that you think might be relevant for a district sales unit in a firm selling pumps, compressors, and air drills to industrial customers.

7. What are the advantages and the disadvantages in assigning to a sales group highly quantifiable objectives?

8. What is the value in setting quotas for individual salesmen? Can you imagine any problems in setting them? Why?

7

Planning:
Strategies at
Management Level

A critical link in the chain of conceptual thinking to actions to achievements is the process of *planning*. Here, drawing from *Webster's*, a *plan* is simply defined as a method of achieving something or a way of carrying out a design. Or, planning is a systematic formation of a campaign or a program of action.

Note that three elements are implied in these definitions. First, there is an *end*, or an objective. Second, the element of *time* is involved; the objective will be achieved sometime in the future. Third, because *action* must ensue, decisions are involved and people are committed to respond with some kind of behavior. The concepts of this chapter therefore must be interwoven with those in Chapter 11 ("Decision Making") and in Part IV ("Leadership and Motivation"). Yet the *process of planning* is so vital to successful sales management that it merits a sharp focus for its own sake.

Still another idea is implicit in the definitions, but deserves particular attention. It is the idea of *strategy*, a concept borrowed from the military and now in rather wide use by businessmen. Strategy is the art of devising and employing plans of action, created to achieve a goal. The basic idea here is similar to that of planning itself, but several additional aspects are implied. Again borrowing from the military, strategy implies the consideration of *alternative means* to achieve the given end, with given resources. It implies the requirement to imagine *obstacles*. It implies *potential retaliation,* given the fact there are rivals with capabilities to react. It implies *"tailoring" and integrating resources and efforts to* preselected targets. Finally, it implies *flexibility,* a capability of shifting and adjusting the programmed actions as needed, to continue "on course" toward the goal.

ADVANTAGES OF PLANNING

The advantages of effective planning are multifold and are widely touted by sales managers everywhere. Some of these are as follows: [1]

1. *Gets more done.* Planning improves the efficiency, hence the productivity of individuals and groups. There is less "wheelspin," fewer false starts, and less wasted effort.

2. *Enhances goal achievement.* Goals are more effectively reached by effective planning. Capability to set even more ambitious (and desirable) goals is increased.

3. *Generates alternatives.* Future events are always tenuous to some degree, and their prediction always involves risk. Planning generates alternatives for these predicted risks.

4. *Anticipates obstacles.* Effective planning flushes out obstacles and defines and evaluates them, making possible their elimination or the preparation of alternative defenses against them.[2]

5. *Enhances control.* Effective planning enables the sales manager and the salesman to maintain better control over their ever-changing environments.

6. *Improves personal achievement.* Effective planning has personal values for the individual. It helps him be more thoughtful and more creative in his approach to his business world. It reduces the pressures on him, enhancing his achievement potential.

However, planning also has some potential disadvantages, which must be understood and weighed. For one thing, planning may introduce a tendency to make behavior patterns quite rigid. In this case, the plan might become an end unto itself, rather than a matching of ends,

[1] The following examples come from statements made by sales managers participating in sales management development seminars, and from my sales manager colleagues in the General Electric Company.

[2] Pan American Airlines put this idea neatly with their statement, "We want pilots who fly out in front of their airplanes." This is also the idea behind "defensive driving."

opportunities, and means. For another thing, the plan may become a means to rationalize an objective. Or, the plan may become a means to rationalize decisions. Actually, there is often only a fine line between planning and decision making.[3] But in some cases, after a decision is made plans may be concocted primarily to justify the decision. Finally, for action-oriented sales units and people, planning may overstress strategy at the expense of tactical reactions that must be made in the here and now of the marketplaces.

THE DIFFICULTIES OF PLANNING

Despite some disadvantages, the many recognized advantages of effective planning make it an essential step. Nevertheless, the process seems to be very difficult for most people. For some reason, many people seem to resist the planning process. Even in the military, where human lives and the outcomes of battles hang significantly on planning, it is done under compulsion. For that matter, students of military history claim that more battles and more lives have been lost because of the inadequacy of planning then for any other single reason. Similarly, in business, probably more orders and more customers are lost because of the lack or inadequacy of planning than for any other reason—price, product design, competitive action.

Planning seems to be elusive—something amorphous—to many people. There appears to be something magic or esoteric about it. This is especially true, and understandably so, for many field salesmen and first-line field sales managers. These are "do it" people, leading action lives in the cross fire of the competitive marketplaces, dedicated to the here and now.[4] Yet a dilemma exists. The real payoff for all the firm's master planning, commitments of resources, and innovations and strategic programs hangs on the tactical behavior of these key individuals in the field. Inadequate planning by these people creates a very crucial flaw in the firm's whole scheme of things.[5]

---

[3] Alderson calls a plan a "bundle of interrelated decisions." See Wroe Alderson, *Dynamic Marketing Behavior,* Richard D. Irwin, Homewood, Ill., 1965, p. 292.

[4] Because of this, field salesmen and field sales managers for the most part become intuitively excellent *tacticians.* That is, they learn how to "roll with the punches" most capably. But *tactics* are reactions, behaviors, responses. Tactical skill is exceedingly important, but in the final analysis, effective tactical skill can really evolve only within the broader framework of an effective strategy, or plan of action.

[5] Many marketing executives believe—and I concur—that significant improvements in sales performance and goal achievement can be gained by more effective planning. Paradoxically, the increasing complexities of the competitive marketplace (making it difficult to plan effectively) are the very compelling reasons why more effective planning *must* be done.

Thus an ambivalent attitude about planning has developed in many line sales operations. On the one hand, it is fashionable to proclaim its values and its legitimacy in a contemporary, sophisticated selling organization. On the other hand, often only lip service is paid—again because the process seems to be elusive to many action-oriented people.

WHAT PLANNING REALLY IS

Planning need not be elusive. After all, it is simply a thought process. It is a logical pattern of thinking, which is simple in essence and which is learnable. It is a mental process involving creative (or imaginative) thinking and problem solving—which, for most sales planning, can be posed as a logical, reasonable, simple step-by-step rationale.[6]

This chapter proposes therefore some relatively simple but rigorous frameworks for thinking about planning sales strategies—or programs of action designed to achieve given sales objectives. These frameworks are widely applicable to all kinds of firms, selling organizations, and markets. Three aspects of planning are considered: first, sales management's broad planning for the optimum allocation of selling effort; second, sales management's planning for "repetitive action"; third—and perhaps the most critical aspect—the salesman's and his immediate supervisor's creation of selling strategies for specific customers (this aspect is discussed in Chapter 8).

PLANNING THE ALLOCATION OF SELLING EFFORT

In Chapter 2, it was proposed that before marketing strategy—the broad plans and programs of action to achieve marketing objectives—can be created, two strategic sets of decisions must be made. First, the firm must decide specifically what market segments or categories of customers it elects to serve. Second, or perhaps concurrently, the firm must determine a line of products (or services) in order to uniquely serve the wants of selected customers.

At the level of sales management,[7] the same sort of process must occur. That is, before specific selling strategies are developed, decisions must be made about how selling effort is to be targeted. These are *strategic deci-*

---

[6] Planning may also be viewed as the process of creating a set of alternative actions to achieve an objective, the determining of the consequences of each, and the selection of the "best" strategy. See the decision-making model, Chapter 11.

[7] Again, we are assuming a marketing management and a marketing organization, of which the selling operation is a part.

sions, which affect the course of all subsequent sales planning and involve decisions about categories of customers and about product lines.[8] It is the genesis of sales planning, and must be accomplished if future planning and action at the customer-contact level is to be optimally tailored to sales objectives.

Customer Selectivity—A Strategic Decision

In the marketing process, the firm has already elected identifiable, definitive market segments or market targets at which its total efforts will be aimed.[9] But this is usually done in a rather "macro" way. That is, the firm may select *kinds* of customers without necessarily specifying individual customers, by name, within the category. For example, in its marketing process, a computer manufacturer and may select "financial institutions" as one unique category of customer to uniquely serve. But at this level of strategy creation, specific customers such as The Bank of America, or Chase Manhattan, or the Dakota City State Bank will not usually be designated as target customers.

In the selling operation, further selectivity is necessary. Based on the missions given it, sales management must begin, at headquarters level, to define more narrowly and specifically the target customers. Here, in a sort of "macro-micro" sense, some differentiations must be made *within the selected market segments.* Thus, within a given segment, customer groupings may be established according to such criteria as size of customer, potential volume of annual business, type of customer technology, and competitive activity. For example, at this level the broad customer category of "Financial Institutions" may be further categorized as follows:

1. Commercial banks with assets exceeding $1 billion.
2. Commercial banks with assets exceeding $500 million but less than $1 billion.
3. Other commercial banks.
4. Saving and loan companies

Obviously, this more definitive categorizing begins to further shape subsequent strategies.

At still another level, either at a regional level or the district level,

8 Here, of course, the products are "given." But how much and what kind of selling effort will be allocated to the various individual products must be rationally determined.
9 This will have been done to enable the firm to zero in on market segments in which it can find uniqueness and ongoing profit.

even more narrowing is required, until at the district level the categories are broken into the names of specific customers. Even here, additional narrowing is done. For example, category 2 above may include, by name, customers with assets between $500 million and $1 billion in the following subcategories:

1. Those having computer equipment who can be regarded as favorably inclined toward our firm.
2. Those having computer equipment who can be regarded as favorably inclined toward a rival firm.
3. Those having no computer equipment but having experience with computer programs purchased from a "computer service center."
4. Those having no experience whatsoever with computers or programming.

Again obviously, this oversimplified targeting of uniquely defined customers still further sets the stage for strategies that are to be tailored uniquely to each customer.

The Customer-Prospect Mix

The defining and categorizing of customers at all levels of sales management result in specific *targets*—each target is uniquely different from all others, but each contains customers who have relatively homogeneous needs, wants, and problems. Resulting strategies, therefore, are not "buck-shotted," hence inefficient; nor are they, at the other extreme, so aggregate that they stimulate stereotyped market actions that satisfy no customers fully. Instead, resulting strategies are aimed at clearly defined, rationally selected targets. This selection of market targets may be called the *customer-prospect mix* [10]—the word "mix" implying that there is an *array* of customer target-groups, with some relative ranking in importance. Again, the criteria used in categorizing the groups within the mix must be left to the judgment of the manager, and will vary considerably from industry to industry. For example, the field sales manager for a soap products company will likely use different criteria in determining his optimum customer-prospect mix than will the sales manager of a machine tool company.

Likewise, the number of categories in the customer-prospect mix should be some optimum, arrived at by management judgment. Too few categories might result in strategies and actions that are too general and

[10] In the following pages, we closely follow W. J. E. Crissy and R. M. Kaplan, "Matrix Models for Marketing Planning," *Business Topics,* Michigan State University, Summer 1963, pp. 48–66.

not uniquely enough tailored. This enhances the possibility that a rival firm may satisfy customer wants and problems more uniquely, even with similar product offerings. On the other hand, too many categories might require too many separate sets of strategies and actions, quite possibly dissipating the resources of the selling operation.

The Product Mix [11]

Most firms market more than one product. Usually the firm markets a line of products, and quite often a number of distinctly different product lines, as potential need satisfiers for its selected market segments. The array of product lines may be called the *product mix,* again implying a relative ranking. How the products are classified into categories, or product "lines," is again a matter of management judgment. This may be done purely on accounting bases, according to the firm's accounting control systems. But it may also be done by unique type of product—unique, that is, in its customer-need-satisfying characteristics. For example, a gas turbine manufacturer may in his product mix separately categorize gas turbines for power generation and gas turbines for oil pipeline pumping, regardless of the accounting system and despite some relatively minor design differences. The extent to which the customer mix is broken down is based on the same judgment factors discussed in the customer-prospect mix. Certainly, the firm's "major" product lines should be included. For example, the manufacturer of large electrical home appliances would probably include in his product mix refrigerators, ranges, washers, driers, and the like, as a minimum.

The Matrix Analysis [12]

The customer-prospect mix and the product mix cannot be considered in isolation or individually when developing sales strategies. Each vitally affects the other. Put another way, the planning of actions to achieve sales objectives cannot be effectively devised by thinking only of customer categories or only of product lines. These two elements are interactive. Each must be considered vis-à-vis the other. This may be done by using a matrix model, as shown in Figure 7-1.

In the matrix, the selected customer target-groups are placed across the horizontal axis, and the product lines are placed along the vertical axis,

[11] For firms marketing "services" (banks, airlines, etc.) this concept becomes the "service mix." If both physical products and services are marketed, the concept may be called "product-service mix."
[12] Crissy and Kaplan, *op. cit.*

		Customer-prospect mix			
		Customer category A	Customer category B	Customer category C	Etc.
Product mix	Product line 1				
	Product line 2				
	Product line 3				
	Product line X				

FIGURE 7-1   The Customer-Prospect-Product Matrix.

forming a "grid." If the firm embarks upon market diversification, the new market segments are added as new columns along the horizontal axis. If the firm embarks upon product diversification, new product lines are added as new rows along the veritical axis.

Analysis of cells. The sales manager now may, as a start of the sales planning process, consider each customer segment vis-à-vis each product line by analyzing each of the cells in the matrix. This individual cell analysis is done to establish a clear understanding of the situation in each market-target segment for each product line.

Two separate analyses may be made *for each cell*. First, questions similar to the following should be answered about the specific customer group and the particular product:

1. Is demand for the product increasing, remaining constant, or decreasing?

2. What are the specific needs, wants, and problems of customers in this group, which this product is capable of satisfying or solving?

3. What forces are at work to change these needs and wants, and how might they be affecting such change?

4. How are the needs and wants now being satisfied? What competitors are there, and how do they operate? What are the capability and likelihood of their changing their strategies and operations?

5. What effort are we now expending on behalf of this product line for this customer group? Should we increase it, keep it as it is, or decrease it?

6. What relationship does this product line have with other product

Customer category B

	Past	Future	Trend
The industry	Market $	Forecast market $	n.c.
Our company	Sales $	Forecast sales $	n.c.
%	Market share %	Forecast market share $	n.c.

FIGURE 7-2   Cell analysis.

lines, and this customer group with other customer groups? What effect if any will any change we make in this cell have on the other cells?

7. Are our efforts in this cell compatible with our overall sales objectives?

8. Is this cell "paying its way" in contributing to our profit goals?

In addition to these questions, another kind of analysis can be made for each cell in the matrix. Figure 7-2 is an enlarged view of one cell, with an additional matrix introduced into it.[13] Here again, this additional matrix analysis will be done for each customer group in turn and for each product line, cell by cell. Note that horizontally we are considering the time element—past and estimated future—hence the trend. Vertically, we are considering performance and potential future performance of the entire industry (our company plus all our rivals). In the inner cells of the grid, appropriate data are written in.

The time periods selected for "past" and "future" depend on the sales manager's judgment. For many types of products and customer groups, the previous year may be used for the past period and the coming year for the future period. Shorter periods may be desired for some mass-volume products and longer periods for others. For some products (such as very large capital equipments), average annual volume for the past five years might be used.

Industry total sales (market $) may be known quite accurately in some

[13] Crissy and Kaplan, *op. cit.* Note that although the ensuing analysis is in terms of sales volume in the markets and revenue to the firm, the data are inputs to the profit equation. Hence, if costs can be calculated for each cell, the grid analysis can also be profit-based.

cases (e.g., the automotive industry). Some industries have trade associations that compile such data and distribute them to member firms. In many cases, however, the data may have to be estimated, as best as possible. But in one way or another, these data must be obtained, since they are crucial for planning.

Company sales for the selected past period are, of course, accurately known by the company; the sales forecast for the future is also known. Hence both for actual past performance and for estimated future performance, the market share, or the company's percentage of the market, is easily calculated.

In examining market share, and the "trend" column, very important planning facts fall out. For example, if for a specific customer group and product line, the trend for the entire industry is down ($\downarrow$), consideration should be given to the possibility of withdrawing (or at least reducing) effort to this segment, or cell, *regardless of the company's sales.* That is, the forecast of company sales for the next period may be up a healthy 10 percent. But if the total market is decreasing, the company may be beginning to "work a dead horse." Conversely, if the 10 percent increase in company sales were the only fact considered, the sales management might feel quite proud of itself. But if the total available market *enlarges* by 20 percent, the company sales increase is plainly inadequate, and worry and new planning and action must be substituted for the pride. This analysis, cell by cell, assures that sales management will avoid stereotyped or "boxcar" thinking and planning.

After this analysis is done for all cells, a vertical summation for each column will place each *customer segment* in proper perspective. The sales manager can thus evaluate objectively (rather than emotionally, as is so human to do) the customer category in terms of its future potential—hence in terms of the effort that should be expended. Such summation leads directly to decisions committing resources and to programs of action—equivalent sales manpower, servicing requirements, promotional programs (those implemented by the selling operation, such as customer mailing programs), and the like. Such analysis spotlights those customer groups that have increasing potential and value and those whose potential and value is on the wane—so that the flexing of effort can be determined rationally and objectively.

A horizontal summation for each row will place *each product line* in proper perspective. Such analysis flushes out product lines on the uptake and those on the wane, so that planning of allocation of selling effort can be determined rationally and objectively.

Looking both horizontally and vertically at the same time provides still another valuable analysis. Assume, for example, that one *customer segment*—say, customer category B—has been determined to be very important to the firm and "on the uptake." Important and additional resources will be allocated to it, and aggressive programs of action will be devised to exploit the predicted opportunity. But assume also (and this is a perfectly reasonable assumption) that one *product line*—say, product line 2—is on the whole diminishing in value. It is on the wane. Sales resources and efforts would normally be reduced for this product line. But a consideration of the decreasing importance of the product line vis-à-vis the growing importance of the customer segment may well show that effort must continue to be exerted on the product line—or at least that any decision to drop the line should be deferred. See Figure 7-3.

In the case shown in the figure, product line decisions must be influenced to an important degree by their effect on customer groups, hence the subsequent reaction of other product lines. For example, suppose that this firm markets a diverse line of pumps and compressors. Assume that Product line 2 is a line of centrifugal pumps and that by previous analysis the line has been found to be decreasing in value to the firm—to the extent that management is considering dropping the line. But assume also that Customer category B is Heavy Construction Contractors and that previous analysis has found it to be very important to the firm, contributing significantly to volume and profit and with much potential to grow.

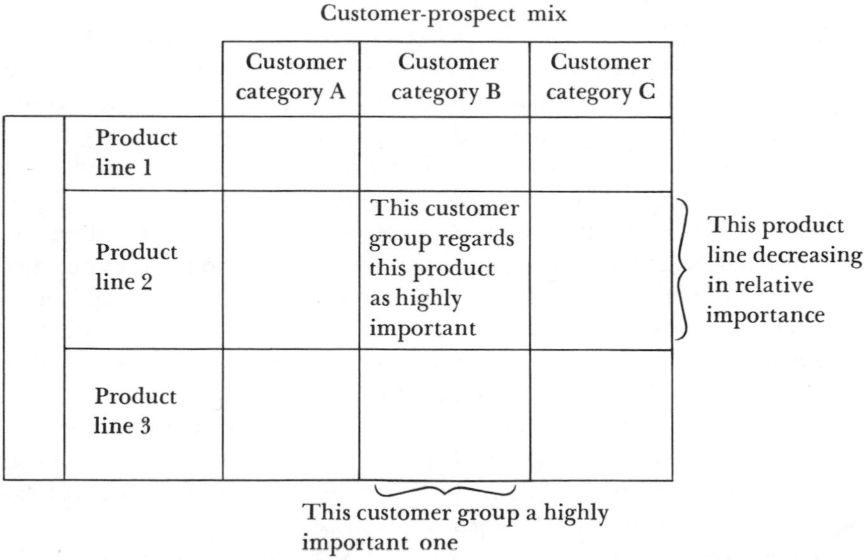

Customer-prospect mix

	Customer category A	Customer category B	Customer category C	
Product line 1				
Product line 2		This customer group regards this product as highly important		This product line decreasing in relative importance
Product line 3				

This customer group a highly important one

FIGURE 7-3   Customer segment versus product lines.

In addition, assume that these customers purchase large volumes of the firm's other product lines. Assume further that although the centrifugal pump line is weak in summation across the market, it is purchased in some volume by this customer group—not enough to warrant retaining it, per se, perhaps. Now assume finally that by the very nature of their business and its growth, construction contractors regard centrifugal pumps as an important, basic resource. Dropping the line will require these customers to seek the product from rival firms, most certainly affecting their purchase decisions for the firm's other product lines. The cell analysis forces an objective consideration of this fact.

Advantages of the Matrix Analysis

The matrix analysis provides a planning framework that helps prevent "boxcar" thinking. By the very nature of the sales-forecasting process, sales management will usually have aggregate or total figures with which to deal. Rather than start the action-planning with totals—or even breaking the totals into parts—it is better to start with the basic building blocks, the individual cells, assigning objectives and plans of action to each, and then totaling.

As an example, it is better to build up sales manpower requirements cell by cell than to start with a total and break it down by some arbitrary method. To be sure, the sales manager may have as a "given" the number of sales personnel available. The cell-by-cell building may exceed this allowed total. But in this case, the sales manager can now go back over the matrix, reducing his original manpower plans where the reduction will hurt the least. Assume, for example, that by the cell-by-cell analysis, he has arrived at a total equivalent salesman requirement of 165 field salesmen. Furthermore, assume the constraint of an expense budget that will permit only 145 field salesmen. The sales manager need not make a blanket, pro rata reduction across the board. He need not "guess" at which customer groups or product lines he must pull away some manpower resources. Having done the matrix analysis and having a cell-by-cell, a product-line–by–product-line, and a customer-group–by–customer-group determination, he can now allocate his 145 field salesmen maximally. He can distribute their efforts so as to focus on market segments previously selected as prime targets.

This rationale and this method of sales planning maximize objective decisions, avoiding the extremes of too broad (or "boxcar") thinking or "shot-in-the-dark" decisions. It keeps the blinders off. It enables analytical determination of the placing of effort where subsequent action will help optimize market objective achievement. It provides a flexibility, permitting rationally based decisions for shifting effort as the sales manager gets feedback from the marketplace. It provides a valuable input into the firm product line and product strategy decisions.

PLANNING FOR REPETITIVE ACTION

Another important aspect of sales management planning is the creation of standing plans—that is, plans to cover certain situations which will hold and can be invoked whenever the situation arises. They are plans that are "on tap," so to speak, and guide action in a predetermined way so long as they are in force. Standing plans are of two general types—policies and procedures. They can be powerful influences on sales organization behavior, and the sales manager must understand their potential and their limitations.

Policies

A policy is usually defined as a general guide to action. Actually, it is more than that; it is also a decision, or a "predecision" for specified situations, which will remain in force. This will be explored further in Chapter 11. But policy making is legitimately considered to be a type of planning, because it does determine behavioral responses in the organization. As such, a policy usually takes the form of statements telling individuals the general bounds of action.

A policy is broad, or general. It is a *guide* to action. It differs from *rules* or *procedures* in that it does not tell individuals specifically what to do. Yet it does predetermine general action, or a framework within which action will be predetermined. As such, a policy is a control device, influencing behavior. Or, it is a statement of decision-rules for "programmed behavior."

In addition to providing a guide to action, a policy may also establish the *philosophy* or the *attitude* that management wishes to pervade the organization. For example, a policy might be the following: "It is our constant desire to be a good corporate citizen in the communities in which we have offices and plants." Such a policy expresses a stance or an attitude and will influence behavior without specifying the behavior.

The kinds of situations covered by policies and the number of policies in force vary widely. This is particularly true for sales policies. Some sales managements have policies in force for many selling situations: pricing tactics, warehouse activities, credit, reporting, customer contact frequency, and on and on. Others have only a few major, broad policies, giving more latitude for behavior to subordinate units and to individuals. Obviously, where a firm should stand on this spectrum is a matter of management judgment, depending primarily on the nature of the organization. One would expect, for example, that a highly sophisticated, highly trained, highly competent professional selling operation (say, the technical sales force for a large computer-systems manufacturer) would be bound by relatively few sales policies.

Ideally, the number of policies should be on the minimum side, rather than on the maximum side. This is true because for all their value and necessity, policies have a number of disadvantages and even dangers:

1. *Acceptability.* If a policy is broad, as it should be, its acceptance and following may be endangered if too many policies exist. "Policies are made to be broken" is not an uncommon thought in the rank and file.

2. *Conflicting policies.* Setting many policies increases the danger that one will conflict with another—again, a common occurrence. For example, one sales policy may encourage the opening of new customer accounts; another may tend to restrict credit. What will the field salesman do?

3. *Inflexibility.* Once established, a policy may hang on and on. The situational world may change, making the policy ineffective or even damaging. Of course, astute operating people may disregard the policy, but this may destroy the validity of the firm's entire policy system.

4. *Substitute for decisions.* Akin to inflexibility is the danger that policies may become substitutes for needed decision making which admittedly involves risk. There may be a temptation to "hide" behind policies. Furthermore, by definition a policy is set or fixed, hence *is not strategic* in character. And one of the pervasive concepts in this book is the need for strategic flexing of behavior, by way of managerial decisions.

Procedures

Procedures and policies are similar in that each establishes a pattern of behavioral response, but they are different in the degree to which they do so. Policy establishes *guides* to action, leaving to the individual who implements it a choice of alternative actions. It will usually not specify *how* it is to be followed. *Procedures* are also guides, but they more rigidly specify what actions are to be taken, hence more rigidly control the end behavior itself.

Even procedures have a spectrum of definiteness and specificity. A "standard method" is a procedure by which a "best way" to handle a situation is established. It may not absolutely determine end behavior, but is more controlling than a policy.

Somewhat even more rigid in control is the "standard operating procedure." Here the solution to situations or problems is spelled out definitively in a sequence of steps to be performed. Obviously, such procedures must be determined for many, many activities in a sales operation, or there would be chaos. Standard operating procedures for *internal* activities are essential. Examples: handling of expense accounts, handling and routing of customers' orders, billing of customers, forecasting. For *external* activities—that is, for field sales managers' and salesmen's customer-contact activities—standard operating procedures must be used with caution, to ensure that creative, strategic thinking and tactical behavior is not inhibited by them.

In summary, the process of setting policies and specifying procedures is a highly important managerial planning tool. By their judicious use, the sales manager can preplan attitudes and responses or behavior of groups and individuals for predetermined situations. Properly devised and used, this planning tool will enhance the match of behavior to objectives.

For suggested readings on planning, see the combined list at the end of Chapter 8, page 122.

QUESTIONS AND PROBLEMS

1. Define "planning," as a sales manager might use the term.
2. Why is planning important? What advantages does it provide to a sales manager?
3. Why do you think it is that in some sales units only lip service is paid to planning?
4. What do you think of the often quoted statement: "Plan your work and work your plans"?
5. Describe what is meant by the "customer-prospect mix." How is it devised?
6. List what you think might be a logical customer-prospect mix for the following companies:
    a. An airline (with coast to coast routes)
    b. A typewriter manufacturer
    c. A full-line department store
    d. A computer manufacturer
    e. A state university

7. Select any firm you wish. Devise a customer-prospect mix and a product mix. Imagine some logical data and construct three matrices, as shown in Figures 7-1, 7-2, and 7-3. Put your imagined data into each of these matrix charts (trying realistically to have both "good" and "bad" market conditions). For each matrix analysis, state your conclusions and how you think they should influence your planning, were you the manager charged with so doing.

8. What is the relationship, if any, between planning and policy setting?

8

Planning:
Selling Strategies
at Customer Level

Without belittling the importance of planning at the marketing management and top sales management levels, we can say that the real payoff for planning strategies comes *at the level of the customer*. In Chapter 3 it was stated that all the innovations, strategies, and programs of the entire firm have their culmination at the "magic moment" when a salesman is face to face with a customer—saying things, doing things, behaving, and reacting to what the customer says and does. This is the payoff moment, on which the success of the firm may well depend.

Planning by the salesman (and by his immediate superior) for this moment—the planning of strategies or programs of action—for each specific customer is one of the most crucial determinants of the effectiveness of a selling operation. And it is probably less well done at this level than at any other.[1] This is not difficult to understand. For one thing, the planning process itself is elusive and hard to grasp, as discussed before. For another thing, the salesman and the district manager are action

[1] This is conjecture, of course, but it is based on my experience in sales management and in consulting with many major firms. There is much evidence that strategy is not very well conceived at the salesman level in many firms.

A Selling Strategy for the XYZ Company

1. Identify customer objectives
2. Define specific goals for this customer
3. Compatibility of your goals with customer's
4. Gather relevant data
5. Evaluate the data
6. The means end chain
7. The master strategy

FIGURE 8-1   The selling strategy rationale.

people, caught up in the pell-mell of *tactics,* or behaviors in the market-places. Yet there is probably more potential for increased business and improved customer relations in more effective planning at the salesman level than in any other factor. It follows that one of the most significant elements of the sales manager's job is to ensure that such effective planning is continuously done by salesmen.[2] This process of creating a strategy, or plan of action, for each specific customer is learnable and understandable. This chapter presents a logical, step-by-step framework of thinking for such planning. It is a "format," or scheme of thinking that is universal and consistent. That is, it can be used with equal effectiveness by salesmen and sales managers of all kinds of firms for all kinds of customers. It is a thought process for presale planning which has been tested by actual use and found to be universally effective.

The elements of this planning process are shown in Figure 8-1.[3] Note that the strategy is being devised and tailored to a *specific customer*—here the XYZ Company.

1. Identify Customer Objectives

At first thought, it would seem logical to define one's own objectives as the first step in creating a strategy. After all, a strategy is a plan of action to achieve objectives—and how can one start without the targets at which to aim? Yet, if the "marketing concept" has any validity—if the firm is

---

[2] In this discussion, we shall be concerned with planning strategies of action with customers. We shall not discuss other kinds of planning by the salesman, such as route-planning. The latter is important, but the former is crucial.

[3] The rationale for this process has its origin in the U. S. Army's "Estimate of the Situation," one of the elements learned by field commanders in the creating of battle plans. Considerable credit also must be given to John McCarthy, formerly a marketing staff consultant in General Electric, who adapted the "Estimate of the Situation" to sales planning and who introduced me to this approach to thinking about strategy.

truly market-oriented and customer-oriented—it follows that one should start with the *customer's objectives* and tailor the ensuing strategy to them.[4]

By "customer's objectives" is meant something much more than the customer's corporate, or total business, objectives. Certainly, every customer firm does have a set of objectives such as profit, volume, and market share. But it would be relatively meaningless for the salesman to meditate about them—at least as far as a meaningful strategy is concerned. *Customer's objectives* here refer to the subobjectives for those particular elements of the customer's organization that have any influence on purchase decisions for the salesman's products. Chapter 6 described the "hierarchy of objectives" evolving in the hierarchy of organization. Each of the work units of the customer organization will have some unique set of goals for itself, and its management or personnel will perceive the salesman's products and proposals in terms of their potential value in achieving these goals. These are the objectives to be identified as a starting point in strategy formation.[5]

Different elements of the customer organization will have different objectives (and different needs, wants, and problems), as well as different perceptions of the salesman and his offerings. The salesman's end strategy, therefore, must take this into account, requiring him to tailor his actions uniquely. For example, consider that the customer, XYZ Company, is a manufacturing firm and that our salesman is selling a line of industrial machinery. Although the actual act of purchasing may be accomplished by the customer's purchasing department, many other elements of the customer's organization may have direct or strong indirect influences on the purchase decision—for example, plant management, plant engineering, quality control, and design engineering. The salesman's planned ultimate behavior must be aimed at satisfying the unique requirements (goals) of all these diverse units.

2. Define Specific Goals for this Customer   √

Much of the rationale of Chapter 6 applies here, and not much more needs be said. Stress must be placed, however, on an important point: the salesman must have *definitive goals* for each customer. This must be more than something like, "Well, my objective is to get all the business I can." Such a vague, general statement has no value.

[4] This may be a philosophical argument, in a sense. Actually, a salesman's objectives are often paramount in his mind, and no great harm is done if we interchange steps 1 and 2 in this process.
[5] From these objectives, of course, come the needs, wants, and problems of that customer group to which the salesman will apply his products or services.

The nature of goals for each customer will vary by type of market and product. Presumably the goals will normally be determined by the salesman himself, based on his total quota or his territorial objective. Ideally they should be quantifiable, as well as definitive. They may include such goals as the following: [6]

1. Volume of orders by product line.
2. Improvement of share of customer's total business placed in these lines.
3. Winning of specific orders or contracts.
4. Increase in volume of a selected line with no loss in others.
5. Enhancement of good relations.

Although the breaking down by a salesman of his total objectives for his job into specific goals for each customer [7] sounds like a simple process (and basically it is), in many cases, it is not adequately done, with a resulting detrimental effect on strategy. In turn, inadequate strategy leads to hit-and-miss action, or behavior. If the premise is accepted that the effective salesman does plan strategies, it must be accepted that clear definition of objectives for this customer must be defined.

3. Compatibility of Your Goals with the Customer's

This step in the strategy development is deviously simple, but may provide critical inputs. Here the salesman compares his goals with those of each of the customer groups. Normally, they will be quite compatible. The salesman seeks orders for his products; he offers in return the satisfaction of wants or solution to problems, assisting the customer in achieving his, the customer's, objectives.

But sometimes incompatibilities arise, provoking potential obstacles for the salesman. And this is the point in the planning process at which such potential obstacles should be flushed out, so that the strategy will later include defenses against them. This may be particularly true when the customer organization has diverse elements with diverse subobjectives. Consider, for example, the salesman for a computer manufacturer. Assume that his customer is a manufacturing firm. The salesman may

[6] Some of the following examples are more capable of objective measurement, on quantification, than are others. See Chapter 6 for the effect of this on the salesman's behavior.

[7] If a salesman has a very large number of customers (e.g., 100), he may have to do this only for his "key" customers—say, those who in total give him 85 to 90 percent of his business—and for those few who have a known potential and have been selected for development.

propose to the customer's plant manager that the computer will reduce variable costs via automation—which might fit the plant manager's objectives splendidly. Or he may propose great new facility for design-problem solution to the customer's manager of design engineering—which might be perceived as enhancing the design engineering objectives. And he might propose to. the manager of accounting the feasibility of much improved information systems—which might fit the latter's objectives. But assume that the manager of employee relations is facing the problems of negotiating a new union contract, an increase of grievances, and a possible work stoppage. When he hears that other elements of his firm are considering using a computer and automating certain processes, he may very sincerely object strenuously to the firm's executives. The proposal *in his perception* threatens achievement of his group's objectives and in his sincere opinion those of the firm. He may work hard to block it.

The ultimate strategy and tactics for surmounting this obstacle will be determined later. There will be several alternatives,[8] but they must be considered when strategic decisions for other actions are made (in step 6). Nevertheless, every effort must be made by the salesman, at this point in his preplanning, to flush out such incompatibilities. The case given above is overly obvious. Such incompatibilities and their resulting obstacles may be much more subtle than this. We can hypothesize that they do occur and with more serious import than most salesmen and sales managers realize.

4. Gather Relevant Data

Every component of the strategy-developing process is important, but perhaps the most critical one is the proper amassing of relevant data.[9] After all, the aim of this process is for the salesman to determine his tactical behavior with the customer. His planned tactics can be no better than the data on which they are based.

[8] For example, the strategy may include the following alternatives with varying degrees of risk, depending on the situation:

1. Do nothing. Assume it will not arise.
2. Attack it. That is, approach him and strive to get him to change his views.
3. Attack his views through other persons in his firm. For example, solicit the aid of the plant manager.
4. Go "over his head." Presell his superiors.

[9] Here we include in "relevant data" not only what the salesman believes to be facts, but also the "maybe-facts," the "intelligent guesses," and even the intuitive "feelings about things."

In every selling situation, there is a maze of data. A complex web of data surround a customer, his organization, his people, their objectives, processes, and problems, his market problems, and his contact and dealing with competitors. Some of the data are clear; some are hazy. Some are highly relevant; some are less so. Some are persistent; some change. But all to some degree affect what will happen in the future. And the better one's knowledge of the data bearing on a situation, the better one can predict outcomes and control the situation.

Some effective salesmen seem to intuitively cut to the core of essential data, greatly enhancing their ability to manage situations. But intuition does not evolve easily and is almost impossible for a sales manager to "teach" to his salesman. Here again, however, we can turn to the idea of constructing a "framework" for gathering relevant data which is logical and consistent. Using the technique of analysis, we can pierce the complexity by proposing first that the salesman will need data in several categories. These are, as a start:

Data about competition — *who, what, trends, rival sales people, locals*
Data about the customer's business
Data about the customer as a unique individual

Within each of these categories, the salesman notes data known to him. He may do this mentally, for relatively simple selling situations, or he may do so formally by using a format like that shown in Figure 8-2.[10]

Data about Competition (Direct Competitors). Even this substep is too complex to be approached without further analysis, or without breaking it down into subcategories. Figure 8-2 proposes only a few such subcategories—by no means an exhaustive list. Here we are merely opening the door with the following kinds of data about the competitors:

1. *Who.* Obviously we must consider each competitor by name. Note that we are interested in those rivals who are *actively calling on this customer.*

2. *How much.* How much business each rival secures is an important datum for the future strategy.[11] For example, assume that we believe that rival ABC is securing 50 percent, DEF 20 percent, and RAT 5 percent. We, of course, are getting 25 percent. In our future strategy we *may* decide to focus on the rival who is doing the most business with this

---

[10] Again, credit to John McCarthy who first introduced me to this thinking.

[11] It is rarely possible to learn accurately and precisely how much each competitor is receiving from a customer. Usually, then, these data must be estimated. And care must be exercised here, because it is quite normal for a salesman to think he is getting a larger share of the customer's business than he actually is.

STEP 4: GATHER DATA

ABOUT COMPETITION					ABOUT THE CUSTOMER'S BUSINESS	ABOUT THE CUSTOMER AS AN INDIVIDUAL
Direct Competition				Indirect Competition		
Who	ABC Co.	DEF Co.	RAT Co.		• Organizational	For each customer individual having any influence on decisions re our offerings:

• How much
• Trend: up, down, N.C.
• The salesman
  Call patterns
  Strategies
  Entertaining
• District Sales Manager
  Who he calls on
  Frequency
• Location of the nearest
  office
• Service
• Pricing
• Product
				• Here enumerate the possible alternatives being offered to customer which, if accepted, may decrease his interest in our offering	• Technological
					• Financial
					• Marketing
					• Policies, procedures, and buying patterns
						• What is he like?
						• What are his patterns of behavior?
						• How does he perceive, think, respond?
						• What seems to be his set of needs, motives, or personal aspirations?
						
						1. Purchasing Agent
						2. Chief Engineer
						3. Plant Manager
						4. Etc.

FIGURE 8-2   A method for assembling data.

customer.[12] This competitor may be complacent, and the customer may decide that we have earned additional business and that it is this rival from whom it can most easily be taken away. On the other hand, our end strategy *may* be aimed at displacing RAT, who is hanging by his teeth anyway. It must be remembered that the gain the salesman makes relative to his rivals will always be at the expense of one or several of the rivals. This must be cranked into strategy.

3. *Trend.* The trend of each rival's achievement with the customer may be an important datum. The anticipated strategies and retaliatory behavior (to our strategies and actions) of a rival may be quite different when his own business with this customer is on the uptake than when it is not.

4. *The rival salesman.* A battery of questions about each competitor's salesman must be answered. It would be naïve to regard him as anything but an adversary attempting to gain additional business at our expense. What kind of a man is he? How old? How long with his firm? How long calling on this customer? What is his education? His technical skill? On whom does he call? What are his personal relations with them? Whom does he entertain and in what pattern? What is his call frequency, and is there any consistent pattern in it? What appear to be his strategies? Additional questions to be answered about each rival salesman will undoubtedly spin off from these.

5. *The rival sales manager.* A whole set of questions similar to those above must be answered about each rival sales manager. A few additional strategic facts may also be helpful. For example, if a rival sales manager periodically accompanies his salesman when calling on the customer, it will be very helpful for one's own counterstrategy to know the following: How much does the sales manager "take over" for the salesman? Does he make many critical decisions? Does he control important elements of strategy, such as pricing decisions?

6. *Location* of each rival's offices, warehouses, order-handling facilities, and the like, is among the important facts to be learned.

7. *"Service"* is a subcategory that must be further broken down into, and sets of facts determined about, such kinds of service as order handling, delivery, in- and out-of-warranty product service, and service record of equipment performance.

8. *Pricing* also requires a wide array of facts. For each rival, what is his price? How does he use price as a competitive strategy? How does he meet

[handwritten margin note: most important]

---

[12] Note that ABC Company is the big rival as far as this customer is concerned. He may or may not be the firm's biggest competitor in the aggregate. But it is his position here, with this customer, that affects our strategy for this customer.

price competition? What non-price-tag elements does he strategically employ (discounts, extra services, transportation costs, etc.) ?

9. *Product.* Obviously, much needs to be known about each rival's competing products. This kind of "technical" information ranges from the relatively simple (e.g., competing producers of anthracite coal) to the quite complex (e.g., manufacturers of nuclear power plant apparatus). Usually, firms marketing more or less complex product lines will have a procedure for supplying to the field sales force detailed information about rival's competing products. Hence we are assuming that the salesman will have knowledge of competitive products at his disposal. But this can be a complicated and bulky list of facts. A handy idea here, for the "data sheet," is for the salesman to note only the prominent or salient features of each rival's product that differ from his firm's product. Never mind here whether the difference is advantageous or disadvantageous; this will be considered later.

Data about Competition (Indirect Competition). Although it is admittedly elusive, *indirect competition* may sometimes raise more difficult obstacles than do direct rivals. Here by indirect competition is meant that which springs from offerings made to the customer that are not substitutable nor directly competitive—but whose purchase will adversely affect decisions about the salesman's products. This often occurs because of the customer's always limited resources. Thus the salesman who is hoping to sell a new and uniquely designed large boring mill may have relatively light competition from direct rivals, but, utterly unknown to him, real competition for the customer's dollars from an automatic conveyor-system manufacturer. Sometimes, too, stiff indirect competition may arise because some noncompeting firm sells something to the customer that changes his processes, his procedures, or even his philosophies. Consider, for example, how the installation of a computer system can adversely affect potential business for many, many suppliers with products completely alien to the computer. Such indirect competition is difficult to foresee—but the astute, effective professional salesman should at least keep his antenna tuned to this contingency and take it into account when creating his strategy. He may rarely be able to attack it frontally, but he may maneuver differently because of it—particularly with respect to timing of actions and with respect to those individuals in the customer's organization (and their objectives) on whom he elects to focus his actions.[13]

13 For example, if the boring mill salesman of whom we spoke earlier learned that he might face indirect competition from a conveyor system, he might center on the customer's plant management and try to arm them with powerful technical and economic ammunition with which to battle, say, the physical distribution management who want the conveyors for their warehouses.

Data about the Customer's Business. If the salesman follows the "marketing concept," he will shape all his end tactics to the customer's needs, wants, and problems. He will strive to present his propositions, his products, his company, and himself in such a way that the customer will perceive all these to be in fact need satisfiers or problem solvers. But to do this, the salesman must know and understand much about the customer's needs and problems. He must be able not only to perceive them, but also to discuss them with the customer in the customer's language. Ideally he becomes an expert in the customer's business. Or, as proposed by such outstanding sales managements as those of Mobil Oil, General Electric, Ford, and IBM, the salesman must function as a consultant to the customer—a management consultant, a technical consultant, a financial consultant, and so on. He needs a wide array of facts about the customer's business in order to do so. Again, this rather complex category can be broken down into simpler and more meaningful subcategories:

1. *Organizational facts.* The salesman must know the customer's organization structure, or at least that part of it which is relevant to his products. He must know which are the decision centers and the decision-influencing points in the structure. He must know who does what and he must understand the relationship between customer groups and individuals, one to another—not only as shown on an organization chart, but as they really are. This knowledge is vital for the development of an effective strategy. In a sense, these organizational facts plug in not only here, but must have been already considered in determining the customer's hierarchy of objectives, in step 1.

2. *Technological data.* If the salesman's strategy is to solve problems and satisfy needs, he must have more than technical knowledge of his own products. He must thoroughly understand the customer's technologies—his technical processes, procedures, and operations of all kinds.[14] All business firms have "technologies"; even such firms as insurance companies or department stores will have technical devices, systems, and processes—hence technical problems that the salesman must know. How else can he develop strategies and tactics that ensure acceptive customer perception?

3. *Financial data.* Often the salesman must gather an array of data about a number of financial aspects of the customer's business. Involved here is more than simply the customer's credit standing, though at times

---

[14] For example, a General Electric sales engineer having a steel mill firm as a customer becomes an expert in steelmaking. He knows the technology (and the language) of steel as well as do the customer's engineers and mill-operating people. Hence he thoroughly understands the *application* of his technical products to the process of steelmaking, and *customer individuals perceive that he does.*

this may be very important. Many other financial data may have influence on how the customer will perceive and respond to the salesman's propositions, and therefore should be cranked into his strategy. All firms —even very large and strong ones such as General Motors—have flexing financial atmospheres at times. Such elements as cash flow, cash position, capital expenditures, and inventory levels all may have influence on purchase decisions. In every firm, for example, it is not uncommon to witness at times a "pulling in of the belt," if cash flow is momentarily unsatisfactory, if inventory is unbalanced, or if a capital budget is exceeded. Whether such financial facts are obstacles or opportunities depends on many circumstances, but they may be very important inputs to the strategy formation.

4. *Marketing data.* In some cases, the effective salesman must gain data about his customer's marketing operations. How the customer stands in his marketplace, what he is trying to do, what his competition is, and similar factors, may be valuable inputs to strategy. This is particularly true if the salesman's product is incorporated into the customer's end product.[15] Not only will the customer's marketing people be interested (hence will seek influence in purchase decisions) in how the salesman's product will affect *their* customer's perception of their product, but they will also be interested in such marketing activities as service and repair parts. Thus under some circumstances, the customer's marketing people may have strong influence, and such facts should be incorporated into the salesman's strategy.

5. *Policies.* Data must be gathered about the customer's policies and procedures. The salesman must strive to know what the policies are (which affect buying procedures and patterns, as well as actual purchase decisions). He must know the written and unwritten policies, who shaped them, who can change them, how they are variously perceived by and influence customer individuals and groups.

Data about the Customer as a Unique Individual. Looking again at the chart (Figure 8-2), the salesman in his data-gathering process turns to the last category: data about the *customer as an individual person.* Here we enter the domain of psychology. In Part III, "Leadership and Motivation," we shall delve rather deeply into human behavior. Although we shall focus on the leadership and motivation by the sales manager of his

---

15 An "original equipment manufacturer's" (OEM) marketing department will be much interested in products that their firm purchases to be incorporated in their own, particularly if such products are a large element of the end product (example: the jet engines purchased by Boeing or Douglas), or if the performance of such products vitally affects the performance of their own product (example: electric motors purchased by a manufacturer of room air conditioners).

followers, the principles also apply to the understanding (and influence) of behavior of individuals in the customer organization. Suffice it to say here that each customer who has any influence on purchase decisions must be understood as a unique individual. Men in business positions are not different from what they are in their other roles. A purchasing agent, for all his outward demeanor, does not come to the office at 8 A.M., close the door on the rest of the world, and become an economic robot, or computer. The plant engineer is not just a human calculator, or a rational system-controlled, decision-making device. These men are human. They have not only business objectives; they have personal aspirations, needs, motives, fears, anxieties, drives. They perceive, think, and respond not only to economic and rational stimuli, but to emotionally based sets of stimuli. Into the salesmans' strategy, therefore, must go an input of all the data that he is capable of generating about how each of these unique, goal-seeking individuals seem to think, perceive, and respond or behave. If the salesman can gain such insight into behavior patterns, he can come closer to predicting what the responses or behavior will be, under situations that he is going to create. And "he who can predict behavior is in a position to influence behavior." Certainly, it is an accepted fact that the salesman's job is to influence behavior. And certainly in our society, where the customer has great freedom of choice, such influence must result in end behavior and end results that satisfy both customer and salesman, or the salesman's success will be short-lived indeed.

How to Gather the Data. The rationale behind this fact-gathering step is sound, but one can legitimately ask, "But how do all this? And how much time and effort should be expended?" These are good questions, because the data-gathering process for many customers and for many selling situations can be massive and burdensome. To further complicate it, the process is never-ending; new facts are always arising and old data change or disappear. Yet the process is vital for effective strategy, and management judgment must be used to decide to what degree it is to be implemented.

To gather the data, several means can be used. One way is to obtain them by *asking*. Many customers want their suppliers to have facts, and readily provide them. Sometimes, of course, certain data may not be freely given, and some degree of tact and subtlety must be used. The degree of personal rapport between salesman and customer is a factor. Sometimes the salesman's manager on a customer visit may be in a strategic position to ask questions and get answers in a way the salesman cannot.

Another way to gain data is by *observing*. It is startling how data can be garnered by keeping one's eyes and ears really open. What goes on in the customer's plants, what can be seen in his warehouse or stockrooms, how he responds to propositions, all can generate facts in all the categories of Figure 8-2. Even such a simple thing as noting in the reception room register who has been calling on whom can be an important information source.[16]

Still another way to obtain data is by the *process of induction.* That is, if A is a fact and B is a fact, then C must be true. For example, assume that a salesman is selling a product that is purchased in quantity at frequent intervals and is stocked by the customer. The salesman learns that the customer has reported decreased earnings for the past quarter, has deferred a proposal to modernize his plant power system, and has canceled some orders on other suppliers (for unrelated equipment). The salesman might induce that inventory levels for products similar to his own might be lowered—and he therefore inputs this *induced* fact into his adjusting strategy.[16a]

With regard to the knotty question of how much time and effort the salesman should expend on data gathering, we must again defer to managerial judgment. Obviously, the salesman cannot spend more than some small percentage of his time in this process. But this emphasizes the importance of having an analytical technique for doing what he does do—and Figure 8-2 provides one. Quite possibly, most salesmen may be able to do a fairly complete job of this for only a few of their major accounts or for specific important proposals. For example, a salesman of organic chemicals located in central Michigan might do an exhaustive job of fact gathering for one of his customers, the Oldsmobile Division of General Motors in Lansing, and a less exhaustive job of it for another, the Central Canning Company in Jackson. Or a turbine-generator sales-

[16] Somewhere in this process, morals and ethics must enter. Where is the dividing line between moral and immoral behavior in fact gathering? Certainly, bribing a customer is clearly immoral, and as far as this book is concerned, must be rejected. But what about glancing at a letter from a competitor, lying on the customer's desk? What about leafing through the reception room register? What about taking a stockroom clerk out to lunch, expressly to seek information? There are gray areas in this regard for which clear decisions cannot be determined here. We are talking about a process for creating a strategy. We cannot duck the issue of morals and ethics, but it is not within our scope at this point to do more than place the decision squarely in the lap of the sales manager himself.

[16a] We propose that if he does this better than his rivals, he might be able, in planning ultimate tactics, to retain his share of business and let his rivals suffer the decrease in purchase rate, or he might be able to arrange a larger "backup" stock in his own firm's warehouse and strategically suggest a different buying-frequency pattern to his customer.

man planning for the sale (he hopes) of a $15 million turbine to Commonwealth Edison in Chicago will likely spend great effort on such fact gathering, and do it quite formally.

But perhaps the real key here is that the salesman and his district manager must develop a *framework of thinking* about this data-gathering process and, regardless of the time and effort consciously expended, always be acutely receptive to changing facts or new facts. With a framework (such as Figure 8-2) in which to accommodate them, the process can be ongoing without significant effort robbed from some other vital process. It is not very demanding for a salesman to say to himself as he crawls into his car after a customer visit, "What new data did I learn today?" Or to ask himself for but a moment on the night before an important customer visit, "Where are the gaps in my knowledge? What kinds of data should I be trying to get, so I can better plan what to do?" Again, a framework for these data greatly facilitates their identification and collection.[17]

5. Evaluate the Data

Once the data have been amassed, the next step in the strategy-building process is the assessment of the meaning of these data. Such evaluation translates *information* into *intelligence*. Borrowing from the military, this step evaluates not only the meaning of each fact, but the relationship between sets of evaluated facts. Put simply, in this step the salesman says to himself: "I observe these data. . . . Some are helpful to me, some harmful. . . . What combinations of them might cause situations that might help me? What combinations could hurt me? Then I can decide better what I should do."

A simple way in which to evaluate the data is to examine each one in turn and ask these two questions:

(*a*) Is this datum an *advantage* to me, and just why?
(*b*) Is this datum a *disadvantage* to me, and why?

An additional shading of evaluation is provided by asking two more questions:

(*c*) Is this datum a *potential* advantage?
(*d*) Is this datum a *potential* disadvantage?

[17] Another significant reason why field sales managers must have salesmen gathering such data is to provide vital market knowledge feedback to the firm, as proposed in Chapter 2 and discussed in the Epilogue. This is only a part of the sales manager's responsibility in regard to feedback, but he must have this knowledge in order to feed back vital competitive intelligence.

This "plus" and "minus" evaluation of all known data will provide several important benefits. When done, whole patterns of advantageous data will appear to fit together, evolving into areas of opportunity that the later strategy can exploit and for which specific actions can be planned. Patterns of disadvantageous data will also emerge, flushing out potential obstacles and areas of danger, for which defenses can now be planned, should they arise. Thus a salesman cannot only create plans of action to achieve objectives. He can also prepare plans of action, or programs of response, to have on tap should they be needed—rather than being caught "flatfooted" and having to react impulsively.

6. The Means-End Chain

The concept and rationale of this step must be emphasized. It is a unique step; it begins the developing of actual actions or a program of action. Here the strategist is beginning to determine what steps he should take to achieve his objective.

He could say that in some fashion, given the objective out in the future, he must take certain sequential steps (Figure 8-3) in order to achieve the objective. That is, he might say, "To achieve my objective, I must first accomplish Step 1, then Step 2, then Step 3, then Step 4—and I will then have achieved my objective." Thus a salesman might say:

"To get that order I want, I must first get the customer's Purchasing Agent to agree to considering my proposal, and approve my contacting the Engineering Department and Plant Management. This done, I must then get Engineering to accept and test a sample, and put it on their approved list. Then I must get the Plant Management to visit one of our plants and inspect similar equipment, to get their acceptance. Then I must make the formal presentation to Purchasing, and if all this is successful, I should get the order."

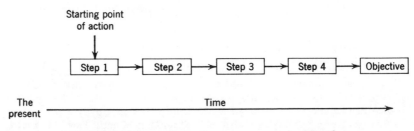

FIGURE 8-3   Stepping-stones to an objective.

Now, these steps may have to be taken, and perhaps even in this order. *But the manner in which they are determined does not follow this A-B-C sequence.* Rather than start from the present and plot one's way toward the objective (as at first seems reasonable), the reverse of this should be done. The neat mental trick here is to project one's self out into the future, to the time when the objective is to be reached, and say, "If I have achieved this objective, what must I have done to get here"—*and then back-plot to the present.* In other words, although the first step of *actions* must be in the present, as shown in Figure 8-3, *the beginning of planning the strategies for such action is in the future and works back to the present.* This is a key idea in developing a strategic program of action. Borrowing from the "means-end chain" concept of decision making, Figure 8-4 shows graphically how the stepping-stones, or intermediate goals, in a plan evolve in such "backward plotting."

In Figure 8-4, the strategist starts by projecting himself mentally out to the end objective. He determines (as an example) that in order to have achieved this objective, he must have first achieved two major subobjectives, or "goals." He determines, in other words, that *if he accomplishes these two things, he will be able to accomplish the end he desires.*

Now, he takes another "backward-plotting" step. What must he do (in his judgment, based on all the foregoing steps of this strategy rationale) to accomplish each of these "goals"? *For each, he again "plots backward."* For goal 1, he must decide (again based on judgment and knowledge) the necessary steps (or "subgoals") to be accomplished.

Now for each of these "subgoals" ("subgoals" 1, 2, and 3 for goal 1 and "subgoals" B and C for goal A, in Figure 8-4), he again decides what stepping-stones need to be covered to achieve each of them and thus determines a set of "sub-subgoals." He continues this process back to the moment of the present and thus has derived a plan of action—a set of targets—to be achieved. He can now begin tactics, or actions aimed toward the sets of goals. What he has done is to develop a whole "tree," with many branches, of logically derived steps to be accomplished. Each element is a *means* to achieve an *end,* which becomes a *means* to achieve another *end,* and so on to the *end-end.* But this "tree" is designed and branched out by *starting at the final objective and working backward to the present.* In Figure 8-5, two "branches" of the tree are shown—one branch for the goals to be accomplished in the customer's purchasing department and one for the goals to be accomplished in his engineering department. In many cases, there will be other branches. By relating the timing of subgoals in each of the "branches," the salesman can, in his preplanning, determine in advance which missions should be sought prior to others. In many cases, it may be strategically very important to

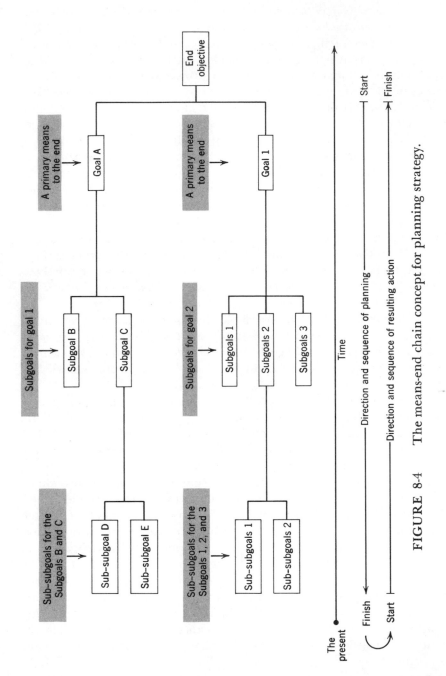

FIGURE 8-4   The means-end chain concept for planning strategy.

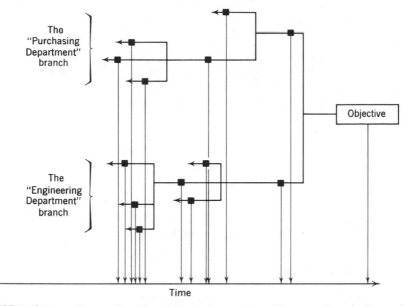

FIGURE 8-5   Interrelated timing of goals leading to the timing of "missions."

achieve one thing before another. For example, it may be advisable to secure approval for one's product from the customer's engineering department before attempting to achieve certain other goals in other customer departments. Or it may be important to achieve a certain goal before trying to achieve a related goal, even within the same customer department. For example, it may be important to "sell" the customer's engineering department on criteria for testing and approving a product before securing agreement to the test itself. The advantages of this timing of interrelated goals are quite obvious—but the process itself may be difficult without an analytical framework such as this. Ideally, each of the subgoals in all branches *becomes a mission for a salesman*. Practically, of course, blockages will occur, and sometimes the salesman must decide whether to continue "attacking" the obstacle, whether to find another approach, or whether to ignore it and proceed with other goals in the "tree." This does not detract at all from the framework, inasmuch as such deviation from it will now be done knowingly and rationally, with defenses prepared for potential, known problems arising from the deviation.

As each of the individual goals and subgoals is considered, the tactics for their achievement are devised by considering all the prior steps of this strategy process. That is, the customer's objectives (at that specific point in his organization), the salesman's own objectives, possible incompatibilities, and all the relevant facts from step 4—all enter into the determination at this point of *alternative actions* that the salesman can use to achieve the individual subgoal. In a way, this may be a sort of microscopic repetition of the means-end chain concept: "To get the engineering department to agree to these criteria, what must I do?" Thus the decisions about *action* have been developed within a strategic framework optimizing a total *pattern of action*. The means-end chain helps eliminate false starts, unnecessary actions, actions that endanger future goal achievenent, or actions that create obstacles in other elements of the action pattern. The concept provides a framework that enables the meaningful introduction of facts into the planning process. It enables the creation of a network of decisions, each of which has a relation and a complementary value to each other.[18]

7. The Master Strategy

The final step, creating the *master strategy,* is almost anticlimactic and redundant after having established the means-end chain in step 6. In a way, the means-end chain does become a strategy—it is a *program* of interrelated and integrated actions to achieve an objective, which is how strategy has been defined here.

Yet one additional strategic element needs to be employed. In the means-end chain, the salesman has considered goals and missions to be accomplished, their interrelation, and alternative actions to achieve them. But in this final step he introduces the element of people and

[18] The means-end chain concept for decision making (or strategy creating, as used here) is similar to several other planning models that are gaining wide use in business. One is the Program Evaluation Review Technique (PERT). Another is the "critical path method," a planning and timing format used in large construction projects. Consider, for example, the NASA Apollo program. The objective is to safely land men on the moon, by a certain date. Now, the Gemini flights were not simply independently devised as steps that will lead to a future step; they have been rationally implemented from a "back-plotted" planning program in the overall Apollo program. Or, for still another example, consider a complex production line such as that of Oldsmobile. At the end of Oldsmobile's assembly process, automobiles of different design drive off every few moments. Now, Oldsmobile does not start at the *beginning* of the process and say, "We must have a foundry, and send its castings to the machine shop, and then to the engine shop, and then to the assembly line. . . ." Or, "And we must have a stamping plant, and send body parts to the body plant, and then to the paint shop, and hope the right body hits the assembly line for the right chassis. . . ." This is the way the *process* is sequenced. But it would be utter chaos if its planning had not been *back-plotted.*

resources. The salesman is not alone; he himself is not his only resource. Here in the final step, he "orchestrates." He is the "leader of a whole orchestra" and can call in the strings, the percussions, or the brass. He can decide that to help reach some particular subgoal, he will call on some particular individual in his company—an application engineer, a financial specialist, or a product specialist. He may call on his management, fitting their particular expertise to selling situations wrapped around the achieving of a particular goal. Or he may call on the physical and process resources of his firm—technical information, product testing, mailing programs, and so on [19]—to aid in achieving a given goal. Thus in developing the "master strategy," culminating from all the foregoing, the strategist has evolved a master pattern or program of action by following a logical, consistent framework of thinking that leaves little to chance. He becomes truly a *manager of situations.*

SOME CONCLUSIONS

Who is to say which is the most important element of the sales manager's job? Or of the professional salesman's job? It has not been proposed that, planning, or developing strategies, is any more important than other processes. It is suggested, however, that in most selling operations, more potential for increased effectiveness exists in better planning than in any other process. In short, more effective planning—*particularly at the customer level*—will result in more effective objective achievement.

How far should the sales manager go in formally employing such a framework or thought process as proposed here? He and the salesman are pressured by many forces demanding their time and effort. There are just so many hours in the week. Only the sales manager himself can solve this ever-present dilemma of allocating thought and effort. But this is precisely the reason why a rational, logical thought structure for planning must be developed and used. It need not be precisely the one suggested here. In fact, the planning format can be adjusted to fit unique selling operations.[20] The important thing is that a consistent framework for planning be used.

[19] For example, General Electric sales engineers were able to have their own purchasing management discuss the concept of "value analysis" with customer purchasing management. General Electric's purchasing management had developed and implemented this concept to great advantage—and this was a "resource" strategically used by GE sales engineers.

[20] For example, sales managers for public utilities such as a telephone-operating company may want to adjust the "competitive" portion of the fact-gathering format. Yet they most certainly have important considerations about indirect competitive forces.

How deeply should it be used? Again, who can say? Certainly, on very key propositions, or for very important customers, it could well be used formally and in depth. But almost more important is actively using it enough so that *the process itself becomes a thinking way of life,* so that even in the hurly-burly of the world of action the strategist unconsciously follows it, and so that when a completely new and unpredicted situation blows up in his face, he has a *way of thinking* with which to deal with it.[21]

Why should it be consistent? That is, why should the same mental process be followed by all salesmen in a sales group and by each salesman for different selling situations? Repeated use reinforces the adaptation of a logical thought process to one's mental scheme of things. Furthermore —and this can be highly significant—consistency creates a communality of language between members of the sales team. A sales manager and his salesman, each of whom uses the same logic in analyzing selling situations and planning strategy for them, can mutually reinforce each other.[22]

SUGGESTED READINGS
(For Chapters 7 and 8)

The Planning Process

1. LeBreton, P. P., and Henning, D. A., *Planning Theory,* Prentice-Hall, Englewood Cliffs, N.J., 1961, Chapters 1 and 12.
2. McFarland, D. E., *Management Principles and Practices,* Macmillan, New York, 1958, Chapter 4
3. Crissy, W. J. E., and Kaplan, R. M., "Matrix Models for Marketing Planning," in M. Alexander and E. M. Mazze, *Sales Management: Theory and Practice,* Pitman Publishing Corporation, New York, 1965, pp. 151–172.
4. Anthony, R. N., *Planning and Control Systems,* Harvard University Press, Cambridge, Mass., 1965, Chapters 1 and 2.
5. Brion, J. M., *Corporate Marketing Planning,* Wiley, New York, 1967.

[21] Some salesmen develop over time an almost intuitive ability to do this. But an objective, learnable planning rationale such as this can greatly reduce chance in this important strategic ability.

[22] The selling strategy proposed here is a very effective supervisory tool for a sales manager. As he visits customers with the salesman or as he discusses customer situations with him, he has here an analytical device of great value. If both he and the salesman are using it, the communication between them is greatly simplified and improved.

6. *Problem Definition,* American Marketing Association, Chicago, 1958 (a paper prepared by a "Problem Definition Sub-Committee").

QUESTIONS AND PROBLEMS

1. Comment on the statement: "If adequate and effective planning is done at the higher managerial levels of a firm, the planning process is not so important at lower levels."

2. You are a salesman in any firm you wish to select (with the condition that your firm's products are sold to other business firms). Select an important customer to whom you are assigned (using imagination if you wish). Draw an organization chart for the customer, with at least four levels, at least three operational functions (e.g., "production"), and at least three staff functions reporting to the top executive.

   Assume a set of corporate objectives for the customer. Now list for each organizational element the "hierarchy" of objectives—again using imagination.

   How would you as a salesman use this information?

3. For the same customer, pick out organizational elements who might have objectives that are not compatible with your objectives. Why might they not be? Of what importance is this to you?

4. For the same customer, construct a "data sheet" similar to that in Figure 8-2, inserting facts that you think might be logically true. (Again, imagination is necessary here, although if you were really the salesman, you would want real data.) Why is this an important thing to do?

5. Show how evaluating the data above provides critical inputs into your strategy. Extract a number of your facts (in each category) that you think, when put together, will provide an area of potential strength for you to exploit. Do the same thing for a pattern of facts that could work together as an area of danger, to prepare yourself against it.

6. Construct a simple means-end chain chart, using the data above. Follow Figure 8-4 in doing this, using only two "branches" in the customer organization and back-profiting only about three or four steps. Include your ideas about time-sequencing the steps in the two branches.

7. As the salesman, however, you "orchestrate." Propose what kinds of resources from the firm you might use in each of the "stepping-stones" of your means-end chain.

9

Organizing
the Selling Effort

The managerial process of *organizing* involves the allocation of resources—human, physical, and financial—with the end purpose of implementing the programs of action planned to meet objectives. Or, planning has to do with work that must be done, and *organizing* has to do with arrangements for getting it done. Organizing is much more than simply organization *structure*, or form. The organization *structure* results from the organizing *process*, which is dynamic, strategic, and adjustive in character.

Great forces for change in the external environment and within the firm itself will always require the sales manager to question the efficacy of the "put-together" of his resources. It would be naïve to believe that a given structure in all its detailed inner forms and relationships will remain the optimal form. Adjustments and sometimes outright changes must be made. Hence the effective sales manager must understand the process of organizing and the various forms of organization structure that can result. This chapter deals with both—process and structure—as never-ending elements in the sales manager's job.

THE ORGANIZING PROCESS

Organizing is the managerial process of arriving at an orderly, accepted arrangement of the independent but interdependent parts of a whole. It can be analyzed in five steps:

1. Determining the total work to be done.
2. Classifying and arranging that work into manageable parts.
3. Defining the work (or missions) to be done by each part.
4. Determining the resources and facilities necessary for the work of each part to be done.
5. Selecting individuals to fill the resulting positions.

1. Determining the Total Work to Be Done

This, of course, comes from the objective-setting process. For the total selling operation, a set of missions will have been specified, including such objectives as sales volume by product line, market share, and development of customer accounts—both short-range and long-range. Also factored into this total work are the plans and programs that have evolved from the planning process (e.g., from such a framework as the matrix analysis discussed in Chapter 7). Time and spatial elements must also be considered—answering the question, "When is this work to be done, and where?"

2. Classifying and Arranging into Manageable Parts

A rational division of work to be done has long been known to be necessary. In a business component such as the selling operation, this division of work entails more than a consideration of manageability due to size. It may be done by classifying the different types of work, or *functions* to be done, as a first step. Thus a selling operation may have the following categories of functions to be done: [1]

> Direct personal contact with customers
> Contact and influence of distributors
> Order handling
> Customer service

Each of these categories is a "manageable part."

[1] The example is a very general one. Obviously, selling operations will vary widely in the way their assigned work may be subdivided. This is why one can observe a *product* focus or specialization as one category of activity versus geographic specialization as another. See pages 144–146 for examples.

This is the idea of "departmentation," or the grouping of functions within an organizational element. It is, in fact, the basis by which the selling operation itself has been singled out as an organizational component, requiring further organizing within itself. These categorizing decisions result in a logical "horizontal" division, as shown in Figure 9-1 Note that the horizontal departmentation establishes work components that are *uniquely different and necessary* to the achievement of the selling operation's objectives. If any of these categories is too large for effective manageability, it may be further broken down—hence establishing a vertical, or hierarchical, division (Figure 9-2).

The "mesh" of structure with objectives——Chapter 6 discussed the "hierarchy" of objectives that emerges from the objective-setting process. In a sense, this organizing step of "classifying and arranging the total work into manageable parts" must work hand in glove with the objective-setting process. The "departmentation" process cannot be thought of in isolation. In actuality, it is the process of determining the proper implementing of resource allocation to achieve a mission. Thus at every step and substep in building the "parts" of the organization tree, the objectives for each part are the forerunner of the work classifications for the part.

This "meshing" of the objective-setting and organizing processes is a simple concept—so simple that it is sometimes forgotten, causing conflict when changes in organization structure may be sorely needed. The organizational elements evolving from this second substep are *functionally oriented*. That is, they are groupings that are designed to *work* in some way to achieve some *mission*—again, the objective/resource-allocation idea. Thus the organizational element, which shows up as a "box" in the orthodox organization chart, must always be thought of in terms of its function, or in terms of what it does, *with respect to the mission* assigned to it. Furthermore, the mission must be given primacy. If this were not true, an organizational element might perpetuate itself with no change even after the reasons for establishing it are no longer

FIGURE 9-1   Horizontal "departmentation."

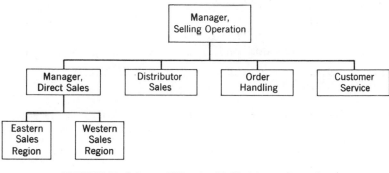

FIGURE 9-2   "Vertical" division of work.

valid. This does not mean that there must be a change in the structure of an organizational element every time the missions given it are changed. It does mean, however, that the structure per se is not sacred and that the rationale behind it must always visualize first the mission and then the optimum put-together of resources for its achievement.

3. Defining the Work of Each Part

In a sense, this is akin to the developing of missions from objectives, as discussed in Chapter 6 (pp. 70–83). But here, even beyond the determining of a mission for a subgroup (which the subgroup will take as its objective), the manager must specify the broad functioning of the group. For example, if a sales manager has decided to organize a customer service group separate from the direct sales group, he will assign to it unique missions and also define its function or work. Figure 9-3 shows an extremely simple example.

In this simple example, note that the specifying of the "work to be done" (the definition of "function") evolves from *missions* rationally assigned to the organizational unit. A sales manager at each level in the organizational hierarchy should always link, in his thinking, missions to be achieved with the definition of work to be done by the subordinate unit. This process should be carried down to the individual sales job itself.

4. Determining Resources and Facilities Necessary for the Work of Each Part to Be Done

The organizing process is concerned with more than people. Certainly, people are the most important resource in any goal-oriented work group.

CUSTOMER SERVICE DEPARTMENT		
Mission (Ends)		*Definition of Function (Means)*
To enhance customer satisfaction	by	providing prompt, effective after-sale service
Mission		Function
To build product and company image	by	servicing in a way to reduce complaints
Mission		Function
To help build increased sales volume	by	establishing proper work relations with Sales Department
Mission		Function
To assure continuing goodwill	by	maintaining a technically competent but customer-oriented organization
Mission		Function
To accomplish the above within cost and profit constraints	by	establishing efficient organization structure, proper procedure, efficient use of manpower, and use of proper control to remain within assigned expense budgets
Mission		Function
Ends to achieve		Broad charter, and broad manner of work

FIGURE 9-3   Missions and definition of work.

But there are other resources, and these, too, must be secured and allocated throughout the organization. It is not enough to break the total work into parts, assign missions to each part, and define the work of each. Along with this must be determined the resources of people, money, and physical things that are to be provided to the organizational element, so that it can accomplish its given tasks. Furthermore, the amount of resources to be provided must be feasible with respect to the assigned missions.

5. Selecting Individuals to Fill Resultant Positions

Only after all the steps above have been followed is the manager ideally ready to fill positions with individuals. Even here, an additional substep is advisable. In step 3, the "work of each part" has been defined, and this presumes that each individual job resulting from the process has been defined. This structuring of the individual job is discussed in more detail later in this chapter.

SALES ORGANIZATION STRUCTURES

The *process of organizing* results in organizational *structure, or form.* The type of the structure is not left to chance, but is rationally determined. Furthermore, the structure may be adjusted from time to time. The types of structure may be classified as follows:

Line organization
Line-and-staff organization
Functional organization
Committee organization
Combinations of the above

Line-Organization Structure

This is the basic type of structure and exists in all business organizations. It is the simple line relationship, in vertical structure, of "boss and subordinate." Thus, in its simplest form, a line sales organization consists of a sales manager and the salesmen who report directly to him (Figure 9-4). A "line of command" exists; the Sales Manager is the direct superior of Salesman A, B, and C. The line of authority runs

FIGURE 9-4   Simple line structure.

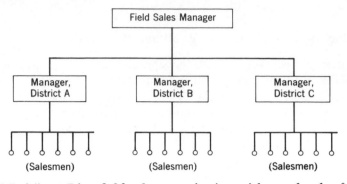

FIGURE 9-5 Line field sales organization with two levels of management.

from superior to subordinate from the top to the bottom of the organization structure.[2]

If the sales operation is larger or more complex, the *organizing process* may have required that the work be divided into additional manageable parts. Thus an additional "level" of management may have been introduced as shown in Figure 9-5. Here, the addition of the three District Managers in no way changes the fact that this is a simple line organization. Tracing the line "up" from each salesman, it is clear that the District Manager is his "boss" and that the Field Sales Manager is the District Manager's "boss."[3] Obviously, other levels can be introduced, if necessary—for example, several "Regional Sales Managers" to each of whom a number of District Managers operationally report. The legitimacy of adding this additional level is subject, of course, to the same criteria as those for adding any other level.[4]

The line structure is critical. It is the backbone of any sales structure, from large and complex sales operations such as IBM or du Pont to small and simple ones such as a three-man "local" distributor sales operation. It is the line structure that provides the downward flow of delegated

[2] This gradation of authority in the line structure is found in all organizations, as a hierarchy or Scalar arrangement. See H. Koontz and C. O'Donnell, *Principles of Management*, 3rd. ed., McGraw-Hill, New York, 1955, p. 263.

[3] Several reasons exist for introducing additional levels of management. Some apply to "staff" management as well as "line" management and, therefore, are discussed later in this chapter under the subjects of "span of control" and "levels of management." We might presume in Figure 9-5, however, that the additional level of *line* management is needed because the nineteen salesmen are spread so far geographically that they need physically closer management contact, direction, and supervision.

[4] Again, see discussion on "span of control" and "levels."

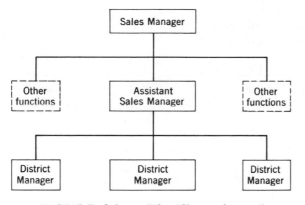

FIGURE 9-6   The "line assistant."

decision-making authority, the upward flow of accountability,[5] and the vital two-way flow of communication between the marketplaces and the firm. However sophisticated the sales operation structure becomes, its line elements must be clearly defined and understood at all levels of the operation.

One special case of the introduction of line management deserves attention—the so-called Line Assistant, as shown in Figure 9-6. If the *function* of the Assistant Manager is clearly a command, or line function, he is in a line position; subordinates report directly to him and only to him, and he reports to the Sales Manager. Unfortunately, the word "assistant" sometimes carries overtones of *assisting* the Sales Manager in *his* direct command function (a "staff" function). There is good argument for using a more descriptive title than "assistant" manager for *line* functions. Thus, in our illustration, this line position might better be called, for example, "Field Sales Manager" (assuming that the other functions reporting to the Sales Manager are headquarters functions such as Customer Service and Sales Administration) .[6]

Line-and-Staff Organization Structure

A line manager delegates to his subordinates in the line organization certain authority for operating duties. Certain parts of his authority, however, he will retain for himself. Furthermore, the line manager may

[5] See Chapter 11.
[6] The General Electric Company, in its vast reorganization of the 1950's *completely* eliminated the word "assistant" from its vocabulary. This huge company with more than a quarter million employees and tens of thousands of managers did not have one single position with a title of "assistant."

have some administrative duties that are not feasible to delegate "down-ward" to line subordinates. If he wants to relieve himself of some of these duties, he may assign them to a "staff assistant."

The concept of staff is quite simple, but is frequently misunderstood. Consider it in this way. A manager of sales has had delegated to him a certain authority to act, to command the line operations "below" him. As a manager, he follows the "managerial process" and engages in:

Objective setting
Planning
Organizing and coordinating
Directing and decision making
Policy setting
Controlling

Even though he delegates prescribed areas of authority to subordinate managers, he must continue to wear several "managerial hats." Thus a sales manager may be involved personally in such aspects of the manage-rial process as forecasting; quota setting; strategy creating; territory analysis and determination; relationship definition between subordinate groups; command decision-making; policy setting in such diverse areas as pricing, customer service, warehouse inventory levels, and customer selec-tion; and bugdeting, sales analysis, and sales control. And we have only scratched the surface. He must also maintain some degree of customer contact, evaluate and motivate his subordinates, keep abreast of techno-logical developments, and analyze competitors' market actions. Obvi-ously, unless the sales organization is very small, the sales manager simply cannot effectively do all these things. He must have some help—and that help may be in the form of "staff."

The fundamental idea of staff, or the staff position, is that of an *assisting* or *facilitating* service to the line operation. The deciding of what staff positions should be created, their functions or duties, and their relationships to other positions is a managerial responsibility and follows the organizing rationale discussed above. The staff positions take two general forms:

1. Staff assistance to the manager
2. Functional staff assistance to the line organization

Staff Assistance to the Manager

This is self-defining. The sales manager hires someone to work ex-pressly for him, to be his "right hand" on some specific aspect of the

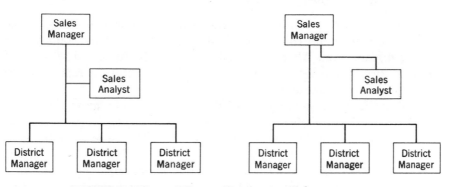

FIGURE 9-7   The staff assistant to the manager.

managerial job. For example, assume that the sales manager is receiving from the firm's Accounting Department basketfuls of information on sales results. Such information is highly valuable, but must be sifted, sorted, categorized, analyzed, and interpreted before it can be a valuable input to objective evaluating, planning, decision making, or measuring. The sales manager may be justified in hiring a "sales analyst" to perform this work for him. Perhaps oversimplifying somewhat, the sales manager may tell the sales analyst; "This is what I want you to do with these data. Here's the form I would like your analysis to take. This is when I want it. Here is an office for you. You need not be concerned with anyone else in the organization—just me." The sales analyst is in the purest sense *a staff assistant to the manager.* Strictly speaking, he has nothing to do with and no communication with anyone else in the sales organization. By organization chart, this can be shown in either of two ways, as illustrated in Figure 9-7.

In a selling operation, the sales manager may legitimately have a wide variety of staff-assistant positions, which are "extensions of his arm," performing for him such functions as forecasting, market analysis, sales planning, competitive analysis, expense control, compensation administration, selection and training of salesmen, and performance evaluations. This is only a partial list and will vary widely with size of organization, complexity and diversity of products and markets, competitive behavior, and the like.

Criteria. To what extent should the sales manager go in creating such staff-assistant positions and to what extent should he permit subordinate line managers to do so? Unfortunately, no magic formula exists. But there are some simple considerations:

1. What alternatives are there? Can the sales manager obtain some degree of help at no cost or less cost by utilizing services outside the selling organization? Alternatively, should there be further delegation of other duties to the subordinate line managers? [7] Can he reallocate his own allocation of time and effort?

2. What is the specific nature of the burden to be removed from the sales manager? How much time is he now spending on it (or should be spending on it) ? Specifically, how will the new staff position free the sales manager for what specific other managerial duties? How will it improve the overall effectiveness and efficiency of sales management?

3. Adding staff costs money. This cost may be considered as an investment. What is the return in the added sales that accrue from this investment? [8]

A rational, hard-headed view suggested by these considerations is a *must* for effective sales management.

This does not infer that staff-assistant positions are difficult to justify. Of course, one can find some "staff-happy" selling operations. But by and large, it can be observed that many line sales managers at headquarters and even at regional levels are overworked and are spread too thin—with some loss of the real effectiveness for which they have potential. As a result, many line sales managers are bogged down with day-by-day operating minutiae, which detract from the crucial demands on them for creative thinking, innovative planning, problem solving, leadership, and motivation. The effective sales manager must develop a clear understanding of the staff-assistant concept and of its place in the overall organizing process. Obviously, the optimal "mix" of line-management and staff-management funds is based on the optimal contributions to revenue and profit.

Functional Staff Assistance to Line Organization

Perhaps an even more common use of the staff concept is found in many selling organizations in the form of the *staff specialist*. Here the staff position is created to provide to the entire sales operation a special

---

[7] For example, might the sales manager delegate more of his sales planning duties to district sales managers, thus freeing himself for his sales analysis duties?

[8] Obviously, only in rare cases can this be quantified. Nonetheless, this is a fair question, which the sales manager must somehow answer, even if subjectively.

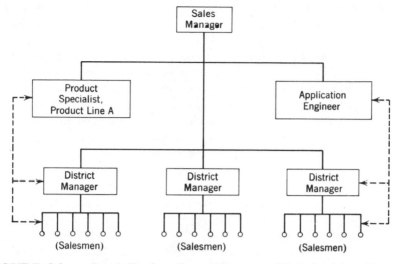

FIGURE 9-8   Specialized staff positions, providing functional services to the sales organization.

expertise. This is particularly useful, since more complex product and market technologies place increasing demand on individuals in a sales operation. For example, a salesman for a machine tool manufacturer may be required to have more specialized technical knowledge of diverse customer applications than one man can possess—hence may need some "backup" assistance from product or industry specialists, who as staff persons are available to him for specialized technical help. For another example, a sales representative for an electrical appliance manufacturer may need a staff specialist to help in devising and conducting distributor sales meetings. Adding this element of staff to the line organization creates the line-and-staff organization structure, which is probably the most prevalent organization form in use today. An example is shown in Figure 9-8. Note a major difference between this line-and-staff form and the line form with staff assistance to the manager (Figure 9-7) . Here the specialized staff position provides an expertise to the *entire sales organization.* The dotted arrows (which normally do not appear in orthodox organization charts) symbolically indicate *an interrelationship and a two-way flow of communication* between the specialist-staff and individuals in the line organization. *No formal authority exists, however, of staff over line positions.* The authority and accountability networks for the line operation follow the line organization, up and down. The specialist-staff positions, therefore, can be viewed as *service or facilitating agencies available to line positions*.[9]

The criteria for the legitimacy of specialized staff positions are essentially the same as those for staff-assistant positions. Here again, all alternatives should be considered. For example, rather than adding staff product specialists as product technology increases, consideration could be given to reorganizing sales positions on a specialized product basis. Certainly there are pros and cons to be weighed for each alternative. The *prime criterion* always is—which is the most efficient way to achieve the ends being sought?

Again, there is no one answer, nor even a common pattern for the specialized staff structure. Even relatively similar sales operations in the same industry may quite rationally arrive at different "put-togethers" of the sales organization equation.

Another thing to consider is the possible "drift" of a staff-assistant position to a specialized staff position or even a combination of the two. For example, a sales manager may have established a staff-assistant position solely to assist him in his sales planning function. Conceivably, over time the sales manager may also make the assistant available to his subordinate district managers, to assist them in their planning functions.

Structure of the Staff "Group." The specialist-staff function need not consist of only one individual. Commonly, the organizing of this staff function will result in a number of positions. Here, really, is a "little line organization," which as a *unit* functions in a staff capacity. Thus in an industrial selling operation the specialist-staff function may appear as shown in Figure 9-9. In very large and complex organizations, such as IBM, General Electric, or du Pont, it is quite conceivable that this staff group can be so large and important that it may have some specialized staff positions within itself! Complex as this seems at first glance, a mastery of the relatively simple principles of organizing as discussed in this chapter provides a clear understanding.

Functional Organization Structure

The two forms of organization, line and line-and-staff, typify almost all structures in use in American business. From time to time, however, one

---

[9] The interrelations, mutual obligations, and communication flow between line and staff often pose difficult problems. To define them, the managerial process of *coordinating* is required, which is discussed in depth in Chapter 10.

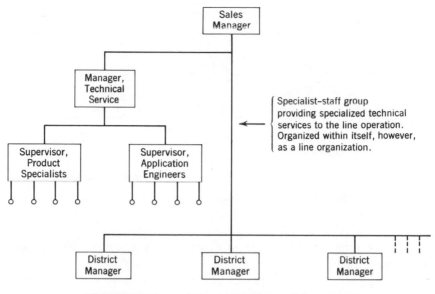

FIGURE 9-9   The specialist-staff function.

hears discussion of another form, the *functional organization* structure. In its purest sense, this structure focuses on the job of the worker—and if this job has a number of distinctly different elements, a "boss" will be installed for each.[10]

An argument can be advanced for this functional form of organization. For example, consider the job of the sales engineer for an industrial machinery manufacturer. In his territory, he is assigned to specific industrial customers, whom he must contact on a direct manufacturer-to-customer basis. But additionally, his firm's marketing management has established industrial-type distributors whose mission is to sell the firm's products to customers not being contacted "direct." The sales engineer is also assigned the mission of calling on distributors in his territory and influencing them to expend more effort and increase their volume. Thus this sales engineer has two uniquely different aspects to his job, each requiring uniquely different expertise. From the sales engineer's view, the demands on him look as shown in Figure 9-10. There is some logic in providing uniquely different sales management in a case such as that illustrated in Figure 9-11. The conditions in this example are by no

[10] This stems from the "scientific management" proposals of Frederick W. Taylor.

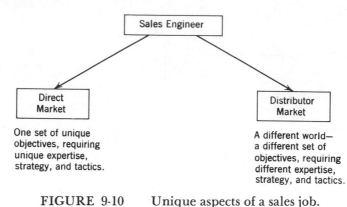

FIGURE 9-10   Unique aspects of a sales job.

means uncommon. In fact, the sales engineer's job may often be even more complicated.[11]

But whatever the advantages of providing "specialized management," they are outweighed by a wide margin by the disadvantage of such an organizational scheme. The "functional organization structure" violates the generally accepted principle of *unity of command,* which proposes that no worker can serve more than one boss. The occasional adherents of functional structure argue that the advantages of specialized management can be had *if the management jobs are adequately coordinated.* The problem is that the management jobs are almost impossible to coordinate, if any degree of authority and accountability is left in them (because they are filled by fallible human beings) —and the very advantages accruing are destroyed if authority is not left in the jobs.

One answer to the dilemma is the use of the line-and-staff form of organization, with very special attention paid to the proper establishment of relations between line and staff-specialist groups. This is discussed in detail in Chapter 10, since it involves the coordinating process. Another answer to the dilemma may lie in the restructuring of the sales positions to product or customer bases (discussed later in this chapter).

[11] For example, the author served in General Electric's apparatus sales organization at a time when a sales engineer could be assigned to (1) industrial distributors, (2) industrial users, (3) industrial machinery manufacturers, and (4) electric utilities. These are widely different types of customers, requiring widely different expertise.

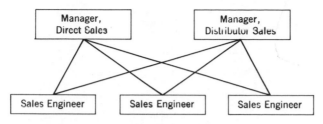

FIGURE 9-11   Functional organization structure.

BASES FOR SALES ORGANIZATION STRUCTURE

Headquarters Sales Organization

Strictly speaking, the only organizational element definitely and always required at the top level of the selling operation is the sales manager himself (Figure 9-12). Anything added is staff, either in the "assistance-to-manager" category or in the functional-assistance-to-line category. *The actual structuring of these "facilitating" elements depends on many factors.* What specific "facilitating" elements are added and how they are structured also depend on many factors—nature of the product line, of the industry, of company size, of markets, of competition, of the marketing organization, to cite a few. No "pat" answer is available for the structuring of these facilitating elements.

Some of the common facilitating units found in headquarters sales organizations are credit, customer service, product sales, and technical assistance.[12] If all these units are organized and manned at headquarters only, the structure is *centralized.* In large or complex sales organizations, however, these service units can be physically spread to the field sales organization on one of two bases:

1. *Geographically* dispersed, but still "centralized," the managerial control remaining with their respective managers at headquarters. Figure 9-10 shows such a structural arrangement for a credit group. "Regional credit managers" are *physically* located at the same place as regional sales managers in order to be closer to field credit problems, hence be more effective. The relation between the regional sales managers and regional credit managers is no different from the arrangement under which credit

---

[12] This presumes a *marketing* organization, of which sales is a part and which, therefore, has other facilitating or service units in it, such as forecasting, market research, product planning, and marketing personnel administration.

FIGURE 9-12   The minimum structure.

managers are located at headquarters—although admittedly the communication between them is enhanced by this physical closeness. (See Figure 9-13.)

2. *Decentralized* service units, with managerial authority over the unit given to the lower-level line management. In this case, the credit function is not only physically dispersed to the regions, but the function and personnel at regional level are placed under the regional sales manager, as shown in Figure 9-14.

Either physical dispersal or decentralization of the headquarters service units instantly create several disadvantages:

1. *Cost.* It will almost always cost more in manpower expense to disperse a headquarters unit to the lower-level line groups.

2. *Managerial efficiency.* In most cases, *decentralization* of the service unit hangs additional managerial duties on the lower-level line manager —which will demand the managerial attention that he is now giving to directly supervising his selling operation. Moreover, decentralization may require technical expertise that he may not have. In Figure 9-14, for example, the Regional Sales Manager certainly will have to develop the managerial skill necessary to manage a credit function (even with a regional credit manager reporting to him) in addition to his normal sales function.

3. *Communication restrictions.* In the *decentralized* organization, the number of channels of communication up and down the organization structure is limited, compared to the number available in the organization in which the service units are only physically dispersed but not decentralized. Figure 9-15 shows the decentralization of only one facilitating unit—credit. The communication problem is much greater as other units are also decentralized. For example, at one time, General Electric's Apparatus Sales Division had decentralized at the *regional level*

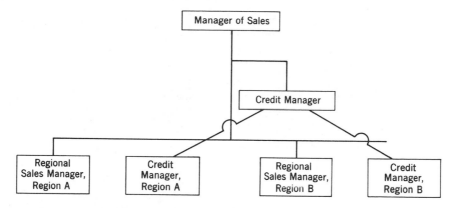

FIGURE 9-13   The physically dispersed but not decentralized service unit.

the following facilitating units in addition to sales, all reporting to the manager at regional level: application engineering, service engineering, repair shops, warehouses, credit and collection, order handling, billing, accounting, and personnel administration. At a later date, these facilitating units were left physically at the regional level, but reported operationally through their own channels to their own headquarters management at sales headquarters. Reason: the regional manager was simply "spread too thin," and his prime function of *sales* management had been diluted.

On the other hand, even though the dispersal or decentralization of headquarters facilitating units is at a cost in dollars and in complexity, such structuring may often, in the net, provide overbalancing advantages. The advantages themselves are the criteria that must be used to justify the dispersed structure. "Payoff" must come from the following:

1. Increased customer satisfaction.
2. Better customer service.
3. Competitive advantage over rivals.
4. *Increased efficiency and productivity of the salesmen.*

The Field Sales Organization

The field sales organization may be structured in a number of ways. The key idea, of course, is to establish that unique structure for the particular selling operation which will enable it to do the best possible

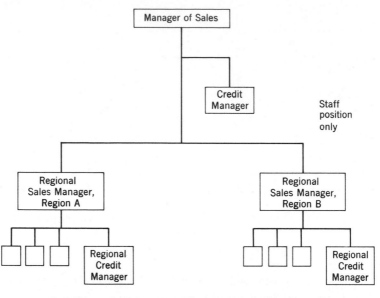

FIGURE 9-14   The decentralized service unit.

job of earning business from its customers. Again, there is no one organizational strategy for this goal. Many factors are at play—nature of the customers, of the product line, of competition, configuration of the market, degrees of technology involved, to name only a few. In general, however, field sales organizations follow one of several basic forms or some combination of them, based on the following factors:

1. Territorial division.
2. Product specialization.
3. Customer specialization.

Territorial Division. Assuming that the firm has some sizable number of customers, its field sales organization will nearly always be structured in a geographical sense. This "dividing the work into manageable parts" logically takes geography into account—because if customers are geographically dispersed, so must be the means of serving them. In its purest form the territorial or geographic basis for structuring will extend throughout the entire field sales organization, as shown in Figure 9-16. Obviously, the amount of territorial extent contained in each region, district, and sales territory will vary depending on the potential volume of business available, number of customers, ease of access to customers, and other factors. For example, the Chicago District of an office machine manufacturer

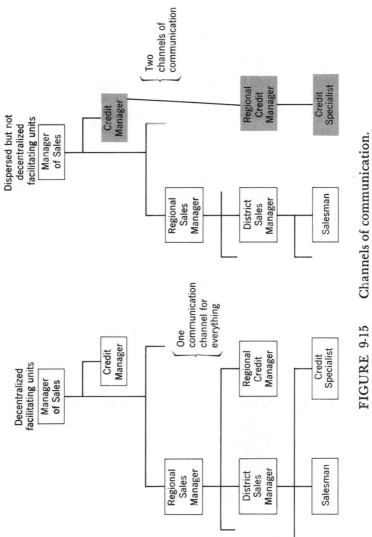

FIGURE 9-15   Channels of communication.

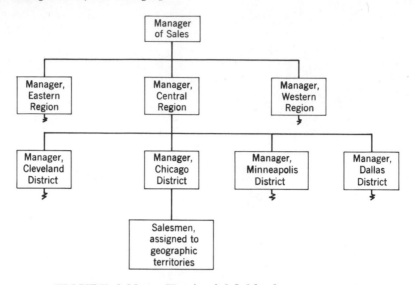

FIGURE 9-16   Territorial field sales structure.

(typewriters, adding machines, etc.) may be limited to only three counties in northeastern Illinois, whereas its Omaha District may include all of Nebraska and Iowa.[13]

The purely territorial basis for the field sales structure is best suited for firms whose customers are widely dispersed (as is the case for most consumers goods manufacturers) and for firms whose products are relatively similar. It is probably the simplest form to create, to administer, and to adjust.

Product Specialization. Another basis often used for structuring the sales organization is by *product*. Organization by product line may be efficient under the following conditions:

1. *The product line is complex from a technical viewpoint.* For example, a chemical company may structure one field sales unit around "organic chemicals" and another unit around "inorganic chemicals." Or a machine tool manufacturer may establish one field sales unit for automatic, programmed machines and another unit for the more prosaic lathes, drill presses, and the like.

2. *The product line is very diverse with many differing products.* For example, an office supply firm (functioning as distributor and dealer for

---

[13] See Suggested Readings at the end of this chapter for specialized techniques in determining sales potentials and territory size.

many different suppliers), may have one sales group selling business machines, another group selling office furniture, and still another selling supply items. Or a "full-line" appliance manufacturer, such as General Electric, or Hobart, may have one sales group handling major appliances (e.g., refrigerators) and another group handling small appliances (e.g., toasters and mixers).

Product specialization may shape organization structure at any level, starting at that of the salesman. Note that at any level where it is applied, it results in product-oriented organization *below* that level and territory-oriented organization *above* that level. Figure 9-17 shows a field sales structure with product specialization at the salesman level only; Figure 9-18 shows the product specialization moved up to include the district management level. Moving farther up the organization hiearchy will appear similar in structural form. Note that when product specialization is "moved up" the organization structure to include management —that is, when even field sales managers' positions are specialized by product line rather than by territory—this structure will inevitably require more managers' positions, hence be more costly. The manpower cost must be outweighed by increased efficiency, and normally this will be

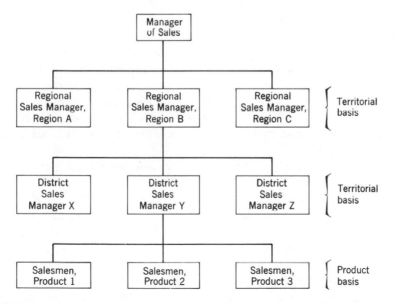

FIGURE 9-17   Product-based sales organization at salesman level.

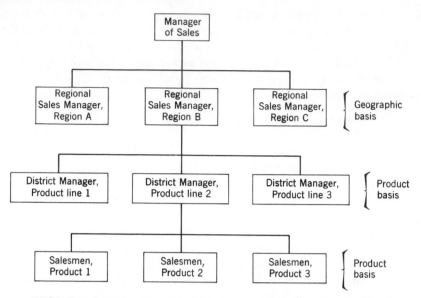

FIGURE 9-18   Product-based organization at district level.

possible only if the product lines are extremely complex and diverse.

Note also another major disadvantage of using the product basis for structuring the field selling organization. When salesmen's positions are established by product rather than by territory (as in Figure 9-17), *territories probably will overlap.* More than one salesman may be contacting the same customer, a situation that many customers resent. Moreover, it is entirely possible that two (or more) salesmen from the same firm calling on the same customer could compete with one another. An additional difficulty with this multiplicity is the lack of one all-embracing "picture" of the customer company, making the creation of effective strategy very difficult.

This does not mean that the product basis is not the most effective one for structuring the organization in some cases. These cautions, however, should be considered by the field sales manager. He will probably need to do much more "quarterbacking," particularly with regard to selling strategy, for product-based salesmen than for territory-based salesmen.

As produce lines become more complex and diverse, but are still short of the point at which the product basis becomes effective, an alternative is to make broader use of "product managers" at sales headquarters and of "product specialists" in the field organization. These are staff positions, providing facilitating or functional service to the field salesmen.

For example, assume that a machine tool salesman is planning to call on the engineering department of a large industrial customer, with a mission of gaining engineering approval of the tool's automatic tape control system. As a "general" salesman handling his firm's entire, complex product line, he may need to have special technical assistance and skill *for this particular selling situation.* Hence the salesman as "quarterback" calls on a product specialist technically skilled in this feature to accompany him on his call.

Customer Specialization. Structuring a field sales organization by *differing types of customers* is becoming increasingly feasible in many industries. Consider for a moment one of the basic premises of effective selling—the salesman must perceive and understand the customer's needs and problems, be able to apply and translate the firm's products and services to these needs and problems, and get the customer to so perceive them. It is highly important that the professional salesman know the customer's technology, process, policies, and so on. *He must be able to talk the customer's language.* This is becoming more and more difficult in many industries as customers are becoming bigger, more diverse, and more complex technologically. Consider, for example, the difficulty facing a sales engineer who is selling packaging machinery in a territory such as the City of Chicago—as he calls on (and attempts to understand) such diverse customers as Motorola, Florsheim Shoe Company, Swift and Company, and Dean Milk Company.

Here an organization structure based on customer category may be feasible, if adequate potential sales volume exists in each category. Then one salesman might be assigned only to steel mills, another only to oil refineries, another only to fan and blower manufacturers, and so on. Each salesman can *"specialize" in his customer's industry,* and become better equipped to understand customers' problems and processes and to successfully apply his products to them.

The customer basis is equally applicable to customer industries other than industrial manufacturing. An apparel manufacturer might have one salesman contacting only large department stores, another contacting only chain stores, and another contacting only wholesalers. An appliance wholesaler might have one salesman contacting retail dealers, another contacting building development contractors, and another contacting large commercial institutions.

Combinations of Territorial, Product, and Customer Bases of Organization. A mix of these forms of organization structure is completely feasible. Suppose that a drug manufacturer has a district sales office in Chicago, covering the state of Illinois. The district sales manager may have two salesmen in Chicago (territorial) selling only three categories of new drug products (product) only to hospitals and laboratories (customer). He may have four more salesmen selling the entire line, each calling only on physicians (customer) in given areas of Cook County and Lake County (territory). He may have two salesmen covering the entire line to all customers in "downstate" Illinois. This is a combination of all types, *tailored to the variables of the market places*. Here again is the strategic sense and dynamic aspect of organizing—that of *strategically tailoring* the structure to optimize achievement of objectives.

ORGANIZING THE INDIVIDUAL POSITIONS

Only after these steps in the organizing process have been completed can the manager consider the subprocess of selecting *individuals* to fill resultant positions. Here again a logical set of steps can be used:

1. General position guides
2. Specific position descriptions
3. Job specifications
4. Selecting the individual

General Position Guides

The position guide is a broad functional description of the position. It is general in character and defines the *type* of position wherever found in the organization. For example, a field sales organization may have evolving from the organizing process such positions as general sales representative, missionary salesman, product specialist, and parts specialist. The position description broadly defines these jobs. That is, it in essence says, "Here's what the meaning of this type of job is, in this organization."

Position Descriptions

However, although the *type* of position may be the same throughout the organization, each specific position *may be quite unique*. For example, the nature and meaning of a "sales representative's" job may be the same for a sales representative assigned to a New York City territory and for one assigned to a territory in eastern Kansas, but what is specifically expected from these two positions may be quite different. Hence there is a need to "spell out" the unique assignment. Here the sales manager must introduce variables beyond the nature of the job. Such variables as the following must be defined for *each* job:

Objectives of the job [14]
Definition of territory
Assignment of customers
Product responsibility
Service responsibility (if any)
Credit responsibility (if any)
Requirements for feedback of information
Definition of the job's relationship to other elements of the organization
Authority delegated and authority reserved
Standards and measurements of performance

Such a position description enables the *incumbent* of a job (as well as his manager) to say: "Here's what my job is. Here's what I am expected to achieve. Here's how I must work with others. Here's my set of freedoms, and my set of constraints. Here's how I am going to be evaluated."

Perhaps a word of caution is in order with respect to the concept of the position description. At one extreme, a sales manager may utterly ignore its use. In that case, he may be hampered in his accomplishment of the next step in the organizing process—the optimal matching of man to job. Furthermore, he may be hampered in his decreased ability to measure objectively and rationally the performance of the individual in the job. Perhaps more serious, he and the individual in the job *may have different perceptions of the job,* which is hardly conducive to efficient operation.

On the other hand, a sales manager may focus so much importance on the position description that it becomes a fetish almost for itself. He may overmanage and overcontrol. Or perhaps more serious, the individual in the job *may perceive the position description as all-holy* and any behavior not specifically in tune with it as unwanted. The position description in this sense may stifle creativity.

Some middle ground between these extremes is advisable. One cannot say just where it should be, because sales organizations vary greatly. Even elements within a sales organization differ so much that the optimum use of job descriptions may vary. For example, assume a selling operation that has been in existence for a relatively long time. It may well be that little formal use need be made of position descriptions for the salesmen.

[14] Objectives for the job are based on the hierarchy of missions evolving from the objective-setting process. However, for the individual sales job, other factors must be considered. What is the *potential* of the assignment? What is the nature of *competition?* What is the nature of the *major customers?* What are the relevant *market forces* at play—demand, cycles, and patterns of buying, trade customs, and so on? All these factors are unique for each sales job.

Now assume that sales management for a number of reasons adds some new, different positions—say, product specialists in the field office. Definitive position descriptions probably should be used for these new positions. But beyond this, even the "old" salesman positions may now have to be redefined quite formally—with respect to the relationships desired by sales management between the two types of positions.

Finally, in finding the "right" spot between the two undesirable extremes, a certain *minimum* use of the formal position description by the sales manager is advisable. It should be used in accomplishing the next step in the process—the development of job specifications, an important step preparatory to matching the job and the individual.

Job Specifications

Having determined the general, broad definition of the type of job and having then more definitively described the specific job itself, the sales manager must now take one more step before selecting the individual to fill that job. This very important step involves the deciding of precisely *what kind of an individual* might best fulfill the requirements of this job. Or, the managerial step here is to establish a set of "specifications" for the "ideal" person for this defined position.

At this point, the sales manager in effect asks himself (without thinking of any particular person), "Given this job, how can I describe the ideal individual for it?" And *without reference to any known individual,* he objectively sets up a set of "specifications" for such a person. Depending on the job, he considers such personal qualifications as age, appearance, personality, and drive. And he considers such other qualifications as experience, education, and technical expertise (or potential for it). In some cases, he considers even other personal traits that would be ideally required, such as family, community interests, and other extra job interests. All this is plotted, of course, in the context of the broad position guide and the specific position description. It results in a clear, definitive picture of the ideal person for the job. Its purpose is to come as close as possible to matching the selected individual to the rationally determined job—and it is an important step in the organizing process that is often brushed over.

Selecting Individuals to Fill the Jobs

At this point, the selection of the individual to fill the job is a relatively straightforward procedure. The definitive set of specifications is at hand; the individual coming closest to it is selected. This does not mean that the techniques of finding candidates and evaluating each of them is a simple and easy one. It is not. But the clear defining of what mix of characteristics is sought is a huge step toward the successful filling of the job. The process of selecting itself is discussed in Chapter 14.

SOME CONCLUDING THOUGHTS

With so many firms growing in size and complexity, the managerial process of organizing is vital. The effectiveness of a firm in achieving its objectives depends on many factors, but certainly the efficiency of the organization structure—the system and subsystems of the firm—is a key factor. This chapter has proposed some "steps" in the organizing process. But the manager must think about more than these steps alone. He must think and act about the organizing process in the total framework of the firm and all its environments.

Organizing is not a one-shot process which provides a lasting structure. It is not even a once-in-a-while process. It is a dynamic, never-ending process. The sales manager must think continually about his organization structure in a strategic sense. This structure is just as much an asset or resource as are the firm's computers, cash, or people. And like all other assets, it occasionally must be strategically adjusted. When this is necessary, and even when organization alternatives are considered, the rationale proposed by this chapter is a fruitful one.

Almost all firms of all kinds face changing environments. Inevitably organization adjustments must be made. However, there are two sides to this fact. Although flexibility of organization must exist, paradoxically some reasonable stability must also be present. Changes in organization are rarely made without causing some degree of conflict, anxiety, and resistance and often some confusion. In many cases these disturbances can create serious loss of efficiency. Obviously they must be minimized.[15]

Finally, another word of caution is necessary. Even though steps in the organizing process are sound and even though the resulting structural arrangement between individuals and groups is necessary, the manager must not make a sacred cow of the organizing process or the organization structure. Structure is binding and constraining. Structure controls and inhibits. In many cases—and this may well be true for many selling operations—the degree of structuring may best be "tailored" to unique demands on a particular organizational element. Perhaps in many sales

---

[15] Part IV deals extensively with these behavioral and motivational aspects of management and proposes strategies for coping with conflict arising from necessary structural or procedural changes.

organizations the job of the salesman should be relatively unstructured—with objectives, to be sure, but with relatively little constraining influence on how the salesman is going to accomplish them, thus permitting and even encouraging his creative potential.

Perhaps the really key aspect of organizing is the effective structuring of *groups* and the establishing of *relationships* between them. This idea of intergroup relationships introduces the managerial concept of *co-ordinating,* a process to be discussed in the next chapter.

SUGGESTED READINGS

The Organizing Process, General

1. McFarland, D. E., *Management Principles and Practices,* Macmillan, New York, 1958, Chapters 8 and 11.
2. Newman, William H., *Administrative Action,* Prentice-Hall, Englewood Cliffs, N.J., 1951, Chapters 16 and 17.

Line and Staff in Organizations

1. Newman, William H., and Sumner, Charles E., Jr., *The Process of Management: Concepts, Behavior, and Practice,* Prentice-Hall, Englewood Cliffs, N.J., 1965, pp. 17–36, 76–94.
2. Moore, Franklin G., *Management,* Harper and Row, New York, 1964, pp. 435–489.
3. Koontz, H., and O'Donnell, C., *Principles of Management,* McGraw-Hill, New York, 1964, pp. 208–215, 231–295.

Job Descriptions: Matching Job and Individual

1. Newman, W. H., and Sumner, C. E., Jr., *The Process of Management: Concepts, Behaviors, and Practice,* Prentice-Hall, Englewood Cliffs, N.J., 1965, pp. 217–237.

Selection of Salesmen

1. Stanton, W. J. and Buskirk, R. H., *Management of the Sales Force,* Richard D. Irwin, Homewood, Ill., 1964, pp. 148–287.
2. Pederson, C. A. and Wright, M. D., *Salesmanship, Principles and Methods,* Richard D. Irwin, Homewood, Ill., 1961, pp. 624–637.

QUESTIONS AND PROBLEMS

1. You have just been promoted from the job of salesman to that of district manager. You are assigned to head the North Central District, taking the place of the former district manager who, after fourteen years in the position, has retired. You have twelve salesmen reporting to you. You also have the customer service and warehouse operations within your responsibility. All the salesmen and the supervisors of customer service and warehouse have been in their present positions a minimum of four years. You are taking over a "going" organization. In this particular case, might you not be justified in not concerning yourself with the organizing process?
2. What relationship does the process of organizing have with the objective-setting process?
3. Comment on the statement: "Organizing is really synonymous with staffing. That is, organizing is really getting the right people in the right jobs."
4. You are a regional sales manager for a large firm marketing industrial chemicals. You report to a headquarters sales manager located at executive headquarters. You have reporting to you twelve district sales managers and one secretary. Your regional sales budget is $30 million. Your market has been growing; your competition is vigorous and competent. Considerable pressure is on you from headquarters for flow of market intelligence, forecasting, sales planning, motivation of district managers, and so on. You feel that there are not enough hours in the week to do all you believe needs doing. What are some of the criteria you might develop to justify to your headquarters management the addition of a staff assistant?
5. Consider each of the following forms of sales organization structure. For each form, cite a company that you think would likely be using that form. Name the company's products and/or markets and indicate why the form used is best suited, giving also the advantages and disadvantages of the form.
   a. Territorial organization
   b. Product-specialized organization
   c. Customer-specialized organization
6. What are the pros and cons for job description?

10

Coordinating the Selling Activities

A story is told about a large computer manufacturing firm that found itself in deep trouble with an important customer because of two widely differing views of the computer system being installed. The customer was a large oil refinery, and the securing of the refinery's first computer system was a real coup for the computer firm. The system was designed to do all production scheduling at all of the refinery's locations, even the routing and scheduling of tankers on the high seas. A long and very good selling job had been done. But after the computer was installed, difficulties developed in its operation, and the customer called the firm, in distress. A team of service engineers was dispatched to the customer's computer center and began working on the malfunctioning system. Several days went by, with the customer's antagonism mounting. Tankers at sea were being held up; refineries were about to run short of crude. The top executive management of the customer was being given hourly reports. In near desperation, the customer management exhorted the supervisor of the service team to bring in whatever talent was needed from his firm to get the system running. The supervisor reportedly replied in this vein: "No use getting excited. All these systems have to go through this kind of shakedown."

Well, the supervisor of service never saw a system that *was not* in trouble. That was his world, and trouble was simply normal. But during the selling negotiations, the great reliability of the firm's computers had been stressed. Not trouble. Hence the customer's top management was infuriated at this reaction and telephoned the chief executive of the computer firm. He, of course, had not been informed of the serious trouble in the great new system—a fact further infuriating customer management. The chief executive then telephoned the division manager, who had not been informed. The division manager called the sales manager, who was ignorant of the problem. No one in the firm had been alerted to a drastic situation that threatened serious loss of prestige—and perhaps future business—in the industry.

This is lack of coordination. One element of the firm—service engineering in this case—went about its business *as it legitimately saw fit*. It sought its objectives in its own "world" of perception, belief, and action. But its actions were not compatible with the objectives and actions of another unit—in this case, sales. In fact, its actions *threatened* the selling operation's objectives.[1] Some manager had not adequately meshed the two units together.

In firms of any size and complexity at all—and this means most firms—the *coordinating process* has significant effect on the firm's efficiency. Simple as the idea of coordinating is, it is a process that is often overlooked or done poorly. The process may be defined as follows:

> Coordinating is the process by which the executive develops an orderly pattern of group effort among subordinate units, and secures compatibility of action in the pursuit of common goals.[2]

Here again the "systems" notion is at work. From the objective-setting process and the organizing process evolve organizational elements, each with its unique set of missions. But they are interacting units and have relationships one to another. The creating, defining, and managing of these relationships form the root of the coordinating process. It must not be left to chance to secure *compatibility* of action—so that each unit does achieve its objectives without conflict and so that the larger component of which the units are parts achieves its larger objectives.[3] The key concept

[1] This set of problems was corrected by the firm. Field service engineering was organizationally placed under field sales. Communication procedures were defined. Service engineers were required never to visit a customer without having a sales engineer present.

[2] Here we are basically following Dalton McFarland, *Management Principles and Practice,* Macmillan, New York, 1958, p. 268. McFarland proposes that "unity of action" is secured. Probably "compatibility of action" better portrays what ideally should happen.

[3] Occasionally some manager will get the idea that *interdependent* subordinate units should "compete" with each other, so that each will "try harder." This is patently ridiculous.

is the meshing together, or tailoring, of the objectives, communications, and actions of the diverse units.

Coordination is not the same thing as cooperation. It would be a bit naïve for an executive to rely entirely on cooperation for this compatibility of effort. For example, he might say:

> "Jim Larson, the Credit Manager is a fine chap. And Mac McDonald, the Sales Manager is a splendid person. They're both loyal company people, and I'm sure we can rely on them to cooperate and iron out any problems between credit and sales."

Assume that they are fine, loyal chaps. Nevertheless, they are normal (and fallible) human beings. Larson's *real* business goal is to get his group to reach the credit goals. This is his world. MacDonald's real goal is to lead his sales group to achieve *its* goals. This is *his* world. *Cooperation is a voluntary behavioral act.* It is a fine thing to possess in an organization, but the manager cannot leave to it the vital interaction of organizational units. He must develop *coordination*—an objective, definitive set of *organizational* relationships between units.

COMMON POTENTIAL AREAS OF CONFLICT
REQUIRING COORDINATION

The very nature of the selling operation requires activities both within and outside the firm that need careful coordinating by sales managers. The following intergroup relations are common to many selling operations. Later in this chapter some special cases are considered.

Coordinating between Groups within the Selling Operation

Within the selling organization itself, the sales manager may have diverse subunits for which interrelationships must be spelled out. Some of these are:

Sales–Service
Sales–Order handling
Sales–Warehouse operation
Sales–Customer billing and collection

Many potential incompatibilities exist here. For a simple example, consider a regional manager of warehousing. He may legitimately perceive that he and his group are evaluated (among other things) by stock turnover; hence he may wish to eliminate "slow-moving" items. On the other hand, a district sales manager wants to have an edge on his competitors and to be able to ship *anything* from stock that a good customer may want. Even such simple incompatibilities often go unresolved. In this case the first management level *above* the warehousing and sales should "coordinate" the objectives and relationships of the two and define a policy that is consistent and compatible to each.

Coordinating between Sales and Other Elements of Marketing

Rational and objective coordination is also required between the selling operation and other functional groups within marketing. Some examples are:

Sales–Marketing Research
Sales–Forecasting
Sales–Marketing Personnel
Sales–Product Planning
Sales–Headquarters Product Management
Sales–Pricing Units
Sales–Factory Liaison Groups
Sales–Advertising

Again, the objectives perceived by sales management and the ensuing actions to achieve them may not be necessarily in tune with the objectives and ensuing actions of other units in the marketing organization. For example, a sales administration unit responsible for pricing strategy and tactics may very legitimately implement pricing actions to achieve the objectives of higher revenue via higher price, the achieving of price leadership, the stability of pricing, and the general lifting of price levels in the industry. But at the same time, the sales department may seek the objectives of greater market share, higher volume, and increased customer goodwill. It is completely conceivable that this normal situation could create conflict between the two marketing groups, to the detriment of each.

Coordinating between Sales and Elements in the Firm outside Marketing

Again following the "systems" idea, the marketing component of a firm is a system unto itself. But it is an "open" system, and inputs from outside can and do impinge its "subsystems" of sales, market research, product planning, and so on. Some of these inputs come from other elements of the firm outside marketing. In most firms the selling operation interacts with many nonmarketing units of the firm—and here again is a crucible either for potential conflict or for mutual enhancement. Coordination may spell the difference. A few typical examples follow.

1. Sales and Production. Production management may legitimately, as they perceive it, seek the objectives of lower unit costs by way of long production runs of one model, low levels of factory inventories, low inventories of raw materials, and the like. These actions to achieve the "lower cost" objective may be detrimental to sales management facing severe competitive situations. Example: some competitors may be able to ship from stock a variety of models, whereas this firm may be out of stock of some units because of the long production runs of one specific model. *Note that we are not saying here that production management is wrong.* Nor that sales management is wrong. What is wrong is an inadequacy of *coordinating.*

2. Sales and Credit. Many credit managers understandably perceive themselves as protectors of the firm's financial position. They may seek such objectives as the minimizing of "bad debts" and the elimination of "bad accounts." Hence they may reduce risks on some new accounts or on some customers' orders by restriction or refusal of credit. On the other hand, the sales manager is striving to increase volume, bring new accounts into the fold, and so on, and may find that the firm's credit policy is placing him in a disadvantageous position competitively. Here again is the need for coordinating.[4]

3. Sales and Engineering. Much potential conflict exists between sales and the design functions of a manufacturing firm. To achieve their objectives, engineering management may develop product designs for internal purposes rather than for competitive purposes. For example, it is quite necessary that a product be designed for as low a manufacturing cost as possible. But without adequate coordination, this objective may be so sought that the product suffers a competitive disadvantage in the marketplace. Or the engineers may design a product in a certain way

---

[4] Such conflict need not exist, of course. A splendid example is found in a General Electric experience. Soon after World War II, the executive of an industrial manufacturing firm visited several electric motor manufacturers, hoping to secure motors for his ingeniously designed product, even though his firm's cash position was not good. An alert, sales-minded credit manager in General Electric looked beyond the obvious credit restrictions and at the customer's great potential. He not only arranged special credit terms (at a professional risk to himself) but lent GE technical assistance to the customer, helping him in his financial management. The customer obtained his motors, produced a highly marketable product, and in fifteen years grew to become a giant in his field and one of GE's largest industrial customers. GE billed him in the millions of dollars per year.

simply because they have some kind of technical idealism that directs them to do so. Sometimes this results in a product whose operation or servicing suffers in comparison to competitive products.[5]

Coordinating Line and Staff

A special need for effective coordinating exists in the securing of optimal relationships between line groups and staff groups. In Chapter 9 the need was discussed for staff assistance to line groups. Assuming that normally all authority for decision and action is vested in the line management, it requires *formal coordinating* to define and obtain the relationship desired between line and staff.

To be sure, many executives leave it up to the *individuals* concerned to adequately mesh together. The staff man is admonished that he (1) has no authority and only represents the boss, (2) must submerge his own personality and be a "teamworker," and (3) must rely largely on persuasion.[6] But in many cases, this puts the staff man in a sort of contest with the line manager, and he who has the more forceful personality may well have influence over the other *but not* necessarily to optimum advantage as far as the meshing of line and staff work groups is concerned.

The following statement may have some bias in it and, therefore, should be taken only as a possibility. It seems likely that despite an understanding of the process of coordinating in many parts of the firm, some executives leave much of the line-staff relationship to chance. Or perhaps worse, they approach them as personality relationships rather than job relationships.[7] As a result, some firms can be described as line-

[5] Almost every homeowner has experienced this as he attempts to service such equipment as an automatic washer, an air-conditioning unit, or an oil furnace. Or consider how many equipments have the nameplate data (model number, etc.) in an inaccessible part of the equipment. This might lend simplicity in some manufacturing operation, but cause irritation in the marketplace. Even professional, trained service technicians growl about such design problems.

[6] W. H. Newman and C. E. Sumner, Jr., *The Process of Management*, Prentice-Hall, Englewood Cliffs, N.J., 1961, pp. 83–84.

[7] The executive may face some difficult problems in establishing line-staff relationships. Perhaps in his firm line managers are strong, dominant persons who, the executive thinks, will resent "outsiders" (staff men). Or perhaps the executive himself came up through line management and consciously or unconsciously places line management in a superior status. Or, conversely, perhaps he rose through staff ranks, but hesitates to "force" staff men on line managers whom he perceives as strong and individualistic. For these and other reasons, therefore, he may leave it to

management-dominated or, conversely, as staff-dominated. In either case, the advantages of an optimum line-staff relationship may be lost. Again, this is not saying that a firm should be line-dominated, or staff-dominated, or neither. It is saying that relationships between line and staff units should be defined and implemented objectively, with a view to the achievement of objectives.

WHO IS RESPONSIBLE FOR COORDINATING?

Direct Responsibility

Every manager is directly responsible for the coordinating process if he has subordinate to him *diverse units or positions that have some effect on one another*. The key here is either actual interaction between two units (e.g., headquarters product specialists and regional field sales groups) or, lacking actual interaction, the affecting of one group's performance by the behavior of another (e.g., field sales and the headquarters forecasting and budgeting group). This is not always obvious in the organization chart, which does not usually spell out the *relationships* between subordinate units. To determine if coordinating is required between organizational units and to specify what managerial position is responsible for the process, several additional factors must be added to the bare bones of the simplified organization chart, as shown in Figure 10-1. To determine which managers are responsible for coordinating, and the specific degree to which they are responsible, start at the bottom of the organization chart and work upward. At each level, beginning with the level immediately above the worker, the manager of that level must ask the following questions:

1. What are the objectives and the work necessary to achieve them for this subordinate position (or group) reporting to me? [8]

2. *Will the work done in any position (or group) have any direct or indirect effect on the work of other persons (or groups)?*

If the answer to the second question is "no"—that is, if whatever each group does in seeking its objectives has no effect on any other group—no

the persons themselves to work out some sort of cooperative basis. This is abdicating his coordinating responsibility.

Probably the answer lies in the meaning itself of coordinating. That is, the executive will find it easier to achieve the right "mesh" if he thinks and communicates in terms of groups and group objectives or jobs and job objectives, rather than in terms of personalities or personal behaviors.

[8] This, of course, is one of the basic elements in the dynamic process of "organizing," hence is presumed to have already been done and to be known.

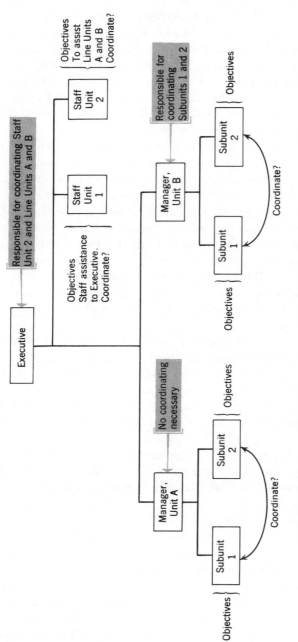

FIGURE 10-1 Managers responsible for coordinating. The key question that each manager must ask regarding units subordinate to him, whether staff, line, or both, is: Will the actions of one unit to achieve its given objectives directly or indirectly affect the plans and actions of any other unit in achieving *its* objectives? If "yes,"—must coordinate the two. If "no"—no coordination needed.

direct coordinating of subordinate units is necessary for that manager. For example, in Figure 10-1, assume that the "executive" is the Manager of Marketing and that Unit A is a headquarters administration group, with two subunits. Subunit 1 is Marketing Administration, which includes market research, forecasting, and budgeting. Subunit 2 is Marketing Personnel Administration, responsible for recruiting, hiring, and training of marketing personnel. Now assume that the Manager of Unit A answers "no" to the second question (which is quite likely). He need not be concerned with *coordination* between the two subunits. Each can "go its merry way" without any effect on the other.

Now suppose that Unit B is the Sales Department. Its Subunit 1 is Field Sales with its several sales regions. Subunit 2 is Customer Service Department, with a corps of service technicians at headquarters and in the field, all reporting to the manager of Customer Service. Now, as the manager of Unit B (Manager of Sales Department) considers his two subunits, he answers "yes" to question 2 (which is highly likely, since both groups are in contact with customers). In this case, what the Customer Service Department people do in their customer contacts to achieve their objectives will affect (favorably or unfavorably) the operation of the field sales people. Coordinating will be necessary, and the manager of the two groups requiring it has the complete responsibility for it.

Consider the staff units in Figure 10-1. Again, we go to the first managerial level above the units of concern—in this case, the "executive." As he asks the two questions, he may answer "no" to the second in regard to Staff Unit 1. Here we can assume that this unit provides staff assistance only to the executive and that its actions do not affect in any way the operation of other units, staff or line. No coordination with other units is required.

However, assume that Staff Unit 2 was formed in the organizing process as a facilitating unit to provide specialized assistance to the line organizations. For example, assume that it is a Product Specialist group, with subcomponents or individuals holding objectives of increasing volume on specific product lines. These staff people are in contact with field sales people, counseling and persuading. Here the manager of the next level above the group is the Executive (in our case, the Manager of Marketing). He must answer "yes" to question 2; hence he is responsible for proper coordinating of Staff Unit 2 with the field sales personnel. However, in this case, the Marketing Manager must *implement* the coordination between the respective managerial positions—the manager of the staff unit and the manager of Unit B. Note that he does not bypass the Manager of Unit B and attempt to coordinate the Staff Unit and *subordinates* of Manager B. And note that the *Marketing Manager is directly and completely responsible for the establishment of coordination.* The managers of Staff Unit 2 and Unit B are responsible for *implementing* the coordinating directives (just as they are for any other directive.) Again, it is well to point out that *groups and positions are coordinated, not persons.*

VOLUNTARY COORDINATION

Consider this hypothetical situation (which is by no means unusual). An aggressive, competent field sales manager is eager to achieve his objectives of higher volume, increased market share, and so on. He has frequent contact with production management and often tries to persuade them to do something unusual, in order to gain some bit of extra business from a specific customer. For example, he may request that they ship the product earlier than normally by putting on a night shift or that they include a nonstandard item into the production schedule. Now, he finds production management to be quite "hard-nosed" about this and unwilling to "cooperate" with him. What should he do? Bow to them? Go to his superior and demand that top management "put them in their place"? Deliberately "needle" them?

It is hard to say what he should do, based only on these bare facts. But certainly, the sales manager is a human being, with drives and motives to do a competent job. Certainly we can sympathize with his feeling of frustration.

Here is a situation which requires coordinating, but in which the co-ordinating executive has failed to achieve it. Perhaps—and note that we say "perhaps"—the sales manager might voluntarily impose on himself the task of coordinating policies that some higher executive should have performed and take it upon himself to establish a workable relationship with production management.

This does not mean that he capitulates or becomes subservient to another group. He can be very cold-blooded about this, and consider the greater ease with which he can achieve his *overall* objectives, *over the long range.* He may find that by sitting face-to-face with production management, accepting with understanding their objectives and problems, clearly portraying his own, discussing the greater objectives of the firm itself, and proposing ways in which the two groups can communicate and interrelate, he can obtain more understanding and help from production than if they had been ordered from above. If he can somehow induce production management to think that he and they are on a team, a more compatible relationship will probably develop.

This is voluntary coordination. It is the managerial coordination that should have been done by a higher manager, but has not been.

Countless examples of voluntary coordination can be seen in many firms. After all, everything cannot and probably should not be defined, and there are many instances where interrelated work is voluntarily coordinated. In the case of the credit manager cited in footnote 4, for example, no superior had told him that he should "coordinate" his work with sales; he did so voluntarily, and sincerely in the best interests of the company.

But this does not mean that a sales manager can leave coordination of vital relationships to chance. Subordinate managers may perceive voluntary coordination as a risk. That is, they may perceive it as appearing "weak" or not adequately "competitive" to their own associates. Even if they do try in some way to achieve it, they may do so inadequately. Hence the sales manager certainly cannot abdicate the direct, formal process of coordination on important issues and group relationships.

HOW COORDINATING IS DONE

It does not make much sense to attempt to develop a step-by-step formula for the coordinating process. Business firms vary greatly in type of structure, managerial style, traditions, and age. In many cases, in "old" organizations, customs and traditions have developed over time, and adequate coordination between groups has evolved. Or, in some cases, the sheer power of the personalities of persons might shade or influence the coordinating process.

Nevertheless, in "newer" organizations or when organization structure is changed, new technologies and processes are added, personnel changes, or a manager "audits" the effectiveness of his organization, a managerial coordinating process may be required. Hence a set of basic principles (if not an actual "formula") should be considered by the manager. Although it is not proposed that these will "fit" in every case needing coordinating, the following principles can help the sales manager:

1. Conceive all possible conflicts that might arise between groups or individuals.

2. Define and clearly communicate downward the objectives of the larger unit of which the subunits to be coordinated are a part.

3. Define clearly authorities, relationships, and policies.

4. Develop an information system flowing to the coordinating executive.

5. Establish communication nets between coordinated units, and facilitate them.

6. Consider coordinating when organizing.

7. Motivate, through leadership, for voluntary coordination.

1. Conceive Conflicts

In the organizing process, the executive has carefully and analytically broken the total work to be done into "manageable parts." He has then assigned a mission (or set of objectives) to each part. In this process, he must use imagination, to conceive not only the mesh of these objectives given to subordinates units, but also possible conflicts between them. Put very simply, he must ask himself: "How do these units interrelate? Can there be any effect, one on the other? In what ways might the work of one conflict with the work of another?" Thus the starting point for the coordinating process is the *identifying of possible areas of conflict that could arise* between positions or groups. To give an oversimplified example, a field sales manager may say to himself: "We have set up a field sales organization, with specific objectives. Separately, we have determined the need for a field service organization to service our products after they are sold. How will these two groups interact? How do they relate? Can the work of one affect the other? In what ways? Under what circumstances? What possible conflicts might arise?"

2. Define and Communicate Objectives of Larger Unit

The only reason for the subunit's existence, with its separate sets of objectives and allocated resources, *is to enable the larger unit of which it is a part to achieve its greater objectives.* Even though the subunits may be given considerable autonomy in some firms, they never exist in a vacuum or in isolation, if what they do in any way has impact of any kind on another subunit. It is not enough for a manager to set the objectives of the subunits. These objectives all mesh, so that if achieved, the larger unit will meet its larger objectives. This is the basic rationale behind the entire *organizing* process. Thus a primary step in the *coordinating* process is to define clearly to managers of all subunits not only the subunits' missions, *but how they mesh together for the achievement of the "parent" unit's objectives.* Again oversimplifying, the field sales manager might say to the manager of regional sales and of customer service: "You have the specific objectives for your groups. Certainly you and I want to see them reached. But the real reason for reaching them is to enable the Sales Department to achieve its objectives." (How he then proceeds to coordinate is discussed in following steps.)

Now, this does not mean that the subunit managers should subjugate the missions for their own groups to anything, even to the larger unit. Ideally, the subunit manager should feel that his group is "his world"— that the most important thing in this world is for his group to reach its goals. But if later this manager must "give" a little in the coordinating process, he cannot do so willingly unless he absolutely understands the vital reasons for it in terms of the objectives of the larger unit. This step does not *implement* coordination; it merely provides a background *framework of thinking* about its necessity.

3. Define Clearly Authorities, Relationships, and Policies

Given the need for coordinating subunits, this next step is rather self-explanatory. As authority is delegated to subordinate units, some restrictions must be made (or sometimes certain authorities withheld) for actions that might conflict with those of another unit. Following the example above, the field sales manager might say to the customer service manager: "You have the authority to go ahead on your own, as long as you meet your objectives, on decisions regarding warranties, return of equipment (etc.). However, you do not have the authority to initiate customer contact. This must be done through the sales regions." [9]

Of course, the field sales manager may not be able to spell this out for all possible areas of conflict. Therefore, he should clearly define the relationships between the subunits—that is, *generally* how they are intended to "live" and work together (see also the discussion of communication below). Also, for the more common and for broad areas of potential conflict, definitive policies should be established.[10] Actually, the statement in the foregoing paragraph about responsibility for customer contact is such a policy.

4. Develop an Information System Flowing to the Coordinating Manager

It would be naïve to believe that conflicts between subunits will always be eliminated by identifying them, spelling out the mesh of

[9] He need not explain *why* authority to contact customers is withheld if the framework of thinking proposed in step 2 has been clearly established. If it has not, probably an explanation is advisable.

[10] The nature of "policies" is discussed in Chapter 11.

objectives, and setting policies. Some conflict may remain—sometimes unintentional and almost unnoticed by the managers of the subordinate units. Therefore, as a control device, the coordinating manager must use the flow of information that he has available for other purposes to detect actions that are out of harmony with one another. This is difficult, because in most organizations a "gestapo" sort of system may be detrimental to managerial relationships and behaviors. However, as the manager sets up the information system that he must have to obtain knowledge of "what's going on," he may well try to define the reports and records with an eye to detecting possible conflict between subunits. For example, many sales managements require that salesmen or district sales managers formally report (on provided forms) certain types of business lost to competitors, as well as the reasons for the loss. Although such reports may not always be completely accurate,[11] an experienced sales manager whose "antennae are tuned" to possible conflicting activity between groups may get signals from such reports.

Observation of activities also provides information to the coordinating manager, again if his "antennae are tuned." During his face-to-face contacts with subordinate managers, he can over time develop a "feel" for potential conflicts. His periodic "review sessions" with subordinate managers may flush out conflicting activities, which he can then correct by means of other steps in this rationale.

5. Establish Communication Nets between Coordinated Units, and Facilitate Them

Perhaps overgeneralizing, we might say that the better the communication between two diverse units, the better the coordination between them. But if left to chance, communication between diverse units that require coordination may be inadequate at best or nonexistent at worst. Here we are speaking of "horizontal" communication directly from unit to unit. The sales manager may facilitate this communication in several ways.

First, he may create a *managerial atmosphere that encourages horizontal communication* without going "through channels." Unfortunately, this is often difficult. Managers are human and fallible, and some may resist any intergroup communication that bypasses them. An understandable retort might be: "I'm accountable for the results my group achieves, and I don't want any outsider influencing my people without going through me." However, the sales manager may change much of this attitude through his managerial "style" and his leadership (to be

[11] Interesting psychological factors underly this statement, and will be examined in Chapter 13.

discussed in Part III). And he may well set the example by encouraging his subordinates to establish direct communication with management of other units. For instance, a sales manager might advise his district manager to establish personal contact and develop a rapport with production management. This is done at some risk, of course, but it is one way to facilitate horizontal communication, thus enhancing coordination.

Second, the use of *committees* facilitates communication. Even if one accepts the arguments of some critics that committees at the operating level are incapable of making binding decisions, the committee does provide a medium for exchange of views, understanding of others' goals and problems, and insight into the fact that others are normal human beings.[12] For example, a sales manager who desires to enhance the coordination between several of his subunits might create a committee consisting of the managers (or their representatives) of field sales, customer service, warehousing, and order service, with a mission to meet periodically, explore innovative ideas for mutual efforts to improve the performance of the department as a whole, and make recommendations to sales management. Certainly, this should not be a "make busywork" project, but should sincerely seek the innovative objectives. Improved communication and coordination will undoubtedly result.

Third, *staff meetings* can provide an excellent medium for horizontal communication. These meetings are usually held on a scheduled basis by a sales manager with all managers of the immediately subordinate units. A prime purpose of such meetings, of course, is *vertical* communication, up and down. However, the staff meeting can be an ideal medium for *horizontal* communication, hence coordination.

---

[12] One of the largest publishing firms in the country uses the committee for facilitating communication between its diverse and semiautonomous groups. For example, this alert company is deeply involved in long-range planning. At the top executive level, the responsibility for corporate long-range planning is assigned to the executive vice-president. He has a small staff of highly expert people for developing such planning. Additionally, the semiautonomous operating divisions—the book publishing division, the magazine division, a microfilm division, and so on—also perform a long-range planning function, specifically focused on the division itself. Clearly, some coordination is required here, or the corporate level might be going in one direction and the operation divisions in another. To facilitate communications and coordination, a company-wide "planning committee" was formed, composed of the executive vice-president, his manager of the staff planning group, and the managers of planning of each division. The committee meets at executive headquarters monthly, interchanging ideas, reporting activities and progress, and making recommendations to executive and operating management.

6. Consider Coordinating When Organizing

During the organizing process, when structure is developed (or when-ever the organization structure is adjusted for some reason), the manager should keep an eye on the ensuing coordination needed between result-ing subunits. If it is feasible to do so, units whose activities will need careful and close meshing should be placed in the same organization component. This permits the ideal situation in which *the coordinating manager one step up* is managing "sister" units. This significantly facili-tates coordination and the compatibility of activities, for several reasons. First, it is much easier for the coordinating manager to predict, observe, and correct conflicts between units. Second, it is easier for individuals within the subunits to see and understand the mesh of goals and the need for coordination. Hence it is easier for them to work toward the higher echelon's goals as well as their own. Third, in a psychological sense, it may provide a feeling of "family" for many individuals, again facilitating coordination.[13]

Even if units are not organizationally placed in the same component, placing them in close physical proximity, if it is at all feasible to do so, may enhance mutual understanding, horizontal communication, and coordination. For example, if it is feasible to locate credit managers physically near sales managers, the credit-sales coordination may be greatly facilitated. It is obvious that a credit manager who passes judg-ment on credit for customers in the Western Sales Region will better "mesh" his activities with those of the Western Region Sales Manager if he is located in the same office in San Francisco than if he is located in his superior's office at New York headquarters. Parenthetically, note that both credit and sales operations profit from this arrangement, even though each manager "reports" up through a different hierarchy. Also note that this can be done only when feasible. There may be valid rea-sons why such physical proximity is not possible, in which case coordina-tion must be otherwise facilitated.

7. Motivate through Leadership for Voluntary Coordination

At the risk of sounding overly idealistic, it must be said that for all the rules, the policies, the procedures, the reports—and for all the valid ideas that jobs and not people are coordinated—activities and inter-group interactions are nevertheless done by individual persons. How

[13] See Chapter 14 for some insights into "group behavior," and its meaning for the sales manager.

they perceive, interpret, and respond to the manager's coordinating efforts may significantly depend on how he presents these efforts to them. Although a discussion of leadership is saved for a later part of this book, it must be emphasized here that somehow the sales manager must by his own managerial behaviors *cause subordinates to want to coordinate with others.*

SPECIAL CASES IN FIELD SALES REQUIRING COORDINATION

In many selling organizations, coordination is not required at the level of the salesman. He is assigned to a territory, he develops business with customers in that territory, and no other activity in the firm significantly affects his work. But in many other cases the sales job is not so simple with respect to its relationships with other activities in the firm. Often the planning and work done by the salesman are significantly affected by others, directly or indirectly, and the regional or district sales manager to whom he reports is responsible for effective coordination. A few typical cases are discussed below.

Team Selling

Frequently the salesman is only one of several individuals in the firm who have face-to-face contact with various personnel in the customer organization. Consider a sales situation in which the customer is an industrial manufacurer and the selling firm is marketing industrial machinery. A number of individuals in the customer's firm must be contacted in the course of selling these technical products. Similarly a number of individuals in the selling firm may have special expertise that can be used to advantage in direct contact of selected customer personnel. These individuals and the pattern of "who contacts whom" are shown in Figure 10–2.

Without careful coordination, the selling operation could be a many-headed monster, and it would take a minor miracle to mesh effectively the individual efforts (even if each one is well done). On the other hand, with coordination, the individuals in the selling firm, coming from different organizational components, can be an *effective sales team.* One individual will be the "quarterback," masterminding the strategy and calling the plays. Normally this will be the individual "closest" to the customer—the salesman. Or it may be the district sales manager. In

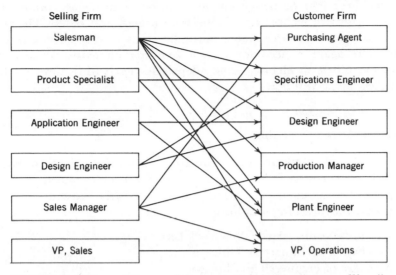

FIGURE 10-2   The need for coordinating in "team selling."

any case, someone must "orchestrate," calling in the various resources of the firm as dictated by the selling strategy.[14] Such "team selling" may take the form of a number of the selling firm's people calling as a group on an individual customer or a customer group. Or it may take the form of different selling-firm individuals calling separately on individual customers. In either case, a master strategy is being followed, and the individual efforts must carefully be coordinated by the "team leader." All the proposals of the foregoing section of this chapter pertain here, and the coordination cannot be left to chance.

Such "team selling" is by no means restricted to the industrial scene. A consumer goods manufacturer (such as Sunbeam with its toasters, frying pans, etc.) calling on a large retailer (such as Montgomery Ward) may have an array of individuals with special expertise visiting an array of individual customers with special interests.

In these examples, members of the coordinated sales team all have direct contact with the customer. In a sense, a "team" may still exist, even when only the salesman contacts the customer. Again referring to the "master strategy" proposed in Chapter 8, the salesman "orchestrates" by calling for help from many people in the firm, even though these people do not call on the customer with him. Feeding information and

[14] This ties back to the "master strategy" step in the selling strategy rationale proposed in Chapter 8.

ideas to him might be design engineers, product managers, production schedulers, service technicians, financial managers, and others. He must have access to these sources and a mutually understood relationship with them. Here again a need for formal coordination exists. If such coordination is left to chance, some adept salesmen will achieve it—but others, less adept, will not.

"National Account" Selling

A special and important case requiring careful, formal coordinating arises when the customer has necessary points of contact outside the territory of one salesman. For example, an industrial customer might extend over the following locations:

1. Executive headquarters: New York City
2. Purchasing headquarters: Chicago
3. Manager of engineering: Chicago
4. Plants, with plant managers, and production management: Roanoke, Virginia; Houston, Texas; Phoenix, Arizona; Seattle, Washington; and Olean, New York.

It may well be that the selling firm must get approval from the customer's local plant personnel; it receives the order, however, from the purchasing office in Chicago; it must also keep contact with policymaking executives in New York City. In this quite simple case, a minimum of three of the firm's sales districts may be involved in a single transaction. Again, coordination is required, or the firm's individual selling efforts at each location may not adequately mesh.

Coordinated "national account" selling occurs also in the retail sphere. Consider selling a consumer goods product to such firms as Sears Roebuck, A & P, Woolworth, or Saks Fifth Avenue—each of whom will have decision-making or decision-influencing individuals spread widely. Considerable selling power can often be generated by a coordinated "team" approach to such geographically widespread accounts.

Parts and Service Selling

In many industrial markets and in some consumer durable goods markets (air-conditioning systems, home laundry, etc.), two markets may exist—one for the product itself and one for renewal parts and service after the sale. Here we are regarding the renewal parts market as one that has profit potential for the firm.

In some cases, the firm may delegate the aftersale parts and service business to another agency, such as independent repair shops and servicing dealers. Even here, coordination is required in a subtle sense, as is discussed later. But in many cases in industrial markets, the firm selling the product also sells parts and service. In industrial markets of any complexity, this is a unique business, considerably different from the new-product business. A customer firm such as U.S. Steel has a vast array of decision-making points that must be contacted by the sales engineers of, say, steel mill equipment. A web of contacts must be built with the customer's operating, engineering, purchasing, financial, and management people. The "sales team" contacting this vast customer organization also has an array of individuals with special technical abilities. After the mill equipment is sold, a large dollar potential is available for renewal parts (sometimes in the tens of thousands of dollars) and service work (periodic overhauls, etc.). But this business is handled in the customer organization by a completely *different array of people* than was the product itself, with different objectives and problems and different modes of buying. This requires a uniquely different selling effort and is usually handled by sales individuals with a different expertise. But to optimize sales to such a customer as U.S. Steel, obviously the competency and quality of performance of parts and service sales people are important, since they can vitally influence the customer's perception and evaluation of the selling firm when the sales team begins its strategic and tactical moves toward the next equipment order. Again, careful coordination is needed, and cannot be left to chance.

COORDINATION WITH BUSINESS ORGANIZATIONS OUTSIDE THE FIRM

Although at first glance it appears that coordination is a managerial process executed only within the firm, it is also an important process in relationships *outside the firm*. Perhaps it can be argued that because the firm's sales management does not have control of business groups outside the firm, it cannot accomplish any coordinating. In a literal sense this is true—and yet *the concept of coordination* and an effort to secure it can often pay rewards to sales management. To be sure, sales management cannot issue directives and policies to ensure proper relations between the firm and external agencies. For this reason, some sales managements have shrugged off the valuable process. Nevertheless, even though sales management cannot command, it can certainly influence relationships

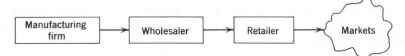

FIGURE 10-3   Elements of the channel system.

in the channels of distribution. It can seek *voluntary coordination,* achieving it by motivation, leadership, and strategic policies. All the proposals of this chapter can be used to this end.

Of course, the sales management cannot set the objectives of the external agency. But it can accept them and mesh with them, even if it requires some compromise on the part of the firm. Unfortunately, the sales management of many firms becomes quite self-oriented and does not really strive to mesh with and tailor its policies to its external agencies. It expects somehow that the external agencies will bend and mesh to the firm. This is usually naïve, and the relationships between the firm and its external agencies are often less than optimal.[15]

An astute sales management creates strategies to influence behavior of firms in its channels of distribution—wholesalers and retailers. Certainly, the conceptual base of the coordinating process can be used strategically. The goal should be an optimum mesh of activities, so that both units (e.g., the firm and the wholesaler) meet their objectives. A few examples follow, showing the structure that needs coordination.

In the consumer goods industries, a common pattern of distribution is that shown in Figure 10-3. In this *system,* how can the interactions of the elements be meshed or coordinated so that each element optimally achieves its unique objectives? How can the firm's actions be strategically oriented so that not only will the wholesaler's actions "fit" the firm's strategy, but the wholesaler's objectives will also be met? These strategic decisions may be more effective if an input is made of the coordinating concepts, tailored, of course, to the relationship sought with a unit outside the firm.

A special case in consumer goods marketing in which very careful coordinating is required occurs when the firm uses "missionary salesmen." Here, in order to influence demand at the retailer level, the firm's sales management sends "missionary salesmen" to selected retailers, to promote the firm's products. Orders received will be booked through the appropriate wholesaler.[16] Obviously, this promotional activity must be

---

[15] For an interesting view of how "middlemen" perceive this, see Philip McVey, "Are Channels of Distribution What the Textbooks Say?" *Journal of Marketing,* Vol. 24, No. 3 (January 1960), pp. 61–65.

[16] The wholesaler, of course, provides the many services of warehousing, credit,

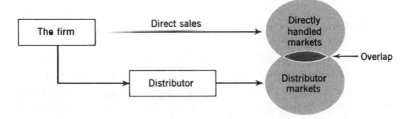

FIGURE 10-4   Competing elements in the channel.

done with the knowledge of the wholesaler; hence it requires careful and sometimes delicate coordinating.

Another set of conditions external to the firm that demands coordinating develops when an industrial firm is selling to industrial markets both through its own direct sales force and through industrial distributors. Schematically this appears as shown in Figure 10-4. The firm may elect to handle "direct", with its own field sales force, certain selected market segments. Usually these will consist of those customers whose potential volume for the firm's product is great enough to warrant having competent salesmen call regularly. On the other hand, the firm does not want to ignore other market segments that contain customers whose purchase volume does not warrant the cost of calling on them. Hence the firm may appoint distributors (or agents) to work these markets, paying them a discount (or commission). The distributor may find such "marginal" accounts attractive, because he handles many products other than those of the firm. But the distributor may find the firm's own selected or "reserved" accounts especially attractive and may try to secure business from them. (He may be calling on these "reserved" accounts for other lines of products. Conflict ensues. The firm cannot legally prevent the distributor from selling goods anywhere.[17]) Hence extremely careful coordinating must be done by the firm. Or, put another way, the coordinating concepts must be considered when creating the distributor marketing strategy.[18]

collection, shipment, and so on. Often the "missionary" idea is used to get a new product started, after which the wholesaler sales force carries on.

[17] This presumes that the distributor has taken title to the goods received from the supplier.

[18] A subtle point develops here *within* the firm. Usually when a firm sells both "direct" and through distributors, the sales department organization within the firm will have one "group" at headquarters and in the field for direct sales and a separate group at headquarters and in the field promoting distributor sales. These groups often become very competitive, to the extent that the total sales performance is impaired, not enhanced. Again, the sales manager must adequately coor-

SOME CONCLUDING THOUGHTS

All elements of the managerial process are important. Who is to say that one is more important than another? We cannot say that the coordinating process is more important than planning, or organizing, or decision making. Certainly it is not more important than motivation and leadership. But—and here is a key idea—in many, many firms coordinating is done more poorly than are the other elements and offers considerable opportunity for increasing managerial effectiveness.

Coordinating is probably more easily visualized and accomplished in small firms than in large firms. Yet, there is a dilemma here. The greater the complexity within the firm, and the greater the complexity outside the firm, the greater the need for coordinating. The greater the need for "horizontal" communication flow, the greater is the need for feedback of information so that all units of the system (which is the firm) can mesh.

There is another dilemma. Most of this chapter hints (sometimes shouts) that coordinating is underdone. But it can be overdone. Coordinating tends to restrict the actions of people. Individual managers in the firm may perceive that their freedom of action and opportunity for creative and innovative behavior are inhibited. Where is the optimum in between? There is no answer. It must be sought in each firm by itself, since each has unique sets of internal and external environments, of customs and mores, of people, of established and accepted managerial philosophy and style. Perhaps the ideas that are discussed in Part IV can reflect back to this dilemma—not resolving it, but hopefully helping in its resolution.

QUESTIONS AND PROBLEMS

1. Does the concept of "coordinating" not depersonalize the organization, giving it too much the feel of the "nonhuman system"? Can we not—in fact, *should we not*—make ourselves rely on human cooperation, human understanding, and human loyalty?
2. In Chapter 2, Figure 2-1 depicts the firm as a marketing system. In how many ways can you see the managerial process of coordinating needed in the process shown in this figure?
3. Where the manager coordinates, just what does he coordinate?

dinate these groups. Conflict is fine, if one group's activities do not adversely affect the performance of another. The loser here is the firm.

4. Since the selling operation is organizationally on the "output" side of the firm, could you say that coordinating is less important to its management than to that of other elements of the firm?

5. Select any company, naming it, its products, and its markets. Imagine yourself as a district sales manager. Stipulate the organizational units reporting to you. List all the possibilities you can think of for possible conflict, which should be minimized by proper coordinating.

7. You are a headquarters sales manager. Among the several individuals reporting to you are five regional managers and the manager of customer service. One regional manager has been complaining to you that the service engineers in customer service are not cooperating with his salesmen, are contacting customers directly, and are setting up their own little "empires." On the other hand, the manager of customer service reports that the field sales people will not provide his men with adequate data on customer problems, do not call them in early enough, treat them in a demeaning way in front of customers, and try to build up little "empires." What is wrong here? How would you go about correcting it?

II

Decision - Making and Delegating

In a typical firm, literally thousands of decisions, great and small, may be made every day. In a large tobacco company, the chief executive is meeting with the executive committee, which is about to make the decision to enter the frozen foods business. In Detroit, the president's advisory council of a large automotive manufacturer has just agreed to recommend allocating $10 million for development of a prototype nuclear power plant for an automobile. These are great decisions, which will have tremendous impact on the firm.

Thousands of not so great but still very important decisions are made. The marketing manager of a cosmetics firm has just approved a $2 million promotional campaign for a new hair shampoo. A production manager of a construction equipment company has just decided to eliminate a second shift because of declining volume of orders. A product manager in a soap company has just decided to change the package design. These, too, are important decisions, which may have considerable impact on groups and persons in and out of the firm.

Many thousands of almost routine decisions are made every day in a single typical firm. A regional sales manager in Denver decides to meet a competitor's cut price. A salesman in Houston decides to "go over a purchasing agent's head" and appeal to customer management at a higher level. A service manager in Buffalo, examining some of his firm's inoperative equipment in a customer's plant, decides that damage was done through carlessness of the customer's personnel, and further decides to so inform the customer. A district sales manager in Milwaukee decides to shuffle and rearrange his salesmen's territorial assignments. These, too, are important decisions. They may have somewhat limited impact, affecting only a very small part of the firm's world. But *in total, the summed-up effectiveness of the many thousands of "little" or "local" decisions* has significant effect on the success of the firm. The effective sales manager must, therefore, develop a logic or a rationale for making effective decisions in the field.

Great emphasis seems to be placed on the "big" decisions. One can be fairly sure that the Detroit automotive executives mentioned above have gone through an exhaustive, rational process to arrive at their great decision. On the other hand, it seems that less emphasis is placed on the small, local decisions—despite their *collective* importance. Furthermore, a feeling seems to exist that in the sales end of the firm, particularly in the field, many decisions are made on the spur of the moment, on almost an intuitive basis. Moreover, the so-called intuitive decisions made by many sales managers are often regarded by management as somehow less valid or less effective than the so-called "rational" decisions made by other managers in the firm.

This idea is worth exploring for a moment. First, what is a decision? *A decision is a commitment to action.* It is important to note that it is *purposeful* action that the decision maker desires. This implies an inseparable link between the elements: objectives, strategy, decisions, action, results. Now consider this in terms of the sales operation. Sales people and sales managers live in the dynamic, pell-mell world of the marketplace. Their actions are aimed at objective achievement, but in complex, ever-changing environments filled with a changing mix of variables over which they have no control. Situations arise involving complex customer and rival behavior, which must be coped with; and they pass and evolve into new, different situations in almost moments. Moments of danger or of opportunity evolve and pass, and must be dealt with defensively or opportunistically without long periods of meditation or analysis. Of course, many sales management decisions are tactical, *seemingly* intuitive in nature—when dealing with dynamic situations.

But this does not mean that such decisions need be based on hunch, or on a shot-in-the-dark basis. It is ridiculous to merely "counterpunch" in a market situation. The so-called intuitive, quick decisions can be based on the same logic as objective, rational decisions. A learnable way of thinking exists about how to make a decision—a framework, or a logical, analytical process. A sales manager can learn this way of thinking, plug into it what facts are available in the moment of time he has, and arrive at a decision that is far from merely "intuitive." The logical decision-making process proposed in this chapter is discussed in depth in the management literature. The purpose here is to adapt decision-making concepts into a fairly simple form and to the milieu of the sales manager. The process will be developed as three major elements:

1. The boundaries within which sales management decisions can be made—constraints and delegation.
2. The decision process itself.
3. The meaning of policy within the decision-making framework.

THE BOUNDARIES FOR DECISION

Consider the position of the sales manager relative to the whole organization. Within the entire hierarchy, sales is an *operating* organization. Furthermore, it is an element of a larger system, that of marketing, and it operates within and as a part of the greater marketing strategy. Marketing management provides certain inputs to sales management—objectives, resources, coordinating requirements, and others. At the very outset, then, sales management has some broad boundaries or constraints within which it must operate.

Moreover, the structure of the selling operation itself has a wide range of managerial and supervisory positions, both line and staff. A vertical hierarchy exists, and many "horizontal" relationships exist. Thus as the top executive of the selling operation sets objectives, plans strategies, allocates resources, and establishes control procedures, managers at lower echelons manage their respective groups as small "subsystems" within the greater system of the selling operation and, therefore, within the greater system of the selling operation. The rest of this chapter focuses on *sales management* as a unique element of the firm, with unique environments in which decisions must be made—environments that are quite different from those of other elements of the firm. Yet even this focusing is rather general, because the particular environments in which the various echelons of sales management exist place very different restrictions and opportunities on decision making.

As the selling operation functions within the greater system of marketing and therefore has certain constraints (since it must mesh with the other elements of the system), so the subelements of sales must operate within the "sales" system. The sales regions, customer service, order service, product specialist groups, and so on, are parts of a greater system which has its "greater" objectives. This is carried on down the hierarchy. The sales region has sales districts whose managers are given certain objectives, resources, and limits within which they may act. The sales district has salesmen who are given objectives, resources, and limits within which they may act. Thus the very process of organizing and the strategic distribution of objectives establish at the outset a set of bounds within which each manager may make decisions, or commit his subordinates to action.

Another boundary or limit within which a manager may make decisions is the amount of resources given to him—in money, people, things, and time. This is covered in somewhat more detail and from a different viewpoint in the next section on the decision-making process. But it is important to note that the resources given to a sales manager at any level absolutely limit his ability to act—and therefore render the decisions made outside this ability meaningless.

Delegation of Authority

Probably the most important limit [1] on decision making is the degree to which authority is delegated to the decision maker. Here we use the term *authority* as permission or the right to make decisions and act. By *delegation* we mean that the authority is given from above.[2] When a manager delegates some of his own authority, he literally gives it and entrusts it to another.

The degree to which authority is delegated down through the echelons of sales management varies widely from firm to firm and sometimes even within the selling operation of a single firm. It is not possible to flatly state how much authority should be delegated downward in the sales organization. Many variables must be considered in this equation:

1. *Always first in this consideration is the attainment of objectives.* How can the subunit best achieve them? How much latitude must its manager optimally have in his power to act?

2. *The degree of complexity* of the product and of the marketplaces is a factor. The more complex they are, the more power to act should probably be delegated. Probably more authority need be delegated to a

---

[1] The word "limit" does not necessarily mean that decision authority is narrow. The "limit" may be very wide in scope.

[2] This is viewing authority from the manager's viewpoint. But there is another crucial aspect of authority as it is viewed by subordinates. This is discussed in Chapter 18.

district manager for IBM's Data Processing Division than to a district manager for a statewide brewery.

3. *The diversity of selling situations* varies greatly. The greater the diversity faced by a sales manager, probably the greater authority should be delegated. For example, a regional sales for a machine tool company selling to many different types of customer industries probably needs more authority delegated than does a regional sales manager for a firm selling accounting forms to banks.

4. *The competitive situation* must be considered. If rivals aggressively maneuver strategically, hence if retaliatory strategies and tactics must be implemented quickly, probably more authority should be delegated to the sales manager in the field.

5. *Competency of management individuals* must be considered. Generally, the more competent the individual, the more authority can be entrusted to him.[3]

6. *Coordination* of the subunit with units outside sales may be a factor. When authority is delegated, the manager receiving it will act upon it in a variety of ways. If some of the ways in which he may legitimately act are apt to cause conflict with other organizational units, the delegation of authority may have to be tempered.

Authority and Accountability

Authority is not granted to subordinates willy-nilly. It is granted to better assure objective achievement by the subordinate unit. To further assure this end, the authority is always granted "with some strings attached." The manager to whom it is delegated is held *accountable* for the results he obtains with it. Here again is the intimate linkage to objectives. A headquarters sales manager may say to one of his regional sales managers: "I will give you the authority to cut prices, to meet a specific competitive price cut, but not to exceed three per cent." This is a delegation of authority. But explicitly or implicitly,[4] the regional

---

[3] This does not infer that *incompetent* individuals are in management positions. Here we are speaking of the competency to handle authority and to make effective decisions. This comes with experience, and, generally speaking, one would expect that sales management might "hold in the reins" for a while after appointing a young manager to his first management job and feed more authority to him as he "grows" in the job.

[4] The accountability is often implicit. This is all right, if it is identically perceived by both delegating manager and subordinate manager. Sometimes difficulties arise when it is not. However, in many "small" cases of delegation, the accountability can be implied. For example, a headquarters sales manager might say to a regional sales manager, "Jim, go ahead and work out this new discount structure with distributors as you see fit." Here it is *implied* that the "working it out" will be satisfactorily done, with no conflict arising.

manager must be held accountable for the use of this authority. The headquarters sales manager and the regional sales manager must each be able to say, after the use of the delegated authority: "What results were obtained? Did the decisions and actions help us get our objectives?" In a sense, therefore, delegation of authority widens the power of the sales manager to act, but the accountability for results in a sense tends to limit it. Put another way, a sales manager delegating decision-making authority to a subordinate can control or limit the scope or use of the authority by the measures of accountability that he places on the subordinate.

Two General Kinds of Decisions

Once a decision is made, and action ensues, it can never really be "undone," if the action proves to be inadequate. However, adjustments can be made, resulting in new actions which might move the unit closer to its objectives. But some "adjusting" decisions are easier to make than others and are more readily accepted than others.

To get at this, consider two very general kinds of decisions that a firm's management makes.[5] One class consists of those decisions (and resultant actions) that are *internally* oriented. That is, they are managerial decisions affecting only people *within the firm* and do not directly affect anything outside the firm. Examples: the sales manager changes the sales compensation plan; he reorganizes the warehouse inventory control group; he approves the purchase of Buicks rather than Chevrolets for regional managers; he establishes a new reporting procedure for competitive activities. All these decisions do affect the behavior of people within the organization and are meant to help move the selling operation closer to its goals.

The other class of decisions consists of those that are *externally* oriented. They are managerial decisions that affect perceptions and responses of people or groups *outside the firm*. They are decisions that affect strategies and tactics (behaviors) of sales persons vis-à-vis customers and vis-à-vis competitors. These crucial decisions will cause customers to react, favorably or unfavorably. They will cause rivals to react in retaliatory manner, defensively or aggressively. They are crucial because it is impossible to undo them.

Generally speaking, the internally oriented decisions are easier to adjust by making new decisions than are the externally oriented ones. This does not mean that internal decisions can be retracted without difficulty, antagonism, or even conflict. But the firm's internal environments are under some degree of control by management. Not so the

[5] Of course, this is only one of several ways in which decisions may be categorized.

external environments. When a sales department announces to customers a new discount structure, a new service policy, a new mode of delivery, or a new anything, it is almost impossible to completely undo the decision if it proves to be an unsatisfactory one. And if the sales management makes a decision against which a strong rival reacts with a retaliatory action with which the firm cannot live, the sales management finds itself in a very awkward position.

Therefore, of all the elements of the firm, it is probably the sales department whose managers most often find themselves in the most critical decision-making situations. This is true because so many of sales managers' decisions result in market actions. Add to this the fact that many of sales managers' decisions must be made almost "on the spot" because of market dynamics, and one quickly sees why these externally oriented decisions must be based on something more solid than hunch or intuitive reflex. This leads us, then, to the vital need for the sales managers close to the markets (customers and rivals) to develop and learn a logical framework of thinking for making decisions.

THE DECISION PROCESS

The logical analytical thought process by which a decision can be rationally selected is a series of relatively simple steps:

1. Consider objectives.
2. Identify and analyze problems or obstacles.
3. Develop alternative solutions.
4. Analyze and compare the solutions.
5. Make the choice (the "decision").
6. Evaluate results and adjust.

Each of these steps, which will be briefly discussed below, is a necessary element in the process. In making a decision, certain of the steps may have more importance in some situations than in other situations. Also, in some situations some of the steps may be taken almost for granted. For example, if only two alternative solutions are available, comparison and choice is a relatively simple subprocess.

The nature of the situation within which the decision is made affects the degree to which each of the steps can be developed. If a headquarters sales manager is contemplating a reorganization of the field sales structure, he may have a relatively long time (weeks, perhaps) in which to explore each step in depth. On the other hand, a district sales manager who, in the presence of the customer, unearths a severe competitive obstacle, may have to touch very lightly (and perhaps almost unconsciously) on each of the steps.[6] In either case, this process is a *way of thinking* which, if consistently used, will improve the effectiveness of decisions—*particularly those that must be made quickly.* Although in actual practice, especially in the tactical excitement of the marketplace, the steps in the decision process may merge into "a way of thinking," it is fruitful to learn it as a distinct set of steps, each of which has a rationale of its own.

Consider Objectives

Sales people are action-oriented. The field sales people in contact with customers and constantly brushed by rivals are particularly alert to problems that fly up in their faces and must be solved *now.* Effective sales people must be good tacticians, able to flex almost instantly with the flow of changing situations. But this can be a dilemma, because the very necessity for quick action may cause a fixation on the tactics themselves. That is, the solving of problems and obstacles may become an *end* unto itself—whereas problem solving really is only a *means* to an end.

In almost every selling situation, any one event is only one in a whole series of events. The solving of problems during one event sets the stage for the next event. *Important as the solving of a problem is, and important as the reaching of a decision for this moment is, the real and crucial question is: how does it advance the decision maker toward his end objectives?* Elementary as it seems, the constant consideration of one's objectives is often forgotten. As a result, problems are solved for their own sake, and the solution may or may not advance the decision maker toward his end objectives. This appears to be disturbingly prevalent in decision making and problem solving in field sales groups.

In Chapter 8, the proposal for creating a selling strategy for each customer focused strongly on the salesman's objectives. Objective orientation was threaded through the ensuing strategy. The key step in this rationale was the determining of "intermediate goals," or the stepping-

---

[6] Many competent sales training programs propose that a salesman, when he encounters an obstacle voiced by the customer, "spar" for a moment by a tactical response of rephrasing the obstacle or expressing his understanding of the obstacle. There are several reasons for this tactic, but an important one is to gain a moment of time so that one "segment" of his mind can flash through his alternative ways of coping with this obstacle. In essence, he goes through some process quite similar to that above in arriving at a tactical decision for coping with the obstacle. Of course, he cannot go deeply into each step, but even a quick and subconscious following of this learned rationale is a far cry from "counterpunching."

stones, or *missions,* to be accomplished one by one to reach the *end objectives.* These are the guiding beacons for action, and to be effective, decisions should be made in their light. As the salesman or the sales manager copes with momentary situations, consciously or unconsciously, a starting input into his decision thinking should be, "What is it I really want to accomplish? Or what ends must I focus?"

The difficulty here is a subtle one. For example, a district sales manager may observe (with legitimately grave concern) that a competitor is making inroads into his firm's good customers. He must react. But in his understandable competitive zeal, he may focus entirely on the problem, "How can I combat this competitor?" This is *not* an end. It is a *means* to some other end (as district sales volume, district market share, etc.). The decisions made for tactical reactions must be made with respect to end objectives, not with respect to the competitors. Of course, it may happen that decisions and actions focused on combating the competitor *might* fit the means-end chain toward the end objective—but they might not, and the sales manager might later find himself trying to undo his previous decisions.

Identification and Analysis of Problems

This step is self-explanatory, but again it is one with subtle overtones. An end decision can never be better (except by chance) than the clarity with which the problem to which the decision is aimed is defined. The key here is for the sales manager to take at least one step beyond the observing of a problem itself. His world is full of events that he observes. Some are problems, or obstacles. For example, he may observe that the sales volume achieved by the Mid-Central District is slipping, with respect to sales potential. This is a problem. But before corrective decisions are made, the problem must be analyzed. The sales manager must say to himself: "*Why* is this district slipping in its moving toward the objectives given it? What are the causes? Changing customer situations? Local competitive tactics? Performance of the district sales people? Quality of management? Inadequacy of service? Any lack of headquarters cooperation?"

Thus the sales manager goes through a *diagnostic* procedure before even beginning to devise solutions. This analytical step is often brushed over, with the result that sometimes the symptom is treated, rather than the cause. The force of this step lies in getting at the *cause* of what is observed.

The degree to which this diagnostic step is followed depends on the facts known and the time available. Harking back to the selling strategy of Chapter 8, here is another strong reason for fact gathering, because the more facts are available, the greater the facility of finding underlying causes for events. More time available also facilitates the diagnostic process, but this does not mean that this valuable tool cannot be used in fast-moving situations. It simply means that the "computer" in the sales manager's brain must scan quickly. And even in fast-moving situations, a sales manager who is aware of this process can often "hold up" the situation for a moment of time, to allow his "computer" to work.[7]

Develop Alternative Solutions

In this step the decision maker searches for alternative solutions. Usually, in any sales situation, a number of solutions or approaches will exist. No simple, "pat" method can be advanced for doing this. To mentally search for and find an array of alternative ways of solving a problem requires imagination and a completely open mind. Perhaps one deterring force that prevents a reasonably complete search is the premature evolution of the solutions as they are imagined or devised. That is, as soon as a "satisfactory" solution is conceived, it is selected, and the search for alternatives stops. Probably most sales-situation decisions are made this way. This is not necessarily bad. After all, a "satisfactory" solution is reached, and the decision should "work." But this premature evaluation and selection may prevent the decision maker from reaching a "better" decision. Ideally, therefore, the decision maker strives to develop as many alternatives as possible without evaluating each one.

For example, assume that a sales manager learns that a competitor suddenly is offering to key customers a consigned stock.[8] He may say: "Bad. We must retaliate some way, or we'll lose business. What can we do? Well, we can do nothing, and appeal to the customer to remember all the service we've given him. [This is alternative number one.] But this probably wouldn't work. [Here the sales manager has made an evaluation.] Or, we could offer these customers a better-quantity discount structure making it a better deal to buy from us. [This is alter-

---

[7] For example, in a face-to-face situation with a customer in which a competitive problem arises, he might say, "There's something here that perplexes me, Mr. Customer, and I'd like your advice about it. Can we explore it for a minute?" And meanwhile, his "computer" goes to work.

[8] In "consigning" stock, the firm places a stock of the products on the customer's premises, but retains title. The customer can take what he wants from this consigned stock when he wants it. He then notifies the firm what he has used, and the firm bills him for it. This strategy makes it easy and less costly for the customer to buy and reduces delivery time to essentially zero.

native number two.] This should work, and serve notice to competitor that we'll fight his tactics where it hurts—in price. Let's do it. [Here he has again evaluated, and has made a decision.]" But having found what he believes to be a "satisfactory" decision (and it may be), he now blocks his mind from conceiving other possible solutions. Some of the alternatives could be the following: also offer consigned stock; revamp stock levels in local warehouse to assure eight-hour delivery time; or propose a "blanket order" arrangement—the customer places one order for his estimated use over time and regular deliveries of so many per day or week are made, unless he changes the schedule (by telephone) — which thus relieves the sales manager of the "paperwork" that consigned stocks entail. Perhaps in the end his previous solution of changed discounts turns out to be the best choice, but perhaps not. Ideally, he should consider *all* the alternatives he can imagine before evaluation and choice.

Analyze and Compare the Solutions

After a battery of alternatives are developed, each must be analyzed and evaluated before the "best" one can be selected. In this subprocess of decision making, a number of considerations are necessary:

1. Identify *all* consequences.
2. Measure against constraints.
3. Compare the advantages and disadvantages of each set of consequences.
4. Focus on major considerations.
5. Consider other units of the firm.
6. Consider short-range versus long-range implications.
7. Consider capability to adjust.

1. Identify All Consequences. This is a vital step. Here the decision maker must say to himself, "If I implement this decision, what are all the things which *could* happen?" He projects himself into the future, and again must use imagination to conceive all possible results. Here, of course, he is identifying all the things that *could* happen, not necessarily those that *will* happen. This introduces the idea of *probability*. Thus the decision maker might say to himself: "If I choose this alternative, there are three possible consequences. I would say there is about a ninety percent chance of the first happening, about a fifty percent chance for the second, and perhaps a ten percent chance of the third." [9]

[9] This is a simple and naïve example, but it is the way in which many "quick" tactical decisions in sales must be made. If very important, major decisions are

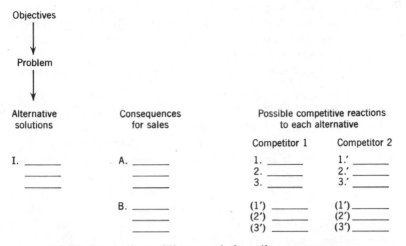

FIGURE 11-1   The search for *all* consequences.

This search for *all* consequences is particularly vital for the "external" sales decisions that will cause reactions in the marketplaces. Here, not only must all the direct consequences for the firm be unearthed—but also *all the possible reactions of customers and rivals must be imagined.* This can be seen in Figure 11-1. Putting this chart in narrative form, the sales manager might think in this manner:

> "I see an obstacle, a problem in the field, blocking us from reaching our objectives. Let me search for alternative solutions. We can come up with possible solutions I, II, and III. [For simplicity, only solution I is shown in Figure 11-1.] Now, I will consider first alternative I, and imagine all the consequences which could occur if we do this. There are two, A and B."

At this point, the decision maker could move on to alternative II and conceive its various possible consequences, then move to alternative III, and so on. However, in sales decisions, before leaving alternative I and its consequences, the sales manager should reason as follows:

---

made, for which some amount of time is available for analysis (example: changing an entire price structure) , the identifying of consequences, the assigning of probabilities, and the rational choice can be done on a more formal basis. Then the new techniques of "decision making under risk and uncertainty" can be employed. See Suggested Readings at the end of this chapter. But the major point is that the *rationale* of this technique can be used by the sales manager even on a quick, informal basis.

"But if I *were* to choose alternative I, and if consequence A *did* occur, it would be observed by competitors. They would have to react *some* way. How do I *think* they *could* react? [10] Well, I think competitor 1 might react to A in one of three ways; 1, 2, or 3. And I think competitor 2 might react to A also in three ways: 1', 2', or 3'."

Here is the great game of chess, or poker, or "war" which is played in the marketplaces. Even when quite informally done, as above, the consideration of competitive reactions to each consequence of every alternative *may flush out possible competitive retaliations which the firm might find it extremely difficult to live with*—or extremely difficult to adjust to. If this is true, *this alternative must be marked as suspect even though its consequences to the firm look attractive on the surface.* The sales manager now goes to alternative II (not shown in Figure 11-1), and repeats the process. He is not yet *choosing* an alternative—he is *analyzing and evaluating* each one.[11]

One more step can be taken in this line of reasoning (not shown in Figure 11-1). For *each* of the possible competitive reactions, the sales manager could ask himself: "*If* they reacted this way, what would be *our* possible alternative 're-reactions'? How could we respond to each of their possible retaliations?" And again, this is a search to be sure no alternative is selected and decision made that would "paint the firm in a corner" with no way to escape.

This presents an interesting strategic concept. For a moment, move over to the position of sales manager of Competitive Firm 1. He sees our firm implement alternative I, and sees consequence A begin to happen. He must react some way. This is *his* problem, and he begins *his* search for alternatives and consequences. He may come up with alternatives 1, 2, and 3 (which may or may not coincide with our predictions). As he considers the consequences to *his* firm for each alternative, he might think this way: "As I weigh each of these consequences for each alternative retaliation, which one provides the greatest embarrassment for that

---

[10] These predictions of possible competitive reactions must be estimates, of course, based on the sales manager's knowledge of rivals' past strategies and actions and their present capabilities. This is a strong point balking the need for an effective market-intelligence system.

[11] Here again, a higher level of sophistication can be achieved by adding not only the *probability* of each consequence, but also the probability of each competitive reaction. Obviously, if possible reaction 3 of competitor 1 is a very serious one, but has only a very, very faint chance of occurring, and if consequence A is an extremely attractive one for the firm, alternative I may be evaluated highly. But if this competitive reaction is very serious and promises great difficulty for the firm, and if it has a relatively *high* probability of occurring, the attractiveness of consequence A is offset significantly and alternative I receives a lower evaluation.

firm who started this? How can we move so that he is in an untenable position and will suffer whatever he does to respond to our retaliatory strategy?" In our evaluating process, therefore, we must give the rival sales manager credit for being this perceptive and try, therefore, to flush out all such possible moves on his part.

2. Measure Against Constraints. As each alternative solution and its consequences are conceived, each must be evaluated against two sorts of constraints.[12] First, the feasibility of the consequences must be checked. If the consequences of a given alternative are clearly not feasible, the alternative can at this point be discarded. For example, in one of the foregoing examples, if the sales manager comes up with an alternative of changing discounts to combat a competitor's consigned stock strategy and then determines that such an action is in violation of, say, the Robinson Patman Act, he can immediately brand the alternative as not feasible and eliminate it.

Another set of constraints is the limits or boundaries within which the sales manager is *capable* of acting. An alternative and its consequences may be feasible for their own sake, but outside the boundaries of the sales manager's ability to act. The array of possible actions he can take is limited by the resources (men, money, and "things") that have been given to him. For each alternative he must ask himself, "Do I have the resources to do this?" If he does not, the alternative must be discarded. Furthermore, the sales manager has limits on authority to act. He must ask himself, "Do I have the authority to make this decision?" If not, he must request a higher level of management to make the decision. If this is not feasible because of time or other internal factors, the alternative must be discarded. Also, each alternative must be measured against policy. That is, the sales manager must ask himself: "Granted this alternative is feasible, and I have the resources and authority. But does it 'fit' us? Is it within our policy to behave this way?" If a "no" answer emerges, probably the alternative should be discarded.[13]

3. Compare Advantages and Disadvantages of Each Set of Consequences. For those alternatives that remain in the "feasible" category, the sales manager now lists the advantages and disadvantages of each set

---

[12] It can be argued that this step should precede the foregoing analysis. Either sequence, or even a blend of the steps, is all right, so long as the reasoning of each step is cleanly and clearly set apart.

[13] For example, Marshall Field or Nieman Marcus *could* have retaliated against the discount operators by reacting in kind and going into a discount strategy. However, this alternative did not "fit" the image these great stores wanted to protect. The alternative was *feasible* but not *desirable*.

of consequences. Again, this may be a very formal and explicit analysis if the decision is a major one and if time is available, or it may have to be a quick mental analysis. In a way, the various consequences themselves for any alternative may be placed in either an "advantage" or a "disadvantage" category. For example, in the previous example in which the sales manager is searching for a decision to cope with a competitor's consigned stock strategy, he may list the consequences of each alternative as either advantageous (moving toward the objectives) or disadvantageous (moving away from or threatening objectives). Thus for the alternative, "Reduce discount structures," he might list consequences as follows:

Alternative 2: Reduce Discounts

Advantages	*Disadvantages*
1. Serves notice on competitor	1. Decreased revenue, if quantity increase does not outweigh "price" decrease
2. Shows customer we want his business	
3. Prevents loss of business to competitor; holds market share	2. May start a "price war" with other competitors
4. Leaves inventory levels where we want them	3. Illegal unless given to all competing customers—but competitor has consigned stock to all of them
	4. May cause problems in other distribution channels

The items in both columns are possible outcomes, or consequences, arranged as advantages or disadvantages. Other evaluations of the alternative are suggested in the sections that follow, but on the basis of outcomes alone the sales manager can at this point place the advantages against the disadvantages. If the latter obviously outweigh the former, the alternative *can* be discarded at this point.

Parenthetically, if after completing the rest of the decision process, this alternative is chosen, the sales manager will want to return to this step and reexamine the disadvantages. Preparing defenses against them will be an essential part of his strategy. This step, therefore, has the additional value of minimizing the rude surprises that could shake him.

4. Focus on Major Considerations. For many alternatives, a host of consequences, both advantageous and disadvantageous, may be possible. Somewhere in their devising, the sales manager must draw a line and say, "This possible outcome is not a significant one." For example, one advantage that could have been included above might be, "Less paper work for headquarters than by also consigning stock." This may be true, but its value as an advantage is very small. The sales manager must "weigh" the possible outcomes and to some extent rank them in relative importance. It is the major or significantly important outcomes that should significantly evaluate the alternative. For example, the "disadvantageous" outcome of "may start a price war" might be highly significant to the sales manager and more than overbalance several lesser "advantages." Here is still another reason why it is so crucial in decision making to *search* not only for alternatives but also for all the consequences that the situation permits.

5. **Consider Other Units of the Firm.** Often decisions made by sales management will have effect on other units of the firm. If the formal coordinating process (discussed in Chapter 10) places certain restrictions on the sales manager, such limitations should have been considered when listing his constraints. But lacking formal coordination, the sales manager may often find it meaningful to consider what could be the inputs to other units of each of his alternatives and what possible reactions might be triggered. In a sense this is "voluntary coordination." But from a completely rational point of view, now is the time to evaluate each alternative with respect to its impact on and response by other organizational units. For example, a decision to change regional warehouse inventory levels (which may be completely within the sales manager's authority) might at a particular time put stress on the production scheduling functions. At least, the sales manager should "crank in" this possibility as he weighs the alternatives.

6. **Consider Short-Range versus Long-Range Implications.** A problem or an obstacle existing at the present moment must be dealt with. If a competitor makes a move that threatens a firm's position in any way, the firm must react. Yet sometimes the "best" action for this moment may not be the best action "for the long haul." Usually a selling operation will have one set of immediate, short-range goals and another set of longer-range objectives.[14] How the short-range goal is achieved *may* have a bearing on how later the longer-range objective is achieved. *Actions that effectively achieve short-range goals may not be compatible with long-range objective achievement.* Perhaps they may have to be taken anyway, but as a minimum the sales manager must do so knowingly with his eyes wide open. But it may be that another alternative, perhaps slightly less desirable for the immediate action, is significantly

---

[14] Definitions of "long-range" and "short-range" depend on the firm. Usually even "long-range" in sales is not too far out in the future. But sales managers realize that what they do in the market today can have very definite bearings on the situations they will face next year with the same customers and competitors.

better meshed with long-range objectives, hence in total is a better choice.

As a very simple example, consider the regional sales manager's problem when he receives a directive from higher headquarters to reduce his expense allocation by some certain percentage for the balance of the year.[15] He may have a variety of alternatives for complying: discharge a salesman; discharge some clerical people; close a district office; require salesmen to travel less; reduce salesmen's customer-entertainment expense; prohibit use of long-distance telephone; and so on. As he considers each of these alternatives in the light of its effectiveness at the moment, he must also say: "But what effect will this alternative have on our potential business next year? If I reduce the sales force, I can easily meet the new expense target. But on the other hand, this will spread us thin, and reduce our customer contact, and over time our competition will surely gain on us."

Even for the spur-of-the-moment decisions made in the presence of the customer, this short-range, long-range balance needs to be considered, even if only in a fleeting moment. Thinking back to the sales strategy of Chapter 8, the means-end concept of the "intermediate goal" step provides help here. At a given moment, the salesman (or sales manager) is seeking to achieve a specific mission which is a *means* to some further end.[16] As he must tactically choose from alternative approaches or responses, his eye must be not only on today's mission, but tomorrow's and the next day's, in the rationally determined "tree" of events ahead. This is similar to the old military adage: "We aren't here just to win battles—we want to win the war." It is probably uncomfortably true that in the hurly-burly of the competitive market world, a sales manager may focus so closely on today's battle that he may have trouble winning the longer-range war.[17]

7. Consider Capability to Adjust. In a way, this overlaps some of the thinking of step 1. But here, in a more specific way, the sales manager must say, for each remaining alternative and its set of consequences: "If I choose this alternative, and commit action to it, can I still adjust it, or change it, or make some new adjusting decisions? Or, if I commit to it, am I 'stuck' with it?" It would be naïve to believe that for a given alternative, every reaction to it within the sales organization, within the

---

[15] This is not an uncommon event.

[16] Even the end of getting an order or a contract is not a finality, but a step in beginning the progress toward the next order or contract.

[17] This is still another reason that demonstrates the urgent need for planning of the sort described in Chapter 8.

firm, from customers, and from competitors will be *exactly* as predicted. Most decisions and ensuing actions, however good, will require some degree of tactical adjustment. Ideally, the decision chosen and its ensuing action should not "tie the hands" of the sales manager, but leave him wide latitude for tactical maneuvering via new, adjusting decisions. If an attractive alternative does promise to "set the sales manager in concrete" for some period of time, some of its attractiveness wanes. If enough attractiveness wanes because of this confinement of future behavior, the "next best" alternative may become the most attractive. At the risk of overgeneralizing, any decision and ensuing action that takes away the sales manager's freedom to act tactically in the marketplaces are detrimental to sales effectiveness. Obviously, many decisions must be made that will do just that, to some degree. But, certainly, the sales manager's *own* decisions should as a minimum take account of this important concept.

Make the Choice

Having followed the decision process, the sales manager can now find that the choice of the "best" alternative is easier, but more important and more likely to really be the best solution. This becomes his decision.

In this last step, he assigns a final value to each alternative. Again, he links the alternatives back to the objectives, both short- and long-range. In a way, this closes the ring. The whole *raison d'être* for the sales manager's group is the optimum achievement of objectives. To reach these objectives, many things must be done and many means must be employed. These individual things, and means, each require a small strategy, set of tactics, and decisions. They are very important, because their successive achievements will facilitate the end-objective achievement. But they are always *means* to the end and, therefore, always must be related to the end. The most ideal decision for one of these intermediate steps is not necessarily the one that best achieves it; it is the one that achieves it in a way that best facilitates movement *toward the end goal*.

As an example, assume that one of the *means* that a sales manager has set for himself to gain an end objective of "increased market share" is "to remain competitive in the eyes of customers." This is clearly a *means* to an end or objective. Now assume that a competitor reduces price by 5 percent, and the firm is no longer "price-competitive." One alternative solution could be to meet this competitive move by also reducing the price 5 percent. Now, this unquestionably "solves" the problem of price

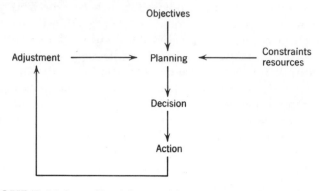

FIGURE 11-2   Decision making as a part of a total process.

competition, but may not move toward the end objective of market share at all. In fact, it *could* move away from it. Hence, though valid for its own sake, this decision may not be the best one for end-objective achievement, *which is the real target.*[18] In this case, perhaps another way of "remaining competitive" might be a better solution.

In final summary, the purpose of the decision process is to generate actions that will move a group toward its end objectives. It is a vital cog in the larger process, as shown in Figure 11-2. Given a set of objectives, the sales manager creates plans to achieve them, within the limits of the constraints and resources given him. Using the decision process, he implements the plans and commits his group to action. He observes the resulting action and its effectiveness in moving the group toward its objectives. If the action is "off target" in any way, he adjusts the action (develops new, different action) by planning strategic shifts and implementing them by new decisions. Thus decision making is not an isolated managerial action, but one element in a dynamic behavioral system. Therefore, all the steps in the decision process itself must have a focus on this greater action-process.

POLICY

Consider this situation. A district sales manager, working in his office, receives a telephone call from one of his salesmen. The salesman de-

---

[18] Of course, it *could* be the best. All we are saying is that the "best" solution for meeting a problem situation per se is not *necessarily* the *"best"* decision for the achievement of end objectives.

scribes a situation with one of his customers and states that, as part of his strategy, he wants to invite the purchasing agent to visit one of the firm's plants with him. The sales manager asks for an estimate of the expense, and the salesman replies, "Seventy-five dollars." [19] The sales manager approves the expense.

Later in the morning, another salesman calls with a similar request— he feels it necessary that three customer engineering people visit with the firm's engineers, on a product proposal that the salesman is making. Asked for an expense estimate, the salesman replies, "Four hundred dollars." The sales manager disapproves the request and says that he will call the firm's engineering management to see if they will send an engineer to visit the customer.

In the afternoon, still another salesman requests approval for taking one of his customer's operating people to a plant to observe the firm's quality control system. Expense is estimated at $100, and the sales manager approves the proposal.

Now, for each of these situations, the sales manager and the salesman have had to spend valuable time to reach a decision. Each occasion requires planning and explanation on the part of the salesman, who may have spent several hours mapping out the strategy even before calling his manager. For each disapproval, the sales manager must provide explanation, and ideally should help the salesman find an acceptable alternative.

But when the sales manager sees that a certain kind of situation keeps repeating and that his decision process is essentially the same for each occasion, he may reason to himself this way:

> "Each time this situation comes up I find I am using the same criteria to reach a decision. It hangs on the expense. I realize that in at least ninety percent of cases, I will approve if the cost does not exceed one hundred dollars per $10,000 of order-value. Therefore, why go through all this fuss? I will put out a letter to all salesmen, telling them they no longer need my approval for customer visits to plants, if the expense is not over this limit. If it is over these amounts, we will look at each case on its merits, and I will make the decision."

The sales manager has established a *policy*. In this case, he has made *one, lasting decision that will have effect for all future identical situa-*

tions. Here, then, a policy is actually a *decision* that will remain in effect until it is changed.

Other meanings are attached to the term "policy" and should be noted to avoid semantic confusion. Often policy is very broadly described as "the basic guidelines within which management must operate." In this sense, policy acts as a constraining influence or a control device. Thus a firm's top management may stipulate that "It is our policy to act with integrity in all our relations with customers, employees, suppliers, and the general public." The "policy" here is meant to be an *influence on the behavior* of persons in the firm. And "policy" is used this way, probably necessarily.

In another sense, management may use the term "policy" almost synonymously with "objective." Thus they may state, "It is our policy to always retain a favorable brand image." Or, "It is our policy to be a leader in this industry." Here not only are guidelines set and behavior influenced, but a target is established.

Sales management itself may use the policy concept in these ways. But perhaps the most fruitful way for field sales management to regard and use policy is as a *decision* device. In the helter-skelter of the marketplace with its complex web of changing situations, the sales manager could be completely bogged down in a swamp of a thousand minor decisions. He can delegate the authority to make some of them. But even for those that he feels he must retain, he might have to spend a disproportionate share of his time and effort. Policy as a decision tool may give him an answer. The key is to find patterns of problems, within each of which *common situations and common criteria* exist. One lasting decision can be made for these common situations. In this case, when a district manager says, "In this district, it will be our policy to do so-and-so in such-and-such a situation," he has used *policy as a decision and has arrived at this policy precisely as he would for any decision.*

Valuable as it is as a decision tool, policy does have some pitfalls. For one thing, an inertia effect may occur. Once established, it often seems to be difficult to change a policy. It may get "lost" in the welter of activity.[20] Furthermore, subordinates get "tuned in" to a policy, its directed behavior becomes *learned behavior,* and even after the policy is

---

[20] In some firms, one often hears the statement, "Policies are made to be broken." Feeling hemmed in by some policy, managers, it is said, sometimes to achieve what they want, must strategically maneuver around the policy, or "beat the system," as it were. This is ridiculous. It means that some old policy, once valid, is no longer meaningful. It may even cause the manager to question some valid policies. Policies should always be under scrutiny and should be swept out as soon as effectiveness is the least bit diminished.

changed, individuals may *tend* to follow the old, learned behavioral path.[21] When a sales manager sets a policy, he should recognize that he may have some difficulty when he changes or rescinds it.

Another difficulty is the problem of so communicating policy that it is perceived by the subordinates precisely as meant by the sales manager. In clean-cut situations, such as the example cited above, this perceptual difficulty may not occur. But in many cases, "policy" can be a rather fuzzy thing and may be perceived differently by different people. Hence their behavior, legitimate in their own eyes, may be quite different from that intended.

The existence of too many policies can be detrimental to the behavior of subordinates. If the sales manager has announced a policy for "this," a policy for "that," another for still something else, and so on, subordinates may begin to *imagine* policies. They may take certain modes of behavior which are not really wanted by management.

Yet in spite of potential difficulties, the concept of policy as a *predetermined and lasting decision* is a valuable decision tool for the sales manager.

SOME CONCLUDING COMMENTS

A selling operation achieves results by *doing* things. It is an action-oriented operation, centered on the *behavioral* actions of its people. For these actions to be optimally effective, the generating or influencing force back of them must be well conceived and executed. All this puts great value on the effectiveness of decisions—the generating and committing of forces for action.

In this chapter we have proposed that the authority to make decisions can be delegated. In most firms, this is true at least to some degree. Certainly sales managers are in a part of the firm's world where actions must flex often, hence decisions must be made frequently. Probably no element of the firm faces so many changing and uncontrollable environments than does the selling operation. Whatever the philosophy and style of delegation, sales management must and does rely heavily on the validity of its managers' decisions.

But there is no special magic in decision making. It is a rational, logical thought process that can be learned. Once learned, it can be a "way of thinking," a framework that can be used, even unconsciously, in reaching a solution to problems or obstacles.

---

[21] Chapters 13 and 14 explore the psychological bases for this.

This leads to another philosophy which is threaded through this chapter. It is likely that most major, very important decisions receive close attention and are rationally and objectively approached. Many persons may be consulted; many alternatives may be weighed; plenty of time is allowed. On the other hand, for every major topside decision of this sort, thousands of day-by-day decisions are made in the rush-rush, bang-bang of the marketplaces—by salesmen and by field sales managers. No one or even several of these decisions is going to make or break the firm. Yet they may make or threaten the planned goals for a local sales office. And *collectively,* throughout the firm's entire selling operation, they may in a summation have very real effect on the firm's success in its markets. The smallest, most momentary decision made in the marketplaces cannot, therefore, be taken lightly. *Every decision should be seriously regarded.* The fact that some decisions must truly be made in almost a reflexive way, almost as a counterpunch, does not reject the concept of this decision-making process. Actually it demands that the process be used. To be sure, time will rarely be available for its formal, paper-and-pencil application. Rather, the sales manager must learn it and internalize it. Like the concept of "defensive driving," it becomes an almost unconscious "program" shaping the sales manager's response.

QUESTIONS AND PROBLEMS

1. What are the pros and cons of delegating authority?
2. Can you think of any kinds of decisions that probably should not be delegated below headquarters sales management level?
3. You are a regional sales manager for a small appliance manufacturer. Your eight sales districts focus on distributors. At your regional level you have a small sales group assigned to "direct sales"—selected large retailers, electric utilities, and so on. You have a significantly higher sales budget and a somewhat lower expense budget to achieve for the coming year, and you are considering the efficacy of your present organization structure. Using some imagination, show how the six-step decision process can be used.
4. You are a headquarters sales manager. You get word from your field sales management that one of your competitors is cutting price and that your firm is losing business to him. How many different alternative reactions can you think of that could be used? What do you think are the pros and cons of each?

12

Evaluating and Controlling the Selling Effort

On a foggy day not long ago, the control tower at a large municipal airport flashed a radio message to the pilot of an inbound private aircraft that he was dangerously low in his approach, and that he needed to flatten his glide. The aircraft promptly responded and landed safely. This is the idea of *control*—the process that detects deviation from the course leading to a target, and makes the necessary correction to come back on course.

The idea of control is indispensable to the effective sales manager. It has two meanings which must be clearly differentiated. In one sense, it is used quite synonymously with "directing"—that is, commanding, or ordering, or imposing demands on another's behavior. In another sense, however, "controlling" is the process that determines if and how a group's (or individual's) actions deviate from the course toward its objectives and provides the necessary corrective actions to come back on course.

This concept of control is particularly valuable for the sales manager —especially the field sales manager—because of its strategic-tactical notion of adjustive or compensating action. Field sales is a set of activities going on in a milieu of changing forces. It would be naïve to believe that sales management in its planning process can plot a course toward sales goals and always find movement on that course straight and

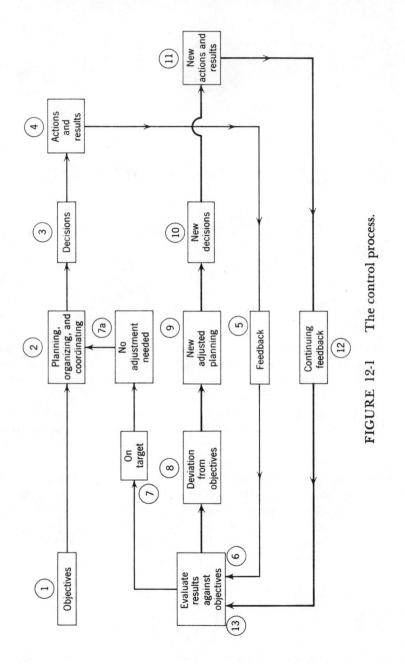

FIGURE 12-1   The control process.

true. As groups and individuals act to follow the plan, customers react in diverse ways. Rivals react, often in less than perfectly predicted ways. To keep zeroing in on the sales goals, strategic and tactical adjustments must be made. The concept of control provides a mechanism for achieving such adjustment effectively. The control process has several inseparable elements: [1]

1. An established goal, a plan to reach the goal, and implementation of actions.

2. A mechanism or device that *evaluates* the action with respect to progress toward the goal. This is "feedback," which specifies deviations from the target course.

3. Corrective action, to adjust actions to comeback on target course. Figure 12-1 shows this process schematically. To trace through the logic of the process, consider a district sales manager as he views the operation of his district: [2]

1. The district sales manager has a number of *objectives* for his district. One, for example, may be an annual total sales volume of $950,000.

2. He devises a number of *plans* of action to achieve the goal. Also, he may adjust the *organization*—for example, he may shift territories or change sales assignments. Furthermore, he assures *coordination* between his sales people and others in the organization.

3. He implements all his plans of action by making specific *decisions* and issuing directives.

4. *Action* ensues. The salesmen implement the plans and decisions. Specific *results* occur.

5. Information about these results flows to the district sales manager through *feedback* mechanisms.

6. The district sales manager now *evaluates* this information. That is, in the sense of "how are we doing," he measures the results against the objective—or against some set of performance standard equivalent to the objective.[3]

---

[1] Many physical systems analogies can be found. For example, in a NASA moon shot, the missle is tracked ("evaluated"); the slightest deviation from preplanned course is detected and described to Gemini Control, where scientists compute the necessary adjusting correction and "command" the missile to so adjust.

[2] The numbers in the following sequence correspond to those in Figure 12-1.

[3] For example, assume that on April 5 he receives from the accounting department a quarterly sales report, showing that in the period January 1 through March 31 his district had book orders totaling $200,000. This *result* is measured against the objective of an *annual* volume of $950,000. The *evaluation* indicates that his

7. If the results indicate that all is well, that the district is *on target* toward its objective, no *adjustment* of plans and actions is needed.[4]

8. On the other hand, if the evaluation shows a *deviation from objectives,* the district sales manager is alerted that all is not well and that something needs to be done.

9. He, therefore, must *adjust* his plans (and perhaps, in extreme cases, his organization). Or he must create *new programs for action,* taking into account the deviation and the estimated reasons for it.

10. *New decisions* are made and *new directives* are given.

11. Salesmen follow these directives and implement the new plans of action. Their "new" actions bring *new results.*

12. The continuing feedback process provides new inputs to the district sales manager.

13. Again, he evaluates the "new" results against the objective, to determine if the deviation has been corrected.

Thus the *control process* is not unlike a radar, sweeping the course to be followed and flashing back the degree and amount of deviations— together with a gyroscope that shifts or adjusts the district back on course.

LINK TO THE OTHER MANAGERIAL PROCESSES

It was proposed at the outset of this book that the "managerial process" is *not* a set of discrete, sequential steps. The process can perhaps be better understood by analyzing it, that is, by breaking it down into the subprocesses of objective setting, planning, organizing, coordinating, decision making, and controlling. But none of these subprocesses occurs in a vacuum. Each involves the others; each has impact on the others.

The sales manager must have an eye toward the subsequent control process as he considers each of the others. As he devises objectives, or missions to be assigned to his subordinates, he should consider how the specific missions can be measured—or how they can be translated into performance standards against which results can be feasibly measured.

district is falling far short of target goal, in that after three months it is securing orders at an annual rate of only $800,000. (This assumes a straight-line relation between orders and time, with no traditional "seasonal" fluctuations in demand.)

4 For example, if the quarterly sales report indicated sales for the first quarter of $250,000 (instead of $200,000 as in footnote 3), or an *annual rate* of $1,000,000, the district sales manager could say, "We are on target," and would not need to make any corrective adjustments. (Note, however, the ensuing discussion of the "iceberg principle" and of the "box-car trap.")

As he creates plans of action to achieve the objectives, he should imagine what kinds of actions might ensue from these plans and whether such actions are in fact capable of measuring and evaluating against the objectives—so that deviations can be detected. As he makes decisions and issues directives to implement the plans, he should imagine how action stemming from these directives will lend itself to evaluating. As he provides methods or systems of feedback of information, he should be certain that the feedback will in fact reliably detect and measure deviations from the target course. Thus the control process must be an input to the development of each of the other managerial processes, and not an afterthought tacked on after all other elements have been determined.

IMPORTANCE OF THE FEEDBACK SYSTEM

The mechanisms of the feedback system cannot be left to chance, or built in a makeshift way as a last resort. They must be rational, planned, and built in at the outset of the overall process. That is, even as a district sales manager considers his objectives and alternative plans and actions, he should also consider for each alternative set of plans and actions the kind of information needed to evaluate them, in what forms it should be, and how it will be obtained.

EVALUATING AND CONTROLLING SALES UNITS

One of the worst things a sales manager faces is the uncertain, uneasy feeling that all is not well. Equally disturbing is his *knowing* that all is not well, but not knowing what to do to correct the situation. The ability to evaluate and control the performance of sales units eliminates this dilemma and helps the sales unit to stay "on the track." The first step in doing this will usually be an *analysis* of the information on performance coming back from the feedback channels.

Sales Analysis

The most vital set of data returning to the sales manager as information on performance is that for actual sales. By and large, it is *actual sales* that are the prime objective of any sales group.[5] If actual sales are on target, all is well in the minds of sales managers. If actual sales are

5 Refer to Chapter 6. This bold statement does not mean that other objectives, and longer-range objectives, are not important. They are.

not on target, sales managers begin adjustive, corrective action.

Yet the evaluation is not this simple in most cases. *"Box-car" (or aggregate) figures may be very misleading and may cover up serious deficiencies in performance that need corrective action.* The raw data on sales usually must be *analyzed*—that is, broken down into various elements and subelements—before the sales manager can evaluate the sales performance with any degree of accuracy.

Consider, for example, a company marketing a varied line of electrical apparatus products to the electric utility industry. Assume that the sales department has as a prime objective a sales quota for the year of $65 million. Assume also that the quota for the first six months, ending June 30, is $30 million. Now, further assume that on July 6 the national field sales manager receives a budget report from accounting stating that actual sales in the first six months were $31 million—comfortably over the six months' objectives.

Does this indicate satisfactory performance? Perhaps it does, *but perhaps it does not.* Assume now that the sales manager does not leap to any conclusion, but *begins to analyze the sales results.* He asks for and gets a breakdown of the actual sales by sales regions, as shown in Table 12-1.

TABLE 12-1   Total Sales Received, by Region,

First Six Months, 19— (All Dollars × 1,000)

Region	Quota	Actual	Budget	Realization (Percent)
New England	5,000	5,500	+500	+10
Atlantic	6,000	5,700	−300	− 5
Central	8,000	8,600	+600	+ 8
Southern	3,000	3,100	+100	+ 3
Rocky Mountain	1,000	1,400	+400	+40
Western	7,000	6,700	−300	− 4
Total	30,000	31,000	+1,000	+ 3

This analysis, breaking down total sales into regional sales, throws a different light on sales performance. Two of the six regions—the second and third in rank among the regions with respect to quota—have clearly unsatisfactory performance. Atlantic is 5 percent off quota, and Western is 4 percent off. The actual dollar deficiency for these two regions is $600,000—*an amount equal to 5 percent of the total company sales budget.*

The analysis cannot stop here, of course. At this point, although *overall* sales performance looks quite satisfactory (3 percent over budget), the performance in two regions is less than satisfactory. Management attention may now be zeroed in on each of these regions and the questions asked: "Why is this region below quota? What can be done to correct it?" Before the second, "corrective" question can be rationally answered, the first one must be—and to do so, further analysis must be made.

For example, sales for the Atlantic Region may be analyzed (broken down) by district sales offices (Table 12-2).

TABLE 12-2   Total Sales Received, by Sales District,

Atlantic Region, First Six Months, 19—
(All Dollars × 1,000)

District	Quota	Actual	Budget	Realization (Percent)
New York	2,000	1,960	− 20	− 2
Philadelphia	1,500	1,240	−260	−18
Baltimore	1,400	1,410	+ 10	+ 1
Atlanta	1,100	1,090	− 10	− 5
Total	6,000	5,700	−300	− 5

It is clear from this analysis that the Baltimore and Atlanta districts are essentially on target. New York District is off a bit, although not seriously.[6] But it is obvious that something is seriously amiss in the performance of the Philadelphia District.

Now the spotlight of managerial attention has further narrowed its focus. But the analytical process is not yet finished. The Philadelphia District sales can be analyzed, by individual sales territories. It may well be that the deviation from quota may be traced to one or a very few sales territories. This brings the analysis down to the individual sales-man, *focusing the need for corrective action on the spot where it is needed.*

Analysis by Product Line. The above analysis of sales (for evaluating purposes) is based on a geographical breakdown. Another way in which total volume can be analyzed is by *product line.* Again, consider the headquarters sales manager in the same company, as he views the sales report for the first six months, stating that actual sales were $31 million against a budgeted quota of $30 million. Is this *really* a good enough

6 See later discussion on the limits of deviation which can be tolerated.

performance? What about the performance on the *individual product lines* that make up this total? What will be his evaluation and his focus for corrective action for individual product lines? Assume that he asks for and gets the additional sales data shown in Table 12-3, analyzing the

TABLE 12-3   Total Sales Received, by Product Line,

First Six Months, 19— (All Dollars $\times$ 1,000)

Product Line	Quota	Actual	Budget	Realization (Percent)
Distribution transformers	10,000	11,500	+1,150	+15
Substations	8,000	8,600	+ 600	+ 8
Capacitors	5,000	4,900	− 100	− 2
Watt-hour meters	7,000	6,000	−1,000	−14
Total	30,000	31,000	+1,000	+ 3

total volume reviewed by *product line*. The analysis is very revealing. Sales results have been excellent for two product lines—distribution transformers and substations. One product line, capacitors, is slightly off, but not seriously. However, one product line, watt-hour meters, is drastically and alarmingly off and obviously needs corrective action.[7]

The analysis may now be deepened by a combination of product line and territory. For example, the watt-hour-meter product lines alone can be analyzed by sales district, to see if the below-quota performance is general in all districts (leading to one set of possible corrective actions) or if it is primarily restricted to one or two districts (leading to a different set of corrective actions).

Analysis by Customer Categories. A third way to analyze sales, in addition to analysis by geographical units and product lines, is by customer categories. This may take several forms. The sales manager can request sales data broken down by:

Individual customers
Key customers
Customer types
Channels of distribution

---

[7] Further analysis and investigation may reveal that the market demand for this product is down and that all competitors are suffering a drop in sales. *But "corrective action" may still be initiated*—in the form of new, more aggressive marketing and sales strategies designed to increase market share.

Individual customer data are practical only if a firm has relatively few customers (e.g., a machine tool manufacturer selling primarily to the automotive industry or a railway supply manufacturer selling only to railroads). In the examples above, if the electrical manufacturer were selling only to the investor-owned utilities, it would be very practical to analyze sales by individual customers, since there are relatively few such customer firms in the country. Recalling the below-quota performance for watt-hour meters, the territorial and product analyses may be coupled with the customer analysis—and it may be found (for example) that four large electric utilities in the Philadelphia office of the Atlantic District had sharply decreased purchase of meters from this company. Thus the focus for corrective action has significantly narrowed to the real root of the meter problems.

Analysis of sales by *key customers* is another possible focus. Almost every selling operation will find that a significantly large proportion of its sales comes from a relatively small proportion of its active customers.[8] These are critical market spots, therefore, and analysis of orders received from them may be a significant input into quick corrective action, if the analysis hints any falloff of sales to them.

Certain customer categories or types may be critical to sales success, and analysis of sales by these categories is highly important. A manufacturer of industrial pumps, for example, may sell his pumps and allied products to a number of industries. Certain of these may be more critical than others to the company's success; hence the sales manager may want feedback of sales data on these customer industries. He may have found, for instance, that historically the following categories of customers contribute as indicated to total sales:

Customer Industry	Percent of Total Sales
Oil refining	30
Gas pipelines	20
Chemical	20
Paper manufacturing	10
Other	20

If analysis of sales for these industries shows danger signs, corrective action should begin immediately.[9]

[8] In General Electric's apparatus sales, for example, it was found that only about 15 percent of customers being called on historically contributed about *85 percent* of the orders received.

[9] In our example, sales data would probably include a sales quota for these key industries—coming probably from the sales districts where district management has

It should be obvious that analysis of sales can take all these forms, or combinations of them. The important concept here is the shaping of the sales data so that the sales manager can flush out critical spots, identify them, *and focus on them narrowly enough to begin tailored corrective action.* The nature of the firm, its products, its selected markets, its customers, its competitors, and its unique market conditions will determine what the "best way" is to accomplish this. Most firms have adequate accounting facilities and management intelligence to help the sales manager establish the kind of sales analysis he needs—to keep him from having to "shoot in the dark" and to prevent the myopia caused by looking only at aggregate data.

Market Share Analysis

So far we have examined various ways in which the sales manager can analyze sales volume to trigger corrective, adjustive actions. Often, however, analysis of sales, no matter how detailed, may not be enough. It is conceivable, for example, that any combination of these ways of analyzing sales may result in a favorable picture as far as sales volume versus quotas is concerned. *This does not necessarily mean that sales performance is adequate.* Actual sales can be equal to or over quota—or they may be over the same period of a previous year—and yet the firm may be losing position to a dangerous extent.

Consider, for example, a firm with a first six months' sales budget of $30 million. Assume that on July 5 the sales reports show sales received of $31 million, or $1 million over the budget. Analyses by districts and also by product lines show performances equal to or above quotas. Assume further that in the first six months of the previous year, $28 million had been booked. Hence the sales manager can truthfully say that the selling operation is not only 3 percent over budget, but also a whopping 11 percent over the performance of the previous year.

Now, further assume that in the previous year this firm and all its competitors combined had sold a total of $280 million. Of the total demand facing this firm's industry, therefore, *this firm's market share was 10 percent.* Finally, assume that the demand facing this industry during the first half of this year has increased from $280 million to $360

assigned quotas for the customers in these industries. It should be noted also that in such a clear market segmentation as this, specific marketing strategies have already been devised for and aimed at these industries. Thus not only will the sales operation be initiating corrective *sales* action, but other marketing functions will also adjust (advertising, sales promotion, etc.)

million.[10] *The firm's market share has dropped from 10 to 8 percent.* It is losing position in the market, vis-à-vis its rivals. Its rivals (certainly some of them) are doing a more effective marketing job—*a clear signal of danger* to this firm, which must begin corrective action quickly.[11] Thus analysis of sales volume alone may not be enough for adequate sales management control process. Market share analysis may often have to be used in tandem with sales analysis.

THE EVALUATION OF PERFORMANCE

The foregoing analyses provide *information* categorized in meaningful ways. The performance itself is *evaluated* against some predetermined set of performance standards, to determine its degree of effectiveness. Thus to bring the sales manager up to the point of determining what (if any) corrective action is needed, the control technique deals with three elements: *information* on performance, *standards,* and *evaluation* of performance (against the standards). Actually, all three of these elements were present in the foregoing examples of sales analysis, as shown in Figure 12-2.

Performance in pursuit of *quantitatively* based objectives particularly lends itself to evaluation in this manner, providing a quite clear input into the sales manager's decision process for corrective action. All performances that are budgeted in "numbers" are in this category. Such "numbers" to be achieved are the *performance standards*—the resulting performance that higher management expects. Typical of quantitative performance standards for sales units are *sales quotas* (sometimes called sales budgets), *expense budgets,* and *manpower budgets.* Sometimes some sales departments assign quantitative measures of *sales effort* to be allocated among various product lines. Some companies are able to set up accounting systems that can measure sales units' *contributions to profit.*

All these performance standards (target against which results are measured) are "black or white," and so is the performance. They

[10] Many factors may cause the demand that faces an industry to shift sharply. It is by no means uncommon to observe a 10 percent shift in demand, plus or minus for some products, in a year's time.

[11] At this point we cannot suggest what the corrective action should be. It may well be that the sales performance is completely adequate, and corrective action is needed elsewhere—in product design, customer service, advertising, pricing, or a combination of these. *But probably sales strategy will have to shift* regardless of the course of the market share loss. Hence this analysis is an input to the sales manager's control process.

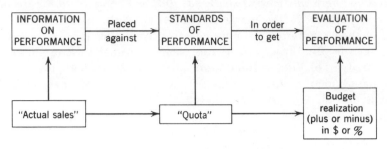

FIGURE 12-2   Elements of control.

probably receive primary attention by most sales managers—under-standably, because they boom out "loud and clear" for everyone in the company to see.[12] And they probably stimulate the major share of corrective action in most sales operations.

Yet most sales operations assign objectives to sales units which are not quantitative and cannot be quantitatively or objectively measured. But it might well be that less than adequate performance against such "qualitatively based" standards could harm the company more in the long run than less than adequate sales quota achievement. What of company image? Brand image? Rapport with customers? Furthermore, suppose that all analyses of quantitative performance and evaluation against quantitative standards appear to be adequate. This is a photo-graph of the past. What of the future? What effect will the sales behavior to get this past performance have on the future perception and response of customers?

If expectations are placed on sales units (or individuals) for non-quantifiable ends, performance toward those ends must still be evalu-ated and sometimes corrected. The establishment of standards is admit-tedly a difficult task in this case. Because it is difficult and because the standards themselves are often quite amorphous, the sales manager must develop a sort of visceral "feel" for them. This is not bad—as long as he can go about developing this subjective "feel" in a rather objective way. This is less confusing than it sounds, meaning simply that he does not let his *bias* overcome his *subjective sense*.

In summary, it is proposed that a sales manager evaluate the perfor-mance of subordinate sales units against not only quantitative standards, but also qualitative standards. The latter include not only the non-

---

12 Recall the discussion in Chapter 6 on the dilemma between "quantitative" and "qualitative" objectives.

quantifiable goals, but also the sales unit's own objective allocation, planning, organizing of resources, decision making, and sets of resulting behaviors. All this is necessary so that the sales manager can devise and propose corrective or adjustive strategies and/or actions.

SEARCHING FOR CORRECTIVE ACTIONS FOR THE SALES UNIT

The final element of the control process is the correcting or "controlling" action itself. The previous elements—analysis and evaluation— help to focus and refocus on efforts being made to achieve objectives. These are inputs to the corrective-action phase of the control process (see Figure 12-1). Note the sense of *time* in this process:

$$
\begin{array}{lll}
\text{Analysis} & \longrightarrow & \text{examines } \textit{past} \text{ actions} \\
\text{Evaluation} & \longrightarrow & \textit{present} \text{ judgments} \\
\text{Corrections} & \longrightarrow & \text{generates } \textit{future} \text{ actions}
\end{array}
$$

Tolerance for Deviation

Deviations from the target course may not always demand corrective action, however. Assume that a sales unit has a sales quota of $650,000 for a certain time period. Now assume that after the period is over, analysis shows an achievement of $649,800. A very slight miss. Obviously it would be a bit ludicrous to initiate corrective action if a group misses by only $200 out of $600,000. But suppose that the analysis shows an achievement of $649,000—a "miss" of $1000—an achievement of 99 percent. Probably corrective action is still unnecessary. After all, forecasting cannot be perfect; demand fluctuates a little; a few customer orders which were to be received late in the period may have been delayed.

Obviously, some degree of tolerance should be permitted before corrective and controlling actions are started. Some range or band of permissible deviation should be established, and any performance within this range should be accepted as adequate. The "floor" of this range of tolerance must be determined by the sales manager himself (though the demands or tolerance of his superiors are inputs into his decision regarding it). How much can a sales unit miss its sales quota before starting appropriate controlling actions depends entirely on the sales manager's judgment. The range of tolerance will normally be different for different firms, for different situations, at different times, and for different performance standards (e.g., a 5 percent deviation may be allowed by a sales manager for sales quota, but only 2 percent deviation for expense budget) .

A Preface to the Actual Control Itself

If a sales unit's performance falls below the range of acceptable results, corrective action should be initiated. For example, assume that a sales district with a quota of $650,000 for a time period achieves only 94 percent of it, below the previously determined tolerable limit. In many cases, the headquarters manager may not need to *initiate* corrective action—this may be done by the manager of the sales district without any impetus from headquarters. This implies the absolute necessity of fast and accurate communication in both directions. First the subordinate sales manager must know clearly what is expected from his unit, the range of tolerable results, and *the expectation that he will correct deviations beyond this.* Second, the subordinate manager must receive quickly, accurately, and analytically the information on his unit's performance and the higher management's evaluation of it. (The sales reports used in the sales analysis discussion earlier in this chapter are examples. They are triggering devices for the subordinate unit.) Third, "upward" communication is necessary from the subordinate manager to the higher manager, reporting what corrective actions are being taken.

All this apparently "automatic" control does not just "happen." It is a way of managerial life, which the higher manager has deliberately and rationally developed specifically to achieve control.

Sales managers cannot expect this kind of "automatic" control to simply happen. It occurs only in managerially mature organizations and when it has been worked on diligently.[13] In many cases, therefore, corrective action must be initiated and rather carefully followed by the higher manager. This may take several forms. In the discussions that follow we shall use the term "sales manager" to mean the headquarters sales manager and the term "district manager" to mean his subordinate who is in charge of a subordinate unit.

"Downward" Communication. When the sales manager detects deviation from desired results, he must communicate this information to the district manager. This means something more than simply having the district manager placed on the distribution list for periodic sales data. The sales manager must in some form (formally or informally) com-

[13] It probably does not often apply to control or *corrective action of the* correction of the actions of the individual salesman. See the later section on the evaluation of the individual.

municate to the district manager that (*a*) the district is below par and that (*b*) he, the sales manager, is keenly aware of it. Furthermore, the sales manager should receive some kind of acknowledgement that the district manager perceives this.

"Two-Way" Communication. As a logical next step, the sales manager and the district manager, *focusing on the sales unit,* begin a dialogue, the sense of which is as follows: "We see that results are not satisfactory. We must do something to correct them. What is it that needs correcting?" This may be an informal dialogue, as it is in many mature sales organizations.[14] Or it may be a more formal dialogue. In many competent sales organizations, the sales manager holds a continuing set of "review sessions" with his district managers. Again, this *formal* two-way communication about objectives, plans, results, and control may be formally or informally conducted. Some sales managers have periodic formal meetings with district managers during which past, present, and future plans and actions are reviewed. Some sales managers accomplish this more informally while "visiting" with individual district managers.[15]

Factors on Which to Focus

To tailor the corrective actions to a new target course, several factors should be considered. Very often the *kind* of corrective action and *who* must accomplish it will quickly become apparent from the consideration of these factors by the sales manager (ideally together with the district manager).

Feasibility of Objectives. The need for corrective action is generated by the sales unit's failure to adequately achieve its given objectives. But before going too far into the initiation of corrective action, the objectives themselves may require an examination, to be certain that they are still feasible. There is nothing holy about objectives, and sometimes after they are set, changing conditions may affect their validity. It is ridiculous for a sales unit to be required to "beat its head against a wall," continuing to seek an ancient objective that is no longer feasible. Of course, change may occur in the other direction, too—rendering an old objective invalid because it is now *short* of what can be accomplished. Unfortunately, managements seem much more willing to raise

14 Example: a sales manager may telephone a district manager and say, "Jim, I note that you're six percent off in sales for the last month. Why don't you dig into this and call me back in the next couple of days—and we'll talk it over."
15 "Managerial style" is an important consideration here. See Chapter 19 for some key ideas about this kind of manager-subordinate relationships.

sales targets (in rising markets) or to lower expense targets than to do the reverse. But if new, lower sales targets or new, higher expense targets are called for, they should be recognized.[16]

Efficacy of Planning. Before corrective action is devised, the planning that preceded the sales actions producing the inadequate results should be reviewed. Was this planning adequate? Did it generate the decisions and actions that *should* have produced adequate results? If the district manager were to do it all over again, would he devise the same plans of action? The purpose of this "step" in the control process is to determine whether new plans of action are needed or whether existing plans are valid and some other correction is needed.

Adequacy of Organizing. To carry out his plans of action, the district manager has available a variety of resources—people, money, and things. Some are completely within his command, in his district. Some are available to him from the rest of the firm (headquarters sales staff, headquarters sales management, marketing specialists, etc.). How effectively has the district manager put together and utilized all these resources? Is the organization *structure* of his district the optimum one? [17] Are the sales territories and customer assignments to salesmen optimum and logical? Has his allocation of quotas to his salesman been logical? Are his people making optimum use of resources available to him? Are the positions in his organization adequately coordinated with others, where necessary? Here again, this "audit" of the district manager's organizing function is meant to flush out appropriate corrective action.

Implementation of Plans. A reasonable next step before actual corrective action is taken is to examine the implementation of the plans of action. What were the final decisions made by the district manager? How were they perceived by his subordinates? [18] In addition to questions relative to decisions and their transmittal to subordinates, what specifically were the responses of the subordinates? Did they by their behavior patterns actually implement the directives as intended by the

---

[16] This discussion does not imply that objectives should be flipped around like yo-yo's. On the contrary, they should be *relatively* stable over certain periods of time. But they are subject to review and sometimes need adjustment.

[17] This does not propose that organization *structure*, like objectives, is subject to willy-nilly change. But conditions, both internal and external to the firm, *sometimes* require a frank examination of the validity of structure—particularly if results are consistently inadequate while other managerial and individual behaviors appear to be satisfactory.

[18] Of course, usually this is not very easy to evaluate. Often, however, the sales manager will receive copies of the district manager's *written* directives, he may also hear the *oral* directives as he visits district sales meetings, and so on.

district manager? This is a crucial element. Because human beings are fallible creatures, inadequate results very often come from inadequate implementing (or behavioral response) by individuals.[19] Because individual performance is so important, its evaluation and correction is discussed separately in a later section.

The Manager Himself. The factors discussed so far focused on the managerial process and on its effect on the sales unit itself. A number of more personal aspects of the district manager's behavior *as* a manager deserve attention. Perhaps the model of "the job of the sales manager" (see p. 49) is a good checklist. How capable is the district manager in those "areas of knowledge" that the sales manager deems important for him? How competent is he in the particular "functional skills" deemed necessary for the district management job? How skillful is he in executing "the managerial process"?[20] How capable is he in his leadership and motivational behaviors?[21] How well does he communicate with higher management, keeping a flow, or feedback, of vital information of many kinds?

ADJUSTING OR CORRECTING ACTIONS

The thought process and the search process just discussed—whether done formally or informally—are designed to lead to specific corrective actions, so that the sales unit's performance will become acceptable with reference to objectives. The corrective action itself is conceived, planned, and implemented *precisely as any other action is.*

Thus, based on the foregoing thought and search process, any of the following corrective actions, *or combinations of them,* may be initiated:

- Adjustment of objectives
- New plans of action, taking into account the intelligence coming from the feedback system
- New allocation of the units resources and new uses of available resources from outside the unit
- New decisions and new directives
- Correction of individual behaviors (see next section)
- New managerial behaviors by the manager himself

[19] Many astute sales managers believe that the *prime causes* of inadequate performance in about equal degree are (1) inadequate planning and (2) inadequate individual performance. Based on experience and observation, I lean toward inadequate planning as *the* prime source of below-par performance.
[20] This idea overlaps with the foregoing discussions.
[21] This will be discussed in depth in Part IV.

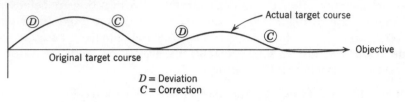

D = Deviation
C = Correction

FIGURE 12-3   The continuing control process.

All of this should be viewed in a "systems" sense, as portrayed in Figure 12-1. Furthermore, like any control system, all this should be *a continuing process*. It can be viewed as a continual "zeroing" in or "homing" on a target. See Figure 12-3.

EVALUATING INDIVIDUAL PERFORMANCE

If a sales unit's performance is below par, corrective action may be needed in any of several categories, as already discussed. Very often, however, it is the correction or adjustment of individual salesmen's performances that has major significance. After all, everything that the firm does in creating strategies rides on the salesman's shoulders. Evaluating and controlling individual performance is one of the most critical *and most difficult* aspects of a district sales manager's job. And by and large, it is not very well done in many firms, probably because of inadequate understanding of the rationale of the control process and its application to individual performance.

The process of controlling individual performance follows the same rationale as that for controlling an organizational unit. That is, the idea of the radar and the gyroscope holds equally well here. The individual salesman has some set of targets to achieve, both quantitative and qualitative. The district manager receives *information* on the salesman's performance—what he has achieved and how he is acting to achieve it. These facts are *evaluated against standards* of performance—the targets he expected to achieve.[22] If deviations are disclosed, *corrective or adjustive action* is initiated, so that the salesman's course zeroes back in on the target.

---

[22] As put by W. J. E. Crissy of Michigan State University, this is placing R_E versus R_A, or "results expected" versus "results achieved." The sales manager seeks to equate these variables.

Information Sources

Information about the salesman's performance—both in results achieved and in the manner in which they are achieved—comes to the district manager from four basic sources, discussed briefly below. The sales manager should not leave these feedback systems to chance. It is essential to his ability to control that they be carefully devised.[23]

Formal Reports. A battery of formal reports is used as evidence of the salesman's performance. Most common are *sales reports,* which show actual sales, usually by product line, achieved in specified time periods by each salesman. *Expense reports* are also common. Usually these two reports are provided by the accounting function. The salesman himself may also provide a number of "activity-type" reports, informing the district manager of his activities in several categories. Firms have varying uses of these salesman-activity reports, but the more common ones include:

- Call reports, showing what customers were visited during prescribed time periods, usually with results achieved and product lines discussed.
- New business reports, showing new accounts or the "break-in" to an account of a product line not previously sold.
- Routing plans, showing how the salesman plans to spend his time with customers in the next time period.
- Lost-business reports, showing what business was lost, to which competitor, for which customer, and why (in salesman's best judgment).
- Competitive activity reports.
- General market condition reports.

These informative formal reports emanating from the salesman himself can be vital sources of performance appraisal and *general market intelligence.* As inputs into the evaluation-control system, they have use *only if in fact they provide information that can be measured against a desired performance standard.* For example, if a salesman is not given an objec-

---

[23] There is no hint here of espionage, or "spying" on the salesman. These are legitimate requirements, and each salesman should know that they are. In fact, intelligent professional salesmen *want* these kinds of information flowing back to their managers, just as they want their managers' evaluations of how performance can be improved. All this is very advantageous to the salesman *who wants to do a competent job*—as I believe most do.

tive of developing new accounts and his performance thus will not be measured against such a standard, it would be silly to require him to turn in periodic "new business reports." Yet some sales operations hang on to reports that are about this useless. On the other hand, a formal report required *for the purpose of market intelligence* is a very valid requirement. But the salesman must know its purpose and be aware that it is not designed to measure him in some mysterious way or to simply make "busywork."

Planning Reports. Activity reports deal with past actions or at best with a fleeting momentary situation in the present. Often, however, it is advisable for the district manager to know how individual salesmen are looking into the future—how they are *planning* strategies of action to achieve their given goals. This can be a highly valuable input to the district manager's evaluation and control system. He has created his own strategies for the district and has issued directives to implement them. But the salesman usually does more than blindly and instantly react to these directives. He plans, in some fashion. Certainly for the more important district strategies, the district manager may find much value in knowing how the salesman is planning.[24] Control (adjustment) at this point (using *anticipated* action) may be infinitely better than control at a later date—if the salesman's plans are not completely adequate.

Observation. In some ways, *observation* by the district manager of the salesman's actions under different conditions may be the most meaningful input into his evaluation-control system. The formal reports with their wealth of data can never breathe the living "feel" of real situations. The district manager may travel in the territory with the salesman—ride the highways with him, visit customers with him, hold postmortems with him at the end of the day. We shall return later to this intimate source of information—personal observation—in discussing "qualitative evaluation" in the next section.

Information from Others. Other individuals may provide a flow of information about a salesman's performance. These may include customers, other salesmen, and various staff people (product specialists, etc.) Here, again, the district manager must completely disavow any sense of spying or "cloak and dagger" tactics, if he wants to retain intimacy, respect, and rapport. Probably a good guide is to *seek* information about a salesman from other individuals only if he would be perfectly content for the salesman to know it.[25] Perhaps *in general,* information from

---

[24] The "selling strategy" model presented in Chapter 8 can provide a good framework for the salesman's "planning reports" to his manager.

[25] Perhaps a more subtle consideration is the effect *on the other individuals* of

others should not be *sought*—but only accepted if given. And even here, the district manager should probably often question its real validity.

Evaluating the Information

Again, two sets of standards exist against which individual performance is measured. One is quantitative in character, and one is qualitative.

Quantitative Measures. The salesman's performance can be quantified by a wide array of quantitatively based factors. Figure 12-4 lists some of them. Few firms use *all* of these, of course; hence many "mixes" of them exist, with varying degrees of importance attached to them.

Boiling down all these quantitative measures to a simple handful, a salesman's effectiveness can be evaluated by the following factors:

- *How much he sells*—his dollar or unit sales volume.
- *What he sells*—the mix of product lines he sells.
- *Where he sells*—the markets and the individual customers that give him most of his business.
- *His profit contribution*—where relevant and where his firm is set up to compute this.
- *How much he costs*—in compensation, expenses, supervision costs.

Qualitative Measures. But quantitative, statistical data do not tell the whole story of performance. Whatever these measures show, he *might* have done better. Or whatever they show, he may have been doing a herculean job to even come up to a bare "par" (whereas another salesman working under different conditions performs in an average way and exceeds "par"). Quantitative measurements are important and will always be essential inputs into the control process, but they simply do not in all cases provide a complete analysis for control purposes.

Many sales operations evaluate the salesman from time to time on the basis of *traits*—for example, integrity, loyalty, initiative, industriousness, and ability to deal with people. Experience and observation show that this kind of "trait" evaluation is usually quite sterile. The terms defy definition commonly accepted by all rating managers, and at best do not help the sales manager very much in determining what corrective action is necessary. A better way exists to evaluate the qualitative aspects of a salesman's performance.

his seeking information about a salesman. The very act *could* undermine confidence in the district manager and in the district itself.

The following list is representative of the various standards that may be used for evaluating salesmen.

A. SALES
  1. Sales volume in dollars
  2. Sales volume to previous year's sales
  3. Sales volume in units
  4. Sales volume to dollar quota
  5. Sales volume in relation to market potential
  6. Sales volume to physical unit quota
  7. Sales volume by customers
  8. Sales volume by outlet type
  9. Sales volume by product or product line
  10. Sales volume per order
  11. Average sale volume per call
  12. Amount of new account sales
  13. Percentage of sales to calls
  14. Amount of repeat sales
  15. Sales volume on promotional items
  16. Amount or percentage of sales made by telephone
  17. Amount or percentage of sales made by mail

B. ACCOUNTS
  1. Percentage of accounts sold
  2. Number of new accounts
  3. Number of accounts lost
  4. Number of accounts on which payment is overdue
  5. Number of accounts buying the full line

FIGURE 12-4   Methods of measuring salesman's performance. Adapted from a Sales Management Seminar presented by Michigan State University, 1966.

Very often *the underlying roots of the quantified results lie in the salesman's behaviors*—his application of knowledge, his defining of goals, his planning behavior, his tactical behavior. These underlying managerially oriented behaviors have great effect on his actions and the results he achieves.

Reconsider Figure 4-2, page 55, which portrays the essential, interacting elements of the job of the professional salesman. If these are the key elements, they logically become the ideal framework by which to qualitatively evaluate the salesman's performance. How *does* he demonstrate his grasp of knowledge and his growing knowledge of his markets, his competition, the product line, each customer's business, and each key customer as a person? How does he apply this knowledge?

C. PROFIT
1. Net profit by salesman

D. ORDERS
1. Number of orders delivered
2. Number of orders booked
3. Number of canceled orders

E. SELLING EXPENSE
1. Compensation in relation to sales volume
2. Salesman's expenses in relation to sales volume or quota
3. Total direct selling expense per sales dollar

F. MISCELLANEOUS
1. Advertising displays set up
2. Number of letters written to prospects
3. Number of telephone calls made to prospects
4. Number of reports turned in or not turned in
5. Number of jobber or dealer meetings held
6. Use of sales aids in presentation
7. Number of service calls made
8. Number of customer complaints
9. Safety record
10. Collections made
11. Training meetings conducted

FIGURE 12-4 *continued*

How does he break down the quotas given him into separate, sought-after goals, customer by customer? How does he create effective plans of action? How capable is he in the "art" of preparing and making selling presentations? How able is he as a tactician, shifting and flexing in the presence of the customer? How well does *he* evaluate his results and begin corrective action?

These are the real roots of qualitative evaluation. Furthermore, they are definitive, understandable, and observable. *Together with the statistical quantified data* they present a very meaningful picture of his performance. As a general "frame of reference" they allow the district manager to see, rather quickly and rather accurately, where corrective, adjustive action is needed.

To be sure, several factors of performance not included in this model might be useful. The salesman's contribution to the flow of market intelligence, his level of motivation, his actions toward continuing personal development, and his managerial ability are factors that sometimes need evaluation and which may provide clues for helpful corrective action.

And to be sure, the personal traits that were somewhat debunked a few paragraphs ago as clues to corrective behavior, still require some degree of evaluation. Certainly, the negative side of some traits is detrimental. And certainly if a salesman has some wholesale lack of certain of these traits, he must either develop them or be invited to do some other kind of job.

The key point is that the most effective evaluation of salesmen's performance—hence the most effective adjustive control—can be achieved by the district manager via quantitative measurements coupled with *logical, definitive* qualitative measurements. And the most productive framework of thinking for logical, definitive, qualitative measurement is the "model" of the professional salesman's job.[26]

CONTROLLING INDIVIDUALS' PERFORMANCE

No set "formula" exists for the actual control action itself, in which the individual's behavior is influenced in a desired way. Every human being is a unique individual, and every situation is really a unique one. Styles of management vary, from firm to firm and from manager to manager. As we shall see in Part IV, the demands by individuals for *different* styles of leadership vary from individual to individual and from situation to situation. There is simply no A-B-C set of tactics with which to approach an individual in such a way as to influence him in a desired direction.[27]

However, some basic "ground rules" do exist, which experience indicates have some practical value. These are *techniques,* or approaches— and do not suggest the actual *content* of the interaction between the district manager and the "corrected" salesman. We shall deal with that broadly in Part IV. The following general approaches are frameworks for the actual corrective or adjustive action (the final link in the control process).

On-the-Spot Correction

Certain kinds of salesman behavior or actions that are obviously "off the beam" must be corrected on the spot, and usually without any diplomatic or subtle approach. For example, if a salesman is behaving in

[26] It need not be identical to the model in this book. A sales manager can construct his own model of his salesman's unique jobs. *But he must construct it* on a rational, inclusive basis, so that its elements thoroughly describe the job.
[27] See Chapter 15 for a detailed discussion of leadership strategies. Its rationale applies here.

direct violation of an expressed policy, if he is failing to follow an explicit directive, or if he is generating customer complaints, his district manager must so advise him and very directly tell him what to do about it. The *style* in which this is done depends on many factors (see Part IV). The "correction" itself may be very gentle and subtle or quite direct and blunt, or even with an explicit threat of discipline. The point here is— sometimes a district manager must make an instant, direct, positive correction.

Continuing Appraisal System

Many firms require periodic manager-subordinate appraisal sessions. The basic idea of such continuing appraisal is excellent; the appraisal should provide a control mechanism for the district manager in the more general "adjustment" of the individuals' performance. However, such formal appraisal mechanics are often rather meaningless, since no clear, definitive framework for appraisal is available. Often the appraisal depends too much on the old "trait" approach. Continuing appraisal is probably more valuable to manager and salesman alike if the combination of quantitative and qualitative factors is used, in the sense discussed in the preceding section. From the salesman's viewpoint, the appraisal session is designed to tell him, "What is expected of me, how am I doing, and how can I do it better."

Review Sessions

In the continuing appraisal system, it is really the salesman himself who is the subject of discussion. In the *review session*, however, the subject discussed by district manager and salesman is a situation faced by the salesman. It may be a general situation existing in his territory (e.g., changing market conditions or changing competitive activity). Or it may be a specific one involving a particular customer. Here the district manager seeks to know the "state of the union" generally in the territory and specifically for key customers or for key pending business. This not only provides important market intelligence to the district manager, but also requires that the salesman rationally analyze his complex job and sharpen his strategies. It further provides the district manager with a superb opportunity to guide the salesman and to subtly influence his strategy and tactics. The district manager can generate important thinking by asking such questions as "How do we stand with our plan of breaking in with Product Line B at the XYZ Co.? What are your major problems with the XYZ Co.? What do you think is the best way to solve them?" [28]

The Joint Call

Traveling with the salesman in his territory and calling on customers with him provide the district manager with an excellent means of control. For new or inexperienced salesmen, the joint call enables the district manager to train, teach, and demonstrate. But the joint call is particularly useful as a control mechanism when making it with experienced salesmen. The focus for both manager and salesman should be the *customer*.

The joint call has three phases. *Before the call,* the district manager should ask the salesman to brief him on the general situation with the customer, problems faced, and the mission to be accomplished in this call. Furthermore, some amount of "rehearsal" should be accomplished, so that both manager and salesman are agreed to a general strategy for the call and on "who will do what" in the customer's presence. [29]

During the call, the salesman should normally "command" the situation. In this tactical phase, manager and salesman will each act as closely as possible to the preplanned strategy, but obviously each will have to flex tactically. Having previously determined the mission and agreed to a broad strategy, it is not likely that tactical maneuvers made by one will foul up the other.

After the call comes the postmortem. The district manager and salesman review the call—the preplanned strategy, what actually happened, how the strategy could have been improved, how the tactical maneuvers in the customer's presence could have been improved, what was really accomplished, and what should be the general plan for the salesman's next visit.

The joint call keeps the district manager tuned to the throb of the marketplace. But beyond that, it gives him a splendid means for suggesting adjustive action, in the control sense. It matters little whether he himself finds some creative idea to suggest or whether he and the salesman fall upon it together. Either way, he has triggered off new salesman behavior designed to improve effectiveness of performance.

[28] Once again, the rationale of the selling strategy logic in Chapter 8 provides an excellent framework for this kind of dialogue and can help the district manager in the control process at this point.

[29] Again, our old friend, the selling strategy, is a valuable tool.

Training Programs

Training toward the end of improving sales effectiveness is a never-ending function. Of course, the primary mission of training is to equip the salesman to do a better job, "before the fact" so to speak. In so doing, training at the salesman level aims at improving proficiency in all elements of the salesman's job.[30] However, training may also have a "control" input. If a district manager perceives broad problems shared by all or most salesmen, it may be efficient to induce corrective action, via training meetings, designed to overcome the problems.

SOME CONCLUDING COMMENTS

The primary mission of every selling operation is *to secure profit and revenue via sales volume now and in the future.* Other missions exist—growth of market share and enhanced company and brand image are examples—but these other missions are really means to the sales-volume end. To this vital end, sales managers at headquarters and in the field develop strategic programs of action, large and small, formally and informally. They allocate and assign their resources, putting together in various ways the people, money, and things given them. They make decisions designed to implement the programs so that people can carry them out.

But the best of plans, the best of organization structure, and the best of decisions will not always assure optimum results. All these managerial processes involve some prediction of the future. And things rarely happen precisely as predicted. Customers react to the firm's actions in various ways. Rivals respond to them not always in the direction and strength predicted. Customers react to *rivals'* responses in various ways. The implementation by the firm's people of the strategic programs does not always go as planned. It is completely normal, then, for the course of strategic selling programs to deviate from what is desired.

The system concept provides a way to minimize the effects of deviation. The cybernetic [31] idea of *control* enables the sales manager to

[30] The model of the "Job of the Professional Salesman" in Chapter 4 provides an excellent "outline" for a training program. See also Chapter 15.

[31] From the Greek word "helmsman," or "steersman." The rather new concept of "cybernetics" in management is basically the control process as described in this chapter.

detect the amount and direction of deviation and make the necessary correction to bring the operation back on target course. The *control process* is simple in concept—as simple as the thermostatic control in a heating and cooling system. As shown in Figure 12-1, the sales manager has objectives—he creates plans of action, implements them, and observes results. Results are evaluated against the desired objectives. Deviations are noted, in size and in direction. These are triggering inputs, requiring adjustment of planning and implementation, and bringing new actions and new results. The control process continues to function—detecting the new results, evaluating them against objectives—and so the cycling process goes on.

The control process answers the sales manager's questions: "How are we doing? Where and how are we off? How can we correct?" The process may control sales units or it may control individuals. Effectively understanding and applying it is one of the marks of a competent sales manager.

SUGGESTED READINGS

The Control Concept

1. Kotler, Philip, *Marketing Management: Analysis, Planning and Control,* Prentice-Hall, New York, 1967, pp. 559–585.
2. Alderson, W., and Green, P. E., *Planning and Problem Solving in Marketing,* R. D. Irwin, Homewood, Ill., 1964, Chapter 12, pp. 332–353. (Mathematical and statistical models.)
3. Optner, Stanford L., *Systems Analyses for Business and Industrial Problem Solving,* Prentice-Hall, New York, 1965.
4. Koontz, H., and O'Donnell, C., *Principles of Management,* McGraw Hill, New York, 1955, pp. 537–558.

Sales Analysis

1. Bell, Martin L., *Marketing Strategy and Concepts,* Houghton Mifflin Company, New York, 1966, pp. 643–657.

QUESTIONS AND PROBLEMS

1. This chapter opened with the statement that the idea of "control" is indispensable to the effective manager. In your own words, state why you think this is true for the field sales manager.

2. You are a headquarters sales manager. Select one specific objective that you think you would feasibly have (e.g., "increase market share from 6 percent to 9 percent"). Using Figure 12-1, briefly list information, data, and so on, for *each* of the "boxes" in the figure (numbered from 1 to 13).

3. An astute manager once said: "The time to start thinking about control is when you think of each other step in the managerial process." What do you think he meant by this?

4. Assume that your company has just established a new product business. That is, it has decentralized engineering, production, marketing, and staff services into a relatively autonomous "profit center." You have been named field sales manager, reporting to the manager of marketing. What kind of data, what kinds of reports, and with what frequency do you think you would request from the accounting department for control purposes? How would you justify each one?

5. Construct an example of your own showing the use of the "sales analysis" concept. Assume five regions, from three to six sales districts per region, four major product lines, and four major customer segments.

13

Managing for Profit

For managers of modern business firms, "the name of the game" is profit. To be sure, many means to the profit end become such important goals, involving complex strategies, that they often seem to be prime ones. Nonetheless, the survival of the firm depends on continuing profitability at some desired level. Although the success of many selling operations may be judged by their *revenue* contribution to profit,[1] the purpose of this chapter is to propose a profit orientation for every selling operation.

The real key to the firm's profit objective is *return on investment* (ROI). One can examine the "profit equations" and see the elements of profit:

$$(1)\quad \text{profit} = \text{revenue} - \text{cost}$$
$$(2)\quad \text{revenue} = \text{price} \times \text{quantity}$$

Obviously, it is desirable to increase the *absolute value* of profit by favorably manipulating the inputs of revenue and cost.[2] But the absolute value of profit in some time period may or may not be truly indicative of the *profitability* of the firm. What does it mean to say that a firm's revenue exceeded its costs by $100,000? This might be a superb annual profit for a neighborhood laundromat, but an almost disastrous level of profit for an airline.

The key is not the absolute amount of profit, but that profit which is

---

[1] For many firms, it is not possible to establish a selling operation literally on a profit-and-loss basis.

[2] Refer to the discussion of the pressure for volume in Chapter 3.

measured as the return on investment made by the owners of the firm. The primary responsibility of management in any firm is to so operate the firm that over the long run the owners of the business receive as high a rate of return on their investment as they might return on similar investments having the same amount of risk.[3] After all, an investor (or a businessman deciding to enter a business) can invest his funds in a number of places and be essentially assured of, say, a 5 percent return *at essentially no risk* (e.g., commercial bank, tax-free municipal bonds). If he were to invest these funds in some business venture *with some risk,* he would rationally expect a return greater than 5 percent, to compensate for the risk. The more risk, the greater he would expect the rate of return to be.

In its simplest sense, return on investment is an expression of the dollars of *profit* generated per dollar of *assets* (investment):

$$\text{ROI} = \frac{\text{net profit}}{\text{operating assets}}$$

Computing ROI in this simple way, however, clouds the meaning of two important aspects of ROI. To see these, we also introduce *sales* into the equation by placing it in both numerator and denominator:[4]

$$\text{ROI} = \underbrace{\frac{\text{net profit}}{\text{sales}}}_{\text{rate of profit}} \times \underbrace{\frac{\text{sales}}{\text{operating assets}}}_{\text{turnover}}$$

Now we see the two contributing elements of ROI. The first fraction, net profit/sales, is the element designating "net operating margin," or the *rate of profit.* This is a measure of *how much profit we make on each dollar of sales*—one important element of ROI.

The second fraction in the ROI equation:

$$\frac{\text{sales}}{\text{operating assets}}$$

is the element designated as *turnover*. Here we are looking at how much *sales we achieve per dollar of assets, or investment.* Obviously, the more sales we can "turn" per dollar of investment, the greater will be the return on investment.

[3] In our analysis of ROI we are generally following Robert W. Johnson, *Financial Management,* 2nd ed., Allyn and Bacon, Boston, 1962, pp. 33–41.
[4] Johnson, *op. cit.,* p. 34.

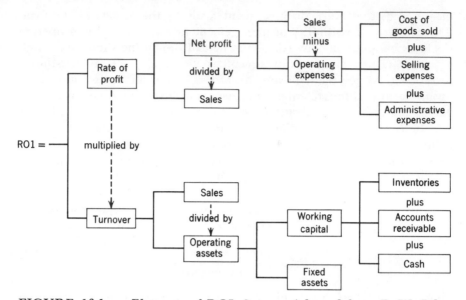

FIGURE 13-1   Elements of ROI. Source: Adapted from R. W. Johnson, *Financial Management,* 2nd ed., Allyn and Bacon, Boston, 1962, p. 36.

Thus ROI depends on two factors—the rate of profit (or profit per dollar of sales) and turnover (or sales per dollar of investment). To improve ROI, therefore, the manager may strategically maneuver within the elements that in turn generate these factors. Figure 13-1 shows these elements contributing to rate of profit and turnover (hence to ROI) .[5]

The elements of ROI shown in Figure 13-1 provide an analytical framework which the sales manager can use in his goal of "managing for profit." It is important to note that many selling operations, even though profit-oriented and profit-motivated, focus on only a few of these elements. There is logic, however, in considering all the elements. ROI can be improved by improving *rate of profit* (top half of Figure 13-1) and also by improving *turnover* (bottom half of Figure 13-1) .

Improving Rate of Profit

Here the sales manager is considering means to improve the profit generated *per dollar of sales*. Note the philosophical twist here—he is not merely striving to increase *sales* or even the absolute value of profit, but rather the *rate of profit,* or the amount of profit per dollar of sales.

The major elements contributing to this rate of profit are *sales* and

[5] Johnson, *op. cit.,* p. 36.

operating expense (see Figure 13-1) . These factors, of course, are familiar to sales managers. Almost invariably, a sales manager will have a sales budget (quota) and, separately, an expense budget. He strives to meet or exceed the sales budget and to meet or be under the expense budget. Unfortunately, he may think of these two elements separately, or in isolation. The real focus should be on the *difference* between these elements: *net profit.*

One difficulty faced by many sales managers (particularly those in the field) can be seen by examining the makeup in Figure 13-1 of *operating expenses*. In many selling operations, these expenses include only "selling expense" (salesmen's compensation, traveling, telephone, etc.) and sales administrative expense (management salaries, training costs, etc.). Often the element of "cost of goods sold" is not used in the financial and accounting management of selling operations. To get the real sense of "operating expenses" (hence later of "net profit") , the *cost of goods sold* must be considered. Here in its simplest sense is meant the factory cost of the goods sold.[6]

Given these elements of sales and operating expense, the sales manager may view his strategies for improving *rate of profit* in several ways. First, it is important to note that the prime goal here is to improve *net profit—* that is, the positive difference between sales and operating expense. This is a critical notion; it is the improved difference between these elements that is important, not the elements themselves. Thus the sales manager strives to do the following:

1. Increase sales more than expense
2. Reduce expense more than sales

Increase Sales More Than Expense. It is the difference between the two that concerns us here. Obviously, if sales increase with no increase in expense, profit increases. Often, however, to increase sales, expense must also be increased. Net profit will increase if sales go up *relatively more* than expense. Thus if the length of the arrows in the following list indicates the size of increase, the following possibilities are possible:

$$(\uparrow) \text{ profit} = (\big\uparrow) \text{ sales} - \text{expenses (n.c.)}$$

$$(\uparrow) \text{ profit} = (\big\uparrow) \text{ sales} - \text{expenses} (\uparrow)$$

[6] I know of several cases where the factory cost of products was a secret, guarded even from sales managers. There may be strategic reasons for this—to keep the firm's cost position away from competitors and from the market itself.

This "relative" relationship between sales and expense should be a normal way in which to consider net-profit strategies. Occasionally, however, for reasons emanating outside the selling operation, a firm will initiate great drives to increase sales—or, separately, to decrease expenses. In implementing such directives, the sales manager should be aware of the impact on the net-profit element of his ROI framework.

Reduce Expense More Than Sales. This may be a strategy to increase net profit by working on the expense element. Here, of course, any loss in sales because of reduced expense (effort) is more than offset by the expense reduction, and net profit goes up.

$$(\uparrow) \text{ profit} = (\downarrow) \text{ sales} - \text{ expense } (\downarrow)$$

Assuming no change in cost of goods sold, such expense reduction must come from selling or administrative expense. Reduction in the field sales force, curtailment of salesmen's traveling and entertaining, elimination of administrative and staff "frills," lessening of internal services, and many other elements may cause some dip in sales, but not enough to outweigh the expense reduction. Profit goes up.

Several cautions apply here. The long-range effect of short-range expense reduction programs must be considered. Even though profit is increased in the short run, can the lost business be regained in the future (without a disproportionate cost) if the firm so desires?

Will an expense reduction program that is perceived by customers (causing reduced sales) damage the firm's image to an undesirable extent?

Finally, looking ahead a bit, consider the effect of reduced sales on *turnover,* in the bottom half of Figure 13-1. Note that turnover is sales divided by operating assets. Assuming no change in assets, note that a reduction in sales will reduce turnover, which in turn *negatively* affects ROI. It may be that the gain in *rate of profit* (top half of Figure 13-1) more than offsets the loss in *turnover* (bottom half of Figure 13-1), and ROI will go up. Or the opposite could happen with some unique mix of all these elements. The critical idea here is that the sales manager should have in mind this framework for thinking about ROI, so that he will understand what will happen to ROI as the various elements are juggled.

Improving Turnover

Improving the rate of profit is only one means to improve ROI. Another is to improve *turnover,* or the dollars of sales generated per dollar of investment, or assets. Here we are concerned with the bottom half of Figure 13-1.

Because most of the elements that contribute to turnover appear to be accounting data for the production (or other operating) components of the firm, rather than for the selling operation, many sales managers may not consider them—and thereby miss opportunities to improve ROI and to create more profit-oriented strategies.[7]

First, consider turnover itself and its elements (Figure 13-1).

$$\text{turnover} = \frac{\text{sales}}{\text{operating assets}}$$

It is clear that if sales increase with respect to operating assets (or investment), or if operating assets are decreased with respect to sales, *turnover will increase,* improving ROI. This simply says again that we are generating more sales per dollar of investment.

Next, consider the elements that make up operating assets. These are *working capital* and *fixed assets.* In turn, the major elements of working capital are, for a selling operation, *inventories* and *accounts receivable.*[8] Decisions regarding levels of inventories, handling of customer billing, and even the very selection of customers for prime focus all affect operating assets. Obviously, strategic decisions in this realm must be made with respect to *improving turnover.* The fraction, sales/operating assets, must increase in order for the turnover to improve—in turn, to improve ROI. It is simply not enough for a sales manager to consider *only* increased sales volume. He must also consider the increased investment to achieve this added volume.

A word about inventories. It is very natural for a sales manager to want a relatively high level of inventory of finished goods, preferably in stock in district (or field) warehouses. The reason for this is that he wants to be competitive (or better) in shipment time to customers. Also, he may want some relatively infrequently called for items in stock, to gain customer awareness that his firm is in business to serve the customer *totally.* This thinking unquestionably enhances sales opportunity. But if the sales manager has a profit orientation, he must weigh not only the increased sales that such inventories might bring (improving rate of profit),

[7] Here we follow Michael Schiff, "The Use of ROI in Sales Management," *Journal of Marketing,* Vol. 27, No. 3 (July 1963), pp. 70–73. In my opinion, this is a "classic," which should be read by all who are interested in sales management.

[8] In the accounting procedure of many firms, inventories and accounts receivable may not literally be carried as part of the selling operation's "books." Nonetheless, they are inextricably involved in the selling operation's responsibility for improved contribution to ROI. They are variables in the selling operations *strategic* equations. They should also be in the profitability equations.

but also the possibility of lower turnover (due to increased inventories) . Which outweighs?

On the other hand, the converse is also true. Operating assets can be reduced by decreasing inventories, or accounts receivable. Turnover tends to increase, hence ROI tends to improve. But again, a balance must be considered. Reducing operating assets is a positive factor. But possibly sales might be adversely affected (items are out of stock and customers turn more to rivals; the credit department gets "tougher" on customers to pay bills promptly) . For turnover to improve, sales must decrease *relatively less* than do operating assets.

Here again the problem of short range versus long range must be considered. And again decisions in the turnover portion of the ROI framework have impact on the rate of profit portion. That is, actions to reduce level of operating assets may cause sales to fall, reducing net profit (assuming no compensatory reduction of operating expense) .

The key idea here is that return on investment is a function of a number of interacting variables, and the sales manager must be aware of this interaction. To maximize his unit's contribution to ROI, he must weigh all elements and select an optimum mix, or balance.

A word about *fixed assets*.[9] In a selling operation, it could be argued, no fixed assets are involved. But fixed assets are here defined as those that will provide services over a period of time greater than a year.[10] Certainly, if one considered any long-run period, the firm's assets invested within the selling operation are not fixed. In the short run, however, at least the *rationale* of fixed-asset management must be considered by the sales manager, to provide a complete grasp of managing for profit. Obviously, the firm's own accounting management will define what is a fixed asset and what is not and will determine the organizational unit to whose financial statement the asset's value is assigned. But the firm *does invest* in relatively immobile assets for the selling operation: warehouses, automatic conveyor systems, internal teletype systems, computers (or "shares" of computers) , district office buildings, and so on. Whatever the account-

---

9 See a provocative article by J. S. Schiff and M. Schiff, "New Sales Management Tool: ROAM," *Harvard Business Review*, Vol. 45, No. 4 (July–August 1967) , pp. 59–66. In this article, which generally follows the previously cited Schiff article in *Journal of Marketing*, the authors use the term "return on assets managed." They use only inventories and accounts receivable as these assets, but propose that this ROI approach has considerable value in decision making. Notable in the article is a description of the use made of the authors' ROAM concept by the marketing management of Sylvania Electric Products, Inc.—in understanding of the meaning of working capital relative to ROI, by field sales managers.

10 Johnson, *op. cit.*, p. 609.

ing method, these all add to operating assets, tending to reduce turnover and the return on investment.

Again, the real key here is for the sales manager to think, as he requests increases in operating assets: "How will this increase affect turnover, and ROI? Will it generate more than enough additional sales to offset its cost? Or if not, will it generate enough additional sales to so increase net profit that added rate of profit will more than offset decreased turnover?"

Managing for Profit

Ideally, therefore, the sales manager orients his selling operation toward the profit objective. Here he plans his selling strategies and operates his sales unit with a view toward his unit's contribution to return on investment. Even if his unit does not have defined for it or assigned to it all elements of the ROI formula (Figure 13-1), it will have many of them—in both the rate of profit and the turnover portion.

All this in no way negates the importance of the classical sales management view of control of selling expense. The expenses stemming from direct selling activities certainly must be budgeted and they must be controlled. But often control of selling expense is so emphasized that it becomes the primary (and sometimes the only) profit-oriented activity other then sales generation itself. Or some target "sales-expense" ratio is devised:

$$\text{sales expense ratio} = \frac{\text{selling expense}}{\text{sales}}$$

For example, assume that a district manager has been given a sales-expense ratio target of 8 percent. Assuming sales of $1 million and selling expense of $80,000, for some time period, he meets his target. If expenses exceed that amount, he must either cut them or increase sales, in order to maintain the required sales-expense ratio.

This kind of expense control may have some value in the short run, for analytical purposes. Taken as the prime basis for strategy, however, it can be myopic and may even result in tactics that reduce return on investment.

Managing for profit assumes that the sales manager has:

1. An actual ROI goal in percent—as a return on actual investment and utilizing all the elements of the ROI formula.

2. Or—a definitive goal of "return on assets managed" in the sense proposed by Schiff and Schiff, using the elements of the ROI formula

appropriate to the particular selling operation. These include both rate of profit and turnover elements.

3. Or—as a minimum—a grasp or a meaningful *sense* of the ROI rationale, so that the strategic meaning of the interaction of all its elements is an input into his decision making.

After all, whatever the accounting techniques of the firm, the *ROI elements do exist* and they do interact. Whatever the techniques, actions of the selling operation contribute to the firm's return on investment—positively or negatively.

In the total system sense of the firm, the modern sales manager must be profit-minded. The ROI rationale is a valuable tool to enable him to better "manage for profit."

SUGGESTED READINGS

1. Johnson, R. W., *Financial Management,* 2nd ed., Allyn and Bacon, Boston, 1962, pp. 33–41.
2. Culliton, J. W., *The Management of Marketing Costs,* Harvard University Press, Cambridge, Mass., 1948.
3. Schiff, M., "The Use of ROI in Sales Management," *Journal of Marketing,* Vol. 27, No. 3 (July 1963), pp. 70–73.
4. "Cost Control for Marketing Operations," *N. A. C. A. Bulletin,* National Association of Cost Accountants, New York, Vol. 35, No. 8 (April 1954).
5. "Cost Control for Marketing Operations," *N. A. C. A. Bulletin,* National Association of Cost Accountants, New York, Vol. 35, No. 12 (August 1954).

QUESTIONS AND PROBLEMS

1. In most firms, the selling operation is not set up on a profit-or-loss basis. Then how can one say that the sales manager must understand the variables of profitability? Why can he simply not focus on getting sales revenue?
2. Consider the equation:

$$\text{profit} = \text{revenue} - \text{cost}$$

How many ways are there to increase profit?
3. Why is "return on investment" such an important criterion for the firm's success?

4. Define in your own words:
    a. Return on investment
    b. Net profit
    c. Rate of profit
    d. Turnover
    e. Operating expenses
    f. Operating assets
    g. Fixed assets

5. Why should the sales manager be concerned with turnover?
6. What kind of "operating assets" do you think might apply to a selling operation? Give examples of some operating assets that might fall within the decision-making responsibility of a sales manager. How will these affect ROI?
7. A company has the following data for a certain time period:

Sales	$100,000
Operating expense	90,000
Working capital	30,000
Fixed assets	20,000

What is the value of:
    a. Net profit
    b. Rate of profit
    c. Turnover
    d. Return on investment

8. The sales management of the same company is, at the end of the same time period, advocating moving into new markets. A market study has concluded that sales can be increased 15 percent (to $115,000) at an increase of operating expense of only $5000. Thus net profit can be *doubled* (from $10,000 to 20,000). Should the proposal be accepted?
9. Assume that in addition to the data given in the preceding question, it is forecast that in order to achieve the additional sales volume from the new markets, warehouse inventories will have to be increased by the amount of $20,000. Also, because of adding many new customers, accounts receivable are predicted for an increase of $20,000. Should the proposal be accepted or rejected?
10. Now assume that in addition it is found that to achieve the new rate of sales on a continuing basis, two new warehouses must be secured in the new market areas (cost of $10,000) and the field customer service centers must be enlarged (cost of $10,000). Assume these two items to be "fixed assets." Now should the proposal be accepted or rejected?

Part III

Personnel Administrative Functions of Sales Management

As proposed in Chapter 4, the job of the sales manager may be broken down analytically into four major categories, all interrelated and interacting:

1. Areas of knowledge
2. Functional skills
3. The Managerial process
4. Leadership and motivation

This book focuses on two of these categories—on the managerial process and on leadership and motivation. This focus is based on the premise that optimum effectiveness of the modern sales manager whose firm operates within the marketing concept depends significantly on these categories.

The theme and the structure of this book follows a rationale that centers on the *managerial* aspects of the sales manager's job rather than on the "functional skills" that he must develop and use. This does not mean that functional skills are not important. They are important and they may even be "crucial."

But they are *technical* skills rather than managerial processes, hence should be subsumed under the *managerial* frame of reference of the sales manager's job. Therefore, they are treated in this book apart from the managerial mainstream. Furthermore, as a set of functions, they are treated in rather broad fashion—again, in the attempt to develop a *conceptual and strategic framework* rather than developing an exhaustive content. After all, each business firm will have unique situations, resources, and *modus operandi* for the implementation of these functional techniques.

The following chapters will deal broadly with these techniques—recruiting and selecting salesmen, training, and compensating. Where appropriate, they will be cross-referred to other parts of the book. Also, for the reader who wishes to go into greater technical depth, references at the end of each chapter suggest other sources of contemporary, more encyclopedic information.

14

Recruiting and Selecting Salesmen

The importance of effective recruiting becomes very apparent when one considers how much of the firm's success depends on what the salesman says, how he behaves, and how he reacts in his face-to-face interrelation with the customer. This is the magic moment—the "payoff" moment. When one also considers the events leading up to this moment, the variable of the individual salesman emerges as crucial. And when one considers the salesman himself, it becomes instantly clear that the input of new salesmen is a vital process. A "new" salesman will, of course, develop through experience and training. But a real key to sales success is the firm's ability to recruit men not only *when* wanted and in the *numbers* wanted, but with the *kinds of qualifications wanted*. This is a rational process.

THE NEED FOR FORWARD PLANNING

As a starting point in this rational process, the sales manager in every firm, large and small, ideally must develop some means of manpower planning. Furthermore, within each firm, sales managers at each organizational echelon, down to the district sales manager, ideally must do such planning. Manpower planning may be a very formal function, often

243

facilitated by staff specialists, in such large firms with vast sales forces as General Electric, IBM, and Metropolitan Life Insurance. It is equally important, even if more informally implemented by the sales manager, in a firm with a relatively small sales force, such as a food wholesaler operating only in the state of Iowa. In fact, the point can be made that the food wholesaler has less margin for error in hiring a salesman than does IBM.

Many inputs are necessary for sales manpower planning. Thus the sales manager must be aware of company goals, company strategies, marketing plans and programs, and product strategies. The sales manager must also analyze the "makeup" of his sales force with respect to mobility patterns —how and under what circumstances existing salesmen tend to move into other positions. Age and experience diversity may affect manpower plans—for example, identification of those individuals who will reach retirement age (or optional retirement age) each year for the next several years.

Some factors outside the firm itself must be considered—for example, the nature of demand and how it is expected to move; the nature of competition and how it is expected to change; the nature of key customers, or customer groups, and predicted changes in their market demands, technologies, and processes. These external variables are inputs for the market-intelligence, market-strategy systems, but often are overlooked as available manpower planning inputs.

Many firms have a large enough sales force to require the recruitment of new salesmen on a regular, planned basis each year. Usually such firms recruit at the college level. A study conducted at the University of Michigan indicates that the companies that are most successful in college recruiting have, among other things, "sophisticated manpower planning" programs. Such companies plan manpower needs five to ten years in advance.[1] The shape of the manpower plan and the extent of its reach into the future will, of course, vary considerably from firm to firm. Manpower planning will also vary within the sales structure of a given firm. That is, it will probably be relatively short-range at the district sales level and will become more extended, more formal, and more sophisticated as one moves up the sales structure to headquarter sales level.

Manpower planning is becoming more important for several reasons. It is increasingly difficult to get men of the quality and in the quantity needed. The cost of getting them is also increasing. (The cost of recruiting at the college level is now estimated to be over $1,500 per person

---

[1] George S. Odiorne, "How to Get the Men You Want," *Nation's Business,* Vol. 52, No. 1 (January 1964) , p. 70.

hired.) In addition, competition for "good" men is becoming more severe. Finally, manpower planning, however formally or informally done, can help to minimize "crash program" recruiting and hiring. To be sure, no recruiting strategy will eliminate all crises or do away with the leaping in near panic when a key sales job unexpectedly becomes vacant.[2]

DETERMINING THE KIND OF INDIVIDUAL WANTED

One result of the manager's organizing process is the identification and description of individual positions (Chapter 9). Before seeking a specific individual for the job, however, the sales manager must consider several factors.[3]

If the sales manager has a definitive job description for a specific sales position, he may start the determination process with it. Even with it, however, and very definitely if he does not have it, it is helpful to start with a picture or "model" of the sales job (rather than the *content* of the job). The model proposed in Chapter 4 is a good example and for convenience is reproduced here (Figure 14–1).

Now, for a particular sales position, the elements are filled in. The sales manager must answer to himself the following questions:

1. For this particular position, what degree of knowledge, skill, and potential is needed in each element?

2. What does the job require in regard to "market knowledge"?

3. How much product knowledge or technical skill with regard to product is required?

4. What is the nature of competition faced by the incumbent of this job?

5. What is the nature of customers to be contacted? What is the range of their technology and processes? What kinds of problems do they have?

6. What kinds of individuals are there in customer organizations? Any "difficult" personalities in key positions?

[2] Parenthetically, one element of manpower planning is to identify the key, or highly critical, sales jobs in the sales force, which cannot be left open or inadequately filled. Potential "runners-up" or candidates for these jobs should be noted from among individuals in the organization.

[3] In this discussion we shall assume that the sales manager hires an individual directly for the job. Sometimes there is an intermediate step, when individuals are hired to enter an orientation or training "pool." Even then, however, a sales manager "hires" a trainee from the pool, using the concepts discussed here. The next Chapter, "Selecting Salesmen," will treat this again.

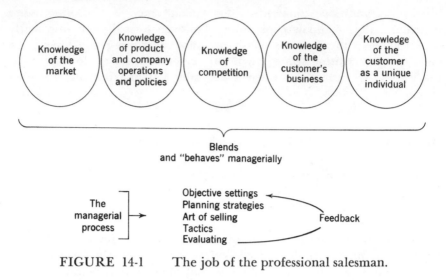

FIGURE 14-1   The job of the professional salesman.

7. What are the objectives of the job? What degree of managerial skill will be required of the incumbent to allocate the job objectives to individual customers?

8. To what extent does the job require the planning of sales strategies?

9. How important is the art of selling—that is, the communicative and personally persuasive skills needed?

10. Based on the customer's business, individual customers, and competition, how much skill in tactics is required?

11. How must the incumbent in this particular job establish the evaluating and controlling process?

Weighting the Elements

Note that examining the job in this manner is different from examining the job description. Two sales jobs may have job descriptions that look very much alike. But when each job is viewed in the above manner, differences may be quickly noted and the jobs made much more definitive. This can be done by evaluating each of the elements with regard to its importance in the specific job. Ultimately, *the elements may be weighted in importance*—a potent clue for the recruiting process.

For example, consider a sales job for a manufacturer of automated machine tools in the Detroit territory. Probably the elements of product knowledge, customer's business, and planning strategies would be deemed the most important. On the other hand, consider a sales job for a manufacturer of fine-grade papers. In selling a product that is really quite similar to that of competitors', it is likely that knowledge of product and of the cutomer's business is somewhat less important, whereas knowledge of customer as an unique individual and the art of selling may be relatively more important.

Evaluating and ranking the job elements are valuable inputs into the determination (to be discussed later) of what kind of individual should be sought. As a sort of managerial by-product, this process also sharpens the sales manager's concept of the diverse jobs under his command.

The Job Description

At this point the job description (either in formal form or as an informal concept) may be examined, because it will normally contain some factors that are not included in our model. The model focuses on the job itself, whereas the job description may also contain some *relationship descriptions*—between the job and management and between the job and other jobs. Thus such additional questions as the following can be answered:

1. What is the relationship of this job to other positions in the sales operation? What communication must be implemented?
2. What is the degree of authority to be delegated to the incumbent?
3. To whom will the incumbent report?
4. What are the measures of accountability that will be applied?

Other Factors

Several other factors should be considered:

1. Based on market potential and probable sales quotas, what will be the range of compensation (salary, commission, or combination) for this job?
2. What are the opportunities for growth (in challenge, responsibility, reward) in this job?
3. What opportunities does this job have for movement or promotion to more responsible or rewarding jobs?

Job Specifications

At this point, the sales manager may turn from the job itself and begin to consider a set of specifications for the ideal man for the particular job.

Simplifying somewhat, he examines all the foregoing questions and asks himself, "What kind of a man is needed for this particular element or relationship?"

This question leads to the *identification of traits* ideally fitted to the job. These traits may be categorized as follows:

1. Intellectual (intelligence, quickness of mind).
2. Creative (ability to think through and solve problems, ability to deal with ambiguous situations, and ability to generate new ideas, new approaches).
3. Physical (age, appearance, manner).
4. Persuasive (communicating ability).
5. Educational (formal education and previous experience).
6. Personal (such psychological factors as drive, stability, aspiration, self-image).
7. Environmental (family, church, clubs, social class, etc.).

The degree to which each of these sets of traits is required is determined by setting each of them against each of the questions (and answers) in the job, the job description, and other factors. Not all of these traits, of course, may be critical in a given sales situation. A set of "job specifications" results—or the description of the ideal man for the particular job. The sales manager can now proceed to the next step—that of generating an array of such candidates for the job.

DEVELOPING CANDIDATES

This is a search process. Its objective is to develop as many candidates as possible for the job, each of whom relatively fits the man-specifications. Many sources exist from which candidates may be sought.

1. The Company Itself. In many cases, individuals with considerable competence and potential may be found in other spheres of the company. Here it is assumed that such individuals will welcome the challenge and the opportunities of personal selling. Obviously, the intracompany search must be made with the agreement of all concerned management. The sales manager may find it helpful to work through the company's personnel function, if one exists.

2. Advertising. Advertising the job in selected newspapers and/or trade publications is commonly done. (Note the Business Section of the *New York Times* on any Sunday.)

3. Educational institutions. Here included are not only colleges and universities, but in some cases high schools and trade schools.

4. Employment Agencies. Some private agencies specialize in professional persons, including those in sales.

5. Professional Associations. Use can be made of such professional groups as Sales and Marketing Executives and the American Marketing Association.

6. Customers. Friendly customers are sources, less for individuals within their own organizations (though they themselves are sources) than through their broad contacts with many suppliers.[4]

7. Suppliers or Vendors. Often a supplier will regard it as an advantage if an individual in his employ moves to one of his customer firms.[4]

8. Competitors. Debate rages on this. Some firms never hire a salesman from a rival firm. Others deliberately try to do so. For example, some small firms seek to hire men from their large rivals who have high hiring standards and excellent training programs.[4]

9. "Off the Street" Applicants. A well-regarded firm may have a flow of voluntary applications.

10. The Present Sales Force. Members of the sales force may be good "recruiters" and develop applicants from among personal and professional friends.

THE MANPOWER "RESERVOIR"

The training "pool" or training "program" is a specialized case. Companies of a size that economically permits it may hire "new" or young sales trainees for an orientation or training program. This is usually a centralized operation, under the direction of a personnel or training staff group. After the trainees complete the program (which may vary from a couple of weeks to a year), they are "eligible" for hire by sales management. Usually, the sales manager still has choice—that is, he can select the individual whom he desires and whom, he feels, best "fits" the job to be filled.

In this case, the man-specifications established by the company recruiting function must be somewhat broader—to fit a more generalized de-

---

[4] It is important to note that this source can produce "discards"; it must, therefore, be carefully considered before being used.

scription of *most* sales jobs in the company. The rationale still holds, however.

The manpower "reservoir" idea is also valid for smaller companies who feel that they cannot afford a centralized training program. Consider a small firm such as an electrical appliance distributor operating in part of a state, with a total sales force of one sales manager and twelve field salesmen. As this firm hires *other* individuals, it may wisely *consider* potential for sales as one criterion. Thus when it hires a stock clerk, an estimator, a serviceman, and even a delivery truck driver, it may strive to select the individual who is not only fitted for the job, but also has the potential ability to move into sales work.

WHO DOES THE RECRUITING?

There is no pat answer to this question. Actual practice by firms varies over an extremely wide spectrum. However, a few general observations can be made.

Functional Responsibility

In firms large enough to have in their organization structure a personnel function, the recruiting responsibility must be clearly spelled out. Most firms place the prime responsibility for sales recruiting in the sales department. Usually the personnel function serves in a facilitating capacity. That is, it may generate an array of candidates, do some initial screening, and then refer qualified candidates to the sales department for final selection.

In small firms with no formal personnel function, the recruiting responsibility is usually vested in the sales operation, although sometimes it is withheld and centralized in the hands of the president himself.

Personal Responsibility

A wide spectrum of practice exists also in the assigning of recruiting responsibility to sales departments. Basically, this depends on the firm's philosophy of centralization versus decentralization.

The case for centralized recruiting centers on the desired need for mobility of salesmen between units of the marketing function and on the desired objectivity in selecting men. Even when recruiting is centralized, however, a territorial sales manager should have a final veto power. No salesman should be "crammed down his throat."

The case for decentralized recruiting—delegating the decisions to the territorial manager—centers on the reasonable premise that the two-way relationship of manager and salesmen will be enhanced if the decision is made at the territorial level. Higher management may establish guidelines and specifications and may retain a final veto power if needed.

Some firms use a combination of these approaches. For certain sales jobs, the territorial sales manager may have prime responsibility. For others (highly important positions or those requiring critical interaction with other sales jobs),[5] responsibility may be withheld by sales headquarters management.

TWO MAJOR PITFALLS

An active, continuous, and rich source of new talent is vital to the viability of any firm. Recruiting philosophy, policy, and procedure are highly important technical elements of the sales manager's job. Two major pitfalls face him—problems that are quite common.

Rigidity of Procedure

The recruiting process over time evolves into a *procedure*—a rather set way of doing something. Sales managers get "locked into" a routine way of recruiting. But many, many things inside and outside the firm are in change. The *mix* of elements of sales jobs changes. The demands on incumbents change. The entire recruiting process must be under continuous examination and appraisal.

The Projection of Self

It is a human reaction for the sales manager to hire in his own image. This is not necessarily bad, but it *may* be. Different sales positions require different "kinds" of people. There is no stereotype that will optimally fit all positions. The sales manager who bases his hiring decisions on an emotional thought such as "He's my kind of a guy," may not be

[5] For example, consider a firm marketing electronic instrument devices. A sales position is open in which duPont is one customer. A salesman assigned to the headquarters of duPont is in an extremely important position, requiring great competency. Probably headquarters will exercise considerable influence in his selection. Furthermore, if this company has another sales job open, in which the contact of one of duPont's decentralized operation is included, sales headquarters management might also exercise influence in his selection—on the basis that he is a member of a *sales team* assigned to duPont.

optimally fitting man to job. The suggestions in this chapter down to the creating of the job specifications are *rationally based*. Subjective considerations, however, enter the creating of the job specifications, particularly those parts of it that deal with the personal or personality traits deemed necessary. The sales manager must strive to avoid projecting his own image to these specifications.

SELECTING SALESMEN

The process of recruiting salesmen and the process of selecting salesmen are closely interrelated. Yet, they are different enough to require separate consideration. The end aims of the recruiting process (Chapter 13) are to determine the ideal kind of individual wanted for a particular job and to make available an array of candidates. The end aim of the selecting process is to screen the candidates, matching each with the man-specifications for the job and actually selecting the individual who matches best.

Selection of salesmen is more than a set of procedural steps. It is a *process*, in which the several steps are interrelated and independent. Each of the steps must be considered to be a further refinement of a matching-screening process. Each can be considered a hurdle which must be overcome.

Nine steps in the process are proposed here. There is nothing magic about this number. In certain cases, some of the steps can be combined.[6] In other cases, some personnel managers propose further subdividing some of them. The nine steps are the following:

The Selecting Process
1. Initial application form
2. Preliminary interview
3. Personal credibility check
4. A longer application form
5. Interview in more depth
6. Testing
7. Physical examination
8. Final interview
9. Decision and placement

[6] For example, steps 1 and 2 can be eliminated if the sales manager has personally sought out an individual whom he considers to be highly qualified. These steps might also be eliminated for applicants within the firm, for whom personnel data are readily available.

Initial Application Form

This is usually a relatively short form, requiring only enough information to determine that the applicant has the *basic* qualifications for the job. As a minimum, it will request name, age, experience, and education. A prepared form may not be necessary. For example, a firm advertising in the trade press may ask that the applicant merely write a letter giving the desired basic information. In any case, this first step serves as a broad screening mechanism and usually will sift out many inadequately qualified candidates.

Preliminary Interview

The purpose of this step is to further screen out unqualified applicants who passed through the first screening. Normally this will be a relatively short personal interview, with the aim of eliminating applicants who obviously fail to meet such preset criteria as physical fitness, generally favorable appearance, generally favorable manner, ability to speak well, and certain standards of experience or training. Note the word "obviously." If there is any question whether the applicant meets criteria, he should not be screened out.

Though the preliminary interview may be short and broad-gauged, the interviewer should make notes for suggested follow-up in subsequent interviews. For example, if the applicant exhibits a defensive manner when questioned about the reasons for wishing to leave his present job, this "clue" should be recorded.

It should be noted here that the techniques for interviewing are complex and difficult. Though training in interviewing is essential, it is beyond the scope of this chapter to treat the techniques professionally. The sales manager who wishes to study them in depth will find the references at the end of this chapter helpful.

Personal Credibility Check

In some cases, in addition to the preliminary interview, the candidate's personal credibility may need to be checked. Such attributes or behaviors as the handling of money (personal credit, e.g.), the use of alcohol, and moral behavior may require checking for applicants for certain sales jobs. Usually this can be done privately by a local investigating agency.

Longer Application Form

For applicants who survive the preliminary interview, considerable additional information will now be needed. Usually, at the end of the preliminary interview, the interviewer will give the applicant the longer application form. Here information in depth is sought, to better enable the evaluation of a match between man-specifications and the applicant. This in-depth information is required in several categories:

1. *Personal Data.* Marital status, family, military status, physical characteristics.

2. *Education.* Information about education is in greater depth here than in the initial application and includes all schools, degrees, fields of study, grades, honors, and languages, as well as any special training programs attended.

3. *Experience.* All positions previously held for all employers, including type of work, dates in job, salary, name of supervisor, and reasons for leaving.

4. *Community Activities.* Activities in civic groups, church and school groups, clubs, and so on.

5. *Health History.* This information may not be necessary if a complete physical examination is to be given.

6. *Reasons for Applying.* This category may provide important clues for the subsequent interview.

7. *Personal Goals.* For some sales jobs, it may be of help to have the applicant state his long-range goals and his income requirements.

8. *References.* Most applications require this information, even though the applicant will surely give the names of references whom he expects to evaluate him highly. The relevancy of the references to his work performance may be a clue, however. If all the references are people who can have no personal knowledge of his work, one might be suspicious.

The Formal Interview

Applicants who have survived the screening so far may now be interviewed in greater depth. At this point, there should be a *reasonably* close match of man and job.

The formal interview is a two-way street, giving the interviewer considerably more information about the applicant to further evaluate his match to the man-specifications and also giving the applicant information about the job, the firm, its policies, and its opportunities. The interview elicits pertinent information in three categories: (1) specific information from the applicant, (2) observation of his manner, behavior, and attitudes, and (3) inference relative to his personal traits. It may follow one of several forms:

(*a*) *Structural interview,* in which the interviewer closely follows a prepared format, recording exactly the answers to specific questions.

(*b*) *Nonstructured interview,* in which the applicant is encouraged to talk by asking him broad, open-ended questions (e.g., "What is it that you like about selling?").

(*c*) *Stress-oriented interview,* in which the interviewer deliberately antagonizes and confuses the applicant, to observe his manner of reacting.[7]

By and large, for the selecting of sales people, the nonstructured form of interview seems to have the most value in helping to evaluate the man-job match.

Again, interviewing and the subsequent evaluation of the interview require considerable technical skill. And again the reader is encouraged to examine the extensive literature on this subject if he feels need to become proficient in this technical skill. Note the specific references at the end of this chapter.

Testing Applicants

Testing is another highly technical process requiring great specialized skill. Probably few sales managers have such competency, and must rely on trained staff specialists or outside consultants. However, testing is such a debatable subject that the sales manager should be at least conversant with current theories and practices of testing—if for no other reason than to evaluate for himself the claims of proponents and opponents.[8]

There are several kinds of tests: intelligence, aptitude, dexterity, personality and interest, and achievement. Some may have bearing on certain sales jobs. For example, a technical sales job that requires a high level of ability in creative problem solving may provide a possibility for testing.

Because of the wide diversity of opinion about the efficacy of psychological testing, it is safe to say that a sales manager whose firm does use

---

[7] "Situational testing" is an application of this technique. Here the candidate is placed in an actual—or sometimes simulated—selling situation, and his performance is observed and evaluated.

[8] The sales manager must also beware of the many charlatans in the psychological testing business.

testing should not base a selection decision only on the results of a test.

Note the reference at the end of the chapter to a good basic source of technical knowledge about the use of psychological testing.[9]

Physical Examination

Most sales jobs are physically demanding and require a full measure of energy and stamina. Almost all firms require a physical examination of the applicant, to make certain that he is physically capable of meeting the job requirements and to protect the company against liability for preexisting conditions.

Final Interview

Often a final interview with the applicant may be necessary to assure optimum job-man match. Although "good" points far outweigh "bad" ones at this stage, the sales manager may wish to be sure that any deficiencies that do exist are either relatively unimportant or correctable. Another reason for a final interview is that several applicants may have survived all the foregoing hurdles, and a final screening out of all but one must be accomplished.

The final interview may be conducted either by the former interviewer or by a "new" interviewer—often the sales manager himself. Sometimes, for key sales positions, several persons in management may separately interview the last handful of candidates, with final selection made in a consensus manner.

CONCLUDING COMMENTS

Within any selling organization there are many kinds of jobs, with varying specifications. Identifying and describing these specifications is a rational process. Matching individuals to the specifications is a less rational, more subjective process. Therefore, following a rationally devised *plan* for selection will help to optimize the match by reducing personal bias and human error.

It is not unusual to observe some firms using such a selecting process when hiring *new salesmen,* but following no such rationale when moving *existing salesmen* to different jobs or when *promoting* a salesman to a

---

[9] For cost reasons, psychological testing should probably not be used unless the number of applicants exceeds the number of open positions by at least three to one.

managerial position. In fact, one of the near tragedies in many selling operations is the promoting of a "star" salesman to a sales manager's position—only to create a mediocre manager at the cost of an excellent salesman.

A rationale similar to that proposed in this chapter can be used in the selection process for *all* jobs in the selling operation. To be sure, some of the steps can be eliminated or altered in some cases. The objective still is to define the job clearly, to develop man-specifications, and to find the individual who most ideally fits the specifications. It is inexcusable to be slipshod about this process—yet many firms do not adequately follow it when filling sales managers' positions.

The key is really quite simple—match the man and the job. The techniques for doing it are sometimes complex, but they are learnable. The references that follow may serve as a door opener.

SUGGESTED READINGS

General Reading on the Selection Process

1. Flippo, Edwin B., *Principles of Personnel Management,* McGraw-Hill, New York, 1961, pp. 177–219.
2. Wolf, William B., *The Management of Personnel,* Wadsworth Publishing Company, San Francisco, 1961, pp. 56–66.
3. Yoder, Dale, *Production Management and Industrial Relations,* Prentice-Hall, Englewood Cliffs, N.J., 1962, pp. 322–351.
4. Jewell, Keith R., "Use Sensible Time Savers," *Sales Management,* Vol. 92 (March 6, 1964), pp. 45 ff.
5. Jewell, Keith R., "Always Check with Others," *Sales Management,* Vol. 92 (March 20, 1964), pp. 49 ff.
6. Jewell, Keith R., "Always Get the Full Story," *Sales Management,* Vol. 92 (April 3, 1964), pp. 47 ff.

Application Forms

1. Marting, E., ed., *AMA Book of Employment Forms,* American Management Association, New York, 1967. (This is a 700-page compilation of actual employment forms of all kinds used currently by major firms. It also includes editorial comment.)
2. Mandell, Milton M., *The Selection Process,* American Management Association, New York, 1964, pp. 158–186.

Selecting Salesmen

1. Haas, Kenneth B., *How to Develop Successful Salesmen*, McGraw-Hill, New York, 1957, pp. 10–13.
2. McMurray, Robert N., "How to Draft a Useful Job Description," *Portfolio of 1964 Selling Plans*, Sales Management, Inc., New York, 1963, pp. 43–44.
3. Hertan, William A., "Eight Pitfalls in Hiring Field Sales Managers," *Portfolio of 1964 Selling Plans*, Sales Management, Inc., New York, 1963, pp. 51–52.
4. Odiorne, George S., "How to Get the Man You Want," *Nation's Business*, Vol. 52 (January 1964), pp. 70–74.
5. Jewell, Keith R., "Let's Take the Hocus Pocus Out of Hiring," *Sales Management:* Part I, Vol. 92 (February 7, 1964), pp. 28 ff.; Part II, Vol. 92 (February 21, 1964), pp. 41 ff.
6. Belasco, James A., "Broadening the Approach to Salesman Selection," *Personnel*, January–February 1966, pp. 67–72. (Emotional and intellectual demands of selling jobs.)
7. Flippo, Edwin B., *Principles of Personnel Management*, McGraw-Hill, New York, 1961, pp. 159–176.
8. Jucius, Michael J., *Personnel Management*, 6th ed., Richard D. Irwin, Homewood, Ill., 1967, pp. 90–124.

Interviewing

1. Fear, Richard A., *The Evaluation Interview*, McGraw-Hill, New York, 1958.
2. Mandell, Milton M., *The Selection Process*, American Management Association, New York, 1964, pp. 187–254.
3. McMurray, Robert N., "Validating the Patterned Interview," in E. A. Fleming, ed., *Studies in Personnel and Industrial Psychology*, The Dorsey Press, Homewood, Ill., 1960, pp. 17–25.
4. Randsepp, Eugene, "How to Hire Key People," *Nation's Business*, Vol. 51 (September 1963), pp. 54–58.
5. Wagner, R., "The Employment Interview: A Critical Appraisal," *Personnel Psychology*, Vol. 2 (1949), pp. 17–46.
6. Mayfield, E. C., "The Selection Interview," *Personnel Psychology*, Vol. 17 (1946), pp. 239–260.
7. Ulrich, L., and Trumbo, D., "The Selection Interview since 1949," *Psychological Bulletin*, Vol. 63 (1965), pp. 100–116.

Testing

1. Barrett, Richard S., "Guide to Using Psychological Tests," *Harvard Business Review*, Vol. 41 (September–October 1963), pp. 138–146.
2. Bender, W. R. G., "Psychological Testing in Industry," *Personnel Journal*, Vol. 43 (April 1964), pp. 203 ff.
3. Miller, Robert M., *Tests and the Selection Process*, Science Research Associates, Inc., Chicago, 1966.
4. Stanton, E. S., "Psychological Testing in Industry: A Critical Evaluation," *Personnel Journal*, Vol. 43 (January 1964), pp. 27–32.
5. Haire, Mason, "Use of Tests in Employee Selection," *Harvard Business Review*, Vol. 28 (January–February 1950), pp. 42–51.

Decision Making

1. Webster, Edward C., *Decision Making in the Employment Interview*, Industrial Relations Centre, Montreal, 1964. (A book of research findings.)

Note

Several excellent journals frequently treat the selection process and its several elements by proposing new ideas or by critiquing current practices. A sales manager who wants to keep abreast of the ongoing study in this managerial field may wish to refer occasionally to the following periodicals:

Personnel
Personnel Administration
Personnel Journal
Personnel Magazine
Personnel Management

Various trade and professional magazines also frequently deal with the selection process:

Dun's Review
Harvard Business Review
Industrial Marketing
Nation's Business
Sales Management

QUESTIONS AND PROBLEMS

1. You are a sales manager for a food wholesaling firm. You need a new salesman to handle a newly established territory, being formed from parts of three other salesmen's territories. You decide to seek applicants through a professional employment agency whose service you have heard is very good. What information would you give to the agency? How would you go about determining this information for yourself?

2. You are a sales manager for a small office-supply distributing firm. You have four field salesmen. In the past, you have had very unpleasant experiences when you lost a salesman with little advance notice. But being in a small firm, you cannot afford to have "stand-by" people in training, as larger firms can. What alternatives might you have?

3. In a company large enough to have a personnel department (or individuals assigned to and skilled in the recruiting and selecting process), what are the advantages and disadvantages in using it for selecting salesmen? What can the sales manager do to strike an optimal compromise between using the personnel department and doing the job himself?

4. State in your own words the value to the sales manager of each one of the steps in the "selecting process."

5. You are a headquarters sales manager. The manager of marketing asks you to prepare a "manpower planning forecast" for the next five years. Of what use is this for your operation? Using imagination, what form do you think it might take? What major variables should be included?

6. Select any company. Imagine two different sales jobs in this company. Describe these jobs and then construct a set of "man specifications" for each.

15

Developing Salesmen

Part I of this book stated that the firm operates in a sea of change. Its external environments are in constant change, requiring adjustive market behaviors; its internal environments react to this and also to the force of changing technology. Customers undergo and react to the same kinds of change, and so do rivals.

The selling operation, as the linking system between markets and the firm, feels the full brunt of all this change inside and outside the firm. It would be naïve to believe that the effective salesman and the effective sales manager need not continually adjust their thinking and behavior. The effective salesman's knowledge, skills, and managerial behavior must shift and must grow, if the selling operation (hence the firm) is to continue to optimally meet its objectives.

The firm, therefore, must view individual's development as a continuous, never-ending process. This development is much broader and more complex than the orientation or induction training of a new employee. It is much broader and more complex than training in the "teaching-oriented" sense of meetings and classroom work. The development process must consider each individual in the firm as a whole person, contributing his mind and body (and even his heart) to a whole job, the real implementation of which is under constant change.

The Objective of Salesman Development

The objective of salesman development is relatively simple: *more effective selling by all individuals in the sales operation*. This requires continuous growth in the attitudes, skills, knowledge, and habits of all sales personnel.[1] *Salesman development* is the long-term behavior change to this end. *Salesman training* is the shorter-term, structured "programs" for learning—or a formal part of the total plan for salesman development.

Note the inclusion of *all* individuals. There should be no debate about who is to be "trained." In today's business world, all professional men must develop, grow, adjust behaviors. Contrary to the idea held by many firms that training should be devised for the new and for the average or below-average salesmen, real payoff may well come even more spectacularly from the continuing or further development of already highly effective performers.[2] To be sure, the goals, content, style, and form of training should vary considerably. But the door-opening ideas in this chapter apply to all individuals in the selling operation—salesmen and field sales managers, product specialists and servicemen, new men and experienced men, outstanding performers and mediocre performers.

A Basic Rationale

Each firm must decide for itself what its basic approach to training will be. A good starting point is to recognize that it is an *individual person* who develops himself, hence that it is his *whole job* that must be the focal point for training, not just some part of it.[3] Thus the basic frame of reference for salesman training is the model of the job of the salesman, reproduced here once more for convenience (Figure 15–1).

This "general position guide" can serve as an outline for training. Here we are assuming that all salesmen follow these elements. To be sure, jobs vary, and for some salesmen certain of these elements are more important than for others. For example—and oversimplifying—assume that in a sales region consisting of five sales districts with a total of forty salesmen, the regional sales manager (perhaps in consultation with his district sales managers) identifies eight of the positions as requiring a very high level of competency in "planning strategies." (Perhaps these eight

[1] Robert B. Burr, "Training and Development of Salesmen, in Robert Vizza, ed., *The New Handbook of Sales Training*, Prentice-Hall, Englewood Cliffs, N. J., 1967, pp. 35–40.

[2] In fact, some sales and marketing managers feel that *most* of their training effort should be allocated to and tailored to the excellent performers. This is on the reasonable premise that even a very small increase in effectiveness of the outstanding performers will far outweigh the gain that can be achieved from mediocre performers through the same developmental effort.

[3] Unfortunately, the great majority of firms overemphasize product training. See Robert Stone, "Eight-Point Checklist for Sales Training," *Sales Management*, Part II, July 19, 1963, pp. 110 ff.

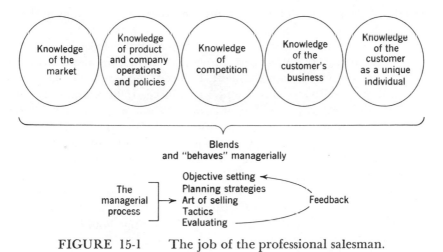

FIGURE 15-1   The job of the professional salesman.

positions encompass the largest, most important, and most complex customers.) This is an input into the training rationale. Probably some kind of training should be considered to help the salesmen in these positions become more effective in planning strategies.

But another variable enters here. To what extent does each of these individuals really need continued training in this element? Recall that in the selection process, a description of the specific job (which puts content and relative weighing into the model) and a set of man-specifications were developed. Presumably the man whose qualifications best matched the man-specifications was placed in the job. But a perfect match is rare. This process, however, pinpoints the gaps, and this is a signal for the need for training in order to plug the gaps.

Furthermore, after the individual has gained some experience in the job, his performance can be evaluated.[4] The evaluation process reveals gaps between performance desired and performance achieved. Often, of course, this is immediately corrected by the sales manager by pointing out the gap and suggesting corrective action [5] (really a "training" device in a sense). However, if the gap seems to be rather common among a number of salesmen, the need for training is indicated.

Thus any one individual may be performing competently in some

[4] Refer to the discussion of "evaluating individual performance," Chapter 12, pp. 218–224.

[5] This presumes that the sales manager knows what areas of knowledge or managerial behavior need sharpening for the salesman to achieve adequate corrective action. This illustrates another value of the "model" of the salesman's job.

elements of his job, but less competently in others. His program of development, therefore, will proceed along two tracks. First, in those areas in which he is doing well, he will need only a skill-sharpening kind of training, at relatively infrequent intervals. Second, in those areas in which there is room for improvement, he needs more specific, more concentrated, and relatively more frequent training. If he is the only individual in this category, the training may be on a personal manager-salesman "coaching" basis. If several individuals fall into this category, a specific training "program" may be devised for a group of salesmen.

This leads to a cardinal concept in training. *Training programs (formal and informal) must be tailored to the needs of individual salesmen.* They should not be created around the image of some manager or around what some manager *thinks* the salesmen should have.[6] The kind, the amount, the style, and the frequency of training should spring from this concept.

GENERAL AREAS OF TRAINING

Just as the firm's overall sales training and development program must have an overriding rationale and a set of objectives, so also must its various elements. Many different kinds of training are normally required, each having its own rationale and goals, but also being interrelated with all the others. The discussion that follows proposes one way in which training and development may be analyzed into key areas, following generally the "model" of the professional salesman's job.[7] It covers:

[6] It has been my observation, both as a sales manager and as a sales consultant to many firms, that it is common for a headquarters sales manager to say, "Let's give them this kind of a meeting," rather than saying, "What do they need? Where are the common, serious gaps?" One would really expect sales managers to be "market-oriented" with respect to training, but many are not. Furthermore, it is often very helpful to have the salesmen themselves recommend what they feel is needed in training.

[7] There are other ways. Many of them, however, turn away from a complete analysis of the sales job, hence are inadequate in coverage. For example, Robert Stone, writing in *Sales Management* (Part II, July 19, 1963, pp. 110 ff), cites "six vitamins" for a good sales training program:

1. Product knowledge
2. Knowledge of company promotions
3. Knowledge of company procedures
4. Management of individual's time
5. Review of selling techniques
6. Motivation of salesmen

A "good" training program may need some additional vitamins, such as strategy creating and knowledge of customers' business.

1. Orientation training
2. Knowledge and skill training
3. Managerially oriented training
4. Market oriented training

Orientation Training

When "new" salesmen are inducted into the company, some basic orientation is necessary. This may take a few days or as much as several months. Many medium-sized and large firms have centralized this training bringing new sales trainees (usually from the college campus) to a central location for the orientation training period. However, even when a salesman is hired for direct placement into a field sales job, he must be given some measure of orientation training, usually by the field sales manager.

The content of orientation training is usually heavily centered on knowledge and skill training, particularly for product technology, and on company policy and procedure.

Knowledge and Skill Training

Note that the elements of this kind of training follow generally the model of the professional salesman's job.

1. Product. This element is basic. Certainly, every salesman must have a complete knowledge of *everything* about his products (or services) — how they are made, why they are made that way, how they may be applied and used, how they are serviced, and so on. This is a never-ending facet of training because product technology is so ever-changing. The possible danger here is an overemphasis on product training at the cost of other crucial elements.

2. Company Operations and Policy. In the model, this element may be subsumed under product knowledge, in a sense. But certainly the salesman must know and understand a wide array of company policies and procedures.

3. Customer's Business. In many cases, some salesmen may require training in customer technologies and processes. It is difficult for individuals to gain this knowledge simply by experience, and it would be naïve to expect that each salesman will adequately keep abreast of rapidly changing customer technologies (hence customer problems and needs, hence new applications of product). For example, consider salesmen selling technical or semitechnical products to such customer industries as aerospace, oil refining, and machine tools. Conceivably, the salesmen assigned to customers in such industries might profit greatly by some occasional training in the changing technology of those industries. The customer need not have an exotic technology for this to be true. It applies also to a salesman who handles several large commerical banks as customers, for example. The world of banking is in change, and the salesman must keep abreast of this change.

4. The Psychology of Selling. Knowledge of the customer as a unique individual is vital. Understanding—or having insight into—how he perceives, thinks, and responds is a crucial input into the salesman's strategy and tactics. This is an area of salesman development that is generally covered inadequately or not covered at all.

5. The Art of Selling. In many firms the salesman is left to his own devices to develop skill in preparing effective selling presentations and in implementing them effectively. Other firms attempt to fill this need halfway by subscribing to some "cookbook" approach ("Ten Proved Ways of Closing a Sale," etc.) that sometimes borders on quackery. This large gap that exists in many selling operations can be filled by using a number of excellent sources. A number of topflight sales training consulting firms are doing fine work in this field. Marketing professors in many colleges of business administration may provide excellent consultation. (See also a later section on "Outside Training.")

Managerially Oriented Training

Few training programs reflect what most modern sales managers recognize—that the effective professional salesman must be more than a "knower" and a "doer." He must think and act as a manager. He is the "manager of his territory" and so behaves. He is the firm's marketing tactician in the field. Understanding of the following managerial processes is essential for the effective salesman:

1. Planning strategies
2. Tactics
3. Creative problem solving
4. Evaluating and controlling

1. Planning Strategies. Most salesmen, even highly competent ones, need continual development in this crucial aspect. Entire training sessions, involving concepts and application, can be built around this area. Chapter 8 of this book can serve as a starting point.

2. Tactics. When the salesman is in the presence of the customer, he observes how the customer reacts to situations that the salesman creates. How should the salesman respond? How should he react to the customer's reaction so that he can make progress toward his mission for that call and not be retarded? This is the realm of *tactics*. It covers all the means by which the salesman rationally flexes or shifts his behavior while with the customer—ranging from the idea of "controlling the interview without seeming to" to maneuvering the discussion down planned paths, to the optimum handling of objections and overcoming obstacles, and to the closing of the sale (or securing of agreement). Again, this is an important element of the sales job that is often overlooked or sometimes handled in "cookbook" style.[8]

3. Creative Problem Solving. Creativity in selling is particularly important in certain sales jobs. This is true in the selling of "intangibles," or services, and in the selling of innovative, new products. It may be true also for the selling of products or services that will require the customer to make drastic changes in his processes or techniques. Developing skill in creative problem solving in a sense is an application of knowledge of the customer's business and of planning strategies. But this element does have a rationale of its own and a methodology that can be learned. It should not be left to chance development in those sales jobs where it is deemed important.[9]

4. Evaluating and Controlling. The professional salesman develops skills in self-evaluating and adjustive behavior. Techniques in controlling, therefore, are legitimate areas for training and development. Again, they should not be left to chance.[10]

Market-Oriented Training

Ability to preserve, understand, and evaluate market forces is important in most sales jobs. To be sure, experience on the job is probably the

---

[8] For example, if one examines the many books on "How to Sell," he is struck with the realization that the area of tactics usually focuses only on some *formula* for the salesman's response to a situation. It never focuses on the *reasons* for the situation. In fact, "formula" tactics never even consider the situation itself or the really key aspect of it—the unique customer. The tie of tactics to strategy and to psychological aspects of selling is almost universally omitted.

[9] A good source is W. J. E. Crissy and H. C. Cash, *Logic and Creativity in Selling*, Personnel Development Associates, Flushing, New York, 1967. This is Volume 8 in the "Psychology of Selling Series."

[10] See Crissy and Cash, *The Salesman as a Self Manager*, Personnel Development Associates, Flushing, New York, 1967. This is Volume 6 in the "Psychology of Selling Series."

best "teacher" of market forces, but training programs can and should treat the techniques and tools that can help the salesman to improve his effectiveness in the following areas:

1. *Market Analysis*—the identification of economic, social, technological, and political forces that may affect demand for his product, their evaluation, and their input into his strategy calculus.

2. *Competitive Behavior*—the developing by the salesman of his own "enemy intelligence" system for his territory, for input into his strategy calculus.

3. *His Firm's Market Programs*—knowledge of the plans and programs created and implemented by the marketing operation, together with his part in them.

FORMS OF TRAINING

Since a large body of literature exists in the realm of forms of employee training, only a broad overview is necessary here. Sales managers held responsible for creating and implementing formal training programs can probably benefit by examining this body of literature, which contains many excellent discussions of *forms* of training. (See the references at the end of this chapter.)

But whereas the literature on formal programs is excellent, nothing much is said about "informal" training. Actually, in the day-to-day personal interaction between sales manager and salesman, great opportunity exists for training—*in the sense that the salesman's knowledge, skills, and attitudes can be enhanced by such interaction*. Again, this need not be left to chance. All the sales manager must do is to realize that his role as "trainer" never really stops and always overlaps all his other interactional roles. Furthermore, if the sales manager in his evaluating of salesmen perceives gaps between performance desired and performance achieved, and if he can "pin down" the discrepancy to specific areas of the salesman's job he need not wait for a training program. He may counsel the salesman. Of course, this managerial behavior is also categorized as "controlling" (see Chapter 12), specifically by way of the "appraisal" technique. It is, nevertheless, *training* in the purest sense, because it aims to continue influencing the salesman's knowledge, skills, and attitudes, and not simply to make a momentary correction. Thus the *managerial-coaching* or *managerial-counseling* interaction between manager and salesman is an essential training device and should be thought of in terms of the foregoing section as well as in terms of the "controlling" process.

Common forms of such informal training include the following:

1. Personal Appraisal. This is the communication by sales manager to salesman of "how he is doing" with respect to the objectives of the job. It is often inadequately done, because many sales managers find it difficult to propose what kind of corrective action should be taken. Again, the model of the job of the professional salesman, consideration of man-specifications, and the rationale of the foregoing section should be helpful.

2. Customer Situation Analysis. The sales manager meets with the salesman to conduct an exhaustive appraisal of market conditions in the salesman's territory and to make a "state of the union" examination of each of the salesman's key accounts. Progress toward goals is reviewed, obstacles are identified, and plans for overcoming them are discussed. This is a "participative" session, in which the salesman himself ideally develops creative ideas for goal achievement, but it is an ideal setting for the manager to "coach" and "counsel." The rationale of Chapter 8 is particularly helpful here.

3. The Joint Call. When a sales manager travels the territory with a salesman and calls on customers with him, an excellent training opportunity exists. It is important to note that a "joint call" on a customer has three phases. First, the "before" phase involves deciding the specific mission for the call, the broad strategy, potential problems, a review of history, a review of customers, a review of competition, and opening tactics. Second, the "during" phase involves the events of the call itself, with the sales manager and salesman enacting their previously planned roles. Third, the "after" phase is the "postmortem" in which the sales manager and the salesman review what actually happened, the degree of success or failure, reasons for either, new facts learned, and mission and strategy for the next call. Again, the customer strategy format of Chapter 8 is an excellent device to use in planning and executing the joint call. Whatever other purposes the sales manager may have for calling on the customer with the salesman, *he ideally should always consider it as a training opportunity.*

Forms of Formal Training

The structural forms of formal training programs (or individual sessions) vary; they are well covered in training literature. The main thing to consider here is that the sales manager must first determine what the desired goal of a particular training program is—and only then should he select a form of the training that uniquely "fits" the goal. Following this idea, we can categorize and list the forms of training as follows:

FORMS OF FORMAL TRAINING

INFORMATION DISSEMINATION

Purpose: One-way flow of *knowledge* to salesmen. Highly structured. Ideal for communicating product information, policy, pricing, procedures, marketing programs, and so on.

1. Lecture
2. Demonstrations
3. Manuals and bulletins

PARTICIPATIVE FORMS

Purpose: Development of *skills and attitudes.* As little structure as possible. Ideal for "situational" and managerial-process training. Considerable participation by salesmen, even in the planning of sessions.

1. Seminar
2. Panel
3. Role playing
4. Group problem solving
5. Cases
6. Task force
7. Gaming

Information Dissemination

A considerable amount of factual information must flow to salesmen. For product, policy, pricing, and promotion programs, this flow can well be one-way. The aim is purely to present information. These forms are useful in orientation training and in keeping experienced salesmen "up to date." The following training forms are the best for this purpose:

1. *The lecture,* in which specific information is presented, usually to a relatively large group and usually by an expert in the subject.
2. *The demonstration,* in which the information is dramatized.
3. *Manuals and bulletins,* in which information is presented in written form and usually in a flow.

Participative Forms

The development of most skills and managerial abilities is better achieved by more "participative" forms of training, in which the individual salesman becomes personally involved, sometimes even before the session by helping to plan the program or by doing "assigned homework." [11] Participative forms are ideally suited to "situational training," or the development of problem-solving and strategy-creating skills. Forms include:

1. *The seminar,* in which a number of salesmen discuss common problems, each contributing to the group. It is usually restricted to a relatively small number (a maximum of fifteen). The seminar should encourage freewheeling discussion by all members, but should not degenerate into a tangential "bull session." A skillful seminar leader thus is essential.

2. *The panel* may be used for larger groups. Here a small number of "experts" give their individual views on a selected problem. Group discussion, addressed to the panel, explores possible solutions.

3. *Role playing,* in which selling situations are acted out by salesmen in front of an observing group of salesmen. Observers critique the role play and made suggestions. There is psychological backing for the idea that it is really the observer who benefits most in this form, since *he imagines himself* in a similar situation. Yet some sales managers and salesmen disparage the role play technique in that it is always too far from "real" situations. When role playing is used, this "make-believe" aura must be accepted and the real focus placed on *observers'* evaluations.

4. *Group problem solving* in which a group is given a specific problem and is challenged to generate alternative selections, to choose the "best one," and to defend the choice. For example, a small group of computer sales engineers might be given this problem:

> "What should be the sales engineer's strategy and tactics when he learns that the customer's Vice President of Employee Relations has expressed violent objection to consideration of a computer purchase until after the new union contract is negotiated six months hence?"

5. *Cases,* in which an entire customer situation, including the competitive situation, is presented in depth to a group of salesmen. In group discussion, the salesmen explore all aspects of the case and attempt to search out all alternatives for successful objective achievement.

6. *The task force,* in which a small group of salesmen (a maximum of five) is presented with some general sales problem or some need for innovative thinking. The group is given some time—perhaps a month—to explore the problem in any way it desires. It is given access to company management and other sales groups for interviewing or idea solicitation.

[11] See W. J. E. Crissy, "Do Assignments Before/After Sales Meetings Make Sense?" in *Sales Meetings Magazine,* March 15, 1967.

At the end of the time period, the task force makes a formal report and recommendation to management. It may also present the findings to the total sales group in "panel" form.

7. *Gaming,* or the simulation of complex situations, is gaining great popularity as a high-potential device for management-oriented and strategy-oriented training. The great advantage of the game (particularly computer games) is that after the salesman (or group) makes a decision for a given situation, customers' and competitors' reactions are fed in and a new situation is created, demanding a new "solution." Teams of salesmen playing in competition with one another (striving, say, for increased share of the customer's business) add spice and life to this training.

External Development Opportunities

The firm's sales training and development programs, both formal and informal, may be supplemented by participation of salesmen in development opportunities outside the firm. Many firms do not leave this to chance, but encourage salesmen to participate, often "nominating" them and covering their expenses. Many such opportunities exist.

1. University or College Courses. Many educational institutions have excellent, highly sophisticated courses in professional selling, sales management, and marketing functions useful to the salesmen. The MBA programs may provide considerable new skill in the "managerial process," particularly in planning, decision making, and controlling.

2. University-Sponsored Sales Seminars. Noncredit seminars are held in some colleges of business administration. An outstanding example is the Advanced Salesmanship Workshop jointly presented by Michigan State University and Arizona State University. Limited to experienced professional salesmen who are certified by their firms to be in the top third of all salesmen in performance, this professional, two-day seminar covers such subjects as:

> Selling Within the Marketing Concept
> Psychological Aspects of Selling
> Sales Strategy
> Creating Effective Presentations
> Creative Problem Solving

These universities, and some others, also periodically present very effective, highly professional seminars in sales management.

3. Other Seminar Sources. Professional associations and trade associations sponsor many sales and sales management seminars and workshops.

These may be staged by the association itself or they may be staged by the firm, using association-developed programs. For example the American Management Association offers an "In-Company Training Program" entitled "How to Be a More Effective Sales Manager," built around five filmed presentations. With the filmed lectures come a discussion outline and leader's guide to assist the firms training personnel. Topics covered are:

How to Recruit, Interview, and Select Salesmen
How to Develop Productive Sales Plans
How to Measure and Control Field Sales Effort
How to Interact With and Motivate Salesmen
Fundamentals of Field Sales Manpower Development

A word of caution: many "sales training" programs are available that are clever and inspirational, but have little objective content and do little more than inspire and entertain. Selection of such programs should be carefully based on training objectives and must be made in terms of tailoring to training needs.

4. Professional Associations. Membership and active participation in such outstanding professional societies as the American Marketing Association and the Sales and Marketing Executives provide a splendid source of personal development. Many headquarters sales managers encourage their field sales managers to become active in such groups.

Distributor and Dealer Training

This training is a special case, but the concepts discussed so far can be adapted to it. Many sales managers direct significant sales effort through distributors' or dealers' personnel. These people, of course, are not under the sales manager's command, and any sales training that they receive from him must come by persuasion of distributor or dealer management. Most distributors and dealers expect their supplying firms to provide *product training,* which is as far as the sales management of most supplying firms goes. Great opportunity may exist, however, for the astute sales manager who can present a balanced, planned, overall training program covering all aspects of professional selling. The distributors' and dealers' salesmen need this as much as any salesmen (and, sadly, often even more so) .[12]

---

[12] The program must be *tailored* to the individual distributor. Unfortunately, a firm's sales manager often presents a distributor program in terms of his own company and of his own perception of need.

Training Tools and Techniques

A well-planned sales training program can be less than optimally effective (and sometimes even an utter failure) if care is not used in *executing* the program *with the right tools and techniques and in the right physical environment.*

A broad array of excellent audiovisual tools are available, ranging from good chalkboards, felt boards, overhead projectors, film studies, and the like to the newer and exciting computer games, video tape with playback, and the like. Much literature is available on proper use of these tools.

In some cases, when a sales manager holds a highly important sales meeting (e.g., the "annual three-day" sales meeting for all field sales managers), he may find it advisable to seek the help of specialists in his firm in the staging of the meeting. But even in the smaller, more frequent sales meetings (e.g., the "monthly sales meeting" held by a district manager for his twelve salesmen), there is no excuse for not using *adequate* tools. Many sales meetings are "spoiled" by poor charts, unreadable slides, lack of an adequate chalkboard, and so forth.

Proper environment is mandatory. Sales meetings that are held in crowded, poorly ventilated, noisy, uncomfortable, or poorly lighted rooms may actually do more harm than good. There is no excuse for not having the right environment for a meeting. This is just as true for the rather "informal" meetings held in the field by a district sales manager as it is for large, formal, headquater-sponsored meetings.[13]

WHO IS RESPONSIBLE FOR TRAINING?

In a way, this is a meaningless question. Certainly, *every* sales manager, whatever his level in the hierarchy, is accountable for the optimal training in all subordinate elements. The real question is, how does he implement it?

Companies of some size may have a headquarters staff unit that spe-

---

13 Even this relatively simple idea needs planning and careful "checking out." I recently attended a meeting in a brand-new "convention annex" built by a motel in Phoenix. The rooms and furnishings appeared quite "plush" on the surface. But soon after the meeting began, another meeting started in an adjacent room. Every word and even the sound of throat-clearing in the next room were clearly audible. Unfortunately, the other meeting was apparently a semisocial one, with much laughter and glass-tinkling. It greatly disturbed our meeting and definitely detracted from its value. Some planner had not checked out the acoustics.

cializes in sales training. This, of course, does not take the accountability, planning, and control away from line sales management. Headquarters sales trainers may implement the initial or orientation training. They may also, on direction of top sales management, implement national sales meetings or uniformly presented regional meetings.

These specialists may also be available to line sales managers (down to district level) in the capacity of cooperating with the line sales manager to facilitate his training decisions. This may be a joint effort, with line and staff personnel combining in the planning and executing of sales training. It in no way takes away the line sales manager's responsibility to make certain that *all training is tailored to his group's needs.*

In a small company, the sales manager may have to plan and execute all sales training himself. He may, however, seek help from some of his salesmen, gaining the additional payoff of motivation through participation.

SOME CONCLUDING THOUGHTS

Finally, the sales manager at any level must always think of the necessary function of training in terms of his group's objectives, short- and long-range. Furthermore, the managerial process of controlling is also involved. That is, he must always think: "What is it we are trying to do? How are we doing? What deviations are there from target course? What changes are needed in performance and in individuals' behaviors? Do individuals now have the skills, knowledge, and attitudes to effect these performances? If not, how to develop them?" Thus training must not be shot at as an isolated target of some kind. It is an activity devised as a result of managerial thinking and analysis and must be meshed into the managerial process.

In the dynamic organizing process, the sales manager must always have a calculus on the missions, charters, and definitions of jobs. As these change, man-specifications change—often subtly. Thus the gap between man-specifications and the performance (and potential) of the incumbent may alter, triggering the need for tailored training.

Even when the *nature* of the job and man-specifications do not change, the *content* may change, requiring training or development. Changes in product technology, market trends, marketing programs and promotions, company policy, customer technology and processes, and competitive activity all are inputs into training plans.

In conclusion, it is well to note that there may be a bit of semantic sloppiness in thinking and talking about *training* salesmen. A danger exists in thinking of training as cramming knowledge into salesmen's minds. Training in terms of "teaching" is oriented toward the teacher side, rather than to the learner side.

Much more meaningful, however, is the idea of *developing* salesmen. Philosophically, development is salesman-oriented. The crucial idea is not what he learns, but how he uses it or how he adapts his attitude and behavior.

Consider the word "educate." Many persons (including some educators) may conceive it to mean merely the imparting of knowledge. But to get at the real meaning of "educate," examine the source of the word. It comes from two Latin words, *é* and *ducere*—*é* meaning "out from" and *ducere* meaning "to lead." Hence "to *educate*" really means *to lead out from.*[14]

So it is with training. Training, even when ideally tailored to the salesman's needs, has fruition only if he takes it and *goes on,* letting it lead his thinking into new channels. This important thought must not be lost in the welter of the details of training.

SUGGESTED READINGS

General Reading for Technical Skill in Training

1. Vizza, Robert F., *The New Handbook of Sales Training,* Prentice-Hall, Englewood Cliffs, N.J., 1967.
2. Hegarty Edward J., *Making Your Sales Meetings Sell,* McGraw-Hill, New York, 1955.
3. Editorial Board of Prentice-Hall Business and Professional Publications, *Executive Leadership Course,* Volume III, Chapter 4, "Training a Superior Sales Force," Prentice-Hall, Englewood Cliffs, N.J., 1963, pp. 65–85.
4. Sales Management, "Portfolio of 1964 Selling Plans," *Sales Management Magazine,* 1964, pp. 53–63, 81–94.
5. Haas, Kenneth B., *How to Develop Successful Salesmen,* McGraw-Hill, New York, 1957, pp. 31–55, 84–182.

University Seminars

1. Andrews, Kenneth R., *The Effectiveness of University Management Development Seminars,* Graduate School of Business Administration, Harvard University Press, Cambridge, Mass., 1966.

[14] I am indebted to Thomas A. Staudt of Michigan State University for this thought-provoking notion.

Sales Management Development

1. Merrill, H. F., and Marting, E., *Developing Executive Skills,* American Management Association, Inc., 1958, pp. 91–198.
2. Adams, Velma, "The Forgotten Field Sales Manager," *Dun's Review,* March 1965, pp. 45–46, 79–80.

Trade Publications

Several excellent trade and business publications have frequent articles on sales training. Notable among them are *Sales Management, Industrial Marketing,* and *Dun's Review.*

QUESTIONS AND PROBLEMS

1. In a mature selling organization, can training be left to individuals, to create self-development programs?
2. How can a sales manager determine what aspects of the sales job need special attention for training?
3. Comment on the statement: "Training programs should be tailored to the needs of individual salesmen."
4. What kinds of training are needed in most selling organizations?
5. Why is it necessary for salesmen to have "managerially oriented" training?
6. What are the pros and cons of using programs generated outside the firm?
7. You are a sales manager responsible for distributor sales. That is, you and your salesmen contact distributors—independently owned firms who in turn have salesmen calling on their customers. What responsibility do you have for training of distributor salesmen? What forms of training do you think you would try to develop? How would you go about it?

16

Compensating Salesmen

Compensating salesmen is one of the most important functional elements of sales management. Yet great mystery and great debate often surround it. There is probably more division of thought (and perhaps more fuzziness of thought) about it than about any other sales management function. The reason may be that the sales manager perceives the sales job and the salesman himself as being utterly unique in the firm (which is undoubtedly true). But this perception of uniqueness often traps the sales manager into bypassing, in his thinking, the basic concepts that underly any system of reward and into considering only the compensation plans themselves and their implementation. Or he may leap to the *tactical* aspects of compensation plans without considering adequately the *strategic* aspects of compensation system within which compensation tactics can vary. Both strategic and tactical considerations must be made, and perhaps too much focus is usually placed on the tactical side. Note Figure 16-1.

UNDERLYING CONCEPTS

A conceptual starting point in thinking about the firm's compensation systems is the individual himself and the work group of which he is a member. The behavior of the individual (i.e., his perception, thinking, and responses or performance) and the influence of the group on this behavior are discussed in some detail in Chapter 17. A fundamental proposition about this interrelation of individual and group is that (1)

278

STRATEGIC CONSIDERATIONS

$\left\{\begin{array}{l}\text{Objectives of compensation}\\ \text{A philosophy of compensation}\\ \text{A rationale for compensation, relating}\\ \quad\text{it to all other elements of manage-}\\ \quad\text{ment}\end{array}\right.$

TACTICAL CONSIDERATIONS

$\left\{\begin{array}{l}\text{Process of establishing a compensation}\\ \quad\text{plan}\\ \text{Forms of compensation}\\ \text{The compensation "mix"}\\ \text{Administration of the selected plan}\\ \text{Evaluation and adjustment of the plan}\end{array}\right.$

FIGURE 16-1   The strategy and tactics of compensation.

the group has a group goal and (2) the individual contributes effort to help the group reach its goal because he perceives that by so doing he will achieve his personal goals better than if he were not in a group. There is a two-way "payoff" notion here. The group needs the contributions (work) of the individual to achieve its goal (else the group would not seek and retain him). At the same time, the individual has personal goals—economic and psychic—and he needs the group and its economic and psychic inducements to achieve them (else he would not join and remain in the group). But there must be some kind of balance or equilibrium in this two-way "payoff." A graphic and basically simple view of this equilibrium is the "Barnard-Simon theory of organizational equilibrium," which is really a motivational view of the firm and which provides a basic philosophy for compensating individuals. Its basic premises are: [1]

1. An organization is a system of interrelated organizational behaviors of a number of persons whom we shall call the *participants* of the organization.

2. Each participant . . . receives *from* the organization *inducements* in return for which he makes *to* the organization *contributions*.

3. Each participant will continue his participation in an organization only so long as the inducements offered him are as great or greater (measured in terms of *his* values and . . . the alternatives open to him) than the contributions he is asked to make.

4. The contributions provided by the various groups of participants are the source from which the organization manufactures the inducements offered to the participants.[2]

---

[1] J. G. March and H. A. Simon, *Organizations*, Wiley, New York, 1959, p. 84.
[2] That is, work produces product, which produces revenue, which provides "payoff" to those who do the work.

5. Hence, an organization is "solvent"—and will continue in existence —only so long as the contributions are sufficient enough to provide inducements in large enough measure to draw forth these contributions.

Here is the startling idea that the success and perhaps even survival of the firm hangs significantly on the effectiveness of its contribution-reward system. This is certainly true of the sales force. Attracting, motivating, and keeping salesmen are essential elements in creating and maintaining an effective, increasingly capable sales force. This is an underlying precept of the compensating system.

Inducements

The *inducements* or payments made by the firm to salesmen (and to sales managers) cover a wide spectrum. Put quite simply, they may consist of economic units and psychic units:

$$\text{total reward} = \text{monetary "payoff"} + \text{psychic "payoff"}$$

Psychological Aspects of Compensation

The model of individual behavior presented in Chapter 17 applies here, and therefore only a brief mention will be made here of the psychological aspects of compensation. Although everyone (sales managers and salesmen alike) places great overt stress on *money,* there is growing belief that in many, many situations, nonmonetary or psychological payoffs may be much more important and influential than ever suspected.

Certainly, some salesmen (and sales managers) have so strong a primary drive for money that it eclipses all other motivations in the workplace. Money is sought as a symbol of success and for the prestige and power that it will provide outside the workplace. This is a psychological set, of course; money is a means to psychic ends. ("I *want* money because I have the *need* for prestige.") But the psychic ends are external to the job; hence within the workplace such individuals may be said to be money-motivated.

However, many sales managers are now postulating that the *majority* of salesmen perceive and value nonmonetary inducements *within* the workplace. Motives other than the "money motive" exist. Some motives that may influence the behavior of (or "motivate") salesmen are the following: [3]

[3] Adapted from W. L. Burton, "There's More to Motivating Salesmen Than Money," in T. W. Meloan and J. M. Rathmell, *Selling: Its Broader Dimensions,* Macmillan, New York, 1960, p. 63.

    Desire for praise and recognition
    Avoidance of monotony and boredom
    Pride (achievement and self-image enhancement)
    Freedom from fear and worry (security)
    Desire to be needed (belonging)
    Conscience (obligation to others) [4]

Any compensation system that does not take account of such psychological motivational factors has some gaps—perhaps serious ones. For all the
importance of money, man's needs, drives, aspirations, fears, and anxieties *as he perceives them in the workplace* must be factored into the
compensation equation. This does not mean that money income should
go down as psychic income goes up. It does presume, however, that
psychological and social values are inputs into the compensation calculus, *particularly* with respect to certain elements of compensation such as
"fringe benefits," bonuses, and special incentive programs. We shall return to this at the end of this chapter.

THE PURPOSES OF THE COMPENSATION SYSTEM

The first step in developing a compensation plan is to establish its
overall rationale by clearly defining the objectives of the plan. Broadly,
these objectives should be considered from two sides—from the firm's
viewpoint and from the salesman's viewpoint.

Objective from the Firm's Viewpoint

Fundamentally, the prime purpose of the compensation plan from the
firm's viewpoint is to help achieve the goal of developing a topflight sales
force, as a means toward the profit end. To do this, sales management
must *attract, motivate, develop, and keep effective salesmen.* This is the
starting point for the consideration of a compensation plan.

Optimum economy of the plan (i.e., the optimum "balance" between
desired results and cost) must always be a basic objective for sales management. Given the objectives of the selling operation, the sales structure
emerging from the organizing process, the specific selling jobs and their
varying requirements, and the man-specifications for these jobs, the individuals placed in these jobs are vital resources. As resources, they are
investments. But they also appear, in a financial sense, on the cost side of

---

[4] Compare these with the "needs" and "self-image" discussions in Chapter 17.

the profit equation.[5] Hence a basic purpose of a compensation plan is to establish levels of pay commensurate with productivity. A selling operation may be on a direct "profit or loss" basis, or it may have some measure of its "contribution to profit," or it may be financially evaluated simply in terms of a sales volume/expense ratio. In any of these cases, salesmen's expense with respect to volume achieved is a critical variable which must be considered.

The *"right" levels* of compensation are necessary goals for other reasons. Monetary pay levels for the sales force are often high with respect to other elements of the firm, and the relationship must be continuously examined in the interest of the entire firm. "Right" levels must also be maintained so that the firm is competitive in its pay offerings and can attract and keep the sales people it wants. Finally, levels must be right so that the rewards are reasonably coordinated with salesmen's efforts and results.

Facility of administering the compensation plan is a basic objective. The plan should be simple to explain, simple to understand, simple to implement, and simple to adjust if necessary.

Control is an extremely important objective. Built into the plan should be control or motivational devices that direct or influence the salesman's selling activities. How the elements of the plan are devised, their "mix," and the quantitative measures used are tools by which the sales manager can indirectly guide the salesman's efforts into avenues desired by the manager—such as guided effort toward certain product lines, certain market segments, certain selling activities (e.g., finding new accounts vs. servicing of existing accounts). Thus the compensation plan can be (and should be) a powerful *influencing* device for the sales manager.[6] Hence it is a *strategic* mechanism as well as an administrative device.

Objectives from the Salesman's Viewpoint

If the sales manager's primary goal of building a topflight sales force is to be achieved and if the firm is to attract, motivate, and keep effective

[5] No inference is intended here that salesmen are regarded as "numbers" or impersonal machinelike resources. On the contrary! But cost is involved and must be considered.

[6] Note, however, that the compensation plan does not operate in a vacuum in this respect, as some discussions of compensation infer. The control and motivational aspects of the plan must be meshed with other elements of the sales management process, discussed in Part II. They must be tied into the sales manager's objective setting (recall also the "hierarchy" of objectives down to and including the sales job itself), planning (the avenues of effort he seeks in market and product areas), and controlling (how he will detect deviation and correct it).

salesmen, the compensation plan must also include consideration of salesmen's objectives, in addition to those of the firm.

Fairness is a must, from the salesmen's viewpoint. Any compensation plan must be perceived by individual salesmen as "about right" in relation to their ability and experience, to the effort they apply, and to the results they achieve. Furthermore, the plan must be perceived by them as *internally consistent*. That is, differences in pay levels between salesmen must have a rational explanation.[7] Also, the plan from the salesman's viewpoint must be competitive with those of other firms.

Regularity of income is usually a desired objective. Most salesmen have regular personal or family expenses (housing, food, education, etc.). There must be some degree of match between income and expenses or the salesman might find himself in a difficult financial position (a demotivating situation!). Therefore, most plans, whatever the form, should assure some base income at regular intervals, which at a minimum can cover his *regular* expenses stemming from the standard of living that his *total* income generates.

Opportunity for additional reward is sought by many salesmen. Whatever the form and the mechanics of the compensation plan, many salesmen strive to be "better than average" and therefore seek a means of achieving greater reward for greater performance. This is particularly true for salesmen working under salary rather than under commission forms of compensation.

Good administration of the plan is as much desired by the salesman as by the sales manager. The salesman seeks simplicity; he wants to understand the plan and be able to calculate or project his income easily and accurately.[8]

Conflicts in the Objectives of the Compensation Plan

As with any array of objectives, conflict or incompatibility may exist between individual objectives. Within the set of objectives from the firm's viewpoint, for example, the desire for control may conflict with the desire for facility of administration. Some optimal balance must be sought, and it must be done on a rational gain-loss basis.

The compensation plan as a whole may conflict with other, noncompensation-oriented objectives. For example, building customer goodwill,

---

[7] For example, differentials in the level of compensation are rational (and usually acceptable) when the demands of jobs vary, different levels of skill or experience are required, different levels of effort are required, and so on.

[8] This becomes particularly important when the plan differs from the "straight salary" form. For control purposes, many plans have several factors or variables and become quite complicated.

company image, and brand image may be an important objective for the sales manager. Elements of the compensation plan must be viewed against such objectives. Will the compensation objectives conflict with such objectives? If so, how? [9]

The firm's objectives for a "good" compensation plan may conflict with those of the salesmen. For example, the control aspects of the plan may conflict with the salesman's desire for simplicity. Again, the key point is to recognize potential incompatibilities and balance them out as rationally as possible.

THE PROCESS OF DEVELOPING THE PLAN

The step-by-step process of developing a compensation plan requires considerable technical expertise, the discussion of which is beyond the intended scope of this book. However, the following framework for this process is sound and has value for a sales manager wishing to evaluate his present compensation plan or to make adjustments. Major overhauls of a compensation plan, however, demand deep study and unique skills.[10] The logical set of steps is as follows:

1. Job evaluation
2. Pricing job value
3. Compensation structures
4. Compensation forms
5. Administration of the plan

Job Evaluation

Basic to any job evaluation is a clear definition of the job—its broad charter, its specific duties, its relationships to other jobs, its degree of

[9] For example, assume that the compensation plan for control and motivational purposes focuses on large volume of orders for certain products for the present and immediate future. Salesmen perceive high payoff in achieving more sales *now* for these products (which is what sales management also wants). But salesmen may then overly concentrate on key customers whose demand for these products is now high—at the cost of not contacting other customers (whose demand for *other* products may be high now and will be in the future). This is a dilemma, and it must be solved by the sales manager from a *planning* viewpoint. Again, the point here is that other managerial-process elements are involved and must be considered if a rational balance of compensation plan objectives is to be obtained.

[10] Excellent literature is available both on general compensation plans and on salesmen's compensation plans. See Suggested Readings at the end of the chapter. Our "Framework" is based on some of this literature.

authority, its means for measuring results. This comes from the organizing process. In addition, certain environmental uniquenesses of the job must be considered. The "climate" of the job and its working environments are aspects to be taken into account (e.g., breadth of territory, amount of travel required, nature of customers, and nature of competition). Finally, the sales potential and expected results must be considered for each sales job.

A number of methods are used for evaluating one job relative to all others. In the simple *ranking system,* the sales manager merely ranks one job against another without any quantitative measurement. That is, two sales jobs are compared, and the sales manager subjectively evaluates one as being more "important" than the other. A third job is then evaluated against the first two and so on, until all sales jobs in the sales unit are rank-ordered from the most important to the least important. This ranking system has several advantages: it is simple, rapid, and inexpensive; it works well for small units such as a district sales organization; to rank one job against another for importance is much easier than to determine the absolute importance of either. The disadvantages are several: it depends on the sales manager's subjective judgment; it is difficult to justify to incumbents; it may not specify why one job is more important than another.

The *point-evaluation* system is somewhat more rationally based and is widely used. Here a group of sales jobs have various "factors" selected and defined. For example, at one time sales engineers' jobs in the General Electric Company had the following "factors" identified:

Education
Experience
Judgment
Dealing with people
Persuasive skills
Counseling ability
Informal speaking skill
Writing skill
Creativeness
Initiative
Industriousness

The next step is to set up a separate yardstick that describes an array of *degrees* of each of the factors and to assign a number of "points" to each degree. For example, for the factor of "judgment" such a yardstick might appear as shown in Figure 16-2. This yardstick is somewhat simplified. It could have more levels of differential. Also, in addition to "degree," the

Factor: Judgment

Degree	Description
1	Judgment not very important. A low level, similar to that for persons who are not experienced in making business decisions.
2	Judgment possessed by persons who have maturity to make decisions in problems in their immediate field only.
3	Judgment possessed by mature persons who have ability to make managerial-type decisions.
4	Judgment possessed by high-level managers who make critical decisions in a wide variety of fields and for many kinds of problems.

FIGURE 16-2   Yardstick in point evaluation.

sales manager may assign "points." That is, the degree of 3 may be broken down to 3+, 3, and 3—, and points assigned to each level. Thus:

Degree	Points
3+	60
3	48
3—	36

Obviously, degree 3 for another factor (say, "writing skill") will have different points assigned to it, if that factor is generally considered to have different value. That is, if in *all* sales jobs "writing skill" is considered to be less important than "judgment," fewer points will be assigned to degree 3 (however degree 3 is described—i.e., even if degree 3 is a "high" ranking for "writing skill"). Thus for "writing skill":

Degree	Points
3+	24
3	18
3—	10

Having set such yardsticks for each factor, the sales manager must determine what degree is desired in each factor for each specific sales job. That is, simplifying somewhat, he may determine that the salesman assigned to a particular territory, with particular potential, particular customers, and particular environments, should possess "judgment" in the range of degree 2+ to degree 3+. This is done for this position for all other factors. Total "points" can be added to give a more or less rational quantification of the importance of the job, hence of its valuation.

Factor comparison is a simple version of point evaluation; it compares the various factors on a job-to-job basis. That is, the sales manager ranks all jobs with respect to one factor, then ranks all with respect to a second factor. The relative weights of the various factors then permit a totaling, to rank the jobs in overall worth.

Pricing Job Value

Given some definition and/or ranking (or evaluation) of jobs, the jobs can now be "priced." Of first interest here is the determining of general *levels of compensation*. As a starting point, the sales manager must go back to the objectives of the compensation plan previously discussed. With fair consideration of both the firm and of salesmen he must find the *general* levels of pay. He must be "in the ball park" so to speak. (This "ball park" may be determined by competitive market forces, as discussed below.) An important factor here is the ranking of importance of the jobs previously done. Whether "job-level" numbers are hung on this ranking or not, some *array* of pay levels emerges. Another consideration is the nature of the job itself and its man-specifications. The "stiffer" the specifications, probably the higher the pay level. Finally, the longer-range manpower plans of the selling organization must be considered. If sales management has an objective of "upgrading" its sales force, for example, general pay levels must flex upward in order to attract sales people with the qualities being sought.

From all this, "bands" or "ranges" of actual pay become evident. Decision about specific pay for a specific job may follow here or it may be made as part of the next step.

Pricing to the Market

All the foregoing discussion of arriving at levels of compensation and the specific compensation for specific jobs is an ideal—a rational framework of managerial thinking. However, its focus is inward, considering only the elements of the firm's own objectives and organization. But *market forces are also at play*, significantly affecting the price levels of jobs.

In many cases, the market forces of demand and supply establish the price levels of jobs. These forces may often *determine* the base price level of certain jobs, and the foregoing concepts of "pricing job level" may be used more to "rank-order" the total compensation structure than to set a value separately for each level.

For example, consider the highly competitive market for college graduates in certain professions. With demand outrunning supply, starting salaries for college graduates have been inching up, putting great pressure on firm's entire salary structures. Thus the compensation for higher-level jobs may be forced up because of this competitive force at some other level.

Another and possibly greater competitive market force comes from other firms, rivals or nonrivals, as they seek some certain expertise. For example, innovative and growing industries (such as electronics, computer, aerospace) have great demand for particular skills. They aggressively recruit personnel from other industries, normally offering very attractive compensation.[11] This phenomenon can be observed broadly.

The workings of the market, therefore, with its high levels of demand for competent people and for particular skills, provide alternative and attractive offerings to individuals. Unfortunately, it is the "better" people in a firm who might be thus "attracted away." The firm must be aware of these market forces and counter them by remaining adequately competitive in its inducements to its valued personnel.[12]

Such market forces are particularly important for the selling operation. Highly competent and effective salesmen are in great demand. Sales management may therefore find the demand to be a greater force than any other in the determining of compensation levels. Furthermore, setting a specific level of compensation for certain key jobs inevitably affects the entire compensation structure. All the "idealistic," internally oriented structuring of compensation must therefore be subsumed under market forces.

Compensation Structures

Job definitions, job evaluations, and classification of jobs into groups now permits the assigning of specific levels and ranges of compensation for all sales jobs.

A rational approach to the development of a compensation structure, given the rank-ordering of all sales jobs, is to "price" each level of the rank-ordered array, following the criteria suggested by compensation objectives and the foregoing discussions of job evaluation and job pricing. Assume that the rank-ordering process categories jobs into five distinct

11 One has only to examine the business section of the Sunday issue of any large metropolitan newspaper to see the great drive for trained personnel.

12 Compensation, of course, is only one element in the "package" of inducements. But there will be *some* level of higher compensation that will tip the scale. Thus a firm may not have to *exactly* meet a competitive offer, but it may have to increase salary somewhat.

categories. Assume that these categories are assigned "job level" numbers: [13]

Job level 10	The most important sales jobs
Job level 9	
Job level 8	
Job level 7	
Job level 6	The least important sales jobs

Within each of the levels, jobs have the same value to the firm. Each level now must be given a "price," and this is usually in a range, starting from some minimum and progressing over time via performance to the maximum, but not beyond it. Further compensation increases can come from earning promotion to a higher-ranked position or sometimes by redefinition (and pricing) of the job.[14]

The compensation ranges normally should overlap. That is, the incumbent in a specific job level should have opportunity to earn greater compensation than is set as the minimum for the next higher level. This is reasonable, since an outstanding performance in one level may well be worth more to the firm than the minimal or perhaps even average performance in the higher level. Also, were there not some overlap between ranges (see Figure 16-3), many salesmen might become extremely anxious to move to other jobs—causing turnover problems if they do and anxiety problems if they do not.

In our previous example, job level 8 may pay a *minimum* of $9000 and a maximum of $11,250. An incumbent must receive at least the minimum, but may over time achieve merit increases until he reaches the maximum of $11,250. At the same time, job level 9 has a minimum of $10,000 and a maximum of $12,500.

Often the *range* in each level increases as job level increases. This follows the reasoning that increasing effectiveness in the more important jobs is worth more to the firm. Thus the range from minimum to maxi-

[13] The "job level" numbers may or may not be made known to the sales force. Usually they are, however, so that salesmen know how their jobs "rank" and what future opportunity exists within that job. In the example that follows one can assume that job levels below level 6 are for nonsalesman jobs, such as order expeditors, "inside" salesmen, or quotation men.

[14] Redefinition and repricing is not unusual. Consider a salesman assigned to the state of Arizona, with a job level of 7. Now assume that over a period of two years, ten large customer firms in other parts of the country open large plants in Arizona. Obviously the importance and value of this job increases, and the job level may be increased to, say, level 8 or level 9. Parenthetically, job descriptions and man-specifications may also change, and the *incumbent* may or may not have an adequate "match."

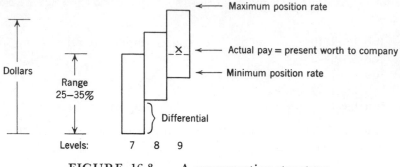

FIGURE 16-3   A compensation structure.

mum at a low level (say, level 5) may be 20 percent, whereas it may be as much as 40 percent at a high level (say, level 12).

Compensation Forms

Several forms or types of compensation plans are used. For all the debate among sales managers and in the sales management literature, *there is no perfect plan.* Every sales manager must adapt and tailor a plan to his unique set of variables. Furthermore, the "best" plan of yesterday may not be the "best" plan for today, and many firms find it advantageous to continually audit and evaluate the plan and to adjust it from time to time. The common forms are:

Salary
Straight commission
Salary plus commission
Salary plus commission plus bonus
Salary plus bonus

Salary

Under the salary plan, salesmen are paid a specific amount of compensation for a specified time period. It is fixed, and is given for time and effort on the job, rather than being *directly* related to sales volume achieved. The salary plan is normally used when it is difficult to correlate the salesman's efforts directly with sales results. This may occur when sales results come from joint efforts (application engineers, product specialists, or salesmen in other territories become involved in the sales transactions); when there is considerable product differentiation and technology; when a relatively large amount of "nonselling" activities exist in the job; or when preselling through advertising and promotions is a significant factor. Also, the salary plan is desirable when sales management believes that it must have freedom to direct salesmen's activities and to strategically alter these duties or their day-to-day tactics.

A major disadvantage of the straight-salary plan is that it does not directly provide an incentive for better than average performance. To be sure, almost all straight-salary plans have provisions for "merit increases," but there is rarely a means to directly correlate actual results with salary. A critical element of evaluation is thus missing. Another disadvantage is that straight salary is a relatively fixed cost—a problem if sales fall.

Straight Commission

This is a plan that compensates the salesman according to some fixed (or variable) rate based on his actual sales.[15] Whereas salary is based on performance and time, commission is based on actual results. It is normally used when there is need for aggressive selling; when results are directly related to individual effort; when nonselling duties are very minor or nonexistent; when salesmen's future achievements do not depend critically on what they do in the marketplace in the present.

Advantages of the commission plan are threefold. First, it has motivational or incentive value, in that the salesman perceives direct payoff for improved results. Second, actual selling expense is more directly related to achieved sales. Third, it has great control value, in that higher commission rates can be paid for those products or customers for which the firm wants special attention.

Several disadvantages must be weighed. Commission plans discourage salesmen from nonselling activities that may be important to the firm (e.g., "follow-up service" to a customer). Aggressiveness may be detrimental, if it turns to "high pressure" in the customer's perception. Also,

[15] The foregoing discussion of "job evaluation" does not *directly* apply here. Job evaluation is a useful tool in establishing a *fixed-rate* compensation (e.g., straight salary), either as a specific dollar amount or as a dollar range. The commission plan, of course, permits the compensation to vary with results. *In a general sense,* however, the rationale of job evaluation can apply. Certainly, the mechanics of the commission plan must be set up with some consideration of the value of the job. For example, suppose that a salesman on commission plan has a customer who receives a large government contract specifying his firm's product—an achievement to which the salesman himself has not contributed. This could be an unearned "windfall" for the salesman. In many cases, therefore, some floor and ceiling must be established even in the commission plan—and the job evaluation concepts can be used generally.

commission plans often become quite complicated and are difficult and expensive to administer. Finally, because of the vagaries of the marketplace, a drop in sales may mean a distressing drop in income for the salesman, affecting his effectiveness.

Salary Plus Commission

A majority of plans fall in this category. Here some base salary is guaranteed—usually at a level that will permit a salesman to meet his normal personal (family) expenses. Incentive is added through commission payments above this base salary. The "mix" of the two plans depends on how sales management "reads" the respective advantages and disadvantages in its own unique sales world.

Salary Plus Commission Plus Bonus

This plan is a combination of three methods of payment. The "bonus" element represents a lump-sum payment made at periodic intervals as a reward for superior performance. The bonus is usually used to reward for performance that cannot be adequately evaluated through either the salary or the commission element. It may be paid to a group (and divided among the members) to reward for group performance in team-selling situations or for accomplishments of an entire group. (Example: a sales district may earn a group bonus that may be based, among other factors, on the number of new accounts opened in some time period.)

Straight Salary Plus Bonus

Under this plan, the salesman receives a stipulated salary, but may also receive a supplemental payment for outstanding contributions by performing beyond the normal expectations of his job (expense control, creative ideas, missionary work, etc.) .

Diversity of Use of Compensating Forms

All these forms of compensation can be found in use. The two most widely used forms are the straight salary and the salary plus commission. One survey covering a wide variety of industries that sell into a wide variety of markets reveals the following use (total exceeds 100 percent because of dual pay plans) : [16]

[16] "How Salesmen Are Paid Today," *Portfolio of Sales Plans, 1964,* Sales Management, Inc, 1963, pp. 73–80.

Basic Methods of Sales Compensation

Straight salary	30%
Straight commission	14%
Salary plus commission	38%
Salary, commission, plus bonus	17%
Salary plus bonus	4%

A more recent survey by Research Institute of America reports the variety of use as follows: [17]

Salesmen Compensation Plans,
National Averages

Straight salary	22%
Straight commission	5%
Salary plus commission	23%
Salary, commission, plus bonus	7%
Salary plus bonus	28%
Commission with "draw"	7%
Other	8%

The wide variety of plans in operation even within a single industry accents the idea that the "best" compensation plan is the one that is most suited to the unique set of variables for a given firm.

OTHER FINANCIAL INCENTIVES

The different forms of compensation provide various degrees of incentive. Beyond the incentive provided by a specific compensation plan, however, almost all firms add other financial incentives—payments in some form to the salesman above and beyond the compensation itself. These are *fringe benefits* and *special incentives*.

Fringe Benefits

The so-called fringe benefits are in wide use and cover a large variety of economic factors. Prime benefits include:

Pensions
Group life insurance

[17] As reported in a special report by *Sales Management,* January 21, 1966, pp. 45 ff.

> Major medical insurance
> Paid vacations
> Paid holidays

Other common fringe benefits are:

> Use of company car
> Special purchase plans
> Club dues

Whatever one thinks of "fringe benefits," they are undoubtedly here to stay. They are important in attracting and keeping good sales people and in maintaining *esprit*. Moreover, the concept of personal security (or freedom from personal financial catastrophe) has become an accepted norm of the society.

Special Incentives

Profit sharing in some form is a means of special incentive used by some of those firms that are able to evaluate quantitatively either an individual salesman's contribution to profit or some sales unit's contribution to profit. In the former case, a "profit sharing" reward is made directly to the salesman—above and beyond his regular compensation. In the latter case, the "profit sharing" reward is made to the sales unit and is then further allocated to individual salesmen by some computation of individual contribution to the group achievement. An important point to remember here is that a salesman participating in some profit-sharing plan must perceive that *his gain is correlated with his effort and results*; otherwise the reward does not really motivate him to "extra" performance.

Many other forms of special incentives exist. Some firms find sales "contests" highly motivating, with rewards going to salesman "winning" by virtue of superior results. The rewards take many forms: specific merchandise items (cameras, color television sets, etc.), cash payments, or trading stamps. Sometimes the awards have more psychic than economic value—for example, the "national salesman of the month" may receive a plaque, a testimonial dinner, or the use for a month of a white Cadillac.

Many pros and cons can be posed for such special incentive plans. Do they really work? Are they worth the cost? Are they degrading to the nature of the professional salesman's job? Debate about them flourishes among sales managers; nevertheless, one sees enough major, sophisticated firms using them to justify their consideration. But again—the real key is tailoring the right kind of special incentive program, at the right time, for the right purposes, to unique sales force situations.

SOME CONCLUDING THOUGHTS

As this book constantly stresses, devising an effective compensation plan is a management function that cannot be done in isolation. It must be linked, in the sales manager's thinking, planning, and implementation, with all the managerial process. It has inputs from and provides inputs into the sales manager's broader objective setting, the planning of programs of action. It closely ties into the organizing process. It is vitally involved with the controlling process.

Furthermore, compensation of salesmen is conceptually much more than simply a mechanism for paying them. Compensation in all its variations is a strategic tool, *providing a means of influencing behavior.*

Finally, it is important that the sales manager recognize the importance of "mix" of elements in a compensation program. This is neatly shown by Keith Davis [18] in his "pay pyramid," illustrated in Figure 16-4. As proposed by Davis, job evaluation *rates the job.* Performance appraisal *rates the man.* Profit sharing *rates the organization* in terms of economic performance, and it rewards employees as partners in it. Together these three systems are the "incentive foundation" of a compensation program, as outlined in heavy lines in Figure 16-4. The three systems are interactive and complementary, each providing a different set of incentives. The "incentive base" is designed to motivate individuals; the "base wage" to progress to greater responsibility; "merit wages" to improve performance on the job; and profit sharing to enhance teamwork and creative thinking so as to improve the sales unit's performance. The "incentive base" may be protected by cost-of-living adjustments to keep the real base wage constant.

Other wage payments, primarily nonincentive in character, are added atop the "incentive base." Seniority increases, overtime or "special working condition" pay, and the "fringe benefits" on the top are not basically incentive in character, since they are not related by the individual directly to his performance. As Davis puts it, they are related more to such broad objectives as fairness, security, and social justice, all of which are strongly present in today's norms.

SUGGESTED READINGS

The personnel management literature is rich in descriptions of the rationale and techniques of wage administration plans. Most personnel

18 Davis, Keith, *Human Relations at Work*, McGraw-Hill, New York, 1967.

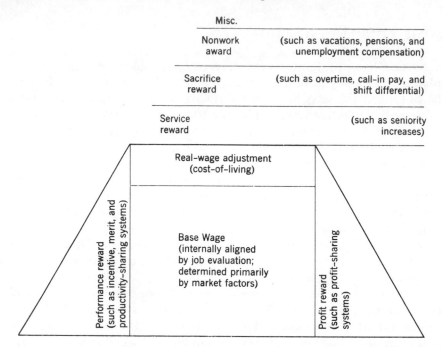

Misc.	
Nonwork award	(such as vacations, pensions, and unemployment compensation)
Sacrifice reward	(such as overtime, call-in pay, and shift differential)
Service reward	(such as seniority increases)

FIGURE 16-4   The pay pyramid: the makeup of a complete wage program. (Read from bottom. Incentive foundation is shown by heavy lines.) From Keith Davis, *Human Relations at Work,* McGraw-Hill, New York, 1967, p. 440. Used by permission of McGraw-Hill Book Company.

management books have chapters devoted to this function. Also, many excellent encyclopedic books exist, entirely devoted to wage administration such as Sibson's book, listed below. The personnel journals frequently have excellent, provocative articles. For sales management, such trade publications as *Sales Management* and *Industrial Marketing* have excellent articles. A few such sources are listed below.

Books Specializing in Wage Administration

1. Sibson, Robert E., *Wages and Salaries: A Handbook for Line Managers,* American Management Association, Inc., 1967, 249 pp.
2. Tosdal, Harry R., *Salesman's Compensation,* Volume 1, Harvard University Press, Cambridge, Mass., 1953, 459 pp.

General Management or Marketing Books

1. Davis, Keith, *Human Relations at Work,* McGraw-Hill, New York, 1967, pp. 406–441.
2. Kotler, Philip, *Marketing Management: Analysis, Planning, and Control,* Prentice-Hall, Englewood Cliffs, N.J., 1967, pp. 516–522.
3. Meloan, T. W., and Rathmell J. M., *Selling: Its Broader Dimensions,* Macmillan, New York, 1960. This readings book has an excellent, integrated section entitled "The Rewards of Selling," with the following articles:
    a. Baer, B. B., "New Light on Salesmen's Compensation," pp. 44–47.
    b. Cost and Profit Outlook, "Incentive Compensation and the Industrial Salesman," pp. 47–55.
    c. Sales Management, "More and More 'Benefit' Factors Coming into Salesmen's Pay Plans," pp. 55–62.
    d. Burton, W. L., "There's More to Motivating Salesmen Than Money," pp. 62–65.
4. Gellerman, S., *Motivation and Productivity,* American Management Association, New York, 1963, pp. 160–169.
5. Herzberg, F., Mausner, B., and Snyderman, B. B., *Motivation to Work,* Wiley, New York, 1959.
6. Patton, A., *Men, Money, and Motivation,* McGraw-Hill, New York, 1961. (For managerial compensation.)

Trade Publications

1. "Compensating Salesmen," a special report in *Sales Management,* Vol. 96 (January 21, 1966), pp. 45–52.
2. "Compensating the Sales-Marketing Executive," a special report in *Sales Management,* Vol. 96 (March 18, 1966), pp. 69–74.
3. *A Portfolio of 1964 Sales Plans,* Sales Management, Inc., 1963, pp. 65–80.

QUESTIONS AND PROBLEMS

1. Explain what is meant by the statement: "Both strategic and tactical considerations are involved in a compensation plan."
2. Explain in your own words the sense of the "Barnard-Simon theory of organization equilibrium" and describe its meaning to compensation thinking.

3. Why must psychological concepts be considered in compensation strategy and tactics?
4. What are the objectives of the compensation plan? How can conflicts arise?
5. Can different sales jobs in the same company have different "values" to the company? Briefly describe three sales jobs that have a spread in value from highest to lowest.
6. What happens when a salesman in a specific job reaches a compensation level equal to the maximum position rate? Is this not a potential problem for the sales manager?
7. Describe in your own words the meaning of Keith Davis' "pay pyramid."

Part IV

Leadership and Motivation

The sales manager's job is complex as well as demanding. In Chapter 4 we proposed that it can be analyzed into several different elements, all of them important and all interacting. The sales manager must amass knowledge in many areas. He must develop a number of technical skills in certain functions. The specifics of this knowledge and expertise will vary from company to company and from job to job within a single selling operation. Common to all sales managers' jobs, however, are two other vital elements—the managerial process, to which Part II of this book was devoted, and the expertise of leadership and motivation.[1]

The crux of the manager's job is "getting things done through others." His knowledge and technical abilities are necessary means to the end of managing. The elements of the managerial process must be understood and well done. But in the end, *the real measure of a manager's ability is the performance and the results of the people he manages.* For all the knowledge and functional skills; for all the planning, organizing, and coordinating; for all the decision making—*it is the resulting behavior of people that provides the payoff.* Organizations achieve results and move toward their objectives through the behavior of human beings, working individually and in groups. Furthermore, each of these human beings in the organization comes into the workplace and responds to it not as a robot nor as an economic computer, but as a *whole* human being—with needs and wants, fears and anxieties, goals and aspirations. Each is a completely unique individual, uniquely perceiving, thinking, and

[1] See Figure 4-1, p. 49, for a model of the job of the sales manager.

responding. Upon his behavioral responses significantly hangs the effectiveness of the firm, and its management. It is vital that the manager have some insight into how normal individuals perceive, think, and respond, if he is to "get things done through others."

Human behavior is exceedingly complex. Even the most learned psychologist will quickly admit that many of the theories of behavior are still open to question. Yet the behavioral sciences do have many concepts that can be directly applied to behavior in the business setting. These concepts are relatively simple, understandable, learnable, and applicable. Our purpose in considering these behavioral concepts in Part IV is to "open the door" for the sales manager to do the following:

1. Develop a "sense" for human behavior—that is, have his eyes open to the behavior of others *in an objective way*.

2. Gain insight into basic concepts of behavior, so that he can begin to understand and explain it.

3. Develop an ability to *predict* how an individual will react to a given situation.

It is on the third factor that we must really focus. If a manager develops the ability to *predict* behavior, he is in a better position to *influence* behavior. And this is the basic meaning of management —to "get things done through others," implying that *others' behaviors are influenced by the manager*. The manager *does influence* the behavior of others. He does so whether he thinks about it or not. The effective manager predicts how an individual will react to certain situations and then creates the kinds of situations to which the individual will react in a manner that enhances group goal achievement.[2] Some knowledge of individual and group behavior is essential to this ability.

To gain insight into this, we shall focus on the individual himself and cite some concepts about his behavior in different settings. We shall propose in Part IV that his behavior is influenced and even shaped by three different sets of forces:

[2] We shall not consider the morality of such influence. We propose that in the business setting, the individual also wants certain "payoffs" or achievements from his work relationships (see Chapter 14) . Furthermore, we can assume that this is not a "slave" society and that the individual is free to move out of his work group. In influencing his behavior, therefore, the manager must make the manager-subordinate relationship *rewarding to both of them,* or the manager's influence will become increasingly less effective. This in itself is a powerful argument for developing ability to predict—so that the ensuing behavioral interaction will be mutually satisfactory.

1. Forces from within the self
2. Forces from the immediate group
3. Forces from the greater society

Chapter 17 discusses individual behavior and examines the psychological forces or drives *within the individual* that temper and direct his behavioral responses. The concepts here come from the science of *psychology*.

Chapter 18 discusses the forces perceived by an individual that impinge upon him from the group of which he is a member. We examine the dynamics of the "small group" and explore basic concepts from social psychology that can help to explain how the group influences the individual's behavior.

Chapter 19 proposes strategic applications of the concepts discussed in Chapters 17 and 18. Chapter 19 also discusses the meaning of *symbols* and how they can help the sales manager to understand the psychological and sociological forces underlying the individual's behavior—hence greatly helping him in prediction of behavioral responses. *Effective leadership* and some application of its elements to some typical situations of conflict are also examined.

Some cautions should be noted throughout these three chapters. First, we shall view human interaction and behavior *only in the business setting*. Much of the conceptual framework may be applicable to other settings, but we shall make no pretense of so extending them. In this business setting, we shall be examining behaviors of the manager and of others in a variety of interrelationships:

Sales manager	⟷	Salesmen
Sales manager	⟷	Subordinate sales manager
Sales manager	⟷	His superior
Sales manager	⟷	Others in firm
Sales manager	⟷	Customers

Another precaution: these chapters *barely open the door* to the fascinating complex of human behavior. The old saying that "A little knowledge is a dangerous thing" has some meaning here. Thus this part of the book is meant only to set the stage for the individual sales manager in his study of human behavior. It is only a starting point.

A last precaution: just as there is no implication here of "manipulating" people like puppets, so must there be no implication that a sales manager can use behavioral concepts *to change an individual*. To be sure, the manager must (and does) influence the individual's *behavior,* or his responses. But the manager must not tinker with the individual's inner self.

Finally a reiteration. In the next three chapters, the pervasive purpose is to help the sales manager to gain insight into how a normal individual perceives, thinks, and responds to situations; to predict how he will do so; and to create, therefore, situations resulting in behavior that will reward both manager and individual.

17

Individual Behavior

Consider the world of the sales manager. At times he may be alone with his own thoughts. But much of the time he is displaying some kind of managerial behavior which intentionally or unintentionally influences other individuals. He communicates with salesmen either face-to-face or by letter or telephone. He gives directives, makes suggestions, seeks advice, or requests information. He proposes strategies, sets policies, gives resources, counsels, appraises, rewards. He explains and he persuades. These are behavioral acts, which in turn trigger some kind of response from individuals perceiving them. These individuals may be salesmen, customers, superiors, fellow managers. His whole world is laced with these social interactions, and his success may well depend on how effectively he manages such social situations.

The purpose of this chapter is simple. A key element of the sales manager's job is to *influence the salesman's behavior*—that is, to "motivate" him. Rather than leave this to intuition, or to cut-and-try methods, the purpose here is to gain some basic insights into how the normal individual perceives, thinks, and behaves—as inputs into the sales manager's "strategies" of motivation. Furthermore, the purpose here is to open the door to a logic, or a rationale, for *predicting* behavior, so that the sales manager might better create situations that will influence the salesman to respond in ways rewarding both salesman and sales manager.

In this chapter we cut a swath through this complex of personal interrelationships and focus on just one—the relationship between the sales manager and one of his subordinates.[1] For simplicity we refer to the

[1] This may be either a salesman or a subordinate manager.

subordinate simply as "the individual." He is the individual whom the sales manager is motivating or whose behavior the sales manager is influencing. In this chapter, we try to get "under that individual's skin," so to speak, and explore concepts from psychology that can help to explain how *he* perceives, assigns meaning to situations in his world, and responds to the manager's behavioral acts. We look at the forces or drives "inside" the individual that shape his behavior. We look from inside him out into his world, as though we were he.

We must start with some basic premises. First, this individual is absolutely unique. There is no one in the world just like him. If the sales manager has ten salesmen reporting to him, this one is uniquely different.

Another premise involves the inner driving force itself that lies behind the individual's behavior. Much of the following "model" of behavior is predicted upon this premise. To get at it, consider for a moment the almost incomprehensible complexity of nature. Nature's great mysteries, from the unfathomable universes to the unfathomable human gene, seem to have a common characteristic—that of a "system." Nature appears to be made up of countless systems, each with an ordered relationship among its component parts. Some are "closed" systems, such as the solar system; others are "open" systems, such as that of climate. Nature seems to maintain *order* within and between the systems by maintaining some set of relationships or *equilibrium* between them.[2]

Of all the systems in nature, perhaps man himself is the most intricate. Consider for a moment what a complex bundle of things man is—*any* man. Think of his intricate subsystems: the motor subsystem that propels him around, which with its muscles, articulated joints, tendons, and sinews is more complex than any man-made machine in the world; the circulatory subsystem, pumping away day and night; the glandular subsystem with ingredients that are vital to man's physical well-being; the nervous system, its sensors flashing inputs from outside[3] to the great computer center in the brain, which directs how the whole organism will react to the inputs.

[2] A *fixed* equilibrium in "closed" systems and a "moving," dynamic equilibrium in open systems.

[3] In this chapter we shall simplify our insights into behavior by considering only the effect of inputs from the external environments on behavior. This is by no means the whole story. Man also has "internal" environments, which influence how he perceives and responds. For a very simple example, consider how a person's behavior is influenced by a malfunctioning thyroid gland. However, here we are interested in how the sales manager's behavior affects the behavior of the individual, hence we can look at it as an element in the individual's external environment.

Stimulus ⟶ Response

FIGURE 17-1

Add to this complex of interaction subsystems still another—man's "mental" or psychological subsystem—and it is quickly seen what an intricate organism man is. To return to the premises underlying our "model" of behavior, we shall assume that within man's psychological subsystem—that of his "psyche"—nature has also built in a mechanism for maintaining an equilibrium. That is, if this open system receives an input from outside itself, its state of "balance" will be disturbed. But nature has provided a mechanism for its coming back into balance—an internal drive that commits the organism to that response (or behavior) which allows the psychic system to find a new equilibrium.[4]

Thus in its simplest form, behavior can be analyzed into two elements —the input, or a *stimulus,* and the *response* (Figure 17-1). This very simple cycle may explain some of the rudimentary forms of behavior in animal or insect life. But it is too mechanistic to explain all of man's behavior, because of man's cognitive or thinking ability and because of his ability to choose alternative responses and to come back into "psychological balance." Man seems to be able to evaluate, or assess some *meaning* to the stimulus input, before he selects some response.

The stimulus (defined and discussed below) is an input from outside the individual (e.g., the voice and manner of a sales manager, giving directions to a salesman). The response, or the behavioral output, is also outside the individual (e.g., the salesman behaves in some way in response to the sales manager's directions). What is it that happens between input and output which influences or even determines the output?

This chapter is concerned with what happens within the psyche of the individual—the "box" in Figure 17-2—because such knowledge will give the sales manager better insights into how that individual perceives, thinks, and responds, that is, the ability to better "motivate" him.[5] First, however, consider briefly the stimulus input itself.

---

[4] The term *homeostasis* is used by psychologists to describe this state of balance or equilibrium, the seeking of which nature has built into the organism.

[5] A caution is needed here. Great debates exist in the science of psychology about what happens in this "box." For example, some psychologists (commonly referred to as "behaviorists") assert that any concepts or theories about what happens within the psyche are incapable of pure definition and relation and, most important, are therefore incapable of observation and measurement. Thus these psychologists reject, in the name of science, anything except variables that can be observed and measured. Hence their theories and observations are focused only on the stimulus

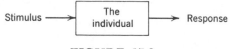

FIGURE 17-2

STIMULUS SITUATION

In our business setting, we are using the term *stimulus* to denote any agent, event, or change in the individual's environment that comes into his awareness.[6] It may be a single, simple thing, such as a loud sound, the temperature of a room, a pistol shot, or the sound of a voice. Or it may be a web of things, all taken together as one event. In this case, the individual perceives a *stimulus situation.* Much of an individual's behavior is generated by a total situation, consisting of many single stimuli that are mentally woven together. Example: a salesman hears his manager's voice. This is a single stimulus (to which he could assess meaning). But many other stimuli also might be at play—the manager's facial expressions, his gestures, the presence of other people, the "setting." The whole amalgam becomes a stimulus *situation,* which the salesman perceives in some unique way and to which he will respond in some way.

Whether he consciously thinks about it or not, the sales manager is continually *creating situations* that are inputs to salesmen's behavioral cycles. Sometimes the sales manager very consciously and deliberately behaves so as to influence a salesman's behavior in some particular direction.[7] But it is important that the sales manager realize that even when he is *not* deliberately so behaving, he will be generating stimulus situations as inputs to the salesman's behavior patterns.

Furthermore, it is important for the sales manager to realize that he is not the only stimulus input. In fact, the situations he creates may be in "competition" with other situations perceived by the salesman (which may have more "strength" as inputs). For example, the sales manager

inputs (which they can manipulate) and on the resulting response output (which they can observe and measure).

The hypotheses and theories in this chapter are not at all presented to engage in debate. They have been developed by those psychologists who seek to understand, explain, and predict behavior even if the concepts cannot be literally, scientifically put to measurement tests.

[6] Stimuli are also present in man's internal, physiological environment, but we are disregarding these in this business-setting analysis.

[7] Whether he is successful is, of course, the whole point of Part IV of this book.

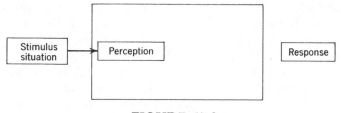

FIGURE 17-3

may request a salesman to meet with him on an evening to discuss next quarter's quotas. But the salesman's wife may have asked the salesman to "be home early that night." Here are two inputs that will influence how the salesman perceives, thinks, and responds. The sales manager is aware of only one—the one he generated.

PERCEPTION

Note that the stimulus situation must be perceived by the individual before it can influence his response. Hence we begin our exploration of "what happens" in the "box"—the psyche—with the concept of *perception,* that is, one's awareness of the world about one. Perception thus is the way in which one experiences the world. See Figure 17-3. Man has a built-in *perceptual apparatus.* This is a key concept in understanding behavior, because it is this perceptual apparatus that translates the outside world into the individual's awareness, triggering the behavioral cycle. Perception has unusual characteristics, knowledge of which can help a sales manager to better understand the individual's behavior.

Perception is unique. Two people *may* perceive the same stimulus situation in the same way, but not necessarily. Two witnesses to the same event may "see" different things. Perception is unique to the individual. How an individual perceives a situation may be quite different from how the sales manager perceives it, resulting perhaps in two different directions to behavior. *The sales manager must not assume that others will perceive things as he does.*[8] For example, assume that a district manager learns of a new managerial training program available to field sales personnel. He may perceive this as a rare opportunity for self-development and announce to his salesmen that he has arranged to have it staged in the district. One of his salesmen, however, may perceive all this as evi-

[8] Clues to how they do perceive are proposed in Chapter 19, under the heading of "Symbols."

dence that he is not doing adequately. Two different perceptions have evolved. It would be naïve for the sales manager to believe that all his salesmen will perceive a particular situation exactly as he does.

Perception is selective. The world teems with stimuli. Fortunately, nature has built a sort of "screening" mechanism into the perceptual apparatus. Some stimuli "bounce off" and do not penetrate the individual's awareness.[9] Obviously, if a sales manager is in face-to-face interaction with an individual, he presents a stimulus situation that does get through the "screen." But many *aspects* of situations he creates may not. Or some things *he* perceives may not be perceived by another individual. One who does not understand this may be quite confused by another's response. For example, a sales manager and a salesman together call on a customer. After the call, as the two of them hold a "postmortem" on the call, the sales manager is surprised (and perhaps irritated) that the salesman has not perceived some things and some aspects of the customer situation that he has. Understanding that this is very normal in human behavior, however, might prevent the sales manager from reacting to the salesmen in less than a beneficially influencing manner.

The "setting" affects perception. A stimulus situation may occur within a larger "setting." Consider the behavior of a sales manager impinging as a situation upon a salesman as the two sit in the salesman's automobile versus the same behavior as the two sit in the office in the presence of other salesmen. Different external settings may result in different perception of the same stimulus.[10]

RECALL OF PAST EXPERIENCE

After the stimulus situation is perceived—that is, when it enters the awareness—a number of interpretative processes begin, either consciously or unconsciously.

[9] We say "fortunately," because if every stimulus about us were perceived and triggered some sort of behavioral response, we would be exhausted before the day was half over!

[10] Consider the very simple stimulus of the sound of a throat being cleared. If this stimulus were emitted by a friend as you were playing golf together, it would probably motivate you very little, if at all. But if you were sleeping alone in your house, awoke suddenly in the middle of the night, and heard the sound of a throat being cleared in the next room, you probably would be highly motivated to do something! Same stimulus—different setting—different perception.

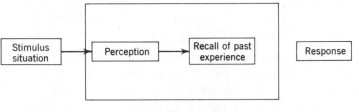

FIGURE 17-4

In a way, the brain now begins to function much as a computer.[11] Oversimplifying, the individual consciously or unconsciously says to himself: "I perceive a situation. My 'psychological equilibrium' is upset. There is therefore a drive in me to do something. But before I do it, let me see what it is I am motivated to do. Will I like it? Or will it be detrimental to me? If it is, what else can I do, to 'get off the hook' and come back into homeostasis again?" Note the basic premise at work here. Once the situation is perceived, homeostasis is disturbed, and *the individual must respond in some way*.[12] But before he does, he interprets the situation, or assigns some meaning to it and its anticipated outcome.

At this point—again admittedly oversimplifying somewhat—the behavioral process may take one of two tracks. The stimulus situation may be perceived as a new, unique one—*a new experience*. Or it may be perceived as *similar to a previous experience*. Here, then, the model proposes that the individual evaluates the present situation through *recall of past experience*. See Figure 17-4.

Normally, an individual perceiving a situation will try to force a "match" or a "fit" with some experience that he has had in the past. He may even try, sometimes quite unconsciously, to warp the perceptual process so that a situation *is* perceived as being "like" a previous one, for which he has some experience—hence some evaluation of "how it turned out." Thus the salesman may perceive a situation posed to him thus:

---

[11] Analogies such as this may be dangerous and can be pushed too far. The computer analogy could erroneously lend a mechanistic or an overly rational sense to human behavior. In spite of this risk, the analogy helps to understand—if not pushed too far.

[12] He might "put it off" for a while. But it will emerge again. He can put it off still again. But being motivated and not following through with a "relieving" behavior is *frustration*. Too much frustration may lead to neurotic states and ultimately to abnormal behavior, when the individual behaves in a maladjusted way.

"I perceive this situation. I must respond. But how shall I? First, I had better check it out. Have I ever experienced it before—or something like it? What did I do then, and how did it turn out?"

Of course, this process may not be quite so simple, and it may take place below the conscious level. But the point here is that we do try to "see what we want to see" and to relate "new" experiences to previous ones, as guides in the response to the presently perceived situation. Thus the recall of past experience influences how the individual responds to situations.

Several factors affect the ease or difficulty with which an individual will recall an experience from the past: [13]

1. All other factors being equal, a happy experience is more readily recalled than an unhappy one. Man hates pain, particularly mental pain. Hence he unconsciously tries to bury painful thoughts—to take them out of conscious awareness.[14]

2. Unhappy experiences are recalled, however. The *intensity* of an experience has a bearing. A *very* unhappy experience may be more readily recalled than a *slightly* unhappy one.

3. Personal involvement aids recall. The more deeply the individual is personally involved in a past experience, the more readily it will be recalled. For example, if a salesman had been very deeply personally involved in a very unhappy wrangle with a customer while the sales manager was only a bystander to it, it is likely that the salesman will recall it more readily than the sales manager when a similar situation arises. Hence recall will tend to trigger a different response by the salesman than by the sales manager. Not understanding this, the sales manager might be impatient with or intolerant of the salesman's behavior.

4. Other factors have effect on ease of recall and, therefore, on the "shaping" of a response to a perceived situation. The more frequent or the more recent the experience, the more readily it will be recalled.

The sales manager must realize that the individual's past experience is completely unique to *him*. To be sure, the sales manager and the individual may have shared some experiences in the past, but even then, he will recall them in a way unique to himself. The sales manager may misread his behavior or wrongly predict it, if he believes that the individual will recall a past experience as he himself does.

[13] Note the use of the word "recall" rather than "remember." Some psychologists believe that no experience is ever forgotten and that some memory trace always lingers. Hence they focus on the ease or difficulty with which these past experiences are "dredged up," or "recalled."

[14] See later discussion of "repression."

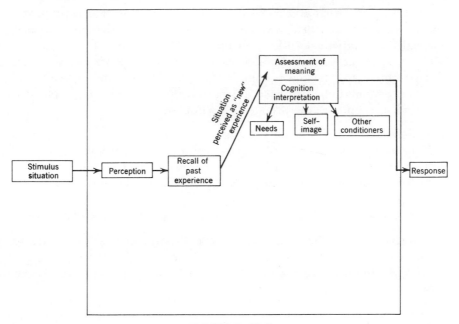

FIGURE 17-5

Obviously, a sales manager cannot have knowledge and objective understanding of all the individual's past experiences. But insight into this important influence on behavior can at least help him. As a minimum it can help prevent him from leaping to wrong conclusions about why an individual is behaving as he does.

Thus the process of recall establishes the presently perceived situation either as similar to a previous experience or as a unique, new experience. Let us consider first how the behavioral process might proceed if the situation is viewed as a new, unique experience.

THE ASSESSMENT OF MEANING

If the individual, through the recall process, cannot (or does not) link the present situation to a previous one, he may likely begin a cognitive, interpreting process. In essence, he attempts to assign some *meaning* to the perceived situation and the drive to respond to it. Consciously or unconsciously, he may evaluate this drive (and anticipated responses) against several factors, or criteria: needs, self-image, and other "conditioners." See Figure 17-5.

First, consider what is meant by a stimulus situation that is perceived by the salesman as a *new, unique experience*. (Later we shall see that normally an individual will try to force a "match" or "fit" with a previously experienced one.) Though most situations that we face are relatively similar to previously experienced ones, some are perceived as different enough to be perceived as new and unique, requiring a particular kind of cognitive interpretation. Examples:

1. Salesman is asked to move to a new territory.
2. Salesman is asked to handle a new, complex product line.
3. The compensation plan is changed from salary to commission.
4. Sales assignments are changed from territorial basis to product-specialization basis.
5. Salesman is requested to take over training of a young sales trainee.

Perceiving such "new" situations, the "computer" again begins to work. A cognitive process starts—one of interpreting and evaluating the perceived situation. Consciously or unconsciously, this cognitive process will *assess meaning* to the situation:

"I perceive this new, different situation. I am motivated to respond, but how? What is the meaning of this situation? What alternative responses are there? What are their consequences, their payoffs?"

This cognitive, interpretative process may evaluate the perceived situation against a number of factors or criteria. How the situation is evaluated with respect to these factors has great influence on how the individual will respond (a highly important idea for the sales manager, since he creates situations perceived by the salesman).

Needs

One factor—and a very powerful one—against which the individual's "computer" will measure a present situation and assign meaning to it, is his need structure at the moment. Here we speak of *needs* [15] as psychological drives, or motives. They are the psychologically based ends, whose satisfaction the individual is constantly seeking. "I perceive a situation. If I respond the way I am motivated to do, will that response pay off? Will it satisfy certain of my needs at not too much cost of others?"

[15] To avoid semantic difficulties, we must differentiate between a "need" and a "want." For our purpose here, a "need" is psychologically based and its satisfaction is an inner emotion. A "want" is for a worldly objective which can satisfy a need. A want is a *means*. A need is an *end*. "I *want* a Cadillac because I have the *need* for prestige."

At times, an individual may be very much aware of a strong need that he desires to satisfy. At other times—perhaps most of the time—needs may be rather amorphous and are lying in the unconscious. Yet they strongly influence how the individual interprets situations and responds to them.

Categories of Needs

Over time, an individual develops a wide array of needs of different character. These may be categorized into several different types. We consider here four general categories: [16]

1. Physiological needs
2. Ego needs
3. Social needs
4. Spiritual needs

Physiological Needs. These are the psychological drives to satisfy the basic animal motive for shelter, warmth, nutriment, and sex. For individuals in the business setting, we assume that these needs are satisfied and have no significant bearing on behavior.

Ego Needs. These are needs whose satisfaction the individual seeks through his own efforts. To be sure, he must achieve them in interaction with others, but he achieves them by his own effort, *through his own behavior.* They are completely self-centered and are sought for the sake of the self.[17] Some forms of ego needs are:

1. The need for *dominance.* This is the need to master one's environment, to influence and control it.[18]

2. The need for *status.* This is the drive for "rank" with respect to others.

3. The need for *prestige.* This is the recognition of one's status by others.

[16] Psychologists categorize needs or motives in a variety of ways. One, for example, is: social approval, status, security, self-realization, and affection. Another classification is: physiological needs, safety, love, esteem, and self-actualization.

[17] This does not mean that they are selfish or that they are "bad." On the contrary, they are the forces that underlie individual creativity, innovation, and individuality. They help men to conquer problems, to create the new, to seek the unknown. They underlie the competitive drive in this society.

[18] Many individuals in sales have a large measure of the need for dominance and derive great psychological satisfaction from solving and conquering tough competitive situations. The management job, of course, provides a potential for satisfying this need. But nonmanagers also may find many ways on and off the job to satisfy it.

4. The need for *achievement*. This is the need to accomplish an end for the sheer job of accomplishing it—for the *self*-satisfaction of achieving it—whether the world knows about it or not. ("I *did* it, by heavens," the individual tells himself joyously, "I *did* it.")

Oversimplifying somewhat, these ego-oriented needs can be considered "in total." That is, a sales manager might observe an individual's behavior over time and conclude that his behavior seems to be *centered upon ego-oriented need satisfaction*.[19] His behavior seems to be *more* centered this way than some other way. This observation is a clue to the sales manager, whose later motivational strategies, vis-à-vis this individual, can take account of this orientation.

Social Needs. These are needs whose satisfaction is also sought, but can come only through interaction with others. It is the *behavior of others* with respect to the individual that provides the satisfaction. Some of the forms of social needs are:

1. The need for *conforming*. Man seems to want *order* in his world and seeks relationships with others. He seeks some approval or validation from others for what he believes and does. Nearly all individuals have some measure of this need to conform to the modes of behavior of some others. Even strongly ego-oriented individuals (like many executives) seem to want to hang together and "act like executives." The strength and the prevalence of this need are probably underestimated. For one thing, some critics of this society have branded it as a "dirty word." Blind, sheeplike conformity is one thing. But there is also "constructive" conformity—a psychological need to be "tuned in" to one's social environments and to be a part of them.[20]

2. The need for *belonging*. This need is kindred to that of conforming. It is the drive, which most people have to some degree, to identify with some group. It can be a very powerful influence on behavior,[21] and very often (sometimes quite unconsciously) a stimulus situation may be

[19] Beware a danger here. We do not mean to imply that an individual's behavior can be stereotyped or put in a neat little pigeonhole. All we can say is that *we think, as of today*, that this individual's behavior *seems to be* more oriented to ego-type needs than to social-type needs. But even this surmise can significantly help the sales manager in planning his own behaviors toward this individual.

[20] Consider the "beatniks" or the "hippies" who rebel against the rules and forces of society and endeavor to shake off its shackles in order "to be free." Yet they hang together, wear the same costumes, and affect the same modes of behavior. They are as peas in a pod—seeking and finding their own brand of "ordered" conformity.

[21] Note, for example, how individuals of approximately the same rank in a given component of a firm, come to act very much alike in many situations, affecting the same manner of speech, the same mode of dress, and so on.

evaluated at least partially by its potential for enhancing or threatening the need for belonging. The threat of being rejected or even criticized by the group to which the individual belongs can be a strong shaping factor on the meaning he assesses to a situation.[22]

3. The need for *love*. This is the need for esteem, respect, and warmth of feeling that the individual seeks from his fellowmen. To be sure, there are some "loners," and there are many individuals who do not openly or even consciously seek the fulfillment of this need. Yet it is present to some degree in many of us and may influence how we judge a situation.

These "social-oriented" needs can also be considered "in total." That is, the sales manager may observe over time that an individual salesman's behavior gives evidence that he seems to be predominately social-need-oriented. Obviously it would be a mistake for an ego-oriented sales manager to *assume* that all his salesmen are similarly oriented and full of interpersonally competitive drives, and to tailor his motivating strategies to this assumption. It is highly possible that some completely competent salesmen may be social-need-oriented. This does not mean they cannot be motivated toward personal achievement. They can be. But the strategy to influence them must be different—*tailored* to social needs, not ego needs. (See Chapter 19.)

Spiritual Needs. These are the needs that man has to relate to God, or the unknown. For many, these are powerful needs, but we shall not attempt to introduce them into our managerial strategies for influencing behavior. It should be noted, however, that these needs and the individual's drive to fulfill them are inputs into his "frame of references," which we discuss later as clues to his behavior.

The "Mix" of Needs

Many needs may be operant at the same time. This is easily understandable when we consider the separate needs within one category. The needs for status, recognition, and prestige all "fit" together. Likewise, the needs for belonging, conforming, and esteem "fit" together. But an individual's need structure can be far more complicated than this. Various ego needs can be operant at the same time as social needs. When the new perceived situation is assessed for meaning against the need structure, one

---

[22] We shall examine this need more closely in the next chapter when we explore the effect of "group's" forces on behavior.

path of response may be directed by the ego needs, but a *different* path may be directed by social needs.[23] This is conflict.

How the conflict is resolved depends in large part on the relative strength of ego needs versus the strength of social needs. An individual may at times assign greater importance to one than to the other. At other times, this valence may reverse. Also, the particular situation and its setting may lend themselves more to the achievement of one than to the other. The key idea here is a strategic one. When the sales manager influences an individual, he must be aware of these vital facts:

1. The relative strength of the sales manager's needs (ego vs. social) is unique to him, and he cannot project it to the individual.

2. His influence may "play" to the individual's potential satisfaction of ego needs, but he must realize that this *could* conflict with social needs, and vice versa.

If over time the sales manager can identify [24] an individual's relative weighting of ego and social needs, his strategies and the situations he creates can be "tailored" to it. This means that his mode of managerial behavior ideally should be shaped differently for each unique individual.

Self-Image

Somewhat akin to needs, another powerful influence is an individual's self-image. Every normal person has some concept of self. He is conscious of a continuing identity. "I am what I am." Psychologists theorize that this is a learned force, which begins in childhood when the young indi-

---

[23] For example, assume that a district sales manager perceives a certain set of competitive and customer conditions that offer him a very unique, but risky strategy. Furthermore, if he pursues the strategy, he realizes that he will probably violate some unwritten policies, or ways of operating. On the other hand, he believes that if the strategy works, its success will be hailed by higher management as a creative achievement. Assume further that he does seek achievement. He wants to be a master of these competitive situations and wants the prestige and growing status that such dominance can bring. Hence his *ego needs* reinforce the motivating drive that he has to initiate the strategy. On the other hand, he has a strong sense of identification with the field sales organization. He has great rapport with his fellow district sales managers and derives much satisfaction from their obvious respect and liking for him. He feels that he is "one of them." As he contemplates the situation and as his "computer" flashes over to *social needs*, he senses a dilemma. If he goes ahead, he may be regarded by his fellows as a "climber," or a "maverick," or an "oddball." *Thus the satisfaction of ego needs may be at a cost to or loss of social-need satisfaction. This kind of dilemma is common.*

[24] A later discussion of *symbols* in Chapter 19 will propose means to help to do this.

vidual starts to interact with others and to see and play various "roles."

The perception that one has of self may be quite amorphous and under the conscious surface much of the time. But it lies there like lava in a quiescent volcano, ready to erupt. At times, however, the individual is very conscious of self.

One's concept of self is complicated by the fact that self-image has more than one form. There is the "real self"—one's concept of *what he really is*. There is also the "ideal self"—one's concept of *what he would like to be*. It is the ideal self—the "one" he wishes he were—that he wants the world to see. He will often evaluate the meaning of a situation and its motivating drive in terms of its enhancement or threat to his self-image.[25] If a potential response promises to enhance it, he may go ahead and do it. If the response has potential to threaten it, he will resist the behavior toward which he is being motivated.

Behavior in defense of the self is very common. A man misplaces his car keys and does not say, "I lost my keys again," but rather, "Who took my car keys?" A salesman who muffs a golden chance to get an order may say to his sales manager, "I goofed," but more often would find many reasons why competition played "dirty," or price was high, or something.

"Saving face" is a behavior that is not limited to our Oriental friends. We all do it. The protection and enhancement of self-image is a normal behavior often done by normal people.[26] It is a powerful influence on how an individual perceives a situation, hence on how he may respond to it.

Other Conditioners

Several other factors condition the way in which the individual assigns meaning to and interprets a situation—hence influencing his response. Each individual has had a lifetime of experiences. He was born to a particular mother, was raised in a particular home, and had a particular family with particular customs, beliefs, and modes of behavior. He grew up in a particular neighborhood, had a particular first playmate, and ran with a particular "gang." He had a particular first teacher, first sweet-

---

[25] This may be an unconscious process.

[26] A sales manager might be irritated by a salesman whose behavior appears to be in protection of self. Obviously, such behavior could be overdone and become almost abnormal. But most of the time it is a very normal behavior and must be accepted as such. The sales manager could easily lose his ability to motivate an individual if he did not quite compassionately understand the self-image concept. Really, all he need do is examine his own modes of self-protective behavior!

heart, and first boss. He is absolutely unique. No one in the world has the same total amalgam of experience and the same background of learning. From all this, he has at this moment of time a *set of values,* which can strongly affect and condition how he perceives, thinks, and responds to a new experience.

A Summary Statement

Thus far in this particular "model" of human behavior, we have seen that stimuli in the outer world first must penetrate the individual's perceptual apparatus. Assuming the premise of "homeostasis," or the seeking of "psychological balance," the individual has a drive to respond in some way. He may perceive the situation as similar to a previous experience, for which he has learned a response (to be discussed next).

But he may perceive some situations as different enough to be "new" experiences. This triggers a cognitive interpretative process, in which the individual weighs responses and then outcomes against his mix of needs, against his self image, and against his beliefs and moral systems.

Sometimes the sales manager cannot gain any knowledge about how the process is working in a specific case. Even then, however, insights into these concepts may help him to achieve an *empathy* for the other person and thus to avoid the pitfalls caused by lack of it. But sometimes a salesman's driving needs and self-image are quite apparent (again, note Chapter 19). Here is real payoff for the sales manager. He can then better predict how the salesman will respond to situations. He can better "motivate" him. He can better influence his behavior, with better chance for psychic payoff to both.

LEARNED BEHAVIOR

Every situation, of course, is not perceived as a new experience. In fact, a significant percentage of situations are perceived as the same as or very similar to the ones that we have experienced before.

As the individual perceives, interprets, and responds to situations, he experiences consequences—payoffs—with respect to needs, self-image, and values. Over time, he *learns* that certain responses to certain situations have certain consequences, and he builds up a repertoire of responses, which are on tap for use in similar situations. If he perceives a situation as similar to one on his "memory drum," for which he has a learned program of response, he will likely select that response without going through the foregoing cognitive process (weighing against needs, self-image, etc.).

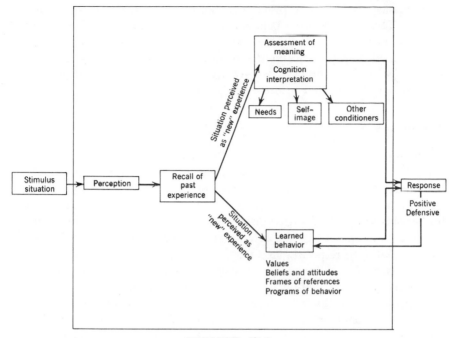

FIGURE 17-6

In fact, the individual often even "warps" or forces the perception of a present situation to make it "fit" his repertoire of responses. "We see what we want to see" and "A fact is what I want to believe it is" are adages reflecting this rather common human practice.

In any case, whether the perceived situation is like a previous experience or whether it is forced to be, the individual will likely respond by selecting a *learned response*. See Figure 17-6.

Over time, the individual *learns,* via payoffs, good and bad. He experiences situations in the world and responds. The consequences feed back to the "reservoir of learning." Through this learning process the individual develops *values* and value systems. He develops whole sets of *beliefs and attitudes* about countless aspects of the world. These may serve as *frame of references*—or a set of *preprogrammed responses*—into which an individual may inject a present stimulus situation without necessarily going through the discrete process of measuring it against past experience, needs, and self-image.

Much of the time, an individual will perceive a situation and, even warping it if necessary, fit it into a set of beliefs and attitudes, or a frame of reference, that has a previously tested and accepted response all ready.[27] Thus the resulting behavior may seem almost reflexive, but it is not. The individual already has (via his experiences and learning) pre-programmed a response, and the stimulus situation triggers it off. Put another way, the individual develops *predispositions to behave,* or tendencies to behave in certain ways, under given conditions.

A Summary Statement

The purpose of this discussion of "learned behavior" again is to help the sales manager understand and predict the salesman's response to situations that the sales manager creates. If the sales manager understands that much of human behavior is learned—that individuals have frames of reference and programs of behavior "on tap" for many kinds of situations—he may be better able to strategically behave himself so as to elicit the kinds of responses he wants.

Sometimes the sales manager may find it difficult to observe clues to a salesman's needs and self-image. But if he can gain insight into his beliefs and attitudes, into his frame of reference, and into his predispositions or programs of behavior, he need not be concerned with the psychological underpinnings for them. Such insight will still enable him to tailor his strategy of motivation optimally *to each unique individual salesman.*

THE BEHAVIORAL RESPONSE

We turn now to the "response" side of our model of human behavior. First recall the important basic premise regarding homeostasis—once a stimulus is perceived, the homeostasis or "psychological balance" is disturbed, and a drive is generated impelling the individual to respond in some way in order to come back into balance. This "someway" is usually quite specific, proposing one particular behavior or perhaps a very few. We proposed that before the individual blindly follows the "direction" to emit a particular response, he either goes through an interpretative process to assess what it is he is being motivated to do or selects an appropriate response from his repertoire of programs. But the key idea is that *a response is called for.*

If by either process the drive directs a response that the individual

---

[27] For example, one can have a simple stimulus tossed to him and in a split second have a mental response. Try this out on yourself. If someone says to you, "Catholic," "the draft," "LSD," "Berkeley," or "big business executive," note how *almost* instantly you have a response on tap for this stimulus.

perceives as a "good" one—that is, satisfying his needs, enhancing the image he wants to present, and "fitting" his values systems—he will go ahead and respond as he is being motivated to do. This is *positive response,* following directly what the drive impels the individual to do. For example, assume that an astute sales manager has perceived that one of his salesmen gives evidence of being strongly ego-need-oriented. Assume further that the sales manager has a particularly difficult mission he must assign to someone and that he poses it to this salesman therefore as a personal challenge, with inferred promise of recognition by higher headquarters. The salesman might think:

> "I perceive this situation. It is tough, and would be done at some risk. But if I do it, I'll have a chance to gain some prestige with my boss and with headquarters management. Let me at it!"

Here psychological payoff far exceeds the risk or cost. What he is motivated to do, he wants to do. No conflict exists. *He responds positively—* that is, in the direction of the motivating drive. This is *positive response.*

Defensive Behavior

A significant percentage of human behavior does not follow this direct, positive path, however. In some cases, as the individual assesses meaning to a situation and is aware that he is motivated to respond in some specific way, he may (for reasons discussed later) perceive that he either cannot or will not respond in this way. This is *conflict.* He "hangs on the brink," propelled by an inner drive to act in some way, but unable to do so. This is *frustration,* and man cannot stand frustration.[28] Too much frustration might cause the individual to become "neurotic" or in the extreme to become mentally ill. Unfortunately, in our social world, man faces many, many situations that have this potential for frustration.

For example, consider again the case in which the sales manager poses an extremely difficult mission in the same challenging manner, but this time to another salesman. Assume that this salesman has a different "mix" of needs and is highly social-need-oriented. He wants order, security, ease of mind. *This does not mean* that he will not work diligently and effectively in many situations. But in *this* situation, the salesman might think:

---

[28] The psychologist defines "frustration" as the blocking of an individual's path toward a goal, whether the goal seeking is conscious or unconscious. (James Drever, *A Dictionary of Psychology,* Penguin Books, Middlesex, England, 1952, p. 103.)

"I perceive this situation. It is tough and would be done at risk. If I do it, I may have a chance at some additional prestige. But at what cost? What if I don't suceed? What will they think? Will they think I'm out for power grabs, which I'm not? I suppose I should do this thing, and don't dare admit I don't want to. But I don't want to. How can I avoid it without saying so?"

Here is a dilemma—an impasse. The salesman is motivated to accept the challenge (positive response), but perceives that the psychological threats to himself exceed the gains. He must do something—but what? (Parenthetically, one might ask whether the sales manager could have posed this situation differently to make it more "palatable" and positively acceptable. It can be done, and Chapter 19 will deal with such strategy.)

Defense Mechanisms

Fortunately, man has an "escape hatch"—a means for resolving this kind of impasse—by resorting *not* to the behavior being inwardly motivated, but to *another different form* of behavior. This is *defensive behavior,* implemented by a *defense mechanism*.[29] It is substitutive behavior, which gets the individual "off the hook," finishes the behavioral cycle, and once more establishes a "psychological equilibrium."

The *defense mechanism* is a mode of behavior adopted by a person to conceal his true motivations or inner feelings, sometimes from the world and sometimes from himself. It can take a number of forms, but only a few of them that seem to be especially prevalent in the business setting will be discussed here.

Two forms are so different from the others that some psychologists

[29] The use of the word "fortunately" at the beginning of this paragraph is open to criticism. Some psychologists and many laymen feel that defensive behavior and the use of the defense mechanism are a *dysfunctional* mode of behavior. Certainly, an individual "overdoing" the use of defense mechanisms—or behaving in almost all his social interaction in a substitutive, defensive way—is hardly what the society calls an "adjusted" person.

Nevertheless, most people whom we would call "well-adjusted" exhibit defensive behavior at times. Whatever the "morality" or the "functional normality" of it, defensive behavior can be observed in "normal" people, such as sales managers, salesmen, or customers! Furthermore, we must consider what a complex social world we live in, with its intricate webs of social relationships. It is ridiculous to think that man will not often face some impasse between his ego and social needs, or between what he is motivated to do and what he feels he can psychologically afford to do. Thus it is argued that within some reasonable limits, defensive behavior is really quite functional and valuable to man.

regard them as "substitutive" forms of behavior. One is *compensation,* in which the individual, sensing inability to reach his goals, tries harder. One might say that there is a blockage between him and his goal, and he rams it harder and harder, to the extent that it is noticeable. Thus a sales manager who has aspirations of promotion (increased status and prestige) but perceives that he is blocked may take work home, spend Saturdays in the office, and join professional associations.[30] A key here is that the individual *is motivated* and also that it is *ego needs* that he seeks. He will very likely perceive situations and assess meaning to them in this light—a strong clue to the strategy of influencing him.

The other substitutive form of behavior when goal blockage occurs is the devising of *substitute goals.* Here the individual experiences the frustration of goal blockage and finally comes to reject the goal and select another. A young salesman may aspire to become a sales manager and to work hard at it. This ego-type aspiration will color his perceptions and influence his behavior. Finally after some years, as he sees younger salesmen promoted, he may turn away from this goal and seek another. He may, for example, begin to take young "cub" salesmen under his wing and groom them, hoping to see them promoted. He seeks to become a "kingmaker." The strategy of influencing him will be quite different in the two different goal situations.

These forms of substitutive behavior apply to the condition of frustration when goal blockage exists. But in our complex social world frustration often occurs not because the individual cannot achieve a goal, but because he does not *want* to do what his inner drive is impelling him to do. This frustration can occur when a perceived situation impels an individual to respond in some way, but he fears that in doing so he may suffer threat to his self-image. Consider a simple example. A purchasing agent inadequately explores a competitor's proposition for a new complex industrial product. He buys it against the advice of others; after it has been installed, he is chagrined to learn from the plant people that it never quite functions as it should, in this particular application. He has made a bad mistake and he knows it. Now suppose that the salesman from our firm wants to capitalize on the competitor's unsatisfactory installation and asks the purchasing agent how it is operating (knowing, of course, that it is operating poorly). This is a stimulus situation, and one can imagine the purchasing agent's mental computer flashing over "needs" and over "self-image." He may be motivated, as he assesses the situation, to respond with "That darned thing. It is terrible! I wish I

---

[30] Of course, it is possible that he simply wants to do these things for their own sakes or that he is escaping an unhappy home situation. But usually it will be fairly obvious if such behavior is compensatory.

had never seen it!" But he may sense that to follow this drive with a positive response will be the same as saying, "I goofed. I, the executive in charge of purchasing for my important firm, made an error in judgment, a lapse in professional care." And this might so threaten his self-image and his needs for status and recognition that he will reject such a response. But he must do *something,* and not hang on the brink. So he may resort to an "adopted" behavior to conceal his true inner feeling and drive. He uses a defense mechanism and gets "off the hook." [31]

FORMS OF DEFENSE MECHANISMS

The forms of substitutive behavior discussed so far are positive in character. The *defense mechanisms* briefly discussed below are somewhat negative. That is, the individual is motivated (as he perceives and interprets a situation) to respond in a certain way. But he foresees that response as disagreeable or threatening—or *potentially* so. In our example, the purchasing agent foresees his "positive response" as potentially image-threatening and as endangering his prestige. *To remove himself from this potentially disagreeable result and still follow through the behavioral cycle, the individual resorts to some other response.* This is the defense mechanism. It is a behavioral response, which may be used consciously or unconsciously. It can take a variety of forms, only a few of which are briefly described here. The following defensive behaviors can be observed as common occurrences in business and particularly sales settings:

Reaction formation
Rationalization
Projection
Regression
Aggression

It is highly important that a sales manager have insight into these forms of defensive behavior exhibited by his salesmen (or subordinate managers). Again, the individual's defensive behavior patterns are valuable clues to his needs and self-image, to his frames of reference. And

---

[31] Of course, he could simply emit the positive response and say that he "goofed." Often a person's status and prestige are so secure that he can admit to a mistake without perceiving that such response will harm his self-image. It may even be reinforced, in the sense that he is *so* competent he can even admit to and graciously accept an occasional "human error." In a great many cases, however, a quite normal reaction in such a situation will be some kind of defensive response. Its forms will be discussed in the next section.

a critical idea is that the sales manager's strategy of his own behavior should ideally be tailored to what *underlies* the individual's defensive responses, not tactically to the response itself.

Reaction Formation

This is a form of defensive behavior in which the individual responds in a manner opposite to that which he is motivated to emit. In doing so, the individual is "fooling the world" by concealing his true feeling—and he is aware that he is doing so. Furthermore, the "opposite" response or behavior must appear creditable or reasonable for the situation, in the eyes of other people. Consider again the case of the purchasing agent.[32] Instead of responding as motivated, he might protect himself by hiding this drive from the world and emit a *creditable but opposite reaction*. He could say when asked about the competitive equipment:

> "Oh, it's coming along [which it is, though he wishes he had never seen it]. The competitive company is a good company [which it is, though he wishes he had never heard of them] and they have an excellent engineering service [which they have, but he wishes it was not needed here]. And you know how a complex new product like this needs some shaking down [which is true, but he thinks this needs too much shaking down]. Now, what can I do for you today?"

This is *reaction formation*. The purchasing agent has really said exactly the opposite of what he would like to say—*to protect himself*. Furthermore, he has now completed the behavioral cycle by means of a response and is "off the hook." Reaction formation is a common model of behavior and must be understood by the sales manager. His strategy to cope with it is discussed in Chapter 19.

[32] This is a true case, told to me by a sales engineer of a large printing press manufacturer. The customer had purchased a competitive press of a new model, costing more than $100,000. Moreover, this was the first press of any kind he had ever purchased from the competitor, and he had done so against the wishes of his own pressroom operating people. The press did not operate as it should, though the competitor kept a crew of his service engineers working on it for weeks. One of the purchasing agent's subordinates told the sales engineer that his boss had called in the competitor's salesman and had given him "a terrible calling down, threatening him that if the press were not fixed to operate efficiently, he would tell everyone in the industry how unreliable the competitive firm is." The sales engineer, hoping to capitalize on this, later asked the purchasing agent "how the competitive press was doing." The purchasing agent smiled and replied as cited above—a typical case of reaction formation used as a defensive response. It dumbfounded the salesman.

Rationalization

In using reaction formation, the individual knowingly "fools" the world. In using *rationalization* he "fools" himself. Rationalization in its common usage is a process of justifying by reasoning after the fact. Very often after an act has been committed, the individual may reason out a justification for it, to eliminate self-accusation or guilt. He does so by divining *creditable* reasons for the act.

The use of reaction formation, where the individual knowingly fools the world primarily to move himself away from a disagreeable (to himself, psychologically) situation, may drift into rationalization. That is, the reasons cited in reaction formation are *so* creditable, that the individual may come to believe them himself. Rationalization has then occurred. Thus our purchasing agent may continue to make his creditable, reactive defensive statements whenever people in his company refer to the misbehaving press: "It *is* a good company. . . ." "It *is* a complex new product, and they *do* need shakedowns. . . ." "They *do* have good engineering service." As he continues to make these reasonable statements, they begin to make sense even to himself. He may begin to think, "After all, these *are* true. My decision wasn't so bad." Ultimately his feelings of shame or guilt for what he previously regarded as a failure turn into good feelings. He has rationalized them.

A critical point of strategy emerges here. If a sales manager senses that an individual is protecting himself by using reaction formation,[33] he knows that the individual is really aware of what he, the individual, is doing. The individual is therefore open to tactical persuasion, if adroitly handled.[34] But if he drifts into rationalization, it is too late. He has now internalized his reasoning, which becomes "truth."

Reaction formation and rationalization are forms of defensive behavior whose use is very normal for many salesmen. It is extremely rare for any salesman to get all the business available. Even highly successful

[33] How he may sense it will be discussed when the concept of "symbols" is explored.

[34] Obviously, the sales manager cannot "pin him to the wall." He must accept the individual's statements, because otherwise he would drive the individual into even greater defense of himself. In the case of the purchasing agent, perhaps his strategy could be to offer the individual the sound, solid reasons why in the future the individual can put great reliance on and feel great security in *this* firm's products. He need not—in fact, must not—tie these persuasive remarks to the individuals previous "poor" decision. The individual himself will do this. Some insight into this kind of defensive behavior can significantly help in understanding the other person and may greatly enrich social interactions.

salesmen lose orders to rivals, sometimes orders that are eagerly sought. A good salesman will always contemplate lost business. Certainly, many factors beyond his reasonable control are involved. But it may be understandably easy for him to protect himself when he does feel some degree of personal blame [35] or when his manager says, "Why do you think you lost that order?" The sales manager's desire to effectively manage, lead, influence, and motivate the salesman will be enhanced by insight into these forms of defensive behavior, used by normal human beings.

Projection

A common form of defensive behavior is another defense mechanism—*projection*. Projection is the externalizing of a feeling or motive—ascribing it to or "hanging" it on something or someone else. It is used to defend the self. A salesman who is losing business and is concerned about it may, when asked about it by his sales manager, blame it on "shady tactics of competition," "unreasonable purchasing agents," or "high price."

A district sales manager listens on the telephone to a headquarters executive who is somewhat critical of the district's operation and is directing some "corrective" steps with which the district sales manager does not agree. The district sales manager perceives all this and feels the strong urge to "tell off" the headquarters manager. His mental computer, however, is also flashing the warning that this positive response has dangers, deterring him from the action. He grits his teeth and says "Yes, sir," but after the conversation is over, he viciously slams the telephone down. He has *projected* his inner feeling to the telephone.

A salesman agrees with his sales manager to a certain strategy with a customer. He puts it off. A month later, his manager asks about its status. He may reply that pressure of business from other customers has prevented him from putting time on it.

It is common for people to "blame" something else or someone else, to protect their own images. This is normal behavior and is exhibited by normal human beings. It is often quite obvious. When the sales manager witnesses it, he should take it as a clue to something deeper than the behavior itself. The behavior is merely a *symptom*, and the manager's strategy must be shaped to its *causes*. (Again, this will be explored later.)

[35] A good salesman will do a "Postmortem." He may say to himself, "How last month, when I learned so-and-so, if I had done such-and-such, etc. . . ." If constructively done, this can be very creative. But it also opens the door for defense of the self.

Repression

When discussing recall of past experience, we noted that, other factors being equal, a happy experience is more readily recalled than an unhappy one. Some psychologists propose that this is because man hates pain, and thoughts of guilt or shame are paticularly painful. Once an individual behaves in some way for which he later feels regret, guilt, or shame, he cannot undo it. As new situations trigger off a recalling of it, he again feels guilt or shame, but is unable to do anything about it—hence he is in frustration.

Here the defense mechanism of *repression* comes into play. Repression is "taking out of the conscious mind" the thoughts of the unhappy past experience. The experience is not forgotten, because situations may dredge it up in some form. It is in the unconscious, and as such (some psychologists propose) still indirectly affects behavior.

Sometimes an unhappy experience will be only partly repressed. The experience may be recalled by some combination of stimuli, but perhaps in incomplete or fuzzy form. The individual may not recall all elements of the past experience, and, therefore, the effect of the past experience may only partially or uniquely influence present perception, meaning, and response.

For example, assume that a capable young salesman, who realizes that he has great potential for advancement, is in a purchasing agent's office. The purchasing agent is called from the office for a few minutes, and while he is gone the salesman notices an opened letter on his desk with a competitor's letterhead. Although something inside him (his "value system," a factor that influences behavior) warns him to disregard it, his desire for competitive information gets the upper hand, and he reaches over the desk to turn the page in order to read it. The purchasing agent comes in at that moment, accuses him of unethical, dishonest behavior, and asks him to leave. The purchasing agent later writes to the president of the salesman's firm and requests that the salesman be taken off the account. The salesman's sales manager defends the salesman and points out his excellent ability and potential for growth. He understands the competitive drive behind the salesman. Over time, the incident is forgotten by the president and by the sales manager, as the salesman continues to perform in excellent manner. But the salesman does not forget it. Because he possesses basic integrity, his self-image is badly hurt. Everything seems to remind him of his terrible blunder. The office secretary will say, "Here's the morning mail," and the terrible experience will well up in his mind. A customer will say, "Excuse me for a moment," and it will well up. But he cannot stand this continued misery, and in time the incident becomes rather fuzzy. Finally, it goes away almost entirely, and even when he does think of it, it seems remote and unreal, almost as though someone else, not he, had done the act. He has succeeded in *repressing* it—a defense of the self.

Regression

Regression is a form of defensive behavior in which the individual returns or reverts mentally to an earlier state. In its severe manifestations it becomes a form of mental illness, but to some minor extent it may be used as a defense by normal individuals in normal situations. It may be used when the individual is motivated to do something that is vague—he feels he must do something, but he does not know just *what*; hence he has a sense of insecurity. He perceives the vagueness and the insecurity as a situation to which he must respond, and he responds as he might have "in younger, happier, more carefree days." He may act in a kidding, playful way, even thought the real situation hardly calls for such behavior. For example, assume that a district sales manager and several of his salesmen are invited to executive headquarters for a seminar meeting with top management, to help devise strategies for improving the district's rather average performance. Assume also that the salesmen have never met the top executives on such intimate basis and that they understandably have "butterflies" in their stomachs as they sit in the plush Board Room waiting for the executives. This is a stimulus situation, but the behavior called for may be vague. A drive is nevertheless there; hence they use the defense mechanism of *regression*. They banter. They crack jokes about executives. One may imitate an executive and "fire" another. One may sit in the chief executive's chair and put on a smug face. Now, the sales manager should not write this off merely as boyish, "cute" behavior—perhaps even feeling critical about it, wrongly sensing a lack of seriousness. These men may be deadly serious and will behave seriously when the meeting starts. At this point, they are simply finding an "escape hatch" and emitting a substitute behavior for relief and protection. Again, the sales manager's strategy should make allowance for this. He would probably make a leadership mistake if he were to rebuke them for "unseemly" behavior in the Board Room.

Aggression

Another common defense mechanism is *aggression*, which is quite literally an attack by the individual on another person or on an object.

(Note that it is *not an attack showing opposition,* which is a positive reaction, in which an individual perceives a situation, assesses its meaning, and senses a drive to attack.[36]) Aggression is a defense mechanism in which the individual attacks not for the sake of attack, but to get out some form of behavior to relieve frustration.

For example, a salesman who has been gritting his teeth and bearing some critical remarks from customers all day, unable to allow himself to respond to them as he would like to, may return to the office and snap at the secretary. Or a sales manager who has been having an unhappy experience with his superior, but has been unable to respond to him as he is motivated, may be sharp and a bit nasty to a salesman who later happens into his office. Or a salesman, after a session with his manager, in which the manager was critical of his performance, returns to his office and viciously kicks his briefcase and slams his file folders down on the desk.

Aggression need not be vigorous. It can be quite mild in form and still serve as a relieving defensive act. Here is a case that actually happened. A regional sales manager developed a simple but potentially promising strategy for promoting a new product. On a visit to the headquarters of the product division responsible for the product, he told the product marketing manager of his plans. The marketing manager was delighted and highly commended the sales manager, stating that he would communicate his commendation to the division vice-president—naturally pleasing the sales manager (ego needs and self-image at work here). The marketing manager then proposed that his own staff prepare some special brochures, personalized for selected customers, to help in the promotion. The sales manager said that they were not really necessary, but might help. They parted with expressions of enthusiasm. The sales manager returned to his region and, for one reason or another, did not get around to implementing his promotional strategy. A month passed, then two months. Occasionally, he would worry about it and think, "I must get at that." But something else always gained priority. One morning about three months after his meeting with the marketing manager, his secretary came into his office and said, "Mr. Johnson, Mr. Smith [the marketing manager] is here to see you." Stimulus situation→meaning→ recall→needs→image→guilt. At almost the same moment, Smith walked into the office, with a wide smile. Without even saying hello, the sales manager snapped, "Where the devil are those brochures you were going

---

[36] For example, a salesman learns that a rival has been spreading untruths about him and his company. Though normally he does not speak of his competition to a customer, he decides he must attack this competitive tactic. This is *not* a defense mechanism, but a direct, positive response.

to send me?" [37] This is aggression—in mild form, but definitely a response taken to defend the self.

A curious thing about aggression is that often an individual will "take it out" on a loved one or on a close friend, unconsciously sensing that such a person will bear the aggression understandingly. An individual's self-image usually will not permit him to aggress against one whom he does not know well. (Except when he is in an automobile, but in this case he can aggress against another without *really* being in interaction with him. The other driver is actually an *object,* not a person.) Some loving wives understand this and learn to be tolerant of a husband's snappishness when he comes home from a rugged day.

The pity is that he may not learn it himself and may react to aggression from friends or business colleagues *with* aggression—a normal reaction. But a sales manager must try to detect if the aggression he observes is defensive in character. If it is, his strategy of influence must be shaped accordingly. As a minimum, he should probably avoid counterpunching.

Apathy and Withdrawal

Two extreme forms of defensive behavior—for which it is difficult to devise influencing strategies—are apathy and withdrawal.

Apathy in a literal sense is the absence of feeling or emotion. It may occur because of repeated frustrations, so that to protect himself, the individual succeeds in erasing any meaning, any feeling for a certain situation.

Withdrawal is somewhat different. Here the individual's defensive response is to take himself away from the situation, so that the situation itself falls out of his perception. He may *withdraw physically.* Salesmen have been known to avoid physical confrontation with their sales managers. Or the individual may *withdraw psychologically.* He may be in the physical presence of the manager, but not be "with it" mentally. He lets his mind escape and go elsewhere, maintaining a modicum of contact so that the manager is not really aware that he has withdrawn.

Defensive Behavior—A Summary Statement

Behavior in protection of the self is common. The various forms that it takes are interesting, and sometimes the form itself may be identified.

[37] The aggressive act was, of course, a stimulus situation perceived by Smith. He had not sent the brochures, for good reasons, but now *he* was concerned about *his* image. In the true case, he stammered and said, "Well, ah, we've had the darned budgets, and a thousand things dropped on us by Division." He used the defense mechanism of *projection.*

However, the key idea is for the sales manager to have a sort of *total view of defensive behavior*. He must understand that the individual is motivated to behave some way, but is substituting some other behavior. If the substituted behavior is not desirable, the sales manager will usually find it futile to attack it.[38] Rather, it should serve as a clue to something that underlies it. The very fact that *he is motivated* to do something (even though he does something else, defensively) means that *the drive is there*, and may be subject to strategic influence.

Above all the sales manager must understand that defensive behavior is a normal response by normal people. Another person's behavior is a stimulus situation for the sales manager. But he might make serious managerial mistakes if he were to unthinkingly respond to that behavior. "Why is he behaving as he does?" is a vital question the sales manager must always keep in mind, particularly as he observes defensive behavior.

CONCLUDING SUMMARY

What has this chapter been really about? Certainly, it would be ridiculous, even dangerous, to try to present here very much about the concepts and theories of psychology. Nevertheless, the effective sales manager must gain *insights* into the people-to-people side of his job.

If Peter Drucker's idea that "management is getting things done through others" makes sense, it follows that the manager influences the behavior of others. The manager continually creates situations to which subordinates react and respond. Here is the very essence of management. The manager motivates. But how?

The purpose of this chapter has been to "open the door" to a few theoretical concepts of psychology, adapting them to the selling operation.

Motivation of salesmen cannot be left to chance. And here we are talking about motivation in its broadest and deepest psychological sense —the total psychology of behavior—not simply some "gimmick-like" motivational scheme. Consider a district sales manager to whom ten salesmen report. Each of these salesmen is a unique individual person. Each has a unique set of needs, motives, drives, aspirations, fears, and anxieties. Each has a unique concept of self, and each strives to enhance and protect it. Each sees the situations in his world (of which the district manager is a part) in a unique way, perceiving them with respect to need

---

[38] Of course, if it is detrimental behavior that affects others adversely, it must be attacked. For example, if a salesman is using aggression on the office stenographers, his behavior must be stopped.

and image enhancement or threat. Each uniquely has an emerging set of beliefs and attitudes, frames of reference, learned programs of response.

How each will perceive the district manager and the situations he creates—*and how each will react and respond*—is crucial to the district manager's success or failure in influencing or motivating. It is vital for the effective sales manager to develop insights—and hopefully, over time, some real knowledge—about how the normal individual does perceive, think, and respond.

Only then can the sales manager not only understand better the behavior of his salesmen, but, even more important, predict it. And the ability to predict behavior greatly increases the ability to influence it—that is, to motivate men. It should be carefully noted and understood also that such knowledge has real psychic payoff to salesmen as well as the sales manager. We all want to be understood, and have situations posed to us that are "in tune" with us and do promise payoff.

One last thought. The concepts discussed in this chapter can be applied to customers as well as to salesmen. Hence these are insights also into some psychological aspects of *selling* as well as of managing. After all, in either case one individual is trying to influence or motivate another.

SUGGESTED READINGS

1. Krech, D., and Crutchfield, R. S., *Elements of Psychology*, Alfred A. Knopf, New York, 1958.
2. Combs, A. W., and Snygg, D., *Individual Behavior*, Harper and Row, New York, 1959.
3. Maslow, Abraham H., *Motivation and Personality*, Harper and Brothers, New York, 1954.
4. Stagner, R., and Karwoski, T. F., *Psychology*, McGraw-Hill, New York, 1952.
5. Sherif, M., and Cantril, H., *The Psychology of Ego Involvement*, Wiley, New York, 1947.
6. McClelland, David C., ed., *Studies in Motivation*, Appleton-Century Crofts, New York, 1955.
7. Douglas, John, Field, G. A., and Tarpey, L. X., *Human Behavior in Marketing*, Charles E. Merrill Books, Columbus, Ohio, 1967 (especially pp. 1–77).

QUESTIONS AND PROBLEMS

1. Why is knowledge of human behavior a valuable asset to the sales manager?
2. Briefly discuss the elements of "perception" that you think the sales manager should understand. Why? Give examples.
3. Assume that a certain salesman's behavior indicates to you (as his sales manager) that he has a strong orientation to "ego-need" satisfaction. How would this affect your own behavior toward him? Give some examples of ways in which you would behave.
4. Assume that another salesman's behavior indicates a strong orientation to "social-need" satisfaction? How would you behave? Give examples.
5. Discuss in your own words the meaning of "defensive behavior." How would you evaluate and respond to a salesman who is exhibiting defensive behavior?
6. You are a sales manager. One of your salesmen has been running under quota for several months. Every time you begin to discuss this with him, he aggressively and with some anger complains about the vigor of competition and the fact that he is cursed with unfriendly purchasing agents. How would you appraise this reaction? What hypotheses would develop? How would you develop a "strategy" for dealing with this salesman?

18

The Group and the Individual

The sales manager manages many things, but the management of *people* is the key element of his job. How his sales group performs and what it achieves in the net are the measure of his effectiveness. The understanding of each person in his group as an individual is essential. But he must have insight not only into individual behavior, but also into *group behavior*.

Many dynamic forces are at work within a group, influencing the individual's behavior. Sometimes these forces may be compatible with what the sales manager is trying to accomplish, and sometimes not. In either case, the sales manager must understand them and how they influence individuals' behavior. To gain some insight into these forces, this chapter focuses on the *group*—what the group is, what the group does, how the group functions, how the group influences behavior. This does not mean that the individual is in a secondary position. Rather, he and his behavior are always of primary concern. We merely shift our focus to the group to examine its powerful influencing forces and then return to the individual's responses to them.

THE CONCEPT OF "GROUP"

A group is more than simply a collectivity of people. Forty-five people seated on a Greyhound bus are a collectivity, or a "bunch," but not a group. They may nod to one another, they may even all have the same

goal (to arrive in Chicago) , but still they are not a group, in the psychological sense.

What other ingredients are needed before a collectivity of people
becomes a group? Imagine that the Greyhound bus runs into a blizzard
and becomes stalled in a snowdrift. Individuals on the bus, anxious to be
free of the problem, begin interacting together, working together, with
the end goal of getting out of the drift. The "bunch" has become a
group. Each person contributes effort, so that the group can reach its goal
and he himself can get what he wants. Specifically:

> A group is a number of people, together in social interaction, each of
> whom seeks personal goal achievement (or need satisfaction) but
> perceives that it can be achieved only through group effort and the
> group's movement toward the group goal. Hence the individuals stay
> in the group and contribute to it, because in so doing they can
> obtain something that they could not otherwise easily achieve.

Note that there must be social interactions for a group [1] to exist. All
the surfing enthusiasts in Santa Barbara are a collectivity, a bunch. But
those who form and participate in the Wholly Rollers Surfing Club are
members of a group. The fact that face-to-face interaction is a necessary
ingredient of this concept of a group limits the size of a group, or the
number of people forming a group. No definite limit exists. Probably if a
group grows beyond thirty or so persons, interaction sharply decreases,
the dynamic characteristics of a group diminish, and the group's influence on members' behavior also lessens. In this sense, an entire company
is something other than a group. It does have some influencing forces on
behavior, but it is more a social system than a group. More specifically, it
is a social system containing many small groups. It is the small group,
and its strong influence on the individual, on which this chapter focuses.

Many kinds of groups exist. There are social groups, family groups,
work groups, community-affairs groups, educational groups, church-
oriented groups, and so on. Any one person is a member of many different groups. Some groups are very formally organized (such as task-
oriented business groups) , whereas others evolve, or simply come into
being (such as a street gang) . Some groups, like our Greyhound bus
group, emerge, operate for a brief time, and dissolve. Others persist for
long periods of time, with individual members coming and going.

The business group is a formal task-oriented, goal-oriented group,
which is relatively long-lived.[2] It has been rationally structured. It can be

---

[1] Henceforth the word "group" will always be used in the behavioral sense of this
definition.
[2] This is not necessarily true. Some groups existing in fluid environments may have

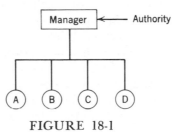

FIGURE 18-1

pictured in the orthodox way, with a "manager" and subordinates A, B, C, and D, as in Figure 18-1. This may be a sales group—say, a district sales manager and a number of salesmen. In this *formal group,* the managerial organizing process has already specified a set of goals for the group to achieve, a set of relationships of manager to subordinates, and missions for each of the subordinates. The manager's position is assigned some degree of authority. He knows, and the subordinates know, that he is the boss and that the incumbent of this position does have certain authorities.

This leads to an interesting tangential idea, which is important for a full understanding of group behavior and particularly leader-follower behaviors. *Authority* is usually thought of as something handed down from above. Furthermore, it is usually thought of as the *right* and the permission to direct, or to command, granted by some higher authority. In this sense, authority is power. *But for it to be followed, the followers must accept it,* and this puts a different light on it. Assuming no conditions of slavery, the *authority must be accepted by the followers.* Authority, then, is *legitimate power*—power given from above, but accepted as legitimate from below. This leads to a somewhat startling thought: authority is as much group-determined as it is higher-management-determined. Some managers do not understand it.[3]

relatively short lives, as managers frequently restructure their organizations. Parenthetically, it may be interesting to contemplate, as one reads the rest of this chapter, the forces of resistance from the group when the manager does decide to reorganize and change the group.

[3] Power-holders have known it for centuries, however. The feudal lords, with their great powers over behavior of subjects, legitimatized their power via the church—the "divine right of kings." If the exercise of power is not accepted as legitimate by followers, sooner or later there will be revolution—bloody or unbloody. It may take very long to occur, but it will occur. Meanwhile, passive resistance, or "psychological" revolt, will take place. *This can even happen in business groups.*

Note also that in Chapter 9 the organizing process was pictured as one that established a hierarchy of rank (hence authority). This view of the requirement that authority be accepted by followers is completely compatible with the view that

Furthermore, different shadings of legitimacy are applied by followers to a manager's authoritative behaviors.[4] Some of his influencing managerial actions are completely accepted as legitimate by followers. Were he to say to his salesman, "Please turn in your expense accounts on the fifth of the month, instead of the fifteenth," they would probably completely accept this directive. However, some of the sales manager's actions may be in a "gray area," where they might be questioned and perhaps followed only reluctantly. For example, were the sales manager to announce a sales meeting every Monday evening, salesmen might grumble and growl among themselves ("What right has he to demand our personal time and encroach on our family life?"). They may follow—but not without questioning and reluctance. Some actions by the sales manager might not only be questioned, but deemed to be illegitimate by subordinates and not followed (actually, therefore, they have "revolted"). Exaggerating to make the point, suppose that the sales manager directed his salesmen thus: "To avoid possible religious conflict with customers, I would like all of you to convert to the Unitarian Church." One can be sure that the salesmen would flatly refuse this directive as not legitimate. This is an extreme, but many more subtle cases can be observed, in which a sales manager's directives are regarded as not legitimate and are not *openly* rebelled against, but simply not followed. For example, a sales manager might say to his salesmen: "I want you to wear dark blue suits, white shirts, and conservative ties when visiting customers." The salesmen may listen to this with bland faces and go out into their territories dressed as they see fit. In a way, perhaps there is little harm in this simple kind of "illegitimate" (in the eyes of subordinates) behavior. But it may have a "summation" effect if emitted very often, so that subordinates may begin to question the legitimacy of more and more of the sales manager's behavior.

But much (sometimes all) of the authority of the manager's position and its use is accepted by subordinates. Together with the missions of the subordinate's job, this exercised authority is the demands on the subordinate, or *expectations* of the subordinate's behavior. In Figure 18-2 the sales manager's *expectations* of the behavior of subordinates are shown at the left. The *group goal* is shown at the top, symbolically indicating that

---

authority is delegated by superiors. Inconsistencies in behavior could occur, of course, if a manager at any level *exercised* power which he thought had been given to him, but which was not regarded as legitimate by followers.

[4] Here we use "authoritative behavior" simply in the sense that the sales manager is attempting to influence others. We are not referring to the *style* with which he does it. That is, we do not infer that he is being an "authoritarian" or a "dictator."

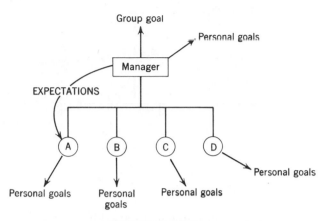

FIGURE 18-2

setting the group goal is a management function in the business group.[5] In addition, each individual's *personal* goals are shown. The difference between group goals and individual goals must be clearly made and kept in mind. Groups form and set a group goal *only* to enable individuals to better achieve their diverse personal goals. The two goals are not synonymous. Hopefully, they are compatible, or the group will not persist. But they are different. A sales manager makes a mistake if he projects to individuals some equating of group goals with personal goals.[6]

The use of authority by the sales manager and his other managerial functions and behaviors are critically viewed by subordinates for another

[5] It may be a group decision in some groups.

[6] Of course, there may be *esprit de corps* and pride in the group. And in group interaction the individual will find satisfaction of ego needs and social needs. But this does not mean that the individual "lives" for the *group* goal. He wants it achieved, to be sure—but so that the group will continue to exist and provide him the economic and psychological "payoffs" that he seeks. This is particularly true at the lower echelons of a firm. The higher one goes in the organizational hierarchy, the closer personal goals of individual managers may come to organizational goals. Thus if one were to ask the chief executive of General Electric what is the most important personal aspiration in his life, he might say very sincerely, "To help this great company be a ten billion dollar firm." But at the salesman level, personal goals usually have little semblance to the group's goals. *This does not mean* that the salesman does not respect (even love) the firm and his job or that he does not commit the whole of himself to his job. This subtle distinction is an important input, sometimes, to leadership strategies. And it is often not very clearly comprehended.

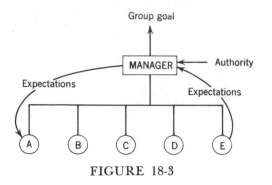

FIGURE 18-3

vital reason beyond that of simple legitimacy. The behavioral view of the group centers in the idea that the individual participates in the group in order to achieve need satisfaction. Consciously or unconsciously, he perceives and evaluates many aspects and situations within the group toward this end. He perceives the sales manager's functions and behaviors and evaluates them with respect to their contribution in moving the group toward its goal—and with respect to his own personal goal achievement. *Thus the subordinate has demands on or expectations of the manager's behavior* (Figure 18-3).

The sales manager is usually well aware of the demands placed on him by his superiors. He may not always be so aware of the demands placed on him by subordinates—and yet these demands may have significant bearing on the acceptance of his leadership and on group performance.

Group Dynamics [7]

As already suggested, the individual perceives and evaluates many aspects and situations within the group. The group is more than the sum total of the behaviors of its members. It has forces at work that strongly influence the behavior of its members. An understanding of these forces, briefly discussed below, is as necessary for the sales manager as an understanding of individual behavior.

The Group Goal

This has already been mentioned. Groups do have goals. A sales group will normally have clean-cut, task-oriented goals—its objectives for

[7] Our discussion will generally follow D. Cartwright and A. Zander, *Group Dynamics,* Row, Peterson and Company, Evanston, Ill., 1960.

volume, market share, new accounts, and so on. Usually a salesman will see how the business goals given him mesh into the group goals. In a task-oriented group, the group goal sets the stage, psychologically speaking, for much of the functioning of the group. Many studies of groups indicate that members tackle their individual parts of the total task better if that total task is well understood. This may appear obvious, but even in some sales groups sales management does not adequately capitalize on this idea.

In many business group situations, a formal group goal is set by management, and individuals contribute toward its achievement, receiving individual need satisfaction by so doing. However, in some situations other, rather informal goals evolve in the common perceptions of members. For example, members of office groups may over time develop great rapport and come to regard the office almost as a "club." They gain great social-need satisfaction from being together, and they develop a set of group goals of their own: camaraderie, social friendship, validation of one's ideas, emotional security. They may perceive everything with respect to *these* goals, not the formal work goal. This may be all right if their work toward their own social goals is not only compatible with but also enhancing to the formal work goal. Unfortunately, sometimes some disparity does subtly result, and performance toward the formal goal is less than optimal.

Furthermore, studies of groups clearly indicate that a sense of *locomotion* toward the goal is necessary for effective group performance. Here again is a valuable behavioral tool for sales management. The periodic "review sessions," or "state of the union" sessions, held by a sales manager are examples. Here we are speaking of the communication to members of how the *group* is doing, where the *group* stands with respect to the *group* goal, not how one individual is doing with respect to his given mission.[8]

Cohesiveness

The ability of the group to continue in existence and while doing so to retain its members is its *cohesiveness*. Although it is not the only measure, cohesiveness does indicate the degree of attractiveness of the group to its members.

The sources of attraction leading to cohesiveness are varied. Locomo-

---

[8] This is not meant to demean the manager's appraisal of *individual* performance. Such appraisal is vital. But it is a different aspect of motivation. Here we are saying that it is possible to generate a psychological drive in individuals to seek to help achieve group goals.

tion toward the group goal, with members consciously working together toward it, may develop a sense of "we-ness." Attacks on a group from outside sources may increase this sense of "we-ness." Often after a group has weathered a severe crisis (example: a sales region under severe criticism from higher headquarters, with threat to reorganize), it may continue with a higher degree of cohesiveness than it had, by virtue of "standing together"—with obvious inputs into regional management strategy.[9]

Cohesiveness is the act of sticking together. Underlying it is a psychological force on the members. This is the concept of *morale*. Morale is the *value* that members place on being in the group. If many or most members place high value on being in the group, the group is generating high morale. High morale brings common enthusiasm, strong regard, and high devotion to the group. The influence that the group has on members' behavior is enhanced by high morale.[10]

The real source of the group's attractiveness to members is the ability of each to perceive that the group satisfies his needs. This ties back to the idea of what the group is and to the model of individual behavior. The group is an object of need satisfaction to the individual. Again, the real key for the manager lies in the compatibility of formal group goals and individuals' personal goals or aspirations (see again footnote 10).

Several sources of unattractiveness can be identified. They can be valuable inputs into the sales manager's strategies of behavior within the group.

1. The basic source, of course, is the inability of the individual to perceive that working toward the group goal will in fact help him achieve his personal goals.[11]

2. Disagreement on group goals can reduce the group's attractiveness to members. Or, if the goals are generally accepted, disagreement on how they are to be achieved (strategies) can cause perception of unattractiveness.[12]

[9] It might, of course, suffer from loss of cohesiveness, if members do not physically and/or psychologically band together during the crisis. Factors that could cause loss of cohesiveness are discussed below.

[10] Hence high morale is beneficial to group goal achievement (performance) *if the behaviors it influences or induces are directed toward formal goal achievement.* Morale per se is not automatically beneficial. It is conceivable that a group could "rebel" against higher authority, disregard the formal goal, strike out on its own, and still have very high *morale*.

[11] He may perceive all this very differently from the sales manager. The sales manager cannot afford to project his own perceptions and meanings of the group to any subordinate.

[12] This raises the interesting (and perhaps complex and debatable) point that when a sales manager devises alternative strategies, one input might be "how will subor-

3. Unpleasant environments can decrease attractiveness. This includes not only unpleasant physical environments, but also unpleasant social or behavioral environments. Physical environmental change can be made only under constraints of time and money. A sales office located in an ugly, run-down, and frightening area can be moved—but it may take time and much persuasion. Furthermore, economic costs always must be weighed against "social" gains, and some balance will exist. Unpleasant social environments, however, can be attacked by the sales manager if he is alert enough to see them and if he understands human behavior.

4. Attempts by members to dominate others can cause unattractiveness. At the risk of overgeneralizing, it may be well for the sales manager to observe the behavior of strongly ego-oriented individuals, who might use other group members as sources for domination. There is a fine hairline between competitive drive and dominance. And members of a group can be very perceptive of this.

5. Poor or ineffective leadership *as perceived by the subordinates* is a prime source of unattractiveness of a group to its members. This is further discussed in the next chapter.

The loss of attractiveness may not always mean a proportionate loss of cohesiveness—with members leaving the group. Sometimes it generates a splitting of a group into separate factions, or cliques. Each will have its own set of subgoals. These "splinter groups" may or may not be in conflict with one another or with the group as a whole. They may be detrimental to the group performance. For example, suppose that in a sales group some salesmen (say, those with college degrees) band together socially in the work environment and give others in the group the perception that "they are different." Bitterness on the part of others can cause some lack of group attractiveness and loss of dedication to contributions to group performance. On the other hand, cliques can enhance group attractiveness, if all members find some "niche" that provides them need satisfaction. In *general,* however, the sales manager should be alert to the forming of informal, "splinter" groups, with their potential for establishing primacy of the "splinter" group goals over the formal group goal and for causing psychological conflict with individuals outside the "splinter" group.[13]

dinates perceive this alternative with respect to group goals, attractiveness, and potential for their individual need satisfaction?" This does not imply that a good strategy will be rejected because of this thought. It does imply that the "tactics" used in its implementation can consider this question. Many a "good" strategy has been less than ideally implemented because it was less than ideally presented to subordinates. To coin a phrase the manager might well think of "the strategy of implementing a strategy"!

13 Again, the idea advocated by some managers of pitting one group against another in a sort of competition is open to question—not only because of possible

In summary, the sales manager should analyze the cohesive qualities of his group from several viewpoints. Foremost is the group performance and its adequate movement toward his goal for the group. Second is the firm's investment in the group. Unattractiveness and loss of cohesiveness mean personnel turnover, with attendant cost, loss of time, disruption of selling strategies, and loss of salesman-customer intimacy. Third, a high level of cohesiveness enhances the desire to enter the group, easing the recruiting problems and in the long run improving goal achievement through desire to stay in and perpetuate the group.

Structure in Groups

All groups develop a set of roles which are interrelated. In a formal business group, this *formal* role structure is rationally devised in the organizing process. But even in informal groups that spring into being, such as the group in the Greyhound bus example, a street gang, or the weekly poker club, a role structure will emerge. In this structure, the individual knows his own role as well as its relationship to other roles. Thus not only do "specializations" evolve, but also the communication nets relating them. Moreover, the role structure and the communication nets enable the individual to identify and call on the human resources in the group.[14]

A "power system" also evolves. Each role in the group has a status assigned to it. Again, this may be done formally in the organizing process or it may evolve informally. Unintended and unknown by the sales manager, members of his group may in consensus ascribe a higher status to some roles in the group than to others.[15]

A very important idea springs from this. The formal roles established by the managerial organizing process have demands placed on them by management, or expectations of their behavior, as noted earlier. But if the individuals within a group also assign their own status levels to various roles, an additional set of expectations exists for an individual.

coordinating problems, but also because of its potential for damaging group attractiveness.

[14] This greatly facilitates the emergence of "informal leadership," to be discussed later in this chapter.

[15] For example, in General Electric's Apparatus Sales Division, the regional operations had a diversity of sales engineer roles. That is, some sales engineers were assigned to a few large and important customers (e.g., steel mills). Others were "general salesmen" assigned to territories with many smaller customers. Others were assigned to distributors. The "job levels," potential salaries, and organizational levels were the same for these sales roles. But members of the sales group ascribed very different status to them, with the "steel mill" sales position in the highest level and the distribution sales position in the lowest.

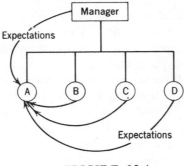

FIGURE 18-4

This set, too, influences his behavior, and the astute sales manager should be aware of this. Thus individual A in Figure 18-4 will be "expected" to behave in certain ways by his manager, *but also in certain ways by other individuals in accordance with their perception of his role.* This leads us to the heart of group dynamics—the regulatory pressure placed on an individual's behavior by the group itself.

Norms of Behavior

Groups develop norms, or standards of behavior for its members. Here we are speaking not of the expectations of management, but the demands that members of a group collectively place on the behavior of others. Furthermore, the group not only determines modes of behavior to be followed by members in various situations, *but exerts pressures on members to conform to these norms.* Behavior that deviates from the norms is undesirable to the group, and the group will use pressure to swing it back to the "desired" behavior.[16]

Over time, the norms of behavior become institutionalized. That is, they become *customs* and almost "unwritten laws." This is so perceived by individuals, who find in this influencing force a satisfaction of the need to conform. Thus over time the behaviors of individuals in a group will become very similar in many situations. The group norms become embedded in the individual's frames of reference, and *the individual develops predispositions to behave in accordance with these norms.* Indi-

[16] The tolerance of deviant behaviors will vary from group to group and sometimes from individual to individual within a group. If members of a group regard one individual as highly valuable to the group, hence valuable for personal goal achievement, they may allow him more deviance from group standards of behavior than they would allow another individual.

viduals in many groups come to dress alike, use the same form of language, and act alike. This adherence to norms affects not only such surface behaviors, but penetrates also to the individual's perceptual process. He may come to *perceive* things as he unconsciously (or sometimes consciously) believes others in the group do.[17]

Group pressures to adhere to group-established norms can powerfully influence the behavior of individuals in many circumstances. A new member in a group is "taught" how to behave in his role often more significantly by the group than by the manager. Setting of output performance often is more a group decision than a managerial decision. Ways of implementing managerial decisions may be more under group control than under managerial control. Acceptance or resistance to change is a group phenomenon, imposing its will on members' perceptions and responses. A young salesman may emulate certain older salesmen (for "good" or "bad") more readily than behave as the sales manager suggests.

This does not infer helplessness on the part of the sales manager. To be sure, the group's influences on individuals' behavior may sometimes be stronger than the manager's influences. And failure to understand this aspect of group behavior opens many traps for the sales manager. But as in many other behavioral aspects of management, for all the hazards, there are opportunities that the alert sales manager can exploit. After all, the sales manager himself and his behaviors are a meaningful part of the whole web of "group life." His behaviors are inputs into the processes by which groups develop their norms of behavior. Again—the key is a strategic one. In this leadership, in his influence of subordinates' behavior toward the ends he seeks, the sales manager's strategies must take into account how established group norms will react to his decisions. He cannot afford to disregard them or to bluntly attack them. He must either shape his strategies as much as possible to accommodate them [18] or, as a minimum, recognize that resistance may occur and prepare to alleviate it. Even to alleviate it, or to strategically attempt to influence group norms, he must understand them and approach them rationally and objectively.

[17] Consider a group like "Hell's Angels." Here is a collectivity of apparently rugged individualists, perhaps rebellious against the shackles of society. Yet look at the power of the group in securing an absolute adherence to group norms—same dress, same motorcycles, same beards, *same behavior*. They are as peas in a pod—and it is via group forces that this occurs.

[18] Again, no effective sales manager will reject a desirable plan of action for fear of conflict with group norms of behavior. But it would be ridiculous to barge ahead with it blindly and be confused or irritated if its implementation is achieved less than effectively.

Rewards and Sanctions

To reinforce its powers to influence behavior, the group develops a system of rewards and punishments. Accepted behavior is rewarded; deviant behavior is punished.

The business group has a *formal* reward and punishment system, of course. "Good" behavior—that which the sales manager perceives as moving the group toward its rational business goal—is rewarded. Reward comes in many forms: monetary (the individual receives a salary increase or money bonus); promotion (raising to higher status, increasing prestige, increasing money income); commendation (enhancing achievement needs, increased recognition); and enriched relationships (being taken into "management confidences," closer contact with management). Punishment also comes in many forms. The extreme is dismissal, and this occasionally happens. But other forms of formal punishment exist: personal criticism, threat to security, cool aloofness, restrictions of resources, movement to a lower-status position (or threat of it).[19]

But the group itself has its own system of rewards and punishments, reinforcing its established norms of behavior. In most business groups, the *formal* reward and punishment system usually dwells on *rewards* for "good" behavior rather than punishment for unacceptable behavior. However, the *informal* reward and punishment system developed by the group usually centers less on reward for "good" behavior than it does on *punishment* for behavior that deviates from group norms. In many groups, individuals perceive *threat of punishment* from their associates as a more powerful influence than the promise of rewards from the formal system. A commendation from the sales manager may not be so highly sought as acceptance by one's fellows. To be sure, this varies greatly from group to group. And it is much more true for an individual whose mix of needs is strongly social-need-oriented.[20]

The punishments meted out by a group against a deviant member are *normally* social in nature. The group may not be able to expel a member physically, but they can "expel" him psychologically by shunning and

---

[19] In many large corporations the practice is sometimes followed to remove an "ineffective" line manager from his high-status position by "kicking him upstairs" to an obscure staff position.

[20] In a selling operation, the strength of the group's punishment system may be less for field salesmen who are in little face-to-face contact with one another than for others in the organization who have close face-to-face contact (e.g., office clerical people, headquarters staff groups, and product specialists). Of course, the sales manager must effectively manage all these groups.

avoiding him. Refusal to allow him social intercourse in the group can be a crushing punishment, particularly to an individual who has any degree of social needs whatsoever. The punishment may take the form of derision, both open and subtle, striking at the deviant member's self-image. It may assume "economic" forms, with the group withholding resources that the deviant member needs to play his role. It may in the extreme take subtle physical forms; the group may leave him no room to park his car, may move his desk to a poor location, or may literally lock him out.

Few individuals are absolute "loners." Even highly ego-oriented individuals have some degree of social needs. Furthermore, they do need the support of the group to achieve their ego needs. Thus the group may develop great power over the behavior of its members, developing it informally and usually without rational planning. *This is a characteristic to some degree of all groups* and is a necessary input into a sales manager's strategies of influence.

Informal Leadership

An essential ingredient of all groups is *leadership*. In formal groups, such as the business group, the leadership role is formally structured into management positions.[21] In informal groups, however, leadership will emerge. In fact, it must emerge for the group to be a group. The emergence of leadership behavior is a coin with two sides. It requires the drive on the part of an individual to emit influencing behavior. But it also requires the need for that behavior and its acceptance by the followers.

Informal leadership sometimes emerges also *in formal groups*. Leadership behavior that directly influences the responses of others can be emitted by an individual other than the manager himself. In many groups, members will turn to some individual fellow member under certain situations for counsel, guidance, and direction. Sometimes they will turn to one member for leadership in one kind of situation and to another in a different situation. Because of their experience, knowledge, age, status level, or relationships with management, certain members may become "thought leaders" in a group. They may come to "translate" the formal management directives into the norms of the group and in essence decide the degree to which the norms will be accepted and followed.

Informal leadership of this kind is common in many sales groups. Some one salesman may have strong influence over the responses of others in certain situations. For a simple example, assume that a sales manager is

[21] How the manager is *perceived* as a leader by his followers is a different matter, however, and is out of the hands of higher management. We explore this in the next chapter.

in the process of reorganizing the territorial assignment of salesmen. Some salesmen may perceive this with anxiety, but rather than exhibit anxiety to the sales manager, they may turn to one of their fellow salesmen, seeking his advice on how to respond. On another occasion—say, when the compensation plan is under revision—they may turn to still another fellow salesman and seek not only his advice but his representing of the group to higher management. *Very often perception and responses of individuals in the group will be influenced by the attitudes and behaviors of a fellow member,* and very often this will be consciously sought by the group.

From a strategic viewpoint, it may seem at first glance that such informal leadership can undermine the formal leadership and the planned influence of behavior by the sales manager. Of course, it can. But to "stamp it out" would be a futile effort, because this is a very normal and natural characteristic of group behavior. Attacking informal leadership will simply reinforce it. Rather, the effective sales manager will over time identify the informal leaders in his group (for various situations) and strategically plan his relationships with them accordingly. Rather than threaten this group relationship, he will as a minimum not appear to be striking at it and as an optimum utilize it for group goal achievement. It oversimplifies to say that he should have the informal leaders "on his side," but in essence that is precisely what he should strive for.

This view of the sales manager's strategy can be quite important for a headquarters sales manager whose line managers (regional and district sales managers) are widely spread geographically. Members of the headquarters staff (product managers, service mangers, etc.) who range the territories and probably have more frequent face-to-face interaction with the field managers than he does have a potential for informal leadership roles—whether they consciously seek them or not.

This final element of group dynamics—that of *leadership*—is so vital that it will be discussed in greater depth, from a strategic view, in the next chapter.

THE MANAGER AS A LINK BETWEEN GROUPS

With regard to his leadership, the sales manager plays a unique dual role, since he is always a member of more than one group. He is always the leader of his own managed group, and he is always a subordinate in another group. Consider a district sales manager's dual role,[22] as shown in Figure 18-5.

[22] See R. Likert, *New Patterns in Management,* McGraw-Hill, New York, 1961.

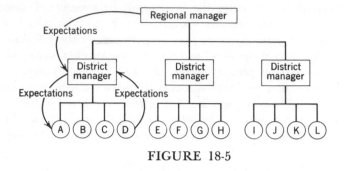

FIGURE 18-5

The district sales manager is a *subordinate or a follower in one group* —that composed of the regional manager, as the leader of the group, and his fellow district managers. This group will have its unique characteristics, and each of the elements of "group dynamics" discussed earlier will be operant. The district sales manager's behavior will be influenced by this group, its leader, and its unique norms.

At the same time, the district manager is a member of a *different group and in it plays a different role,* that of leader. Again, this group is completely unique, with its own set of "group dynamics," its own mode of influence, its own norms. The district manager cannot behave in the same manner in this group as he does in the other group. Furthermore, he must accomplish the important ability or skill of *translating* the influence and the behaviors from the higher-echelon group to the lower-echelon group. He must take directives from above and reshape them to uniquely "fit" the individual needs and the group needs of the lower group. Conversely, he must "translate" upward, reshaping the requirements of the lower group to the individual needs and group needs of the higher group. Skill in this *linking* of groups and translating expectations from one to the other is one of the marks of an effective manager. It is probably particularly important at the first level of management above the individual worker level—and it is one of the reasons why a district sales manager's job is one of the most important (and sometimes most underrated) jobs in the selling operation. For it is here that the translation stops, and all the strategies culminate in the contact of customers by members of the group.

SOME CONCLUDING COMMENTS

The sales manager's role is much more complex than his being simply the "boss" of a number of individuals. In fact, his success as a manager depends on more than his separate relationships with individuals. He is the manager of *and a member of* a group.

An individual has some rather consistent pattern of behavior, which is his *personality*. Each group also has its unique mode of behavior, for which the term *syntality* has been coined. Within its inner dynamics the group exerts strong influences on behavior. Individuals respond to these influences because they perceive that by so doing need satisfactions will be more readily achieved. As a unique member of the group, the sales manager is vested with the authority of his office. But he is also in a splendid position to lead the group (influence behaviors) if he understands the elements of group dynamics and considers them strategically in determining his own leadership behaviors. The purpose of this chapter is merely to open the door to such understanding. The purpose of the next chapter is to explore *how* he can use this insight.

SUGGESTED READINGS

1. Bonner, H., *Group Dynamics,* Ronald Press, New York, 1959.
2. Bass, Bernard M., *Organizational Psychology,* Allyn and Bacon, Boston, 1965 (especially pp. 148–213) .
3. Hare, Borgotta, and Bales, *Small Groups,* Alfred A. Knopf, New York, 1965.
4. Homans, George C., *The Human Group,* Harcourt, Brace, New York, 1950.
5. Homans, George C., *Social Behavior: Its Elementary Forms,* Harcourt, Brace, New York, 1961.
6. Gibb, C. A., "Leadership," in Gardner Lindzey, ed., *Handbook of Social Psychology,* Addison-Wesley, Reading, Mass., Volume II, 1954, pp. 877–917.
7. Gellerman, S., *Motivation and Productivity,* The American Management Association, New York, 1963, pp. 19–97.

QUESTIONS AND PROBLEMS

1. How can you relate some of the concepts of individual behavior discussed in Chapter 17 to concepts of group behavior?
2. Why should the sales manager understand the "dynamics" of group behavior?
3. For each of the elements of "group dynamics," give an example from a sales unit and suggest how it can influence an individual salesman's behavior.

4. A sales manager once said: "If any of my men try to act like a boss, or try to influence the other people in my group, I'll get him straightened out in a hurry. There can be only one boss in a good group." Comment on this.

5. What are the advantages and the disadvantages to the sales manager of certain patterns or norms of behavior that develop in his sales unit? Give examples.

6. Give some examples of how "punishment" may be meted out to an individual by members of the group. Explain how this might be detrimental to the sales manager's goals for the group.

19

Leadership Strategies

On the fifty-second floor above Park Avenue in midtown Manhattan, a headquarters field sales manager is earnestly seeking approval for a managerial promotion he wishes to make. As he sits in the executive conference room, he faces across the large table a trio of executives—the executive vice-president for operations, the vice-president of marketing, and the manager of personnel administration. He has proposed a candidate for the position of regional sales manager of the Western Region, a vitally important market area for the firm. The candidate is presently thirty-four years of age and is a sales engineer with an outstanding record of sales accomplishments. For thirty minutes the group has covered in detail the candidate's dossier—his educational background, his service with the firm, his past and present ratings, company training programs in which he has participated, his record of achievements, his extracurricular activities in the industry and in the community, his family situation, his loyalty and integrity. His relative youth has posed some problem in the eyes of the executive vice-president, but not a serious one. Everything in the candidate's past performance seems to favor his appointment, and the group is on the verge of giving approval when the marketing vice-president remarks: "I have only one reservation. How do we know that he will be an effective leader of men? The Western Region has a lot of tough-to-handle people. And they need some guidance. How do we know he can do this?"

At this point, the rational, objective appraisal of the candidate breaks down. The sales manager "thinks" that he will be a good leader and cites the fact he was vice-chairman of the community fund drive. The personnel manager notes that he was a staff sergeant during his service stint. The executive vice-president uneasily murmurs that the last time the firm promoted a "star salesman" he nearly ruined his region by "antagonizing everybody." The marketing vice-president suggests that he might attend some management courses at Stanford.

This group of executives has hit upon a very difficult question. How can one be sure about this almost magical quality of leadership? They know—as all executives do—that many elements exist in the management job, but perhaps the most crucial is the ability to influence others' behaviors in a desired way. "Management is getting things done *through others*." But what does it take to be a good leader?

Men have been fascinated with this question for centuries. From the time of Socrates to today's executive conference rooms, the question has been explored, "What makes a good leader of men?" Is it true (and this myth seems to persist) that good leaders are "born, not made"? Is it true that a few men can become outstanding leaders, but most of us cannot?

The major difficulty in solving these questions has lain in the fact that the "magic" quality of leadership has been explored from wrong points of view. For centuries man has observed outstanding leaders, those whose influence on others was clearly obvious—from Genghis Khan to Julius Caesar to Napoleon to Washington to Hitler to Eisenhower. In the business world, it is relatively easy to identify the great leaders of men, as well as the mediocre leaders. In any firm one can observe a wide range of leadership ability. But in the past the focus of leadership study was placed *on these known leaders* and the question asked, "What qualities do they have?"

Because of this point of view, studies of leadership centered on the traits of known leaders. Many studies attempted to correlate known leadership ability with the leader's personal qualities. Such studies developed proposals that *on the whole* good leaders were a little more intelligent than followers, a little physically larger than followers, and so on. Or leaders were described as persons who have confidence, loyalty, consideration of others, vigor, creative thinking ability, reliability, and so on. But personality traits are vague and difficult to quantify. And individuals can be found who possess all these traits in large measure, *but are mediocre leaders of men*.

Turning away from studies of traits and personal qualities, many psychologists now center on the *behaviors of leaders and the functions of leadership as it affects group performance*.[1] This opens new insights into

[1] The behavioral view of leadership was triggered off during World War II when the armed services generated many studies of leadership. Several universities, notably The Ohio State University, and scores of individual psychologists and social

leadership, allowing its description and analysis as a behavioral relationship between individuals. This does not mean that leadership does not require personal skill. It does. *But it is the act of behavior of the leader as it is perceived by and responded to by the follower that is the key to understanding it.* Leadership is influencing the behavior of another, not some set of qualities. It is *behavioral,* and can be understood within the frameworks of individual behavior and group behavior discussed in the preceding two chapters. Hence it can be objectively analyzed and learned.[2] The concern and the admitted inability to predict, expressed by the executives in the example opening this chapter, can be solved. The potential for leadership can be assessed through knowledge of the candidate's "typical" behavior patterns. Also, the executives can provide him with knowledge of basic elements of effective leadership.

EFFECTIVE LEADERSHIP

As with any other aspect of human behavior and interaction, no simple "formula" exists for effective leadership. A headquarters sales manager cannot say to a district manager, "Now, Jim, here's what you say and how you act." Rather, the district manager must think strategically: "I believe that this individual perceives and thinks this way. I have observed his behavior over time, and I think that he is strongly social-need-oriented. The group means much to him. And I note that he seems to respond to the group, and carefully matches his behavior to that of certain key people in the group. Knowing this, how best can I present a situation to him, to influence him to willingly do what I want him to? Well, I predict that if I present a situation to him in this particular way, he will react in this manner. Or I could present it in another way, and I predict he'd

psychologists contributed to a major breakthrough in understanding this vital behavior.

   It should be noted, however, that some behavioral scientists are uneasy about the "premature burial" of leadership traits. They wonder especially why some men *gain acceptance* as leaders while others do not. See particularly F. E. Fiedler, "Leadership and Leadership Effectiveness Traits: A Reconceptualization of the Leadership Trait Problem," in L. Petrullo and B. M. Bass, eds., *Leadership and Interpersonal Behavior,* Holt, Rinehart and Winston, New York, 1961, pp. 179–186.

2 This is a very important statement. Before leadership was analyzed in terms of behaviors, social interactions, and perceptions and responses of followers, essentially no firms had any effective way of developing leadership abilities. Now some forward-looking managements are beginning to incorporate leadership training into their management development programs.

react in that manner." [3] To go more deeply into this idea, consider three kinds of leadership behavior, which we shall arbitrarily call (1) attempted leadership, (2) successful leadership, and (3) effective leadership.

Attempted Leadership

Consider this example. A district sales manager is holding a sales meeting at the district office, attended by his twelve salesmen, two service technicians, and the office administration manager. He is proposing certain directions for selling strategy, emphasizing the need for additional effort on certain product lines. *He has a goal that he wants achieved.* To attain the goal, he knows that he "must get things done through others" and therefore must influence each of his salesmen to behave in some particular way. During his discussion on one particular product (say, the Model 2450 Office Copier), he addresses a salesman saying: "Mac, next week I think you'd better concentrate entirely on the Model 2450, and put most of your emphasis on the bank customers in your territory."

Now, at this point, the sales manager has emitted a behavior designed to influence another individual to do something to help him, the sales manager, reach his goal (increased sale now of the Model 2450). Also at this point, the salesman has perceived this behavior as a stimulus situation, but has not yet responded behaviorally. His "mental wheels" are turning as he interprets the situation,[4] but he does not respond. If leadership is the influencing of another's behavior to do what the leader wants, this act of the sales manager has not at this point gained such response, hence is only *an attempt to lead.*

If next week the salesman does not respond as the sales manager has asked,[5] the attempt has failed. No leadership has been accomplished. He

[3] The sales manager may not think all this in such A-B-C, academic language. But *in essence,* the effective leader goes through some sort of rationale like this. Those who have intuitively developed it and learned it do so quite naturally and almost unconsciously. But there is nothing wrong with anyone in a leadership position consciously and deliberately *working* at this, until it *does* come naturally.

[4] There are many ways in which he could interpret this situation. He might have already made customer plans for the next week, which he must cancel, causing some embarrassment. Yet he seeks personal approval by the sales manager. Or on the other hand, he may be strongly ego-need-oriented and may resent being told flatly what to do, rather than being given a target and permitted to lay his own strategy. Or perhaps he is in a defensive frame of mind and thinks, "Why did he single *me* out first?" Obviously, there are a great many ways in which he might assess meaning to this situation, weighing against the positive drive that he senses to go ahead and do what the sales manager proposes.

[5] The salesman might evaluate his own plans more highly, rationalizing that in the long run they will serve the group better than the short-range "crash program" the

may simply ignore the directive or he may make a bare, superficial stab at it. His behavior may deviate in some way from what the sales manager intended. The *attempted leadership* then will have been unsuccessful. If the salesman responds only partially in the direction sought, the attempted leadership is really still unsuccessful, since the sales manager's goal is not achieved. It would be naïve to believe that this example is unusual. With all good intent, and with no malice, the response of the follower to the influence of the leader may take a different track than that sought by the leader.

Successful Leadership

But suppose that the next week the salesman does precisely what the sales manager has asked. He cancels previous commitments and concentrates his efforts entirely on the Model 2450, calling almost entirely on bank customers. His behavior is exactly what the sales manager has wanted. This is *successful leadership.*

In successful leadership, the leader emits a behavior designed to influence the behavior of another individual in a certain manner, and the other individual does respond in that manner. *The leader gets what he wants.* His leadership behavior is *successful.*[6]

Effective Leadership

In successful leadership, the leader is rewarded. He gets what he wants from the social interaction. But what of the follower? He has perceived the leader's act of influence; he has been motivated to respond in some manner; he emits that behavior. How does he regard his own act of behavior? If he regards it as rewarding to him in some manner, *effective leadership has occurred.* In successful leadership, the leader is rewarded by the follower's behavior. In *effective leadership, both leader and follower are rewarded by the follower's behavior.* We say "effective," because the consummated cycle of interaction provides a "payoff" to the

---

sales manager has proposed. Or he may value his self-image with customers more highly than a possible rebuke from the sales manager. He may reason that if he does not follow the sales manager's directive, he might "get away with it" or, if discovered, "talk his way out of it." These are only a few of the possible responses.

6 The *outcome* of the other individual's desired behavior is another matter. It may or may not effectively achieve the sales manager's end goal of greater sales of Model 2450. If it does not, his strategy was perhaps open to some question. The real point involving *leadership* is that he did seek to influence another's behavior (for some purpose of his own) and he *was* successful in getting the behavior he wanted.

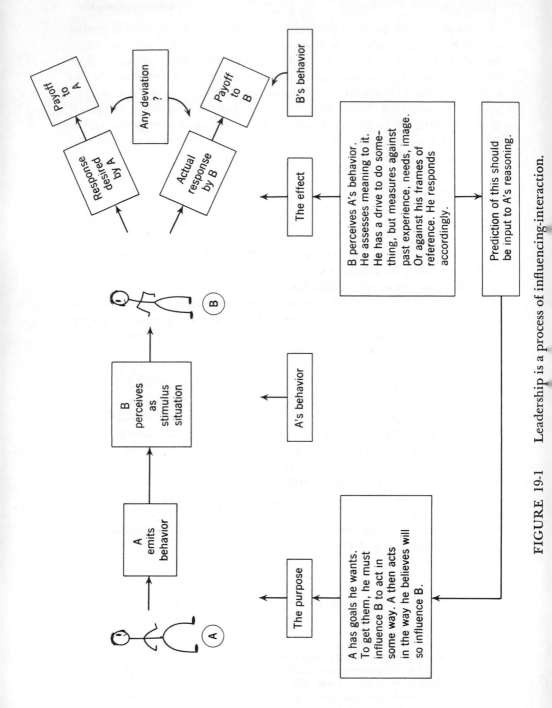

FIGURE 19-1   Leadership is a process of influencing-interaction.

follower. This reinforces the relationship between leader and follower and enhances the leader's behaviors as "good" or as "need-satisfying" in the follower's frame of reference. The eminent George Homans puts it this way:

> Human interaction is an exchange. If I want something from you, I behave in some way to motivate you to behave in some way that will reward me. But if you do emit that behavior I am rewarded, satisfied. But if I don't return some reward to you, you will not respond in like manner the next time I seek it from you.[7]

Figure 19-1 shows this interaction process in graphical form.

The "reward" that the *leader* receives from the interaction between leader and follower is some behavior by the follower that gets or produces something the leader wants. The follower's *behavior* is not what is really sought by the leader. It is merely a means to an end—the end being what the follower's behavior achieves.

What is the reward, however, from the *follower's* viewpoint? It can take many forms, physical and psychological. In a physical sense, it can be an economic reward. A salesman following a sales manager's influencing behavior may receive a bonus or a salary increase, or he may perceive that by positively responding he is taking a step toward such an economic reward. A follower may receive other kinds of physical rewards—better facilities, more resources, tickets to the Series, a martini and lunch.

In the web of sales manager-salesmen (or headquarters sales manager–regional sales manager) relationships, however, psychological rewards are extremely meaningful to the follower and are more widely used than physical rewards. The follower has many needs at play; he has a self-image, which he seeks to enhance and protect. Satisfaction of the ego needs (status, recognition, prestige, achievement) and of social needs (belonging, conformity, security), as they all exist in some "mix," is greatly rewarding and is sought by the individual. The reward perceived by the follower might be that of gaining new stature through the act, of gaining recognition by management. Or it could be merely a "thank you" and a smile from the leader. Or the reward could be a feeling of achievement for the group.

Of course, this can all work in the negative sense, too. The follower might perceive the attempt at influence and think, "If I do this, I don't see any value in it to me." He is not motivated to do it. However, he may then continue thinking: "But if I don't do it, what might happen to me? He is in a position to hurt me some way, if I don't do it. I certainly don't

[7] George C. Homans, *Social Behavior: Its Elementary Forms*, Harcourt, Brace, New York, 1961.

want trouble, so maybe I'd better do it." Thus the follower perceives some threat to himself if he does not positively respond. Hence he follows the influencing behavior, thus rewarding the leader and removing threat to himself. *Removal of threat is a positive reward,* and not a trifling amount of follower behavior is of this sort.

Or consider another aspect of threat removal as a reward. Suppose that the follower perceives neither positive payoff for himself nor threat to himself *from the leader.* He might think: "I don't see anything in it to me. And if I don't do it, I'm not afraid of anything he might do to me." (For example, an old, experienced, and competent salesman, well acquainted with top management, might think this way about an influencing attempt by a young sales manager.) He is not motivated to respond. However, he continues to think: "But if I don't do it, what will the rest of the gang think? Will the other salesmen think I'm jealous, or something, which I'm not? Will they think I'm undercutting the new boss? They might, if I refuse, and I certainly don't want to get the gang down on me." Here is threat of punishment not from the leader but *from the group,* and the salesman may respond positively and gain the positive reward of removal of threat of "punishment" from the group.

All this brings the interesting if startling thought that *effective leadership* is as much follower-determined as it is leader-determined. Certainly the follower must perceive reward (need satisfaction and/or image enhancement) from his follower behavior. Tying this thought into the concepts of group behavior as well as into the psychology of individual behavior, it is evident that

> The effective leader is he who by his behaviors and functions helps to move the group toward the successful attainment of group goals, such that *he and group members achieve their individual personal goals.*

The general claim can be made that followers value most highly that leadership behavior which contributes maximally to individual satisfaction obtained through the group. Thus a leader is more than some person occupying the office of a manager, inheriting certain authorities delegated to that position. From a behavioral viewpoint, the leader is the person who is perceived by followers as the best means available to get them where they want to go at that time.[8] Again, here is a tie back to the

8 These ideas seem quite obvious when one considers "emerging" leadership in informal groups (such as a street gang). However, in a business group, the manager is *imposed* by the firm, so to speak, on the group. But is this really any different? To be sure, the business group members feel impelled to follow the manager to some degree. (There is threat implied, if they do not.) But the degree of the

concepts of group behavior in the preceding chapter. The group has expectations or demands on the leader. In the eyes of group members, the effective leader must fulfill these expectations. They demand more from him than simply to give orders or to be "a nice guy." They expect him to behave in many different ways to contribute to group performance so that the group moves toward its goals [9] and each of them gains the need satisfaction for which he is in the group.

THE ROLES OF THE LEADER [10]

The effective leader is "many things to many people." The expectations of his behavior demanded by group members (and for that matter by his superiors) may be widely diverse. He is an important actor in an important, always changing drama in which he plays many different roles. The group collectively and members individually expect these roles to be played at appropriate times. A brief description of some of these roles follows.

The Executive

Very often the members of the group *desire and expect* the manager to play the role of executive. That is, they expect him to perform for the group the functions of objective setting, planning, organizing, coordinating, and decision making. For example, in a field sales group, whose group objectives are set, individual salesmen expect to have goals meted out to them. They expect to have a broad strategy mapped out, within which each develops his own strategy. They expect proper allocation of resources. They expect executive-level decisions. Furthermore, they realize that external conditions change and that the entire group strategy must occasionally be adjusted.

The Planner

The function of planning is one of the managerial processes. But very often a group, without really wanting a total executive function per-

manager's *real effectiveness* in influencing behavior centers in these concepts. How he performs in the follower's eyes may spell the difference between an average and an effective managerial performance.

[9] The group goals, that is, as *the group members see them*. Hopefully these will be the same as the manager's goals for the group. In most sales groups, they probably are.

[10] This discussion of leadership roles follows Krech and Crutchfield, *Social Psychology; Theory and Problems*, McGraw Hill, New York, 1948.

formed (members may want freedom to make decisions), may want the planning itself done for the group.

The Policy Maker

In the same sense, group members may at times want broad guidelines for action spelled out, within which each is free to make decisions for his own part of group activity. In most sales groups, for example, salesmen and sales managers who must make many spur-of-the-moment decisions in the dynamic marketplaces want and expect some kind of boundaries, so that situations are not too ambiguous. Moreover, the ground rules set by the policy maker give a sort of psychological security to group members.[11]

The Expert

Often the group needs help in solving some particularly difficult problems, and may turn to the leader. The expertise that the group demands from the leader will vary from group to group. In a sales group, the leader is often expected to have a high level of skill in solving difficult competitive problems, in creating effective strategies, and in developing good relations with customers.[12]

The External Group Representative

The group identifies itself as a unique group, existing in many environments, internal and external to the firm. To be efficient and successful, the group *as a group* has relationships with other groups—other sales groups, marketing groups, production groups. At times, members of the group are very much aware of these relationships and demand for the sake of the group that the sales manager adequately represent them.

Here is the "linkage" idea again. The adequate representation by the sales manager of his group to higher management is often perceived by the group as one of his more important roles. This is particularly true either when the group is achieving notable success or when the group is

[11] As an example of this kind of psychological security, consider the skipper of a cabin cruiser sailing in a large, unknown bay. He knows, however, that all reefs and shallow bars are marked by buoys. Not seeing any buoys, he is free to cruise ahead at full speed, without worry.

[12] How much technical knowledge and skill he must have is debatable. Certainly he must have a basic knowledge of technology relevant to his markets, products, and customers. But it would be asking too much that his technical knowledge surpass that of individual salesmen. He probably should possess a high level of skill in the *managerial and strategic aspects* of his job—the main thrust of this book.

in difficulty or crisis. An individual also may often expect the sales manager to "go to bat" for him with higher management.[13]

The Controller of Internal Relations

Members of a group have a web of social relationships. These may not always work smoothly. The group may demand of the leader that he so control these relationships that conflict does not arise. Sometimes if one individual "gets out of line" with group norms, the group may expect the manager as a member of the group to get him back "in line."

The Arbiter and Mediator

Sometimes conflict does arise between individual members of a group, which may be perceived by others in the group as detrimental to group goal achievement, or to group attractiveness (hence detrimental to potential individual need satisfaction). The group may not be able to resolve this conflict or may not want to do so. The group then may expect the manager to judge the conflict and reconcile it, functioning in the role of arbiter and mediator.

Conflict can arise in many ways in a sales group. Two salesmen may be striving for promotion and perceive each other as antagonists. Interpersonal conflict can result. Or one salesman may feel that another salesman is getting more than his share of resources (e.g., stenographic help) and may become antagonistic. Or one subgroup (salesmen) may have conflict with another subgroup (order service clerks). The group has a demand on the sales manager, as leader, to identify and fairly resolve these detrimental conflicts.[14]

The Purveyor of Rewards and Punishments

The group may have its own system of punishment for deviant behavior. The sales manager, however, is the firm's source of reward and punishment. The group expects him to play the role of purveyor of rewards and punishment with equity and objectivity. It particularly expects him

---

[13] To generalize, the ego-need-oriented individual may expect the sales manager to "go to bat" for *him*. The social-need-oriented individual may expect him to "go to bat" for the *group*.

[14] There is a caution here. The sales manager's behavior in mediating conflicts will be perceived and assessed by the individuals concerned *and also by the group as a whole*. In other words, the conflict has greater psychological meaning than simply a dysfunctional relation between two persons.

to mete out the rewards the firm can offer in accordance with individuals' real contribution to group effort.[15] Fairness and prompt action are the keys to satisfaction of group demands.

The exercise of "punishment" by the sales manager can be a ticklish problem. Sometimes, some groups will expect the sales manager to discipline a member without delay and in very certain terms. At other times, some groups may leap to the defense of the member receiving some form of punishment. How the group will react to punishment of a member cannot be put into a formula. It is an "equation" with many variables, which the sales manager simply must picture for himself. The concepts of the previous two chapters, plus the concept of symbols, discussed later in this chapter, may help him predict how the group will react.[16]

The Exemplar

The group may expect the leader to behave as a model for the group. In his integrity, his stability, his honor, his loyalty, he becomes a *symbol* which the group members strive to emulate. This can be particularly important for a sales manager visiting customers with a salesman. His behavior in the marketplaces may have a strong exemplary effect on the salesman.

The Ideologist

Groups develop traditions as well as norms of behavior. They are reinforced symbolically and almost ritually. As a group member, the leader contributes significantly to this, and the group may expect him to help evolve and communicate the group's beliefs and philosophies. "This is what we are, and this is what we do," ideologically, is important to many groups.

The Surrogate for Responsibility

Although a feeling of obligation is normally held by any person in a business job, it may be difficult for most individuals to extend this to the

---

[15] Sometimes with due respect to such compensating factors as age, service with firm, and difficulty of position.

[16] There is no implication here that a member needing discipline or correction should not receive it. In fact, the group may expect the manager to discipline. We suggest, however, that the disciplining act, whether simple or severe, can trigger off defensive overtones in *some* groups.

group. Group members may, therefore, shed the feeling of responsibility *for the group,* even though their composite actions determine group performance, and expect the manager to substitute for them in this responsibility. "Let the boss worry about the group. Let him feel the obligation for what the group does." Bear in mind that group members *want* a feeling of obligation to be had. They may pass it over to the manager.

The Scapegoat

Sometimes the group has trouble, performs inadequately, and comes under some degree of censure from outside. Even though the fault may lie with the behavior and performances of group members, the group may expect the manager to suffer the consequences, to pay any penalty. They may expect him "to take the rap."

The Father Figure

Some group members may, quite unconsciously, perceive a relationship with the manager akin to that with a father. There is much in the business life in a firm to support this. The manager in many cases is perceived as mature, wise, and benevolent. He counsels. He sets a tone for behavior. He commends and he disciplines. He is the link to the outside.

The Importance of the Roles Demanded by the Group

All group members do not demand that the sales manager play all these roles. One may demand only one of the roles or two. Another may demand other roles. Hence the effective leader may have to sense that he must play one role with one member and a different role with another member at a given time. *His strategy of influence and his behavior must therefore be so tailored.* This is a crucial idea in effective leadership. Certainly, it is difficult. It would be asking too much of a sales manager for him to know precisely what role to play and specifically how to tailor his behavior to each individual. But he can try to do it and to come as close as he can, particularly in the important situations that he must create. One of the major reasons for gaining insight into individual behavior (Chapter 13) and into group behavior (Chapter 14) is to come as close as possible to tailoring leadership behavior to the individual—so that the leader's influence of the individual's behavior will optimize group performance and the individual's need satisfaction. This is a far cry from hoping to do it by chance or by intuition. Or from disregarding it.

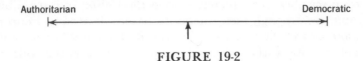

FIGURE 19-2

Thus the sales manager faces a "mix" of roles demanded of him. Salesman A may expect him to play one role and to behave in one certain way. Salesman B may expect a different role behavior, and so on. To complicate this somewhat, *the mix changes over time.* Salesman A may want the sales manager to play a different role tomorrow. Thus the sales manager must keep continuously "tuned in," constantly maintaining inputs into his strategic calculus, so that he can shape his motivating behavior accordingly.

Still another complication can arise. At any one moment—say, when group members perceive that group performance is good and that "all is going well"—a mix of several different role behaviors may be demanded of the leader by different members. And the astute manager may perceive this and so tailor his behaviors to different individuals. Then, assume, some crisis occurs, which group members perceive as a threat to the group. This may develop very quickly into a demand *shared by all members* that the leader adapt his leadership behavior and begin to play new roles. For example, when the group is doing well, members may expect the manager not to play the executive role. They may feel they are doing very well, thank you, without being "bossed." But when the crisis comes, they may not only welcome but demand a strong executive behavior.

AUTHORITARIAN VERSUS DEMOCRATIC LEADERSHIP

This leads to still another view of managerial style, or of how the manager behaves in some rather consistent manner. One way in which his leadership behavior can be described is as either *authoritarian* or *democratic* (Figure 19-2). By authoritarian is meant, in the extreme, that he makes all decisions. He is a "czar." By democratic is meant that he makes no decisions by himself, that the group makes the decisions. Between these polar extremes is a wide spectrum of leadership styles.

In seeking an "ideal" style of leadership behavior, it is probably correct to reject the two extremes. In our society, with the values and norms we have developed, the master-slave relationship is taboo. The authoritarian style of leadership in the extreme (even though the manager acts benevolently or paternally) therefore can be rejected as not desirable.[17] Likewise, for the great majority of business groups the extreme of absolutely democratic leadership is not feasible.[18] (It is a little difficult to imagine a sales manager saying to his sales group, "What should we do? Can you fellows come up with some objectives and some strategies we can vote on?")

The question arises: "But where *is* the 'best' style of leadership? Midway? Toward the authoritarian side? Toward the democratic side?" In any collectivity of business managers, this question stirs much debate, and convincing arguments are posed for various answers. Perhaps *an* answer can be found for a few groups. A foreman of a track gang for the Santa Fe might generally find an authoritative style most productive; the manager of a research laboratory for du Pont might find a democratic style most productive.

For most groups, however, the question of "which style" is meaningless. The preceding two chapters and the foregoing discussion in this chapter all point to the *uniqueness of the individual* and to the differing demands of the group placed on the leader. Whether the sales manager best behaves in a rather democratic or in a rather authoritarian manner, or to what degree in either, will vary. It will vary from group to group (the track gang versus the laboratory scientists). It will vary from time to time (more democratic when all is going well, more authoritarian when crisis occurs).

Perhaps most significantly, the "best" style of behavior will vary from individual to individual. At any one moment of time, one salesman with strong ego-oriented drive may want to be left alone to make his own decisions (within reason, of course). At the same time, another salesman with strong drive for security may want guidance, and in the extreme he may want to be told what to do and when to do it, for certain sales situations. Put another way, one wants democratic leadership and one wants authoritarian leadership, at the same time. Other salesmen will have variations of these expectations of the sales manager.

Here is still more evidence for the vital need for the sales manager to have enough insight into the motivations of the individual and into the dynamics of the group so that he can tailor his behavior to match the expectations of him—*in order to optimize his influence of behavior.*

---

[17] This does not mean that the absolute authoritarian style does not exist. It can be observed here and there. But its existence does not validate it. As a style of leadership behavior, it falls short of optimal effectiveness.

[18] Considerable debate is waged about this. As our society continues to change, and as the technological as well as social milieu of business changes, the trend to more and more "participative" or "democratic" management may continue.

FIGURE 19-3

There is not *one strategy* of influencing behavior. There are *many strategies,* uniquely tailored to unique individuals.

SYMBOLS: CLUES TO LEADERSHIP STRATEGIES

But even if he has some insight into the basic concepts of individual behavior and group dynamics, how can the sales manager identify and evaluate the motivational drives behind one specific individual's behavior and behind this individual's expectations of him? To come at least close to an answer, the sales manager can watch for certain kinds of clues to the forces behind the individual's behavior—clues to his frames of reference, to his "programs" of response, and sometimes to his very needs and self-image. To get at this powerful tool, consider Figure 19-3. If the question were asked, "What is this figure?", most people would respond somewhat as follows:

A Cross
God
Christianity
Christ
The Church

But this is *not* what the diagram is. Actually, the diagram shows two black lines one-sixteenth inch wide, one being vertical and one and one-half inches long and the other line being horizontal and one inch long, the latter bisected by the former, at a point one-half inch below its top. This is a literal description of what the diagram *is,* but the respondents seeing it ascribed some additional meaning to it. They perceived it as a symbol. *A symbol is a sign, plus its meaning.*

$$symbol = sign + meaning$$

Man's ordered life could not exist without symbols. Our social world teems with them, providing inputs of the *meanings of things* to us. Many symbols come to have a common meaning shared by everyone. For example, language itself is a symbol. When you write the squiggly lines C A T on a paper, a reader perceives some meaning *beyond* the squiggly lines; he perceives a pussycat, a feline animal. The sounds of those squiggly lines emitted by the voice box also provide some meaning beyond the sounds themselves—the meaning of a feline animal. A red and green traffic light, the numbers on a taxi's fare box, a coin, a blueprint, a five-color page in a magazine, a monogram on a refrigerator, a lapel button—all these are symbols, or signs with some meaning beyond the signs themselves.

We all exhibit symbols, which can be clues or cues to our inner motives. Sometimes these symbols are very consciously used; sometimes we exhibit them quite unconsciously. But they are there, for the perceptive and alert observer to see. These symbols may be of two general categories —physical symbols and behavioral symbols. Either may offer clues to the individual's perceptions, interpretations, and responses.

Physical Symbols

Every individual exhibits a host of physical symbols. The following are a few simple examples of physical symbols that a salesman might consciously or unconsciously exhibit.

Sometimes the clothes he wears *may* have symbolic meaning. Suppose that he hangs his jacket so that the label "Oxford" shows. Obviously, a two-hundred-dollar jacket. Can he be saying, "Look what I can afford"? Might it be a clue to a status drive, indicating that he is anxious for ego-need satisfaction (status recognition) ?

Consider the neighborhood he lives in, and talks about. If it is an "executive"-type suburb, might he be exhibiting a clue, again showing desire to fulfill status needs?

Sometimes the car a person drives exhibits his psychological needs. Sometimes the college to which he sends his son (and talks about) is a clue to inner drives. Sometimes the people with whom he associates and about whom he talks (name-dropping) have symbolic meaning for his own needs and image.

The trappings that a man exhibits in his office may be clues to his inner self. Trophies, plaques, mementos, citations, all may have meaning. Sometimes the furnishings of the office have symbolic meaning.

A management consultant tells this interesting, true story about how symbols in a client's office gave him significant clues about the man himself, hence leading to an effective strategy. He called on the vice-president of marketing of a firm producing industrial machinery, at the vice-president's request, to explore how the consultant could help organize a sales meeting for the firm's hundred salesmen. The consultant arrived at the vice-president's office with a carefully prepared strategy and a carefully rehearsed presentation focused on the "psychological aspects of selling." He arrived at the vice-president's office and found him to be a kindly, somewhat reserved man in his middle fifties, conservatively dressed, and hardly in the "executive" style. Almost immediately after he had sat down and the two had uttered their first greetings, the vice-president's secretary entered, saying that he had a long-distance call. The vice-president motioned to the consultant to remain seated and began his phone conversation, which lasted about ten minutes. For the first minute or two, the consultant mentally flashed over his carefully rehearsed presentation about application of psychology to selling. Then fortunately he realized he had a golden moment for observing this man's office. He noted that the office itself was very plain, with the brick wall of the old plant painted but not paneled. The floor was old oak, newly varnished and spotless, but not carpeted. Steam pipes ran across the ceiling at one end of the room. The oak desk was an old one, large and functional. At one corner was a stack of papers, at precisely right angles to the side, with the top of each sheet placed one inch lower than the one below. Beside the papers was a row of pencils of identical length, side by side and parallel to the papers—three red, three blue, three black. Everything on the desk, in fact, looked as though it had been trued in with a T-square. No knickknacks were there—like desk-pens sets, family portraits, clever ashtrays. The only unusual device was a well-worn slide rule. At this point, a "light dawned" for the consultant—"this man is an *engineer* through and through." He continued his search for symbols. The walls were bare. Behind the vice-president's desk and within his reach was a bookcase filled with obviously well-worn technical books—*Electric Circuits, Mechanical Engineer's Handbook, Modern System Design*. Across the room from him was another bookcase filled with new-looking books still with paper jackets on, obviously little used—*Marketing Management, Sales Forecasting, Marketing Research*. Along one wall was a counter on which were several cut-away samples of the firm's products. The consultant added all these symbols and hypothesized to himself that this is a man who is engineering-oriented, very rational, pragmatic, and extremely methodical and orderly in his thinking. Based on this prediction, and with not a little anxiety, he discarded his carefully devised strategy and quickly decided on a completely different approach. After the vice-president finished his call, the consultant began to discuss the salesman's job in a very analytical manner, beginning with the requirement for technical knowledge and for analytical planning ability. He *focused* on this theme, rather than on the psychological theme that he had planned to discuss. In fact, he never mentioned the word "psychology" and discussed the salesman's need for "persuasive and influencing ability" as secondary to his technical and analytical planning ability.

This true case is a simple one, using rather simple physical symbols as predictors of an individual's frame of references and likely responses. In this example, the consultant was admittedly "shooting from the hip," without the advantage of having observed the vice-president and his physical surroundings over a period of time, as the sales manager can observe his subordinates.[19] Yet the situation was alive with possible symbols, almost shouting their psychological meanings.

The word "may" has been used throughout this discussion. A diploma on a wall *may* have some meaning about the owner's self-image. But, of course, it may not. It may have been hung merely from habit. Or perhaps its owner did not like a bare space on the wall. Or perhaps his secretary had found it in a file cabinet and hung it. Any time a sales manager assigns possible symbolic meanings to an object, *he does so with some risk*. But, then, risk is involved in most predictions and decisions and is no reason for not using this powerful device, which can give clues to an individual's inner drives. However, some caution is required, and several "ground rules" about the use of symbols should be followed.

1. Do not rely on a single symbol to predict an individual's drives and responses, but build up a set of interrelated symbols. If the sales manager observes one symbol that appears to be meaningful, he can make a little "hypothesis," saying, "I think maybe this thing means that his image is hurting, and his behavior patterns will probably be in defense of himself." *If the hypothesis is correct, he will surely observe more symbolic*

---

[19] In this case, the consultant's hypothesis was correct. He did receive approval to prepare and conduct the sales meeting, and worked with the vice-president's assistant, a young graduate of a large university's MBA program. The meeting did focus on psychological aspects of selling and sales strategy, and it was highly successful. Several months after the sales meeting, the vice-president again called the consultant, to begin plans for a follow-up meeting. He confided: "You know, if you had originally told me you would do all that psychology stuff, I never would have bought it. But now that I see what it's all about, I realize it's pretty important. And my sales managers think it's great."

evidence supporting it. The most valuable use of the concept of symbols occurs when one can observe a whole *set* of symbols, or a *symbolic setting.*

2. The symbols must be evaluated in terms of the other individual's setting, not that of the observer. Put another way, the observer must be careful not to project *his own meanings* to the individual. For example, if a sales manager wants a Cadillac because of its prestige value, he might be wrong if he ascribes a similar motive to the warehouse supervisor, who owns a Cadillac. (It may be that the supervisor has an independent source of income, or that he inherited the Cadillac, or that his wife has money, or even that he simply rationally determined that owning a Cadillac is a wise economic move.)

3. The meaning of the use of symbols by one person cannot be transferred to another. If the consultant in the case above were to visit another office and observe a similar set of symbolic evidence, he should not say, "Aha, here's another engineer, so I'll use that same strategy." *The underlying meanings to one individual may be different from those to another individual exhibiting the same symbols.*

Behavioral Symbols

Important as physical symbols are in revealing clues to an individual's motives and image, *behavioral symbols* may be even more useful to the sales manager. By behavioral symbols is meant the underlying meaning of a behavioral act. Very often the act itself is a significant clue to the individual's need structure or self-image, or to his "programs" of response, permitting the manager, therefore, to better tailor his own influencing behaviors.

Defensive behavior may be particularly important from a symbolic viewpoint. The sales manager may observe a subordinate's act of behavior and hypothesize that it is defensive—an act of reaction formation, projection, or aggression, for example. He tries to understand *what this behavioral act really represents.* That is what will be the target for his tailored influencing behavior, not the defensive act itself.

Again, it is better to observe *patterns of behavior* for an underlying meaning than simply to rely on a simple observed act. Very often an individual will have a pattern, or a "style," of behavior for certain kinds of environmental situations, which may be a clue to his inner motives.

The difference in an individual's mode of behavior in different situations may have significant symbolic meaning. For example, a headquarters sales manager may observe that a regional manager always has a certain manner of behavior when the two of them are alone together (e.g., friendly but businesslike, man-to-man, straightforward) . But then he observes the regional manager's manner of behavior when one of the latter's salesmen is with them. Is it different? How is it different? In still other situation, he observes the regional manager's behavior when the two of them are with the headquarters sales manager's superior, the vice-president of marketing. Is it still different? Out of these different modes of behavior exhibited in different situations may come clues to the regional manager's strength of ego needs, strength of social needs, or drive to protect the self. Hence they may be important inputs into the sales manager's influencing strategy.

The human being is a complex individual. Even the individual himself may often be unaware of the deep psychological drives shaping his behavior. Much of the time, his "mix" of needs and their relative strengths may be very amorphous and indefinable even to the individual himself—even though the needs are highly operant. His belief and attitude structures, his predispositions to behavior, his learned programs of response, his patterns of defensive behaviors, may all operate without his being consciously aware of them. Yet he surrounds himself with many symbols that are signal flags to these motivating forces within him. An astute, alert leader watches for these clues, using them to understand and predict the other's behavior, so that *he* can behave so as to influence the other, to the end satisfaction of both. Here is a most valuable strategic "tool" for the effective leader in his influencing interaction with an individual.

SYMBOLISM IN GROUPS

Symoblism is very important in group life. Individuals need to relate themselves one to another and to the group. They seek the *meanings* of things in the group, and symbol systems evolve to maintain a consensus of meaning, vital to the group's existence.

In a business group, the set of norms developed by the group results in patterns of behavior. These patterns of behavior over time become *customs,* or accepted modes of behavior. From these evolve rituals, traditions, and myths which have symbolic overtones. Many of the repeated, traditional, time-honored modes of behavior of a group have meanings beyond the modes themselves. They say to the group: "This is the kind of a group we are, this is how we act, this is the way we regard each other."

Many of the procedural and administrative aspects of a group develop symbolic meanings of this kind. The procedures of entry, the early training programs, the salary plan, the formal performance appraisal process, all develop meanings. Management meetings, management training programs, management incentive plans, all have symbolic meaning, transmitting an overriding management philosophy, beyond the procedures themselves. All these activities transmit to the individual the group's meaning of things, very often with strong emotional overtones.

An understanding of the traditional and even ritualistic customs of the group as symbol systems conveying the meaning of the group to individuals, may help the manager in understanding the underlying group norms, pressures, punishment system, and informal role structure. The leadership role played by the manager as a member of the group can be better understood, if the manager "reads" the symbolic overtones of group customs and behavior—"This is what we are, what we do, what we want."

All this may be extremely helpful to a sales manager who must introduce *change* into a group. Very frequently, changes in procedures, process, policy, or organization will run athwart of group needs, as perceived by members. Very often, change is resisted—particularly when the proposed change threatens old symbol systems, chops down the old totems. This results in ambiguity as perceived by individuals, and resistance and conflict may continue until new meaningful symbol systems emerge saying in effect, "Now this is what we are. Now this is what we do, and how we act." The traditional, ritualistic modes of behavior of a group may often be understood and predictions of group behavior may be enhanced by observing the symbolic meanings developed by the group.

SOME CONCLUDING THOUGHTS

In this chapter, leadership is viewed not simply as traits or qualities but rather as a behavioral interaction, with the behavior of the leader perceived, interpreted, and responded to by the follower. To be truly effective, the follower's behavior must not only reward the leader (get done what he wants) but also reward the follower (provide some need satisfaction). The mutual reward coming from this behavioral interaction is reinforcing to the relationship between sales manager and subordinate. Each regards the behavioral interaction as a "good" experience, and each will so record it in his "memory bank." When the sales manager again acts to influence the subordinate's behavior, the subordinate will more likely perceive the situation as potentially rewarding and will more willingly respond positively to it.

Each manager-subordinate interaction is a unique, separate experience. Every individual has his own unique mix of needs, his unique self-image that he strives to enhance or protect, his own frames of reference. These may at times be similar to those of others, but not necessarily. At any given moment, an individual in a group may have need structures strikingly different from those of others, coloring his perceptions of the manager and his behavior. Some individuals may be highly ego-need-oriented; some may be highly social-need-oriented; some may be relatively individualistic; some may be highly group-centered. Some may be strongly goal-oriented, with personal aspirations providing great drive for creative opportunities. Others may be security-oriented, with a dread of someone "rocking the boat."

No one mode of behavior by the leader fits all these needs and expectations. The astute leader consciously strives over time to better understand the psychological drives within each individual, so that in seeking to influence him, he may create situations and behave in such a way that he, the sales manager, gets the response he wants, and the subordinate gets something *he* wants as well. This is *effective leadership*—a set of behaviors tailored to reward both leader and follower.

Through insight into basic concepts of human behavior [20] and into concepts of group influence on the individual, and by using the descriptive and predictive tools provided by the idea of symbols, *the sales manager can learn and develop increasing effectiveness* in leading individuals by influencing their behaviors. If he senses that an individual salesman is ego-need-oriented, he shapes his leadership behavior accordingly. He tries to create situations leading to behaviors that will be perceived by the follower as satisfying the ego needs of status, recognition, or achievement. For example, he might say to such an individual: "Mac, I think you could score a real coup if you get some Model 2450 sales next week. The Vice President has the push on, and I'd sure be tickled to tell him your results if you concentrate on the 2450 with the banks next week." This would probably be more effective than merely directing him to concentrate on Model 2450.

On the other hand, to the individual salesman whom he senses to be social-need-oriented and group-influenced, he shapes his leadership behavior differently. He tries to create situations leading to behaviors that will be perceived by the follower as satisfying the social needs of belonging, conformity, respect, or security. For example, he might strategically focus on the *group* in approaching this salesman, saying, "Jimmie, the district has a real tough job to do, but I know the gang will tackle it as they always do. They have the goal of increasing Model 2450 sales next

[20] The concepts discussed in Chapter 13 only barely open the door. Furthermore, many other "models" or conceptual frameworks exist, some of which may be more appealing or meaningful to a sales manager.

week. I know they'll swing away at it, and I'm betting they achieve it. I know we can all count on you, Jim, to work like the devil for us on it." Probably this would be more effective than merely directing him to concentrate on the Model 2450.

Of course, salesmen do not fall into the neat little packages symbolized by Mac and Jim, above. But though the examples are simple, they are not overly so. They demonstrate the leadership strategy of tailoring leadership behavior to the unique individual. This is the very heart of effective leadership.

SUGGESTED READINGS

Leadership Concepts

1. Gibb, Cecil A., "Leadership," in Gardner Lindzey, ed., *Handbook of Social Psychology,* Addison-Wesley, Reading, Mass., 1954, pp. 877–920.
2. Homans, George C., *The Human Group,* Harcourt, Brace, and World, New York, 1950, pp. 172–189.
3. Krech and Crutchfield, *Theory and Problems of Social Psychology,* McGraw-Hill, New York, 1948, pp. 404–439.
4. Warters, Jane, *Group Guidance,* McGraw-Hill, New York, 1960, pp. 27–58.
5. Petrullo, L., and Bass, B. M., *Leadership and Interpersonal Behavior,* Holt, Rinehart, and Winston, New York, 1961.

Symbols

1. Warner, W. Lloyd, *The Living and the Dead,* Yale University Press, New Haven, Conn., 1959, pp. 449–490.

QUESTIONS AND PROBLEMS

1. What is really meant by the term "leadership strategies"?
2. Give examples of "attempted leadership," "successful leadership," and "effective leadership."
3. What concepts from Chapter 17 apply to the idea of "effective leadership"?
4. Comment on the statement: "A good leader always behaves in the same manner. His followers need this consistency."

5. Give an example in a sales group setting of each of the "roles" that may be expected of the leader.

6. Why can we not say that one particular "style" of behavior is the best one for the leader of a specific group?

7. Define the term "symbol" in your own words. Explain how a sales manager can use this concept.

8. Give three examples of physical symbols that you have observed an individual exhibiting, which you think are important clues. State how you might have used them.

9. Do likewise for three examples of behavioral symbols.

10. What do you think is the meaning of the expression "tailored managerial behavior"? How is it important to the sales manager?

11. Discuss, in one page or less the salient points and the real meaning, or the real sense, of Chapters 17, 18, and 19—and their importance to the sales manager.

The Uniqueness
of Sales Management

We are living in exciting times in the world of business. Everywhere one looks, he sees firms in a great battle for growth, for dynamic market power, and for new and expanding markets. One sees new technologies, new innovations of all kinds. With their market orientation—and with markets themselves in flux—firms are in a constant state of adjustive strategic behavior.

The success of the modern firm's strategic programs significantly depends on the effectiveness of its selling operation. And a basic premise of this book is that the effectiveness of the selling operation depends significantly on the effectiveness of its management. *The effective sales manager is a critically important person in the firm.*

Furthermore, the sales manager's job is a *unique* one—perhaps one of the most unique in the entire firm. Hopefully, everything in this book supports this proposition. Certainly, the effective sales manager must possess considerable knowledge in many areas. He must possess technical skills of many kinds. Beyond this, however, he must think and behave *as a manager.* He must understand and be able to implement the elements of "the managerial process." He must have insights into and ability to use the concepts of human behavior, motivation, and leadership. He must also thoroughly understand the systems relationship of his selling operation to all other components of the greater system that is the firm.

THE "ART" OF SALES MANAGEMENT

Throughout this book, the total complex of the sales manager's job has been analyzed and the relating components have been examined in a rational way. A thread of *logic* has run through all the models.

But this is not enough. The truly expert sales manager possesses something that no book and no executive development program can capture. Truly effective sales management is an *art* as well as a semi-science. It requires a flair, a style, an almost visceral ability to respond with precisely the right "touch" to situations. It demands an ability to sense opportunities and to move in at just the right time, in just the right way. It requires, as art does of any artist, a sense of creativity, an ability to break mental bonds to the past and to move into the new. All this can come only from experience—by doing and by learning from what is done.

Parodoxically, these almost "magic" artistic qualities do not diminish the importance of the logical frameworks of managerial thinking and behavior proposed in this book. On the contrary, the need for this "art" in sales management makes them imperative. The "art" must be learned over time. Were it left to cut-and-try methods or to intuition coming from long experience, the true effectiveness of the sales manager might require a long, long time to develop. Frameworks of thinking such as those proposed in this book define processes, thinking schemata, rationales, models—which serve as *foundations of logic on which the sales manager builds an "art."* These frameworks of thinking greatly accelerate the learning process; reduce the cut-and-try methods; and provide a way to understand, describe, and predict phenomena in the sales world. Their use as a thinking-way-of-life enhances creativity, because they permit the mind to take off from a sound, solid, understood base. Both are needed—rational, learnable models of sales management and the intuitive sense gained by experience. Given the first, each will enhance the other.

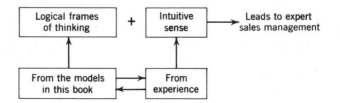

THE GREAT OPPORTUNITIES IN SALES MANAGEMENT

The sales manager has rare opportunities—possibly more than any other functional manager in the firm. First, he can be deeply involved in *effecting change*. Second, he has intimate, *personal contact* with many different individuals in and out of the firm. Third, he can find great personal challenge in the *freedom* that he has.

The Management of Change

Most functions in the firm deal with and contribute to change— changing goals, strategies, and tactics. However, the sales manager occupies a unique position in the *management of change*, because he lives in two worlds—the world of the firm and its processes and the world of the market with its great changing forces. Constantly, he is adjusting the strategies and tactics of the firm's market behaviors. Constantly, he does this to mesh the adjustive behaviors to the changing marketplace. In so doing, his selling operation is itself a force for change, an input of change *to* the markets. And constantly, he is providing *inputs back into the firm* that affect the firm's internal strategy and decision-making processes. The sales manager is in a key position to understand, generate, and manage change in and out of the firm. The systems, managerial-process, and strategy models discussed in this book may be of help as bases.

Wide Array of Personal Contact

Probably no functional manager in the firm has as wide a spectrum of diverse individuals with whom to do business. Great *opportunities for influence* come to the sales manager. He has intimate face-to-face contact with a wide diversity of customers involved in purchasing, engineering, product design and manufacture, finance, personnel, general management—to mention a few, depending on the kind of firm. Consider, for example, the wide array of individuals as customers personally known by a sales manager of General Electric, du Pont, General Foods, or American Airlines. Consider the many different kinds of industries and individual firms—with the array of different wants and problems—with which these sales managers must become intimately acquainted. The effective sales manager is in a position commanding considerable influence for creative, innovative thinking and behavior, which can "multiply" through his customer organizations.

The sales manager's range of personal contacts within the firm itself is also wide. Granting that he may in some cases work through marketing headquarters people, he may have intimate personal contact with management and operating people in production, engineering, finance, and accounting. He may deal with such subfunctions as production control, inventory control, warehousing, product design, sales promotion. Here, again, he is in a key position to influence the perception, thinking, and strategic behavior of important management people within the firm. These are all opportunities—and responsibilities—not to be taken lightly. They present exciting challenges.

Opportunity for Personal Creativity

In all formal organizations, individuals behave within a network of constraints. This is true of all formal organizations—not only business groups, but government, social-agency, military, and even religious. Behavior of the individual is influenced by such controls as organization structure, job description, objectives, budgets, procedures, and policies. Even in management positions, the individual is free to behave only within certain prescribed limits. This is inherent in social and economic organizations.

In most firms, however, the managers in the selling operation—particularly the field sales managers—have relatively *wide fields of freedom* in which to behave. To be sure, policies and procedures, goals and accountability, and organization and resource constraints are present in every sales organization. But the manner in which the sales manager behaves within these constraints has greater latitude than the manner in which most other managers can behave.[1] Put the other way, the sales manager probably has more alternatives open to him for strategic decisions and modes of tactical behavior than do most other managers.

This relative freedom from constraints provides great opportunity for individual expression, but it also poses a challenge and even an obligation to the sales manager. With more alternatives open to him for achievement behavior, the sales manager has opportunity for uniqueness, for creativity, and for problem solving. These are the payoffs for him, for the firm, and for his customers. It is exciting to realize that whereas the success of most firms depends significantly on the effectiveness of the selling operation, sales management also provides probably the greatest opportunity in the firm for freedom of action, alternatives of tactical behavior, and creativity in problem solving. Quite possibly, this is still

[1] Of course, this is a biased statement. But if one observes management jobs in the firm, he can build a strong case to support this view.

another reason for the sales manager to become increasingly adept in the managerial process discussed in this book. He has personal opportunity; he must exploit it by a sound rationale of managerial behavior.

FINALLY AND ALWAYS—THE CUSTOMER

Let us end this book where it all begins—with the customer. On his decisions depend the firm's success in reaching its objectives.

But the customer has much more at stake than simply deciding to buy or not to buy the firm's offering. The customer's own objective achievement is directly affected by the strategy and tactics of the selling firm. The customer has goals, for which he must secure and to which he must optimally apply resources of all kinds. He has needs and wants, conscious and latent. He has problems and obstacles to be solved and overcome. Effective selling and sales management in a supplying firm can be significant to his success.

The selling-buying process is not a confrontation between opposites. It is a process of matching and meshing. This book has viewed the process from the side of the selling firm. But *from the customer side,* effective selling has just as great a value. The selling operation of supplying firms is a vital communicating link for the customer—linking his goals and problems to creative problem solvers. The customer gains knowledge, via the selling operation, of new ideas, new processes, new technologies, and new means. Beyond product and technical knowledge, the customer gains "news" of an important part of the business world. *In a very major way, many creative or innovative achievements by customers are generated by the selling operation of a supplying firm.* It probably does not push this idea too far to say that effective, professional selling (and its management) has a distinctive *social value,* since it triggers new thinking for customers' creativity.

Thus the "systems" idea goes out beyond the firm itself. The firm is a system of business action, but it is really a part of a greater system—the socioeconomic system of the marketplace, a vital element of our society. The firm's link to this greater system is its selling operation. On the effectiveness of its management depends not only the success of the firm, but also the efficiency of the greater socioeconomic system itself.

Finally, consider the importance of effective sales management as a major contributing force for change. We are living in a world of change. With knowledge expanding exponentially, every firm's sources of information and new ideas must also enlarge exponentially. More innovation of great interest to a firm is going on than the firm can possibly learn by its internal information systems. The firm must link itself, however, to the mushrooming technologies outside itself. A prime means to do this is through the sales organization of supplying firms. Imagine, for example, the tremendous advantage to a firm of having *access* to General Electric's great and emerging technologies through General Electric's sales organization.

Thus the selling operation has an obligation not only to its firm—and not only to its customers—but to the total business system as well. The more competent, creative, and productive it is, the greater will be the spread of the new, the creative, the better. In turn, perhaps the business system can become even more vital to the viability of this great, changing society.

Author Index

Subject Index